VOLLEYBALL CENTENNIAL

THE FIRST 100 YEARS...

Byron Shewman

Thank you for supporting the
SAN DIEGO VOLLEYBALL CLUB!
For additional book orders,
please send $19.95 + $3.00 s/h to:
SDVBC, P.O. Box 710098, San Diego, CA 92171
or call Janet Kramer, (619) 284-SDVC.

MASTERS PRESS

A DIVISION OF HOWARD W. SAMS & CO.

D1295685

Published by Masters Press (A Division of Howard W. Sams & Co.)
2647 Waterfront Pkwy. E. Dr., Suite 300
Indianapolis, IN 46214

Published 1995

Printed in the United States of America

Library of Congress Cataloging-in-Publication Data

Shewman, Byron, 1947—
    Volleyball centennial / Byron Shewman.
        p.   cm. — (Spalding sports library)
    ISBN 1-57028-009-6
    1. Volleyball—History. I. Series.
GV1015.2.S44   1995   94-47631
796.325'09—dc20   CIP

Front cover design by Julie Biddle and Phil Velikan

Acknowledgments

From Pop Idell, volleyball's earliest visionary and progenitor of the All-American system, I will appropriate his Red, White and Blue (First, Second, Third Teams) for recognition of contributors to this book. It is in no way a reflection of their interest, only the amount of time and help asked for...and freely given.

BLUE (Third): Doug Avery, Doug Beal, Barbara Boskovich, Victor Botkin, Dick Caplan, Jim Coleman, Matt Gage, Rick Hazeltine, Elmer Johnson, John Kessel, Kerry Klostermann, Janet Kramer, Terry Liskevych.

WHITE (Second): ASICS Tiger Corporation, Peter Brouillet, Bud Fields, Dave Heiser, Holly Kondras, Spalding Athletic Company, .

RED (First): Ken Hansen, Susan Lorscheider, J.T. Ragan, Dick Templeman.

I would also like to recognize the following for their unusually kind contributions of photos to the book: ASICS Tiger Corporation, Doug Avery, Robert Beck, Peter Brouillet, Bud Fields (USA Volleyball photographer), Dave Heiser, Bernie Holtzman, Spalding Athletic Company, Dr. Leonard Stallcup, Style Craft, Volleyball Magazine.

Sources used:

"An Analysis of Volleyball in Various Regions of the World" (1950), Dr. Lu, Hui-Ching

"The History of Volleyball in the United States" (1960), Lance Flanagan.

"The History of Contribution of the United States Volleyball Association" (1968), William Odeneal.

The History of YMCA Physical Education, 1979, Elmer L. Johnson.

Kings of the Beach 1988, Sinjin Smith and Neil Feineman.

For all those who have played the game during its first 100 years.

And specifically for Dick Templeman, who has given more to volleyball and its people, while expecting less in return, than anyone I know or have learned of. So much for nice guys...

Foreword

I've craved a book like this for a long time. Because while you can fill shelves with all the instructional texts and videos available today, discovering books about the early days of volleyball is a much more challenging task. I found reading this book to be an act of renewal, a reminder that we inherited this game from generations of dedicated players and supporters and a reminder of the responsibilities such a legacy implies. And even if you don't find it inspiring, I'm sure you'll find it interesting to learn about the changes, the personalities, and even the constants in the history of volleyball.

The sport of volleyball is a century old, which doesn't seem like such a long time, really. But only now, having read this book, do I understand the profound evolution this game has experienced. Without the vision of people like W.E. Day and Pop Idell, we could be playing a game that seems to be an impossible tangle of rules randomly extracted from other sports: ten players and unlimited contacts on each side of the net (you'll find out how many contacts one particularly scheming—and patient—team in the Philippines used), dribbling allowed, on a net that runs from the floor to six feet high, for a duration of nine innings. Volleyball 100 years ago seemed the ultimate mongrel sport.

But the game *did* change, thanks to passionate people like Mr. Day and Mr. Idell. Idell's innovations will leave you awestruck: rules, lighting, the All-American team concept, the list is very long. And Gene Selznick,

love him or hate him, he cared about what he did and he moved people. The roundhouse serve, the attitude, excellence on any surface. To many in volleyball he was exactly as Byron Shewman describes him: the "reprobate."

Then there are the things that never change. We thought we had the patent on volleyball jargon with terms like six-pack and pancake, but Pop Idell was ahead of us there too—ever hear of a "fracture skull?" It seems consoling to find that even players in the '40s and '50s had problems with referees' tight calls. And cramping in beach tournaments started decades ago, not just in the last few years.

I knew about the rule changes from the 1970s on, enacted to promote defense, in an effort to stave off the unending onslaught of new offensive weapons. Rules like four hits off the block and mounting antennae on the net to narrow the amount of court the defense has to guard. But, you'll find out the problems of the offense overwhelming any defense are as old as the sport itself.

When I first heard about the concept of the book, it was to be an officially-approved USVBA publication—potentially a very biased viewpoint. That worried me. Fortunately, my concerns were for naught, because Shewman does an exceptional job of presenting the *whole* story. Much of the fascination of the early lore is the tension that developed between the Westies (the beach players) and the Easties (the establishment). That tension fostered much of the dynamics and politics of volleyball today.

Amidst that tension, some in the USVBA, surprisingly, acknowledged long ago what a great teacher playing doubles on the beach is (doubles being yet another, and probably the most significant, invention of Pop Idell). Here's the quote from the 1947 Guide: "...beach volley ball develop[s] excellent coordination and ball-handling..." The norm for the establishment, though, was an attitude that detested the game for both its irrelevance to six-person indoor volleyball and for the excess adulation it showered upon the players. Or it used to, anyway. Ironically, the beach game, volleyball's traditionally despised orphan, will be an Olympic sport in Atlanta.

Santayana's warning was, "Those who do not remember the past are condemned to repeat it." I thought the alphabet soup battles like AVP and USVBA and FIVB were curses just for the modern day. But it seems as if we're stuck in an eight-track loop of turf battles— only the letters have changed: the AAU vs. the NAIA vs. the NCAA...

One other fact, the most important, hasn't changed at all. Ultimately for millions of players and fans in this country and many millions more throughout the world, volleyball still does what it did almost 100 years ago: to quote the Handbook of 1903, "It cures the blues."

—Karch Kiraly

Contents

Prologue

Imperial Beach. From the pier, I look out at the same humble court, the frayed volleyball net being buffeted by an uncaring wind. I was a poor kid playing college basketball when I fell upon this new sport, quite by accident, so many years ago.

A scant seven years later in 1974, I was meandering down the Moscow River, one of the players sipping vodka to take the edge off the humiliation of having the Soviets kick our butts night after night. After a few ceremonious toasts, Vladimir Savin approached me: a world-class player, coach and now the man behind the world's greatest volleyball machine—one which had driven international volleyball for most of its 30-year existence. A man with a distinguished presence, one which bespoke not only power but intelligence and sensibility, was speaking in perfect English. Now, he was speaking to me! "How is it that you have two Romantic names?" I fumbled for a reply—no one had ever asked me that. Sure, I had been an English major, and more, wore the paradigm of poetical first names. But that was just an accident—neither of my parents...and certainly not my hard-drinking father who spent too much time in jail—had ever heard of Lord Byron. Nor had he ever heard of a man who shared his anglicized German surname: Schumann...Robert, German composer. Romantic? The Russian stumped me too on that one...and challenged me.

Romantic is a term I've been labeled with much of my life, mostly accused of. Looking back, volleyball was perfect for a romantic disposition—especially a poor one—a sport character-rich, and at 20 I was already inclined, almost unknowingly, to the fascination of human personality...while irrefutably given to sport from early childhood. Sports kept me alive; the other kept me interested in life. Volleyball had it all—all I could never reach I thought. Vibrant and clean competition—in the gym or in the sun—beautiful women and witty urbane ultra-cool guys who intimidated the rest of us. Out of reach.

Not so, finally. I lived it as an insider, or player, for a good decade. I would also become an outsider—a player who struggled against the established system and took a defiant—and romantic—stand. I lost...and won on another level. One upshot was that it took me to many parts to see, and live, and to many immemorable times and people—things one will always carry.

About 13 months ago, one morning I was struck with the idea of writing the Centennial history of the game. Not the normal, insipid gruel but the REAL story: the people and the playing. My idea was received with immediate skepticisim. "Yeah, you might sell a few but you won't make any money." One fortunate result for people who write poetry is that they learn early on certain types of writing bear no financial reward. I'd never written for money— why start now?

After thousands of miles, scores of interviews and countless telephone calls, I now present the game with its first history. It's one with a human face and one which features players in the main; players unmatched in physical renown but also those with characters unparalleled. From the earliest moment of my playing career, I'd heard of the politics, the insular bureaucratic thinking rife within the sport. With age, I learned that particular affliction was one endemic to every human organization: small to large, private to public. One learns to live with it. Still, that doesn't make it right, in some cases. For my own part, I'm sure I have ignored many of those more deserving, even injured the feelings of a few. It was not intended.

Consequently, you won't find much in this book about officials, administrators and recipients of the various awards of distinction in the sport. If you are looking for accounts of those individuals, I suggest you pick up any USVBA Guide for the past 70 years. Those individuals—and many should be saluted according to their efforts—have ample treatment in the official voice. Finally, I recognize a few possible outstanding areas of insufficient treatment: collegiate history is the one most salient. And although women weren't allowed to officially compete until 1949, perhaps I err in that coverage even though I tried to equate historical impact respectively with quantity of material.

I tried to write it with my same early fascination of the sport. And being all too human, it bears my own imprimatur. Sport...as art...as love...are things we practice all too little in a short life. This one's a great game—with great people. I suspect it will be played a lot in the next 100 years. I've written it for those who played it in the first 100—they are deserving.

And now...I'm going surfing.

Byron Shewman

San Diego, January 17, 1994

Chapter 1
1895-1911

"In the beginning..."

"Keep the serve on the mayor! He's in trouble," urged the team captain, John Lynch, to his teammate serving up the ball.

"What about your job?" the server asked in wide-eyed dismay.

Lynch, also captain of the Holyoke Fire Department, bit his lip in second thought. How would Mayor J.J. Curran take to losing? Especially in front of 29 physical directors of the YMCA assembled here just to see the first game ever played as a public exhibition? Suddenly his Irish ire flared and he nodded with grim resolve at the server. "Forget my job. Serve him!"

Sitting in that small gym of Springfield College in the dripping heat of a July afternoon in 1896, sweating in suits and cravats, most of the 29 men seemed genuinely amused by this new game. The crude ball was patted back and forth across a tennis net, strung at six feet, six inches by the ten respectable men who appeared to have potential.

After the final point of the "inning" was scored, the participants politely left the court and toweled off their perspiration. The inventor of the new activity, William P. Morgan, physical director of the Holyoke YMCA, thanked his colleagues for attending. Dr. A.T. Halstead of the Springfield faculty in turn asked young Morgan a penetrating question: Why had he named the new game "mintonette?" Since the nature of the game seemed largely to volley a ball back and forth

across a net, why not call it "volley ball?" Why not, indeed! Morgan agreed and the rest of the attendees at the Physical Directors Conference of the Eastern section of the YMCA christened the new sport.

Morgan and the ten members of his group caught a trolley car back to Holyoke. It seems the good mood of Morgan was infectious as the mayor invited the whole gang over to the town's swankiest pub for a pint of Samuel Adams—much to the relief of John Lynch. After a healthy downing of his glass, a remnant of the brew's frothy head trembling like a caterpillar on his thick moustache, Mayor Curran winked over at the opposing captain of the other team. "Hey Lynch, I bungled a couple out there at the end...just wanted to keep it close!"

"Fighting fat with fun..."

In 1895, William Morgan had to come up with a new idea. Only four years earlier and only ten miles away, basketball was invented by his professor, James Naismith, at Springfield College. In that short span, the germ of the NBA had already assumed a stronghold in the Northeast, particularly in the new YMCA gymnasiums cropping up all over that region. These facilities originally designed for gymnastics, which then dominated indoor exercise, filled a new and growing need in post-Civil War society. Prosperity and expansion in America had given the country a new confidence and placed it on a financial level of its European forebears. Brash and young, the nation was coming into its own.

Promise of new wealth coupled with absence of tradition was a strong magnet to the Old World. Soon immigrants were pouring into Ellis Island in rapt salute to the giant lady of liberty. Transforming from a rural society to one of industrialized urbanization, America was a hothouse for change—the new middle and even lower classes, now with a little money in their pockets and more free time to spend it, developed a new thirst for games. Schools put organized sports in their curriculums; women were freer to be active; a new community parks and recreation program was introduced in the big cities; better transportation allowed for greater attendance at sporting events, and new publications began to feed the tiny embryo of sports information which would become an insatiable monster in time.

Still, it should be remembered that America, and particularly the Northeast, had a strong foundation of Puritan and Calvinist religion. The same people who in colonial times prohibited instrumental music in church as sinful—only vocal or "mouth music" was considered godly—also passed on the influence of their famous Blue Laws which prohibited work or play on the week's only free day. After a Sunday morning of fire and damnation from such snorting evangelicals as the famous Jonathan Edwards, the activity which most provided exercise or amusement was eating or reading the Bible. It was a clash of values but human nature eventually would have its way and the church would perforce relax its attitude. Americans were going to have fun—religion or no.

An organization formed in 1851—the Young Men's Christian Association—sought to provide a place for the newly arriving young men in the nation's cities to find Christian fellowship. Wholesome leisure was the aim: lectures, reading rooms, socials and teas were employed to keep young men away from the corrupting influence of the street. However, the initial attempts to evangelize the young men through sermons was largely rebuffed and by 1880, the YMCA wisely decided to use sports as its vehicle to spread the Gospel and good morals. Although professional baseball and college football had already emerged, the YMCAs built gymnasiums and filled the serious need for qualified instructors. In 1885, the School for Christian Workers was founded at Springfield, Massachusetts (later to become Springfield College) which prepared leaders, steeped in moral as well as physical education, to set America as well as the world on the proper path.

Hence, it was logical that Springfield would spawn new ideas and invent new sports as well. Morgan had hailed from the area and because of his talent at football, Naismith had persuaded him to attend Springfield where he played center for the Springfield Eleven. Graduating in 1894, he quickly took a job as physical director of the Holyoke YMCA. It wasn't long before the 25-year old figured out that for most of the members enrolled in his classes for businessmen—portly and middle-aged—basketball wasn't going to fill the bill. A few sessions of sprinting full-court by these cigar-smoking, sedentary men told him it wasn't working. Basketball was too strenuous and too rough. Besides, some of these guys were pillars of the community—a broken arm or, worse, heart attack would not go over too well—so the director went home convinced that he needed to come up with some new game for the roundly bourgeois clientele. Something to make them sweat a little but allow them to relax at the same time.

"A little 'o this, a little 'o that..."

The original ten rules of the game suggest that Morgan created a concoction of many other sports of the era. In fact, the sport's original name was derived from badminton, "minton", which was brought back from India by a YMCA director. Badminton probably also provided the idea of keeping the ball in the air. Baseball undoubtedly contributed the three servers per inning rule. Taken from basketball, the forerunner of the set was a type of dribbling, or repeated "air bounces" to one's self. A player could only dribble or set to oneself behind the dribbling line which was four feet from the net. Handball loaned the idea of allowing the ball to be played off overhanging objects, walls etc. while tennis donated the two serves for each server. The original dimensions of the court were set at 25 feet by 50 feet. Certainly the most taxing of the "Ten Commandments" of volleyball—at least it would be for modern players—was Rule 10 which stipulated: "...any player, except the captain, addressing the umpire or casting any slurring remarks at him or any players on the other side, may be disqualified, and his side be compelled to play the game without him or a substitute, or forfeit the same."

In the Handbook of 1897, some suggested techniques for playing the new game were printed as follows:

HELPS IN PLAYING THE GAME

♦ Strike the ball with both hands.

♦ Look for uncovered space in opponents' field.

♦ Play together; cover your own space.

♦ Pass to one another when possible.

♦ Watch the play constantly, especially the opponents.

The same publication of 1903 revealed some scintillating remarks. From apparent scientific observation, it was decided that a "player should be able to cover 10 feet by 10 feet of floor space." And ostensibly, medical benefits had been discovered in the new activity: "The game is valuable from a hygienic standpoint, as the chest is never in a contracted position during the play." Other curious items as "correcting round shoulders" were also listed as advantages for young urban professionals of the time. The final claim of volleyball was the most promising and ambitious as well: "It cures the blues."

Certainly it was a far cry from today's volleyball and a lot of experimentation was called upon to evolve the game. The first ball used was a basketball..."but we found the basketball was too heavy and made our wrists sore," reported Morgan. Next a soccer ball was used. This was replaced by the bladder of a basketball, which was better but too flighty. Finally Morgan went to nearby A.G. Spalding Brothers with specifications for a soft calfskin ball which wouldn't float away or break one's fingers. As the purveyor of almost every other piece of American sports equipment, this was easy stuff for Spalding. The new ball was manufactured with specs as follows: 25-27 inches in circumference, weighing 9-12 ounces, with a cover of leather or canvas. Not too different from what a Spalding Top-Flite 18 looks like today, except for the outer lacing. So, the game had a specified ball early on even though most other aspects of the sport would change dramatically.

But trying to invent a new game was not easy, particularly 100 years ago. It's not too surprising that great variations in play, rules and venues were found everywhere. Walking into a gym, an unsuspecting player might be met with a two-inch white mesh net, strung between five and seven feet high, and very likely hanging all the way to the floor. The court length could vary between 35-80 feet. Very likely, gymnastic apparatus protruded onto the court and overhanging running tracks made setters think twice about putting up high sets to hitters—although spiking was indeed rare in those days. Some of the corners of courts were rounded because of space limitations.

The result was that basketball flourished while its cousin, volleyball, remained a slow, monotonous game which soon came to assume the distinguished moniker of a "sissy" sport. One thing that couldn't be argued was that the early rules provided flexibility. So much so, that with no limit on number of players per side, a team might feature 25 men playing at once. Needless to say, things could get crowded. And with no prescribed number of hits or touches of the ball, who knows what tactics that rule— or lack of—led to! Additionally the original

Spalding ball most likely didn't make for receiving or handling it an easy task; the leather cover was laced over a tongue to hide the rubber bladder, leaving a large, protruding bump and a lopsided ball.

One man who took an early interest in the sport and added the first major changes was W.E. Day. Physical director of the Dayton YMCA, Day had attended the Springfield College unveiling of volleyball and took it back to Ohio and his exercise classes. By 1900, his modified rules were accepted and published by the YMCA. Day's innovations raised the net to seven feet, erased the dribbling line and dribbling borrowed from basketball and axed the nine innings rule for a game of 21 points.

As for whom played the sport early on, it stayed almost exclusively in the hands of the people it was designed for—the portly shakers and movers of the community. In fact, these middle-aged gentlemen so cherished the game that they jealously guarded it to the point of discouraging outsiders to play. One of the early, great innovators of the game, A. Provost "Pop" Idell, commented: "It seemed, at the time, they didn't want the rest of the world to know about it..."

And while this element of the "clique" has remained with the game in some places (as any novice who attempts to get in a pick-up game at Manhattan Beach can testify), Pop Idell, at the Germantown YMCA in Philadelphia, led an impressive movement to shake up the sport,

expand it and give it some excitement. Beginning in 1910, Idell, the physical director at the Germantown YMCA, used his venue and its players in an on-going experimentation to improve the sport and its play. Astoundingly innovative, he was a tireless crusader and unafraid to try any new idea. Six-women, women's doubles, mixed-doubles and mixed-sixes were all innovations Idell introduced in Philadelphia while the rest of the country was trying to figure out who served first. Apparently, his enthusiasm infected the Germantown group to the point where they sensed their role in the destiny of the young sport. Idell described the unusual environment surrounding his players which "reflected a cause, a form of religion and a purpose in life which contributed to the fine art of living."

So apart from Germantown—and the heated Fire Department-City Fathers rivalry of Holyoke, which reportedly carried on for many years—volleyball largely languished for almost two decades. Bogged down in a welter of varying rules and a strong partisan attitude of its early male players, there is little mention of the sport to be found in the annals of the YMCA during the period. Even William Morgan left his YMCA post after a few years and took a job at the Harrison Radiator Company. Although he followed the progress of the game, which he created "only for enjoyment and exercise," he soon left its future in the hands of others.

William G. Morgan. The YMCA physical director who invented volleyball in 1895. (Courtesy of Holyoke Volleyball Hall of Fame)

Holyoke YMCA—Holyoke, Massachusetts. The birthplace of an American sport. (Courtesy of Holyoke Volleyball Hall of Fame)

Volley Ball

Volley Ball is a new game which is pre-eminently fitted for the gymnasium or the exercise hall, but which may be played out of doors. Any number of persons may play the game. The play consists of keeping the ball in motion over a high net, from one side to the other, thus partaking of the character of two games, tennis and hand ball. Made of white leather. Constructed with capless ends and furnished with pure gum guaranteed bladder.

No. V. Regulation size, best quality. Each, **$4.00**
No. W. Regulation size, good quality. " **2.50**
No. A. Guaranteed Pure Para Rubber Bladder, for either Nos. V or W Volley Ball . Each, **75c.**

Volley Ball Net and Standards

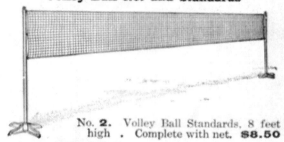

No. **2.** Volley Ball Standards, 8 feet high . Complete with net. **$8.50**

Volleyball and net at bargain prices. Mail order from Spalding catalogue, 1906. (Courtesy of Spalding)

Volleyball's first team, Holyoke YMCA, 1895. Morgan is in upper left. (Courtesy of Holyoke Volleyball Hall of Fame)

Chapter 2
1912-1927

"Honestly..."

No headlines, but at least it made the sports page in some of the nation's major newspapers, and that was a first for volleyball. It happened in 1924 at the cliffhanger finals of the National YMCA Championships in Pittsburgh's Central YMCA; the match-point spike by a Pittsburgh Central hitter landed long, and the Germantown Y six erupted, leaping into each other's arms with the joy of victory—except for one player who remained at the net, immobile, head down. Was he praying? Giving thanks for victory? Not at all. Slowly the captain, Bill Nenner, raised his hand to the referee in admission that he had touched the ball in his attempt to block it. In those days, the "honor system" required a player to call his own touch if unseen by the referee—a single mortal in an epoch of imperfect optometry—and it promoted the high ideals of the YMCA.

Like stunned mullet, the Germantown players returned to the court with a slim 15-14 lead. The shock must have taken its toll; Pittsburgh fired off three straight points, and in a matter of a few minutes, Germantown went from national champs to second place. It's uncertain what treatment the distinguished player later received from teammates but some journalists attending the competition lauded the valorous deed to the skies. Praise was also heaped on the sport itself which so exemplified Christian principles.

"Your rules or mine?..."

After Morgan handed his fledgling game over to the YMCA, it was largely controlled by the Volley Ball Rules Committee made up of YMCA physical directors who met annually to discuss and revise regulations. Beginning in 1897, these were published each year as part of the Official Handbook of the Athletic League of the YMCA. However, the yearly booklet alone did little to change the early inertia which had set in. The aimless drift went uninterrupted until 1912 when YMCA leaders recognized that the wildly different interpretations of rules around the country was strangling the infant game in its cradle. What followed was the first attempt at some uniformity and tightening of the rules' interpretations. The committee also decided to promote volleyball as a national recreational game. After all, there were some advantages: small playing space and inexpensive equipment, women and children could join in the activity, recreational play required no referees, and the co-operation and close proximity of players fostered the social qualities the YMCA stood for. As they were putting in shorter days and suddenly free to enjoy Saturday afternoons, American workers could also jump in those new marvels of invention—automobiles—and go places and do things never done before. Like go to the YMCA! Soon informal, get-acquainted volley ball classes were part of the agenda at many Y facilities.

Unquestionably, the older genteel version of the game was given a boost, but before long the testosterone factor entered the equation—men wanted competition. Quickly, the intensity level rose within the individual YMCA's play and competition with other Ys was organized. Another product of the national push was the first flowering of interest by women. Beginning in 1914 in South Parks of Chicago, volleyball was widely played by ladies, although with modified rules. In deference to the fairer sex, sides were increased to nine players and play was limited to two periods of 15 minutes separated by a five-minute break. As testimony to the wisdom of these watered-down rules, no record of a single case of cardiac failure exists!

By 1916, enough growth prompted Dr. George J. Fisher, president of the Physical Directors' Society, to suggest that the NCAA be invited to share in a new, broader formulation and adoption of rules. The NCAA accepted. At the meeting the two delegates of the YMCA were Dr. Fisher and Christopher Scaife, Chairman of the Volley Ball Rules Committee. The NCAA representatives clearly saw significant potential for a new intramural sport; however, stigmatized as a "sissy" game, athletic directors were reluctant to include it as an intercollegiate sport. The major legacy of the new alliance—the Joint Rules Committee—proved to be a separately published "Official Volley Ball Rules," edited by Fisher. The year of 1916 also found some major rule changes: the net was established at eight feet, the game score was reduced from 21 to 15 points, and the rotation of server rule was adopted. Two out of three games constituted a match, the six-player limit was adopted and the modern version of volleyball had almost arrived.

The "Official Volley Ball Rules" handbook was part of Spalding's Athletic Library, one of many sports handbooks the company distributed through the American Sports Publishing Library. Presumably, it was not a bad marketing strategy since Spalding made the only volleyball. Apart from the rules, various short articles were also included in the annual publication such as philosophical and technical commentaries. It sold for a dime. In 1916, "The New Volley Ball Rules" by Christopher Scaife appeared in the rules handbook which could have served as the sport's credo, trumpeting a philosophy of the YMCA founders which would steer the sport for several decades to come: "To create a game that would be just a play game in every sense of the word; a game in which thousands of men, boys and girls all over the world would indulge with real enjoyment, getting wholesome recreation and hygienic exercise without the intricate and specialized plays developed in other games..."

A closer look at the content of the rules handbook of the same year gives a fair example of what an enthusiast would find in that era's publication. The standard format was rules, articles and regional reports. In 1916, 15 articles appeared in the publication...three of them rather tell-tale: "Business Men and Volley Ball," "Volley Ball and the Development of Character," and "Volley Ball: A Social Game."

"Onward Christian Soldiers..."

The period between 1900-1915 marked the great international movement of the YMCA. Fully committed to employing sports as the tool to spread Christianity around the globe, volleyball was first introduced to Canada in 1900, then to Cuba in 1905 and soon to much of Latin America, including Mexico and Brazil in 1917.

But the sport's most fertile ground was found in the Philippines, where Elwood S. Brown of the YMCA introduced it into the public school system in 1910. By 1914, there were more than 5,000 courts in public schools, playgrounds and private clubs in the Philippines, and it was here that the "Filipino bomb" or first version of the modern spike was unleashed. Other innovations were adopted. After one team set the ball back and forth between themselves *52 times* before hitting it over the net, the local rules committee observing the game demanded the first three-hit rule. It seems that a pressing dinner engagement of one of the attendant officials was only one motivation—a stronger one was that of the opposing team which threatened to walk off the court and go home. The rule was quickly adopted throughout the Orient.

About the same time, the YMCA ambassadors imported the game into Japan and China and these three countries soon competed in the sport's first international play in the Far Eastern Olympics in 1912. However, the game flourished under different rules in the Orient. For example, Asian rules called for nine players on a side. Their playing style was also more sophisticated, with player specialization and team strategies of offense and defense. In fact, in 1920 the YMCA director who introduced the game to Japan, Franklin H. Brown, was so impressed with the play that he took back some of the features to America and suggested their adoption. Curiously, only the important rule of "three contacts" was accepted by the Joint Rules Committee—but nonetheless a very needed regulation. It was the first time that rules or playing changes from a foreign countries would be rejected by the sport's hierarchy...it would happen many times in succeeding years.

"In the trenches..."

With the Declaration of War in 1917, the War Department authorized provision of recreational activities for the troops on a large scale. Quickly, General "Black Jack" Pershing ordered the program to be handed over to the YMCA for implementation—their physical directors had already demonstrated their adeptness for such a task in many parts of the world. The slogan: "Every Man Engaged in Some Activity Every Day" was created and volleyball instantly got a tremendous boost. It was good for mass participation, had minimal equipment needs, and of course the physical directors were not only knowledgeable players but teachers as well.

Initial reluctance by soldiers quickly eroded and in 1919 over 16,000 balls were distributed for play. Between 1918-1919, an estimated 1,500,000 military men participated. Everywhere the American Expeditionary Forces went the YMCA had nets and balls ready. Rest camps, naval bases, colleges, ports of entry,

combat zones—guys learned to play a new game which some would come home to play.

It was also during the war that volleyball gained its first foothold on the Continent. In the summer of 1919, American and Allied troops competed in the Inter-Allied Games—"the Military Olympics"—on the outskirts of Paris. As it was increasingly apparent that Germany was on the brink of collapse, thousands competed throughout the summer in a myriad of sports indigenous to all Allied countries. Spectators fought to get into the 25,000-seat stadium and wildly applauded everything from the Spanish sport pelota to Arabian camel fighting. So in the European theater of war, the American Doughboys not only left behind a trail of broken hearts but a new sport as well. To be sure, many European governments following the war would give financial and educational support to volleyball which led to a high-level competitive sport—something which didn't happen in the United States for decades.

"Pennsylvania—Home of Champions"

The end of the war blew through American society like a tornado. Mustard gas and the unimaginable human carnage put an end to the old romantic notion of war. Disillusionment with leaders, politics and religion found fertile minds and the Jazz Age was suddenly upon the United States. Women not only voted, but they danced the Charleston, bobbed their hair, drank bathtub gin (the Prohibition began in 1918) and listened to the latest contraption, the radio. The sophisticated melodies of George Gershwin were listened to by the metropolitans, and Bessie Smith belted out the blues for the more adventurous. And it was the golden age of sports in the country; Babe Ruth and Red Grange were bigger than life. Times were good again and America went on a fun-ride never before seen in its history.

Volleyball also came back from the fields of France re-energized. In anticipation of the conflict, bodybuilding and calisthenics had been the rage before the war but now patriotic fervor had subsided. People turned to exercise for enjoyment as well as competition and fitness. For volleyball, truly a pinnacle was reached with the establishment of a YMCA National Championship Tournament in 1922. Held at the Brooklyn Central Y in New York, the championship featured 23 teams from 11 states and Canada battling for the title. In a shocker, Pittsburgh Central Y upset the powerful Germantown Y team from Philadelphia which had dominated the Atlantic seaboard for a decade. The loss sparked the first serious rivalry in the sport which would continue for many years.

The man who organized the first competition, Robert Cubbon, pointed out the advent of a new, serious game and the internal conflict which continued to plague it well into the future.

> ...there are a few who regret the passing of the old volleying game, but the new fast and scientific game, with boosters and spikers highly developed, has come to stay and "Servus Ball" and "Pass Ball" will better fill the other need.

That first championship match also featured a handful of men who would influence the game dramatically. Harry A. Batchelor who coached the victorious Pittsburgh team, led by John Weible, soon earned a reputation as one of the sport's first great mentors. After winning that first contest, he added four more national titles in a row to his record. Another graduate of Springfield College (1917), Batchelor and his great enthusiasm sparked the interest which would make The Steel City share status with its neighbor, Philadelphia, as the first two power centers of the sport. A physical education teacher, Batchelor devoted much time to developing the sport at the high school level. He was successful. His own Westinghouse High school was the first to ever adopt volleyball as a varsity sport.

The playing coach of the favored Germantown squad, known as "The Big Red Team," was Pop Idell. The fabled 33-year old already had a long career in volleyball. A local gym rat at his hometown Germantown Y, he began playing the sport in 1904 when he was only 15. In 1914, he took the physical director job at the same Germantown YMCA.

Then...talk about a career! One of the best players of his day, Idell's coaching career was even more brilliant: between 1912-1919, his record with the Germantown Y team was 750 wins and 75 losses. The Official Rules handbook claimed that in 1918-1919, his team compiled a "world's record of 125 consecutive victories!" He was one of the founders of the USVBA. As a referee, he was recognized as the national dean of officials. He was the developer of the first skills tests for players and officials and the designer of the "modern" volleyball produced by Spalding. Idell was the first creator and selector of All-Americans and made the first teaching film in 1937. In short, from 1920-1950, Pop Idell was considered the authority on volleyball in this country. Another important figure of the early game, Robert E. Laveaga wrote: "During World War I, volleyball almost died for lack of leadership here in the United States. Idell pushed it through. He was a player, coach, student and excellent writer who deserves all the credit due him."

Idell was the sport's most creative mind, and he must have run on high-octane—in 1960, he even tried to get volleyball accepted as a commemorative stamp but his request was denied by the U.S. Post Office because the sport wasn't considered "an important enough enterprise." It was for him. He ended his hands-on career as a referee in the 1962 USVBA National Championships—three years before his death at 76. If history has left Dr. George Fisher assuming the role as the George Washington of volleyball, then surely Pop Idell was its Ben Franklin.

As the "Father of Volleyball," George Fisher had a long and distinguished professional career. Graduating as a physician from the Cincinnati College of Medicine in 1898, he gave up medicine for the YMCA where he rose from physical director to Senior Director of the International Committee for Physical Education.

He held many professional and honorary positions of national prominence, most notably one as a full-time executive with the Boy Scouts of America for 25 years. A staunch proponent of the value of exercise and relaxation over competition, Fisher kept the sport on that tack for over 20 years. Under his stewardship, volleyball remained the quintessential YMCA game: pure, egalitarian, and amateur. Amateur in every sense of the word; players should not receive remuneration of any sort, anytime. That was normal thinking for the era, but the idea of true YMCA amateurism extended even to administrators. Consequently, the first full-time administrator for the USVBA wasn't hired until 1973! In 1933, Fisher wrote a curiously revealing report:

> When I was a physical director, I enjoyed playing the game and found it a splendid, though not exacting, recreational game... Its chief use has been an informal, happy, recreative game—a very popular game with businessmen as it lacks the element of strain and physical contact.

So after steering the sport for almost two decades, its appointed caretaker saw it in the same light as William Morgan. Certainly there was no argument that the game "was exacting," at least in its popular version. It was just the way the early gentlemen preferred the sport to be.

Still, the '20s was a time of growth for the sport. In 1923, State YMCA Championships were held in New York, New Jersey, Colorado and Georgia. By the end of the 1920s, volleyball featured an annual YMCA championship in most states. And some of the bosses who played in the YMCAs, infected with a bout of charity, took the game to the workplace. Mineworkers in Colorado, men in steel mills of Pennsylvania, workers in shipyards and canneries on the Pacific coast were converted to volleyball. One industrial leader commented in 1922:

Not only countless twilight and other volleyball leagues composed entirely of industrial workers, but thousands of men and boys are playing the game during the noon hour in spaces between buildings, between rows of box cars, between piles of pig iron, on 18 foot sidewalks...there is no single thing that is doing more to bring management and men together than volleyball...

In the Volley Ball Rules handbook of 1922-23, an article appeared by Dr. Kalengberg as "Volley Ball in Industry," in which he lauds the game in the workplace that "takes the place of crap shooting, dirty stories and unprofitable gossip..."

In perhaps the first big-time industrial league ever formed in 1923 and disputably the origin of the "spike," Carnegie Steel Company had 25 teams paying three games a night, twice a week. Volleyball was prevalent enough with the game's hierarchy that in 1924 Fisher appointed A.H. Wyman to represent industry on the Joint Rules Committee.

The remaining major rules were put in place during this era. The year 1920 saw the end of the "flexible" (any size) courts which were found in every part of the nation. Dimensions were finally set at 30 feet by 60 feet...and helped to eliminate the home court advantage in many cases! Another important advancement at the time (already established in the Far East) occurred when the setting rule was defined. An arbitrary call by the referee, setting was the most difficult skill to officiate and to master as a player. One can imagine what butchering of the ball went on along the long road of evolution to today's "deep dish" of the beach game where even a breath of spin on the ball results in a violation. Yet in the early '20s a major advancement came when "lifting, carrying, throwing, jabbing, slapping" the ball—and even more heinous crimes—were deemed unacceptable.

If the '20s seemed a virtuous age for the sport, one man clearly stands out from all the rest. It was no surprise that the famous honor call of 1924 was made when considering the coach of the Germantown team who instilled those values. It was Pop Idell. Idell continued his tireless campaign on almost every possible level—between 1923-1933, his "Intensive Volley Ball" articles were published in the yearly Official Volley Ball Rules handbook, sharing advancements made from the playing laboratory at his Germantown YMCA. Although not numerous, the articles were regarded as the Bible of volleyball.

In addition to his creative powers, Idell's prescience of the future was truly uncanny. In 1920, he initiated the first Doubles Championship at the Germantown YMCA. It immediately caught fire and the best players from all over Pennsylvania came to consider the annual event as one of the year's highlights. The court was shorted to 50 feet by 30 feet and apparently its creator was no slouch as a player either, even at the age of 35. In 1924, the Handbook reported that Idell teamed with William Buchler to beat Bill Nenner and his partner William Philler, two starters off the Germantown varsity.

What didn't the man do in volleyball? Another first occurred in 1927; Idell took a 7,000 mile promotional tour giving local talks and clinics with evangelical zeal—the first extensive tour ever organized. In turn, he was so impressed with the talent and interest he encountered that he predicted the sport would be dominated by teams from the Midwest and South within a few years. To no one's surprise...he was right again.

Back row (left to right)—Fry, Smith, Idell, Buchler. Front row—Vorberg, W. B. McKaraher, Phys. Dir.; Rappold, Capt.; Wood, Briggs.

BIG RED TEAM OF GERMANTOWN Y.M.C.A.
PHILADELPHIA, PA.

Big Red Team of Germantown YMCA, 1922. Runner-up, first YMCA National Championship. Pop Idell in back row is player-coach. (Courtesy of Spalding)

SCENE IN FINALS, FIRST NATIONAL VOLLEY BALL CHAMPIONSHIP, BROOKLYN, N. Y., APRIL 28-29, 1922.

Germantown Y battling it out with Pittsburgh Central Y in the first finals, 1922. Held at Brooklyn Central YMCA. (Courtesy of Spalding)

First edition of the Offical Volley Ball Rules handbook, 1916. (Courtesy of Spalding)

Pop Idell. The Ben Franklin of the game.

Chapter 3
1928-1936

"Don't block!..."

"I'm gonna block!" whispered a bedraggled Germantown player to his captain, Bill Nenner.

"Why?" asked the incredulous expression of the captain, so drained from the humidity of a hot Chattanooga night that he was too tired to talk.

"Anderson's the only guy who doesn't windmill so they'll probably set the ball close to the net. Worth a try," the tall Marshall Ward added. The captain disagreed. There was a far better chance with six guys arrayed in a half-moon defense at mid-court. Crouched and ready, in hopes that the spike would come right at one of them, to be lifted up just like in setting. Then he could run to the ball and set it to his taller partner for a kill.

"We gotta try something! We haven't scored a point in 20 minutes," Ward braved a reply.

In a rare democratic impulse, or perhaps it was fatigue, Nenner deferred. Silently he recognized that points were hard to come by but he just didn't like the block. Besides, you couldn't even reach over the net to block—or spike—anymore! They'd just passed that new rule. Finally he murmured with a frown: "Go ahead...but you're wasting your time."

In the final game of the 1928 National Championship, Ward homed in on "Andy" Anderson across the net. Behind him he heard the thud of the underhand serve which typically landed in the far corner where a player took it overhead with a "ten-point pass"—satisfying the rule that the ball was "clearly batted" by contacting it on the tips of the ten digits. The ball was delivered to the Hyde Park setter, or "henchman," waiting near the net. It was automatic. In fact, everybody in the gym knew where the ball was going in those days since a team was broken down into three pairs: each pair made up of a setter and a hitter. When in the front row, the henchman of the duo would invariably set the ball straight up from wherever he was along the net; his adjacent and exclusive spiking partner would attack the ball. This made for life-long friendships...or sometimes less friendly relationships considering the practice of substituting both players out if one was playing badly.

True to form, Anderson watched the ball lifted 15 feet directly above his setter—the great Jake Rashkin; it was his job to approach the set which he did by running parallel to the net. Ward matched him step for step—it was mano a mano. Although Anderson used a normal one-foot takeoff, instead of attacking the ball in the windmill motion with an unbent elbow, he lashed out at the ball like he was throwing an object. Putting more heat on the ball, Anderson grunted with the force of his attack, certain of scattering the opponents lined up like six (no, five!...it didn't matter) ducks on the pond. Then the unspeakable happened. Somehow Ward got one of his hands in the way of the ball, it caromed back and landed on Hyde Park's side. A point was scored and Germantown's supporters exploded in jubilation. Well...at least those who were still around after midnight. The match had begun at eight o'clock and had been going on over four hours now. It was an intrepid play but it broke the ice. Germantown revitalized and went on to capture the crown. The first team to ever come through the losers' bracket in the double elimination tournament, they captured the championship winning the final two games: 15-13 and 20-18!

As Ward of Germantown demonstrated, the block was a "surprise" tactic. A leading expert on the game in that era, Robert Laveaga, commented at the time: "In general, blocking is not worthwhile as an acceptable principle of play to be used consistently. There are times when it is advisable, but it is not considered effective as a general policy of play."

"Casting a wider net"...

The year 1928 was a signal one for volleyball. When 315 people were sent invitations to come to New York City for a meeting to form a new national organization, only 32 showed up—31 of them representatives of the YMCA. At the Yale Club, the United States Volleyball Association was founded; Dr. George Fisher, who was already serving as editor of the Official Volley Ball Rules handbook, was elected as the first president. The momentum for the new organization had been primarily an interest to expand the National Championship from exclusively Y teams to Open ones as well. Although some YMCA officials were opposed to the new, independent organization, they were outvoted by other members who favored a stronger joining of forces to further widen the base of the sport. The Volley Ball Rules Committee was opened up to 12 national organizations including: the NCAA, Boy Scouts of America, Playground Association of America, US Army and Navy, High Schools, Industry and the women's division of the American Athletic Federation.

Significant equipment changes also occurred in 1928. Since the new organization promised new growth, a representative for Spalding, George Hepborn, also thought it time for a new ball. He was led to Pop Idell for ideas on how to improve the old one. Idell of course had some. The "balanced ball" was produced by having the plunger type valve moved to the opposite side of the lacing and concealed, distributing the weight more evenly. The old ball when served was often a giant knuckleball coming over the net; now it was only a slow curve at worst. Coincidentally, the overhand serve arose as an offensive weapon at almost the same time as the revamping of the ball. Its employment was first mentioned in the 1929 handbook and represents the first major tactical change of the sport. Developed "out West" in Chicago, within a couple of years the old underhanded serve was cast on the junk pile of history. In 1932, "The Coming of the Overhead Serve," by Robert Laveaga appeared in the handbook to officially recognize the major change in the game.

In 1932, Idell also developed a standardized net of dark-colored, four-inch mesh with wire cable and two-inch white tape at the top; this made for a taut net and clearer vision of the ball. Also during the same period, a certain YMCA physical director, who had some prior years as an indoor decorator, used his talents to study new lighting and paint schemes for gymnasium walls. The YMCA adopted the changes and visibility of moving objects improved dramatically. The same man invented the system of differently colored floor lines which marked the different games: basketball, volleyball, and badminton, to name a few. After providing so many other creations, it's not surprising to learn that the former interior decorator and inventor was none other than Pop Idell. Idell's giving nature surfaced again when he stipulated that all royalties from balls and nets which normally go to the inventor would be deducted from the price of the items.

As the sport was slowly slipping out of the grasp of the older male members of the YMCA, there came a final cry of protest lodged with the organization's directors. Although alarmed by the game becoming "too intensive," the YMCA did not halt the game's evolution and wisely placated the oldsters by creating a Veterans Division in the National Championships in 1928 for players over 35. Those senior players must have been quite pleased—at least that first year. Since only two teams entered the division, every player received a trophy!

Soon after the formation of the USVBA, the Great Depression hit the nation like a sledge hammer. Suddenly, Americans were forced to think more about eating than playing games and consequently the national craze for sports was tempered. By the mid-'30s industrial leagues were gone; in 1937, the position of industrial representative to the USVBA was gone too. Still, part of the FDR Administration's policy was to provide healthy activities for the nation's youth and unemployed. To that end such organizations as the Civilian Conservation Corps, National Youth Administration, and Works Progress Administration promoted recreation around the country. Volleyball, being a relatively cheap activity, gained new converts to the game although on a rudimentary and unexciting level.

A rare fire flickered in the eyes of the USVBA hierarchy in 1932. In anticipation of the Olympics in Los Angeles, a bid was made to have volleyball included in the Games. But Avery Brundage, head of the powerful Amateur Athletic Union (AAU), took little time in turning it down. Instead, the USVBA was invited to organize a demonstration match during the competition. The match took place but few traces of that historical event remain.

However, the AAU with its watchful (some said predatory) eye noticed that the sport was demonstrating some life on the West coast, particularly in Southern California. In the 1938-39 USVBA Official Volley Ball Guide the six leading indoor clubs were listed: Pasadena Y, Long Beach Y, Hollywood Y, Los Angeles Athletic Club, Hollywood Athletic Club and San Diego Athletic Club. However, in the mid-'30s it was the Pasadena Y "Aces" which dominated the game. The article added:

...there have been each season for the past decade one or two or three teams in Southern California capable of placing among

the first ten in national tournament play, but due to the fact that the meets usually have been held at cities some three thousand miles distant, Coast teams have sent a team East each second year, Los Angeles "Y" taking fifth place at Knoxville in 1934, Pasadena "Y" tieing for fifth place at Davenport in 1936, and Pasadena "Y" taking fourth place at Detroit in 1938. In future it is expected to send one or more teams East each year...

As the Pasadena Y managed to keep ahead of the pack, an article in the preceding year's Guide by the team's manager, Ira Swett, gave a run-down of the squad:

Led by the West's most powerful spiker, Captain Wendell Smith, the great offensive power unleashed by the Aces was the determining factor in their victories. Aided by All-America spikers Web Caldwell and Al DeWeese...the Aces were able to subdue their opponents... The three-man block, originated by the Aces in 1936 on the Coast, was continued with telling effect, while the floating serve became more and more into its own.

In time the AAU saw enough action to engineer a breakaway movement in 1935 by forming its own National Championship—claiming jurisdiction over the sport of volleyball and hoping to capture its players as well. Powerful in most other amateur sports, including track and field which it controlled, lines were drawn and a showdown came in 1937. The USVBA had mustered enough support to fend off the takeover, and the AAU was forced to cave in and affiliate with the older organization. Hardly a friendly relationship, they would continue to run separate National Championships into the early 1970s.

"All-American...the shoes count too..."

The tradition of selecting an All-American team was conceptualized by Pop Idell and instituted in 1927. That year the handbook published his Red, Blue and White Teams which corresponded to First, Second and Third teams. Admittedly it was a manner of gauging and recognizing the best players while leaving their hallowed names to memoria. At the same time, the selections by definition were subjective...and often provided torrid topics of debate which could provoke outcries of political skullduggery to outright calumny. From the beginning the exercise stirred controversy, which has continued into the present, and a safe prediction is that it will incite heated discussion as long as it continues.

Idell's criteria for his selections are discussed in his article printed in the 1942 Volleyball Guide, "My 'A' System for Rating Players." He explains:

If the Red, White and Blue Teams should play each other, the skills are so near even that the team having the best morale at that time would probably win... This is my "A" system for rating players who I see:

INTENSIVE VOLLEYBALL

♦ A perfect game equals 100 points.

♦ The game is divided into 6 Departments.

♦ Each Department shows its points of the 100 as follows:

    MORALE...........................15 points
    SERVE..............................7 points
    DEFENSE........................18 points
    PASS.................................7 points
    SET UP............................20 points
    ATTACK............................33 points

(Idell then goes on to elaborate each department with respective points as shown in the following for the attack.)

ATTACK

Reverse According to his Best Hand:

    10....Right-handed and what he does
    10....Left-handed and what he does
    8.....Height, 6 ft., 1 in. (take off
         one point for each inch less)
    5....Shoes

Any round figures of any part of each department are subject to:

    2....Perfect Set-Up
    2....Medium Set-Up to net
    2....Far Away Set-Up to back court
    2....Set-Up to side line
    1....Fracture Skull
    1....Low
Total: 10

I have two systems. I have used the "A" system the longest for rating individuals (since 1911) and which I have made public. However, my "AA" System is my personal property. I intend that the public shall not see it as, in addition it includes the character (in my sight and hearing) and personality of many players, officials, and, in a few cases, even going into their homes. I might be given a hundred-year jail sentence for my "Opinions" since 1912.

A simple glance at this elaborate and arcane scheme reveals an original mind—a perfect guest for David Letterman. As the most innovative personality of the first half-century, Pop Idell's personality continually displays an offbeat element, a quirky touch of the genius. His system is no longer around today. Who could decipher his reasoning behind docking points for being short? *And shoes?* Points for the right fit, cleanliness—who knows? As for "Fracture Skull" and "Low," it is only known that he was referring to difficult sets for spikers to hit. But finally, what a breath of fresh air he must have blown through the game so controlled by those YMCA patriarchs.

Yet, Pop Idell seemed to succumb to attacks of partisan thinking at times. Although done with coaching in 1927, the affection for his old team and state remained. His initial All-American First Team selections of 1927 included six Pennsylvania players from three separate teams. Yet the winning team, Hyde Park of Chicago, placed all six starters only on the Second Team. In 1928, after the miraculous victory of his beloved Germantown team, he included all six

Germantown players on his All-American Red (or First) Team! In justification of his criteria, he cited the 16-year national prominence of the team's greatness, the fact that his team had to play four more games than Hyde Park in the tournament, its sterling character and finally the crowning achievement of rising through the loser's bracket. He went on to admit that, in 100 games, the First Team would beat the Second Team six only 51 times. Perhaps another pang of compunction prompted him to place all six Hyde Park players on the White (Second Team)... again!

He appeared to let his parochial side get the better of him once again the following year when he named his All-Time All-America Teams (for the eight years of existence) and picked Germantown' s spiker, Marshall Ward, as the "world's greatest all-around player," although he claimed that Hyde Park's R. "Andy" Anderson was gaining ground on Ward. Alas, it seems that even Pop Idell was human.

Still, his enthusiasm and flair was a welcome rarity in the annual handbook. While the booklet is made up of mostly prosaic articles on rules and team values, Idell's commentary, "Intensive Volley Ball," always dealt with play of the game—with style. To wit; the introduction of his "Intensive Volley Ball" in the 1925 Handbook:

> Old Men, Fat Men and Children don't play Intensive Volley Ball! Jumping...would make a lake out of a fat man in which his whole team might drown.

Even more entertaining was Idell's other annual article, "Volleys." A type of "Confucius says," the articles were full of witticisms, tips and rules of conduct like the wisdom found in Chinese fortune cookies. Here are a few from his 1923 "Volleys":

♦ A star set-up player is known by what he does with a medium or bad pass.

♦ The "attack" must be like greased-lightning, let loose by a hair-triggered brain.

♦ Set-ups arched parallel with net to the back of attack players are called "fracture skulls." Painful injury can happen to a player making the jump, as he decidedly goes off balance.

♦ The ideal figure for an "attack" player is long legs, short body, long arms, good feet and sound head.

♦ Watch out for those who sulk or make catty comments out of the depths of their jealousy. ...At the first opportunity use your influence to drive these people out of volley ball.

♦ Volley ball players as individuals are always liberal in their financial support of sports.

Vincent Bennett was another early leader of the game whose voice surfaced as one of expertise. An attorney from New York, Bennett was known as an excellent referee and beginning in 1933, his selections of All-Americans appeared side-by-side with Idell's. The two selections would appear concurrently for many years until a selection committee was finally decided upon by the USVBA to pick the best players of the National Tournament. In the 1933 rules handbook, Bennett also included an article describing his impressions of the '32 Nationals. Interestingly, his observations of the San Antonio-Hyde Park finals also pointed out the important role of the referee.

> Unfortunately, Hyde Park has acquired the habit of holding and following the ball... Hyde Park would have won the tournament if it had overcome its "sticky" ballhandling.

The official had a lot on his shoulders in those days. Every serve and set was a judgment call...and how was "sticky" defined? The referee also had to rule on the occasional underhand retrieval of the ball. If a fingernail passed through the plane of the net, he was expected to see it. A game's outcome was highly influenced by the officiating; the fact that different interpretations still varied in different regions of the country made for lively discussion...a blemish on the game to endure for decades.

Sometimes the players' innovations led to rule changes as well. This occurred in 1936 when the two "crosses" became required as part of the official floor markings. The determinant of this ruling could be traced to the Division Street Y team of Chicago which in the Nationals the year before grouped all five players to create a screen for the server. Howls of protest to the referee were ineffectual; nothing in the rules prevented it. Until the next annual meeting of the USVBA when the rule of the crosses was adopted: to be placed 15 feet back from the net and 10 feet from the sideline, the two small markings were used as co-ordinates to divide the court into six equal areas within which each player must stand until the ball was served. Quickly the screen was practically eliminated as a weapon—it was later revived in the 1950s when the crosses were eliminated.

"A Man's Game..."

What about American sport itself in the '30s? Was that only a man's world in those days? And was volleyball any different? The title of the first book ever written on the subject of volleyball could probably help answer that question. It was published in 1933 under the august title: *Volley Ball: A Man's Game!*

Written by a leader in the game, Robert Laveaga, the article must not be judged too harshly. Perhaps a fairer assumption is that the intent of the title was not a healthy shot of machismo, but rather an attempt to persuade American athletes—undeniably men in the main—that volleyball was not the "sissy" sport it had been labeled as for so many years. Still, in retrospect it is not surprising that the prevailing attitude towards women's volleyball, and women's sports, was belittling. In the 1925 handbook appeared an article by Agnes Wyman, Head of the Department of Physical Education at Barnard College (Columbia).

Entitled "Volley Ball for Girls and Women," the article suggested certain modifications of the men's rules. The most notable included the increase of the number of women on the court: from six to nine, twelve or fifteen! The educator also thought "batting" of the ball should be allowed with either hand; women should be allowed unlimited number of hits, and the rules should permit another lady to assist an errant serve over the net with a second hit.

In the 1930 rules handbook, a curious article appeared entitled "Preliminary Game for Volley Ball for Girls and Women." It would appear in several editions of subsequent years.

Cage Volley Ball or Giant Volley Ball is a very good preliminary game for volley ball. It is a game which causes much merriment and laughter and at the same affords some exercise without being strenuous. It is highly recommended for a mass program, as the number of players is limited only by the size of the field and the rules are very simple. Little still is necessary in order to enjoy it..."

"Little still" indeed! The lady educator goes on to suggest a prescribed ball between 20 and 36 inches, constructed of rubber or preferably "aeroplane cloth." It was a giant beach ball three feet across, banged anywhere and everywhere, since no limit on hits per side was the rule. On a court jammed full with as many girls as could fit. The creator of the game remains anonymous—probably with good reason.

With that kind of leadership, women were still far from enjoying serious competition to say the least. The official voice of women's volleyball was the Committee on Volleyball for Girls and Women. Associated with the American Physical Education Association, their adapted rules were published in the official Handbook of Women's Sports. They were printed in the USVBA rules handbook as well and usually accompanied by a short, generic and colorless article on women's volleyball. In fact, in 1928 the women's committee adopted separate rules for women which would last until

1958! Some of the modifications are as follows: eight players per side, two serves, no limit to amount of hits on one side, most points scored in 30 minutes wins (mandatory five-minute break), net height of 7'6". Everything a young girl could have hoped for! At least that's what the prevailing standard of feminine sport prescribed during the first half of this century. Even as late as 1942, Nan Weed, a member representing women on the Volleyball Rules Committee, expatiated at length on the game's virtues of team play and social skills. She went on to describe her own sex as "women being creatures innately social and not seekers after individual prowess..." She described volleyball's suitability for ladies: "...the possibility of a continual development of skill without constant practice, without accompanying development of big muscles, may be another element of appeal for women."

It is all the more remarkable that the enormously popular "novelty matches" organized by Pop Idell in Philadelphia ever took place, much less flourished. As early as 1929, Idell had women playing six against six in serious competition. Not stopping there, in 1930 the visionary persuaded the ladies to play doubles! The following year he crossed the gender barrier with mixed doubles and in 1933, the mixed-six or "novelty matches" took off in the Germantown Y and grew into a well-attended city wide championship. Typically Idell studied hard before altering the rules: the first and third (if needed) games were played on a net of eight feet with only men spiking. The second game was played by only women spiking on a lowered net of 7' 6". A product of a more chivalrous age, Idell stipulated that men could not spike directly at women.

Besides being a brilliant game innovator, Idell seemed to also possess a keen sense of human nature which he employed to promote his beloved sport. His reflections on the co-ed game in 1934 are as follows:

> "Women are now more interested in all-men games. Men are now interested in all-women games. More spectator players are at all games. The women cover more territory on defense and add color to the team's morale (in novelty matches). The men at first tolerate, then quickly respect the ability of the women. Selfishness is quickly exposed and corrected by the system of three touches and alternating the set-up and attack. Men's gym suits are washed and ironed oftener."

"West coast baby..."

At the same time, something new was happening way out on the California coast. Los Angeles in the 1920s was already spinning the luminous shroud which would bedazzle the entire world. Moving pictures were going to "talkies" and new, brighter stars like Clark Gable and Jean Harlow appeared in the firmament. Long, chromed automobiles carried the living icons through the palm-studded boulevards down to the beaches of Santa Monica. While the well-heeled frolicked in the white sand of private clubs strung along the coast like a pearl necklace, the less fortunate could swim and relax at the public beach just south of the Santa Monica Pier (Santa Monica Playground in those days). Normal citizens would hop on the "Red Car" for a nickel and have the public streetcar dump them out at the foot of the Playground—the lively and fascinating place that would transform into Muscle Beach one day.

No longer around today, the gaggle of private beach clubs under the famous Santa Monica cliffs began a long decline with the Great Depression. However, the man who played in the first beach doubles game is still around. Paul Johnson, 83, first played beach volleyball in six-man games at the Edgewater Club in 1927. All of the clubs had a sand court in that era and soon a serious competition was held between four clubs which rotated venues each Sunday: the Deauville, the Del Mar, the Santa Monica Athletic Club and the Strollers.

The popularity of sand volleyball and its youthful lifestyle even caught the eye of the USVBA power brokers back in the colder climes of the East and Midwest. In the 1938-39 USVBA Guide appeared a short article by J. Frank Holt entitled, "The Beach Game Attracting Youth."

> Players at the beach are conspicuous for their youth, some of those on the better teams ranging in age from 18 to 25. Many of the better players at the beach become promising indoor players. Indoor players in the Far West on the average are much younger than on the East Coast and in the Middle West.

> At the beach the soft, underhand floating serve predominates, while most of the indoor teams in this area use the hard overhand serve. There is considerable mixed volley ball at the beach clubs, three girls setting, three men killing, the only restriction being that a man does not spike the ball directly at a girl.

During the week when not enough regular members were around, Johnson and his cronies gradually devised four-man and then doubles formats. It was one summer day in 1930 when Charley Kahn, Bill Brothers and Johnny Allen joined Johnson to play in the first beach doubles game. Looking out on the formidable expanse of sand that fateful afternoon, they decided to play on one-quarter of the court and then tried one-half. But since the other three were all setters—and short—Johnson claimed that they insisted on trying the full court to exploit their greater quickness and ball-handling. "I was the only one who could hit!," Johnson laughs today. A new game was born.

Soon the doubles game spread to the other clubs and by the mid-30s a definite style had developed. On a 7' 10" net, the ball was rarely spiked. After receiving the serve overhand with the fingers, the ball was set to a partner who in turn would set, or "shoot" the ball to an open spot on the court. The third contact was loosely handled without the player required to face the direction he set it. Defensively, the ball could be retrieved overhand as the serve, bumped with

one arm or even run down to "scoop" it back over their head with two open hands.

"Harmonic convergence...in 1935..."

"Would you like to play?" she asked. Like to play! He would have done anything for this lovely dewdrop. Jump off the pier, swim around it underwater...you name it! But Manny Saenz had never touched a volleyball in his life—played every sport the guys played in those days and excelled with quickness and grit. Only 5'6" on a good day, he'd learned to take every advantage growing up with his brothers; all bigger than him, a couple of them became pro boxers and football players. From Mexican ancestry who had lived in Los Angeles since the early 1800s, Saenz's father was the first fire chief of Culver City. He was 21, in great shape and just out of the Merchant Marines in 1935 when he caught himself watching a rare mixed doubles game. At Sunset Pier in Venice he intrepidly stepped on the only court, confident that this running around in the sand would be a piece of cake. Saenz would remember always his first game..."she was gorgeous! "

Love was indeed a strong motivator but competition had its own intense flame. Soon he was playing every chance he could. Jimmy Lennon, father of the harmonizing girl wonders who helped make Lawrence Welk a national TV figure, was Saenz' first partner. He soon moved north with a new partner, a UCLA basketball player named Al Harris, to the tougher games on nearby Venice Beach. By the late '30s, they were playing the best competition around at two places: the Deauville, the private club owned by the Los Angeles Athletic Club where the local heroes of the LAAC indoor team played, and farther north at the public courts of State Beach.

Unbeknownst to either of them, the other half of the first great doubles beach team, Bernie Holtzman, was getting his initiation into volleyball the same year as Saenz. In 1935 the 13-year old Holtzman kid tagged along one day with his older brother down to the pier in Santa Monica. Fascinated by what he saw there, the kid would come everyday hoping to get into the six-man games on the one public court. Nobody invited the little urchin, small for even his age, all that summer. Still, while standing on the road to hitch a ride back to his home in Hollywood because the Red Car was too expensive, he'd dream of getting in a game to perform heroic plays. Especially in one of those games held every Sunday game when co-ed sixes were played. Spectators lined up on the pier to watch the contest below which awarded a case of chilled Jonathan apples. This was the depth of the Depression and food was a premium. Holtzman remembers that "when one of the teams realized they were going to lose in the finals, they'd suddenly start acting nice so the winners would share the apples."

It was the next summer, when one of the adults took notice of the little waif hanging around and gave him a shot. Promptly told that his small stature required him to concentrate only on setting, the shell-shocked kid nodded enthusiastically. He got asked again that summer—he was always there waiting for that magic nod. Since the proletariat had only one court at their disposal, the public court was usually crowded with games of sixes but in rare times, doubles were played like they were in the private club courts. "It rained a lot in those days and that's when I usually got a chance to play doubles. I remember people standing on the pier and pointing at those crazy people down there playing in the rain."

A few years later Holtzman was the best player at the pier while still in his teens. His partner, Carl Stewart, suggested that they venture up to State Beach to try their luck against the heavies. State Beach! It was a bold move. The nets were a little higher and by now the best players there, as at the Deauville, were spiking the ball...and hard! But Stewart had already made the little jaunt north and convinced his young partner that like anything else, it wasn't as bad as one thought. What Stewart didn't reveal is that he had bandied Holtzman's name all over the beach as a young phenom capable of dethroning the best of the State players.

Sam Shargo, the better of the two brothers who made up the best doubles team at State Beach, was waiting for him. "Sam Shargo took this C minus player named Minetti and annihilated me!" Holtzman laughingly recalls. The Santa Monica boy left the beach licking his wounds that day; it would take a couple of years before he would be able to even stay with the Shargo Brothers—both lifeguards who were exercise and diet fanatics which made them oddities—but Holtzman had plenty of time.

George J. Fisher, first USVBA president (1928-1951)

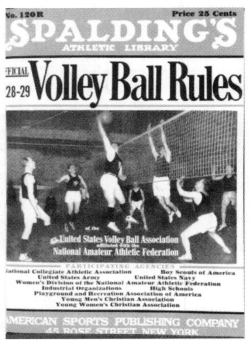

Official Volley Ball Rules handbook, 1928-1929. (Courtesy of Spalding)

1, G. F. Scouten, Phys. Dir.; 2, Max Eble; 3, J. m Nell; 4, S. M. Ward; 5, Wm. Philler; 6, M. Luther, Mgr.; 7, E. Pretty; 8, J. McKaraher; 9, Wm. Nenner, Capt. and Coach; 10, J. Root; 11, Wm. Buchler.
GERMANTOWN Y.M.C.A. NATIONAL CHAMPIONS.

First USVBA National Champions, 1928. Germantown YMCA. (Courtesy of Spalding)

Chapter 4
1937-1945

"Ace of aces..."

From the Official Volley Ball Rules (1937-38):

The opening match was between the defending champions, Houston, and Louisville. No one gave the Kentuckians even an outside chance, but when Houston lined up with only two of last year's veterans and without volley ball's No. 1 spiker, Jimmy Wortham, it was apparent that Houston was not the Houston of old. The hometowners sprung the first surprise by taking the second game from the Texans, extending the match to a three-game affair, which Houston finally won, 15-4. The word soon passed round that this year Houston was just another volley ball team and it was apparent that a new champion would be crowned. The Texans' ace, Wortham, was taken ill before the tournament and after Duncan (Chicago) had placed Houston in the losers' bracket by winning two straight games, Houston in desperation attempted to recoup by using the ailing wortham in their match with San Diego, but Jimmy was a sick man and should never have played. San Diego put Houston out of the tournament in two straight games. A game but listless team was through as champions.

Jimmy Wortham was selected in 1954 by the Helms Foundation as the best player of the first 50 years of American volleyball. He must have been sorely missed in 1937—the Houston YMCA squad had won the National Cham-

pionship every year between 1933-1939 except for the year the first megastar came down sick. The Lone Star hero had already taken center stage in 1931 and 1932 when he led the San Antonio Y to two national titles. Although Chicago had several excellent YMCA teams such as Division Street, Duncan, Larrabee Avenue and Lawson, as well as the largest pool of good players, it was the Texans who hooked almost all the gold in the '30s. How dominant was Wortham? In 12 national championships, he was a selected First Team All-American ten times. During his two off years, he was selected both times as Second Team. One of few surviving players who competed against the great Texan, Manny Saenz as a rookie remembers him "hitting the ball so hard against the outside blocker that it kept going up into the stands and out of play."

"The printed word..."

Perhaps what most marked the late '30s was a strong grassroots movement among serious players which sprouted a series of small volleyball bulletins around the country. Effectively a part-time volunteer organization and run on a shoe-string, the USVBA could only provide its annual Official Volley Ball Guide and look to the YMCA to run the yearly National Championships. Although the limited influence of the USVBA didn't affect the great unwashed majority playing in the YMCAs what came to be known as "bat ball," the competitive players were starving for more competition and knowledge. In 1936, the first local bulletin was published as The Lawson Digest. Others followed:

The Evanston Volleyer, Volley Ball News, and the provocative Dope Sheet (Chicago Central YMCA). An active promoter of the sport, Robert Laveaga, suggested combining the local rags into a national publication. The National Volleyball Review was established in 1941 with Harry Wilson, the founder of the Hollywood circular, as editor.

Robert Laveaga who was a YMCA official and educator pushed to get the sport into the education system. No mean task. An avid writer with his eye open for new trends, he contributed articles regularly to the Guide as well as the Review.

"On the road...3,000 miles..."

In the winter of 1940 when two guys walked in the little Venice gym, the handful of players on the court couldn't help but take a long gander...a few became visibly unnerved. It couldn't be! Orrin Sage in their gym! The top player of the Los Angeles Athletic Club (LAAC) who had led his team to a second place finish in the 1939 USVBA Nationals was now leaning against the wall of the crackerbox building and speaking in low tones to George Miller, his occasional gestures pregnant with criticism. "Why was he there?" went the unspoken question.

The pickup game ended and the demigod strolled into the center of their quiet gaze. He stared down at Manny Saenz, "How would you like to play in the nationals for us?" Nationals! In Philadelphia! With LAAC! Even Manny, the little guy so chock full of moxie, swallowed hard before saying yes to his impossible dream. He'd played against Sage and the other LAAC guys on the sand at the Deauville and he'd run up against some of them in local gym play. He held his own he remembered...but could he really play with these guys? Sage explained that they had lost their one substitute needed for the trip and Manny's talents fitted the bill—someone off the bench to play set-up if needed but mostly to go relieve the big guys in the backrow. The vets knew Saenz was green but also they had never seen reflexes like his. He could crawl under a bazooka and take a direct shot with a

one-arm stab or simply with his strong fingers, absorbing the shock to put up a perfect lob.

In May, the seven Angelenos got in two cars and got on Route 66. Even that wasn't easy. At the last minute, Doc Burroughs had to get the infamous Henry Valle and his lightning-fast left arm out of a scrape in a local bar and into his Ford coupe. Good thing too. Valle and Sage spiked the LAAC to a landmark in the sport's history. No non-YMCA had ever won the USVBA Nationals and never a team from the West coast. At the same time, the Embarcadero YMCA team in San Francisco headed east in their vehicles—all six of them. They had a left-handed hammer like Valle too: Frank Bechert. Bechert helped them prove the surprise of the Nationals by finishing in third place. The Volley Ball Guide the following year printed an article summarizing the tournament. Peppered with examples of hyperbole, the remarks by Adrian Hull were incisive:

> Wortham is still the best all-round player in volley ball, but is being given more trouble by blockers than in former years...Anzuini of Larrabee (Chicago) made one of the most spectacular plays of the tournament by going up the end wall to recover a rebound from a spike. ...The most sensational player in the tournament was Collis of Hughes Tool (Houston). Not as consistent as some of the others, he has the highest, most graceful jump, and the hardest kill of any spiker this writer has ever seen. Some of them hit the ceiling after hitting the floor. When he learns to "crawl" on the ball like Jimmy Wortham, he should become the greatest spiker the world has ever seen.

Greatest players and All-Americans...the year 1940 exemplified the subjective nature of that exercise. In the first place, there were now two separate selections: one by Vincent Bennett and the second by Pop Idell. In typical fashion, Idell's was more extensive and rather convoluted for that matter. Still, he tellingly wrote that he only selected "people for my All-American teams on account of their 'Naked Skill'. There are a few very punk personalities amongst them, but I do not allow that to influence at all."

If Idell ignored personality as a factor in his equation for All-Americans, ostensibly Bennett did not. Volleyball's first bad boy, Henry Valle had great playing ability that was only equalled by his irascible character. The embodiment of pure athleticism, Valle ran the 100 in 9.7 seconds which was close to world record time. Manny Saenz reported that he could have played in the NFL had he been able to pull it all together. Paul Johnson, the early beach doubles player who stayed around the game in Los Angeles for a half-century, said, "he was the best player I ever saw." Valle was fast, spring-loaded and had a whip for a left arm. Idell in explaining his complicated and somewhat arcane system which rated his All-Americans from top to bottom, wrote: "However, the 'Figures' show me that Valle was tops in 1940..."

He was "tops," but the southpaw didn't make either First or Second Team on Bennett's lists! And it happened the year before as well; Valle was on Idell's First Team while absent on any of Bennett's. Observations in an article by Harry Wilson on the runner-up LAAC team of 1939 stated that "the sudden development of southpaw Valle into a first rate spiker was all they needed." Yet, curiously Wilson didn't include him on the California All-States teams selected that same year. Well, maybe not so curious. Paul Johnson remembers "Valle had a short switch and sometimes he'd climb up the referee's stand after Wilson if he made a bad call.... So Harry would try to kick him back down with his feet." Hierarchy aside, the sinewy and muscled Valle must have impressed his opponents. In 1941 the defending champs, LAAC, didn't make the trip to Ann Arbor but one of their players did. Henry Valle was recruited to play for another team outside his home state. Pictured in the 1941 Guide with second place finisher, Houston YMCA, his visage seems a bit crestfallen. Dick Caplan remembers why. "Valle showed up in Ann Arbor and he wasn't allowed to play!" To change teams in those days, a player had to meet strict guidelines and apparently a technicality was missed.

Good thing for Caplan's North Avenue Chicago team—they beat Houston without Valle in the finals 15-12, 16-14.

While keeping in mind that the hierarchy was imbued with the YMCA mindset, no leap of logic is required to see why Henry Valle wasn't viewed as a model citizen. At least that can be speculated. In fact, LAAC's Doc Burroughs had his hands full most of the time; reportedly the avuncular manager-coach got Henry out of local jails once or twice to play. The prototype of the anti-hero, Valle was the first of the counter-culture athletes who would emerge in the '60s to mark the sport, in particular the beach game: undisciplined, play hard...and party hard.

As for the two seperate All-American selections by Idell and Bennett, a distinct improvement was made in 1942 when a committee was appointed to select the best players. That system has remained until the present...but the suspected partisan influences and favoritism in certain choices has also remained to fuel controversy through today.

"Indoor doubles and college..."

One of Pop Idell's inventions found a Pacific coast foothold in 1939. Appearing in the 1940 Guide was an article by Harry Wilson on the first "Southern California Doubles Championships":

> This game is gaining nationwide attention and is almost as popular there as the regulation game. Play is on 25-foot courts, or just 5 feet short of regulation... Eighteen teams entered with play starting at noon...on two courts and kept going for ten hours.

Who won that first doubles tournament? George Miller and the irrepressible Henry Valle. Although he finished somewhere in the lower part of the pack, Harry Wilson also competed and with a not-too-shoddy partner: All-American Webb Caldwell.

The following year the "National Doubles Open Championship" celebrated its tenth anniversary in Wilmington, Delaware. The winners, Hannaman-Melon knocked off the Shuck twins in a double finals. There were two things that apparently helped the victors:

♦ Hannaman who "packed some extra weight," was trailing in the semi-final when he decided to give away the hopeless game in order to save himself for the later final.

♦ Mrs. Mellon, "mother of the champion...proudly showed a rabbit's foot, but admitted she had rubbed the fur thin."

The Guide article of 1941 continued:

> Doubles calls for stamina and skill. The competition brings players down to a level of ability. The tall player cannot get by on his height alone. He must back it up with speed and ball handling. The ball must be well set up by each player... Blocking, single or double, is practically useless. Then there is always the tricky little placement toss. The going is steady and calls for good physical shape.

Both the University of Pennsylvania and Temple entered teams in the 1940 Nationals in Philadelphia. There are records of increased popularity on other college campuses as well, but almost entirely as an intramural activity. The first varsity team formed was at the University of Washington in 1934. With no other varsity teams to challenge, they played in Open tournaments. The few examples of inter-collegiate play happened in 1941 when the University of Pennsylvania played 12 matches, but only two against other universities—Columbia and Temple. Another historic event occurred in 1948 when Florida State University was the first college to hire a full-time varsity coach for volleyball. One of the frequently heard questions following the move was: "Why?" The fact that no league or collegiate competition existed did nothing to discourage Florida State Athletic Director Howard Danford in his quest. A rabid supporter of the sport, he single-handedly got the coach hired—over minimal protests from the powerful football and basketball coaches.

"Blocking and blindness..."

Spiking developed faster than any other skill in volleyball's evolution and this same prowess led to the criticism of the slowness of scoring. Points were hard to come by. Gradually it was realized that one way to get on the scoreboard was to block the ball. Reason also soon revealed that if one blocker could sometimes stuff a hard Spalding 114 for a point (and protect his shell-shocked teammates at the same time), why not try two? They did and it worked. Then a few California teams—open air and sunshine fostering imagination and daring—tried three! Soon too many balls were being hurtled back at the attacker. Some players, coaches and administrators were alarmed. An entertaining article, "Benefits and Dangers of Blocking" by Ross Breniser, appeared in the 1938-39 Guide to set things right.

> But, beginning with the 1937 National Tournament, those present noted a tendency to "gang up" on the block...And so we have the Triple Block, risky, detrimental to morale and adding difficulty to the officiating. But these points, while most important, would not be enough for its elimination. I consider two other factors as delivering its knockout punch—the one is moral, the other physical.

The author goes on to argue the lack of probity in a multiple block by praising baseball's pitcher-batter duel; volleyball should likewise feature a one-on-one contest. However, he ends by caving into a two-man block compromise ruling. As far as his "physical" argument, he cites his knowledge that some men "have lost as much as eight pounds during the two days of the Nationals and I have known of more than one case where near-exhaustion followed for members of teams not in the best of shape." It is intolerable in the author's mind that set-up men who never had to jump, now have "to jump at least eight to fifteen times a game;" and spikers must increase their normal number of lift-offs—15 to 20 times a game—by the same eight to 15. His sympathy almost audible, he concludes: "It isn't any wonder that men play out!"

Yet, the modern mind wonders if these complaints might have found their source in some of the teams with more ample flesh...and shorter players! What is known is that the problem became so acute that the USVBA Rules Committee stepped in with a compromise in 1938—only two adjacent blockers were allowed. A few years later Pop Idell published a short strategy on how to beat the block. He stated that "the height reached by the attack player, with his running high jump take-off with one foot and much greater reach of one hand, gives him the real advantage, if he will only use it." So it was the block which stirred the first rule controversy.

Officiating continued to be a chafing problem; referees from different regions had differing interpretations of the rules. Finally an effort in the late '30s was made to establish hand signals and an accreditation program was incorporated—much to the joy of the players. In a report on the 1940 Nationals, Pop Idell can be referred to once again for insight into the player-referee problem. As his wont, Idell seemed to land on the side of the player in disputes. His observations on the curious honor system found "well over 100 fouls called by the players, thereby assisting the referee. Many games were lost, and even a match, by this extreme matter-of-fact sportsmanship." And as in many other instances, Idell recapitulated the danger of the sport being overly officiated—playing should be foremost.

> The superfluous sharpness of the refereeing had quite a tendency to upset the players and make them feel that they were playing for the referee rather than for themselves and the spectators. I believe there will be a tendency to organize the officials so that they will not be the pre-

dominant third element during the tournaments.

"Amateur at any cost..."

The attack on Pearl Harbor in late 1941 was an alarum which cleared gymnasiums and beaches of volleyball players as well as every other sportsmen. The nation was thrust into war on two fronts requiring a total commitment from all its citizens—able-bodied young men fighting in both Europe and the Pacific and everyone else working in factories at home. The USVBA Nationals were suspended in 1943 and 1944. The only area of growth for the sport was overseas, particularly amongst the troops in the South Pacific. One man closely involved with the military version of the game was Major E.B. DeGroot of the US Air Force. In 1942 when he became Director of Physical Training for the West Coast, the former athlete was looking for exercise when he stumbled into the Olympic Club of San Francisco. An early leader of the game in California, Al Fish, introduced him to a new game and DeGroot began an almost one-man campaign to spread his affection for volleyball throughout the military world. He would be quite successful.

At the end of World War II, the sport of volleyball had certainly undergone a serious metamorphosis during its first half-century. By the time the rules were finally refined to a near-modern version, almost three decades had passed. One thing hadn't changed—the YMCA influence. The game was born in the YMCA, and it was largely dominated by its influence even though the USVBA was the governing body. Almost all of the game's stewards were acting or former YMCA officials, and they were the ones who year after year engaged in the most crucial debate: recreation or competition? As late as 1944, a leading YMCA volleyball figure criticized the trend of "spiking skills" which would eliminate older men's continuing interest. He went on to even suggest that the net be raised six inches in order to do away with the "spike scoring skill" and replace it with "placement volleyball." Fortunately his counsel was not taken but the conservative sentiment still held sway. There were too few Pop Idells around.

It seemed that the old inertia which gripped the game prior to 1928 had crept back. The game limped along in Ys across the United States and occasionally a new pocket of serious competitors would be added to the centers of Philadelphia, Detroit, Chicago, Des Moines, and Houston, but it was slow sledding.

There's not much argument that the precepts of the early fathers were adhered to: "it's a game to be enjoyed...and never to be tainted by money." Thus, growth came hard. The only revenue between 1928-1945 was the 2% royalty payment from the Volley Ball Guide, increased to 10% in 1942. The amount of books sold in 1928 recorded were 11,266 to yield a credit of $225.22—sizeable enough in those days. Expenses that year totaled $78.00 so there was cash in the kitty. In 1942, there was a year-end balance of $194.87 in the treasury. Volley Ball Guides were bought in record quantities by the War Department and shipped overseas with balls and nets. The year World War II ended, 1945, produced a bumper crop for Guides with sales of almost 40,000. The income being a little over $1,800 yielded the highest balance in the history of the USVBA: $1990.48! A look at Guide sales before and after the war is revealing.

Season	Guides Sold
1936	5,178
1941	5,256
1942	5,000
1943	5,043
1944	8,595
1945	39,712
1946	30,487
1947	20,002
1948	15,907

So after 50 years of operation, less than $2,000 was in the bank. The USVBA could proudly say that it never lost money—disbursements in 1945 were only $233.42. Yet critics must have asked: What are you doing to grow the game? If the National Tournament is used as an indicator, the game was anything but booming. In 1922, there were 22 men's teams entered in the YMCA Nationals. In 1936, the number had dropped to 20 and in 1949, only 16 men's teams entered the USVBA Nationals in Los Angeles. The USVBA was concerned with making the rules or changing them, getting them out to the public, hosting a yearly National Tournament with the YMCA, and that appears to be about the extent of its charter. Slow but sure...to say the least.

Playing style was admittedly picking up. The attack which struck such fear in older men had transformed into the two-foot takeoff and spiking motion that is seen today on television— the windmill had gone the way of dinosaurs.

Still, big change in national interest was not very perceptible even though two things were happening: it was moving West—the first western team (and non-YMCA) ever to win the national title was the Los Angeles Athletic Club. And secondly, a new groundswell of interest was seen in younger players, perhaps best represented by the average age of competitors. In 1922 the average age of players competing in the National Championship was 40. In 1941, that age had dropped to 34.

The dynasty of the '30s: Houston YMCA. Led by the greatest player of the era, Jimmy Wortham, this 1938 team blew through the Nationals without losing a game. Front row (from left to right): Noel Crenshaw, Harvey Orrison, Dick Whiting, Coach C. H. Winston. Back row: D.A. Sanders, Carl Owens, C.M. Mailander, Fred Warren, Jimmy Wortham.

Women join in...with modified rules. Exciting play at the Holyoke YMCA about 1940. (Courtesy of Holyoke Volleyball Hall of Fame)

Harold Heller reaching high on a deserted State Beach in 1939. (Courtesy of Bernie Holtzman)

First Californian champions. Los Angeles Athletic Club wins the USVBA title in 1940. The game's first "bad boy," Henry Valle, created havoc for opponents while rookie Manny Saenz was the only sub. Front row (from left to right): Henry Arnold, III, W.P. Burroughs, W. Lawrence Barr, Manuel Saenz. Back row: Eddie Ellson, Orin Sage, Jr., Gordon Smith, Henry Valle.

Some called it "bat ball" but the game was played widely by American soldiers in WWII. (Courtesy of Holyoke Volleyball Hall of Fame)

The last of the great Chicago teams: North Avenue Y. This 1945 National Championship team would repeat in 1947...the last non-California champions until 1989. From left to right: Bill Stratton, Jim Linehan, Leonard SIeben, Dick Caplan, Spartico Anzuini, Bill Alton, Larry Spejcher, Harold Wendt, Walter Brown (coach). In front: Ernest Reniff, Manager. (Courtesy of Dick Caplan)

Whitey Wendt of Chicago North Avenue. The powerful spiker was considered by many to be the best of his generation. (Courtesy of Dick Caplan)

Chapter 5
1946-1950

"Stemming the California tide. . . for the last time..."

In May of 1947, Dick Caplan packed his bags for Houston with an extra bit of excitement. His North Avenue Y team from Chicago had seen its dynasty end the year before when Pasadena YMCA captured the title—only the second time a team from the West coast had done it. The North Avenue team had won in 1941, 1942 and 1945, which was due some said to having a diluted field of competitors because of the war. In 1943 and 1944, the war had suspended the National Championship. At any rate, it was time for revenge.

"Cappy," a skilled setter, was an experienced tournament player having played his first Nationals in 1937 for the Lawson YMCA in Chicago. Following the winning tradition of earlier Chicago teams of Hyde Park and Division Street, the better players had gravitated to North Avenue in the late '30s. One of Chicago's strengths had been great setters: Jake Rashkin of Hyde Park, Nate Mariotti of Lawson, and now Spartico ("Sparky") Anzuini had picked up the mantle for North Avenue. The North Avenue team had worked hard all year and Cappy in particular had something up his sleeve for Pasadena.

The North Avenue team counted among them "the greatest spiker ever until that time" according to Cappy. Whitey Wendt was the big gun and virtually unstoppable at the net. However, he only would hit in two positions, left front and center front, since his "henchman"

always preceded him. At right front, his setter was in the back row. Cappy, who had studied at the Art Institute of Chicago and was now a commercial artist, was struck with an inspiring thought one day at his drawing table. Why not backset to Whitey instead of setting the normal front set to his spiker or "killer" as the attackers had been nicknamed. "Unthinkable!" and "Couldn't be done!" were the reactions of his teammates.

"Why not?" countered Cappy.

His teammates still demurred until the cagey setter finally tried it in practice and Whitey almost took off the hand of one of the defending scrimmager. The only remaining problem was the potential hurt feelings of Cappy's normal spiker—but, in the interest of winning the Nationals, he gladly would play the decoy.

The finals came and predictably North Avenue vied with Pasadena for the title. The backset to Whitey was golden, keeping the Californians off balance. Cappy enjoyed the victory, his "greatest highlight" of the 51 Nationals he was to play in during his career. As a Midwesterner, it would be a memory to hold onto: California teams, both men and women, would win almost every National title afterwards in virtually a total domination of the sport.

The other unforgettable moment for Cappy came in 1970 in Honolulu when he was instrumental in one of the all-time upsets in volleyball. As a 57-year old player, Cappy's role was reduced largely to serving but serving was something he could still do. Coach Jim Coleman of the Kenneth Allen team of Chicago was within a breath of defeat by the powerful Cisco's team of Manhattan Beach—the team probably favored to play against the favored Chart House team. Losing 14-11, Coleman looked over at his veteran, "Cappy, go in and serve!"

Serve he did, five straight floaters, and he also dug a ball for a point. Kenneth Allen won 16-14. In 1988, Cappy served his last competitive ball in Salt Lake City at age 75, his 51st National Championship.

"Going Hollywood. . . "

Los Angeles was Boomtown after the war. A nation wearied by the devastating war was ready for some "R and R" and the still unspoiled beauty and motion picture myth of Southern California made for an alluring place. War industries were converted to making peacetime products. The GI bill made a college education as well as owning a home a dream within grasp. Newcomers, particularly from the Midwest and the South, came in hordes and many of them were GIs already introduced to volleyball overseas. Suddenly, the YMCAs were filled with new players and on weekends the game was taken to the pristine beaches.

The war had also interrupted the national mania for sports—even Ted Williams had flown in combat missions and Joe Dimaggio made his contribution keeping the troops happy by hitting baseballs on military fields in Hawaii. Now the hunger for sports came back with a vengeance and sports marketeers were aware of it. Corporate giants began their long affair with sports advertising. It was at this time that General Mills began publishing its Wheaties Sports Library which was made up of inexpensive booklets on the fundamentals of sports. Volleyball got its turn in 1946 when it was neatly tucked in the "Play and Neighborhood Games" edition. Still no respect. After more than a half-century, volleyball's public image as a picnic activity hadn't changed.

Nonetheless, the year 1946 was a big year for volleyball in the gym and on the beach in

Los Angeles—and particularly for Bernie Holtzman. Having served as a GI in the hot spots of Europe and North Africa, there was even more reason for Bernie to get back to paradise. He'd learned firsthand that life could be short. So off with his khakis and straight to State Beach; Holtzman soon was controlling the hallowed stretch of sand with Manny Saenz. Although Al Harris was still a dominating player, he was entering the long twilight of his career; besides Harris had a wife and kids while Saenz and Holtzman were bachelors. They began to hang out together following the same daily routine: "beach, gym and sometimes a bar afterwards." Eventually they were playing volleyball seven days a week, several hours a day. A prophetic line lifted from a Bernie Holtzman letter penned during World War II read: "Volleyball. . . God's gift to the bum. . . "

But there were some other strong duos ripening, as would be readily apparent when the first bona fide beach doubles tournament was organized at State Beach in 1946. In the finals it was Dick Livingston and Don McMahon against Saenz and Holtzman to no one's surprise. The bigger team showed more power at the net but the two "mighty mites," Saenz and Holtzman, ran down ball after ball, setting each other with immaculate precision on the unprotected, windy State Beach. Two pairs of hands with the touch of piano virtuosos and as the sun was dropping into the Pacific on a late Sunday afternoon, Saenz and Holtzman triumphed. Holtzman would recall winning that first tournament as his most memorable moment in volleyball. He and Saenz would have many more—both indoor and outdoor.

In fact, they both had played in the 1946 USVBA National finals in Chicago earlier that year, but then they were on opposing teams. In the first ever all-California finals, Saenz who had stayed with the LAAC was pitted against his beach partner and the Pasadena YMCA Aces. Pasadena brought a lethal All-American arsenal of hitters: the heavy cannon arm of Webb Caldwell coupled with machine gun versatility of the marvelous Everett Keller took many casualties. In fact, it was Keller who worried Saenz the most. This guy could do it all, both inside the gym and on the sand; Saenz, the fireplug, later named Keller as the "best all-around player he'd ever played against.

Pasadena prevailed; Holtzman did his job predictably well, grabbing a Second Team All-American set-up spot. The tradition of selecting three killers and three set-up men had continued after the war and Pasadena placed two setters on the First Team: Paul Siano was joined by Jim Ward, a fabulous athlete who picked up the game while in his 30s. By the late 1940s he was considered the game's premier setter along with Manny Saenz. As a consolation to losing to his buddy, Holtzman, Saenz got some consolation as the other First Team setter.

The Nationals of 1946 featured the "Golden Jubilee Volleyball Championships" in Chicago. An unusual bonhomie and joy was in the air amongst the 18 teams;the war was behind them and they counted themselves among the fortunate ones who survived it. Dr. George Fisher's introductory to the Guide, "Fifty Years of Volley Ball," called for improvement and invoked the future.

> Tomorrow we will have increasing problems of major importance. We must tighten up our organization. We must define more clearly our amateur basis;and clarify the basis of membership. Our administrative machinery must be perfected so that every part of the country will be adequately covered. . . If such spirit continues Volley Ball will stand out at the very top of the good group games of our times—"On through the next 50 years."

If Fisher could have had a glimpse of the next half-century, he might have left the confines of the YMCA, come out West and perched himself atop the Pacific Palisades, above the Strand at Manhattan Beach, or a host of other places: Santa Barbara, Hermosa Beach, Corona del Mar, Laguna Beach, La Jolla, or Mission Beach—as long as it was in Southern California!The laboratory was there and would

stay there—in spite of the fact that the game's official guardians were sprinkled around the country, largely behind physical directors' desks in YMCAs. Blessed by the climate, West coast players began a year-round schedule of playing. And in typical Southern Californian fashion, the game took on its own mythology. New looks, new phrases, new techniques were created and imitated by the rest of the country. Often a gesture or term would originate in Santa Monica, be presented at the USVBA Nationals in perhaps Detroit, and then be appropriated the following year by players in the rest of the country. Naturally, the game took on some of the Hollywood glamour, and that distinctively cocky aloofness of Southern Californian players which still is around today. It was soon a mini-culture and one hard to break into for an outsider. Hard enough for a non-local from another beach town as Redondo Beach, more daunting for a flatlander from the San Fernando Valley, and for the poor guy on vacation from Nebraska with milk-white legs and too-tight trunks looking to get in a friendly game. . . forget it!

The following came from the Region 12 (including California) report in the 1947 Guide:

> Southern California again enjoyed its beach volleyball. This form of the game goes on continuously the year round with such players of national prominence as Holtzman, Saenz, Caldwell, Sage, Ward, the Kellers and others of equal renown and ability to be found almost any day in the midst of a tough game on the sand. It is commonplace for beach players to begin play in the morning and continue throughout the afternoon until fading light calls a final halt. Doubles is played almost exclusively and those at the national tournaments who were impressed by seemingly impossible "saves" made by western players need look no further than this beach volleyball for the answer. Not only does beach volleyball develop excellent coordination and ballhandling, but it provides coaches in the Los Angeles

area with a seemingly inexhaustible reservoir of new talent.

The synergy between beach and indoor was first seen in two players. As Saenz who had started before him, Holtzman, in part because of their short stature and certainly due to their love of the beach environment, spent endless hours running over the deep sand of State Beach's "A" court. Still there was a difference in the two. Manny controlled the beach;it was his domain. He imperiously made the rules and established the protocol. Bernie, affable and habitually laughing, seemed to play mostly for the joy of it. He did it for free, for fun and it paid off. After beginning with Saenz, he went on to dominate the beach game for its first decade.

"Paris in the springtime. . . "

Ah, City of Light! April, 1947 and the plane trees were budding in the Tuileries. Edith Piaf, the "little sparrow," captured the hearts of a generation with her gutsy vibrato. Django Reinhardt and Stephane Grapelli played "le hot jazz" in the cabarets of Montmartre. Small wonder some of the GIs had trouble leaving Paris. In truth, those who stayed on as well as the new ones shipped over as protectors of the Marshall Plan were received in wide-open arms as liberators. So much so that the climbing rate of venereal disease sounded an alarm with the top brass. Chaplains and physical directors were gathered to deal with the problem.

One man who figured highly in the campaign for sex education was Major E. B. DeGroot, who had been stationed in Frankfurt as Chief Athletic Officer for the US Air Forces in Europe. Arriving a devotee of volleyball and an able administrator, DeGroot had already organized the first European Theater Volleyball Championship in 1946. Since he was already in Europe, the USVBA asked him to attend the first Federation Internationale de Volleyball (FIVB) meeting between April 18-20, 1947. Joining DeGroot as the other American delegate to represent the United States was Royal Thomas, member of the World's Committee of YMCAS working with displaced persons in Germany. Cheap transportation was obviously a prerequisite for the position.

Fourteen countries attended that first meeting:Egypt, Brazil, Uruguay, Belgium, Czechoslovakia, France, Holland, Hungary, Italy, Poland, Portugal, Rumania, Yugoslavia and the United States. Some of the "General Observations" made by Harold Friermood in the 1948 Guide were as follows:

♦ The international games rules permit a three man block at the net with a back court man permitted to come to the net to block (but not spike).

♦ Volleyball has "caught on" as a major spectator and big-time participant sport in European countries for several reasons:There is a lack of team sports. There is no preconceived attitude that it is a "sissy" game.

♦ The top European teams seem to be the Poles, Czechs, and French about in that order.

♦ Hungary was voted into full membership after some argument by the Czechs that they were still an enemy country.

DeGroot made further comments on competition he saw:

The style of play used makes an extremely exciting and spectator thrilling game. . . There is considerable spiking on the first pass which goes directly to the spiker. . . There is considerable full-court changing of positions and variations of arrangement upon the part of all six players.

It was decided that each country advance 100 swiss francs ($25) as well as an annual dues of 100 Swiss francs to run the new organization. Quite a bargain to get in at that time! Paul Libaud, a Frenchman, was elected President and held that position for 37 years—until the 1984 Olympics when he was replaced by Ruben Acosta of Mexico.

Although the international seed was small, tiny sproutings were soon seen in distant lands. The National Volleyball Review which had been edited and published by Harry Wilson since 1939 now dropped the "National" in favor of "International. "Supported on a minimal level by the USVBA, the quarterly publication which had been carbon-copied now took on a printed glossy look. Its average 20 pages were largely running accounts of regional competition peppered with articles, announcements, gossip columns and the standard prosaic blurbs of the USVBA. Initial cost was a quarter.

When Harry Wilson left Illinois to settle in Hollywood in 1939, he was already active in Midwest volleyball. Aligned with the Evanston YMCA between 1931-38, he was a national referee and scorer before serving as an officer for the USVBA in 1936. A philatelist by profession, stamp collecting was eclipsed at times by a consuming interest in volleyball. As the man who "ran volleyball in this country" for close to two decades, he continually added arrows to his volleyball quiver: player, coach, editor, writer, clinician, international representative and equipment importer. With untiring commitment, Wilson's gift of organizing was a rarity in the game's hierarchy and soon produced results. Ambition in a man often makes him also highly opinionated, and to no surprise, his early successes would lead to conflicts, especially with players, in later years.

Never a great player, Wilson in time would make his biggest mark in American volleyball as a coach. It seems he had a vision as early as 1938 which is when a fellow staff-member, George Swanson, remembered that Wilson's "interest in fielding a top-notch representative team at the Hollywood YMCA was born." It would take a long time. With four powerful teams already established in Los Angeles, Manny Saenz remembers that Wilson was known for years as "fifth-place Harry. "But dogged determination and enthusiasm eventu-

ally were good ingredients for Wilson's greatest coaching talent:he could recruit. Yet even a talented recruiter has trouble enlisting good players to a losing team, especially amateurs! Wilson had to wait until 1947 before he finally assembled a team which merited a trip to the USVBA Nationals. With two talented setters, veteran Al Harris and Henry Cardona, Wilson scoured Los Angeles high and low to find 6'9", 280 pound Jack Stetson. Stetson could pound, yet he was amazingly agile as well. Hollywood Y tied for fifth at the Houston Nationals.

Now with some new grist for his propaganda mill, Wilson went on a relentless hunt for new talent upon returning from Houston. Dumb luck played a role too. With the Pasadena Y smarting from its disappointing loss to North Street Chicago in the 1947 finals, a likewise disappointing fourth-place finish for LAAC got both teams talking in the post-season. Why not combine both teams?Go for size, power and take no captives. A new LAAC team was formed and according to Wilson it was ". . . well-known All-Americans to form what is probably the most powerful blocking and spiking team in the history of the game. It included such well-known greats as the Keller brothers, Orrin Sage, Fred Warren, Webb Caldwell, Jim Ward and Paul Siano."

With all that fire-power, some former players were axed. Before the discarded players could toss away their old jerseys, Wilson was on a few choice doorsteps. One was that of the small hitter, Bernie Holtzman, who later wrote, "It didn't take too much persuasion. . . I had just been rudely discarded from the Pasadena Y team, which had formed a six-killer team. . . After a few practice sessions, Harry informed me that due to extenuating circumstances—he had one spiker on the team, Jack Stetson. . . and eight set me—I would be converted to spiking."

Initially Holtzman found it a frustrating apprenticeship but Harry's "enthusiasm inspired me, his patience amazed me." Wilson gladly gathered the other scraps:Harold Heller, a spiker cut from Pasadena was picked up but what was most available was just what Wilson didn't need—little setters. Yet when the littlest is arguably the best. . . even at 5'6". . . exceptions are made. Manny Saenz was gladly snatched up and Wilson went to work with four setters and two killers. With clipboard in hand, he actually orchestrated individual and team drills. "Something no coach had ever done" remarked Holtzman. The occasional night practices in that era were simply warm-up and play games amongst whichever players showed up. This was different; "we worked hard that year," remembers Saenz.

One wonders that if Harry Wilson had happened upon the rarest stamp of the American Revolution period in May, 1948, would it have made him any happier than the final point of Hollywood Y's capture of the gold in South Bend, Indiana. After dropping the first game, they won the next two in 15-12 scores to fell the mighty LAAC killers. Wilson called his squad the greatest defensive team in history and employed what he called "a razzle-dazzle type of play which not only keeps its spikers out of trouble but sometimes makes the spiker hard to identify."

"America today. . . tomorrow the world. . . "

If Harry Wilson had reached the summit, he didn't stay there for long. There were other mountains to scale;that same summer of 1948 Wilson took the first US All-Stars to Europe. The barnstorming began in southern Italy and went north to play 18 matches in 21 days! Playing against National Teams of Italy, France, Belgium, Netherlands and Czechoslovakia, the Yanks posted an impressive 17-1 record—the only loss was against the Eastern Bloc power, Czechoslovakia. The squad was composed of mostly Midwesterners who were required to pay for their own trip. Perhaps those players had more discretionary income; it was certain that the hard-core West coast players like Saenz and Holtzman weren't making any money from all the time they spent playing volleyball at the beach in the off-season. Still, there were start-

ing setters from Southern California on the squad: Bernie Specht and Paul Johnson. Johnson, the man to play in the first beach doubles game, fondly recalls the trip. "We had a great time. One thing that stands out is that we couldn't drink the water anywhere. So in many places, they gave us wine. We were playing slopped up half the time!"

In his Review, Wilson devoted extensive coverage on the trip throughout the year—more comment was given to local color as well as the turmoil and trouble of traveling than actually playing. It was pointed out that "calling voluntarily is not the custom," and that the "referee allowed the usual blocking over which had its usual discouraging effect." An example of Wilson's style and content could be seen in the account where he registered his amusement at the bevy of young Italians girls fussing over one of their local heroes after an American "bloodied his schnozzle" with a spike. . . "when an American would hardly complain of a broken ankle!"

The first crusaders came home with a truckload of memories and victories, but more important than any trophy was the new system of offense expropriated. The Europeans dared to play with only two setters!. . . backsetting as frequently as straight ahead. A bigger spiker could now replace a smaller setter to bolster the attack and block. Dick Caplan remembered being shocked when one of the returning players, star hitter Bill Stratton, announced to the North Street Y team that "we didn't need three setters!" The Chicago team quickly assimilated the new system as did all the dominant teams in Los Angeles.

Before introducing it to the Hollywood Y team, Harry Wilson discussed the new idea at length with his floor general, Manny Saenz. It was normal procedure for Harry. For all his organizational and promotional skills, Wilson's incontrovertible weakness was game coaching. Afflicted with a nervous disorder, Wilson would visibly shake in severe pressure situations. Of course, tense moments arrived often and a trembling coach during timeouts did not have the most calming affect on players. Hence he would turn to a series of great setter-leaders to basically determine positions, strategies and game decisions: beginning with Manny Saenz, Jim Ward would follow and later be succeeded by Rolf Engen.

Elsewhere in the world, the game was being extensively supported. Soon after Josef Stalin walked away from the Yalta Conference, the Iron Curtain was closed. To offset the dramatic and excruciating social changes wrought by the State juggernaut, sport was pushed in a big way. It would be a huge arm of propaganda and public diversion. In Eastern Bloc countries as well as the USSR, national sports programs were trotted out before the world on a level never seen before in history. To put it lightly, the socialist countries were going for the gold—at any price. Volleyball had already enjoyed popularity as well as status as a high-level competitive sport before the war, so it was no surprise that it was designated one of the chosen sports. Besides, it was a very "social" one...

Quickly, the dominant Russians were closely challenged by the East Germans, Czechs, Poles, Rumanians, Hungarians and Bulgarians. The best kids were culled from junior teams and assembled at national training sites to train, travel and compete full-time. Their job was to play—and they got good—fast. There were certainly worse jobs.

The Far East had been the other area of advanced play but World War II had taken a huge toll and political change made sport slow to reform. China was especially affected. The wrenching social changes brought by Mao-Tse-Tung would require many years before the populace could start thinking about such frivolities as competitive sports.

"Finally... women...and students..."

In 1949, the USVBA National Championships came to Southern California for the first time. Held in Los Angeles, the tournament was a watershed event for many reasons but the most pivotal was that after 54 years of official op-

eration, a Women's Division was formed. Eight teams entered the first women's championship at the Naval Armory in Los Angeles. One area where women's (and men's) volleyball had incubated was Houston; the better women players found a sponsor in Seales Auto Company and came out to outduel the women of Southern California. Harry Wilson commented: "Those gals could really spike and field that ball, and it was a revelation to many of the male players and most of the spectators to see such hard spikes..."

The final day featured the Houston six defeating the team from the Los Angeles Police Training Academy. Led by the combination of Louise Lolyspies, "tall, left-handed and with power to burn" with the accurate setting of captain Kathy "Zat" Zester, Seales Auto Company must have recouped their investment for uniforms. The third place team, Santa Monica, was coached by Manny Saenz.

That same Nationals found for the first time also a Collegiate Division when seven West coast colleges entered teams. Won by USC, it was a demonstration of what was to come—California domination. Stanford, led by the great basketball player George Yardley, came up short against the USC Trojans after eliminating Long Beach City College in the finals. Clearly, it was the beach game which had spawned interest in these young converts. USC students went to Hermosa Beach while guys from UCLA spent long summer days on Santa Monica's beaches between three sports—surfing, ogling co-eds and playing beach doubles. It was a lifestyle to kill for...and conducive to building good volleyball players.

"Youth must serve..."

Two guys were 20, two were 21 and all were under six feet except for the tallest who was 6'1". The Long Beach YMCA had been the darling of the Nationals since 1947 when the two Montague brothers, Buddy and Jimmy, only 17 and 18 that year, ran, jumped and had fun like a bunch of kids! "The sensations of the tournament"... "the crowd favorites" were some of the epithets written about them. As quick to smile as to run down a ball, they took a surprise fifth place their first year. Coached by former great player Clive Graham, fostered in the Southern California League with the best competition in the country, and under the superb setter Bernie Specht, they finally stole the show in 1950 by winning the USVBA Championship over the Hollywood Y.

Growing up in the idyllic seaside village of Naples near Long Beach, the Montague brothers' lives were changed forever when the breakwater was built in the early '40s to allow war ships into the harbor. They had to drop those heavy redwood planks called surfboards and find something else to do at the beach—doubles and then six-man games at the Pacific Coast Club filled a void. If the affable Jimmy Montague would go on to have one of the longest and most decorated careers of an American player, his younger brother by a year was a little more subdued and blessed with even a little more physical talent. A lefty and great leaper, spectators loved to watch Buddy uncoil from his contorted spiking position to deliver another rocket. Buddy impressed Bernie Holtzman enough for him to call the left-hander in 1950, "the most colorful player I ever saw. "

With the appearance of a new California dynasty at Long Beach in 1950, the suntanned women from Southern California gave their first notice of the future as well. Santa Monica had beefed up its squad by combining with players from the previous runner-up Los Angeles Training Academy. In the finals they bumped off another lot from Houston, the Red Shields, a team "very much handicapped by their unfamiliarity with 'tight' calling by the officials..." Surely taking serves on the sand and in the wind must have improved the deftness of the champions' touch which was required for serve reception and setting.

The University of Southern California repeated as collegiate champion in what figured as an international tussle. Getting knocked off in the winners' bracket by the University of Mexico, the smaller team from south of the border using low, quick sets eventually succumbed in a double finals. Seven teams had taken time off from their studying to compete.

The widespread popularity of volleyball in the armed forces during the war stayed on the bases around the world. Or at least one man, Colonel E. B. DeGroot, took it upon himself to not let it die. Upon the heels of victory and now with the lead-dog role in the world, the US military had tremendous clout. . . and money. The "Colonel" made sure that one of the army's seven designated sports for worldwide competition was volleyball. The year 1950 saw the first All-Army tournament when eight major commands from all around the world flew into Northern California to wage battle for the gold medal. The finals were played at Fort Ord and immediately the tournament became the largest competitive program ever organized in United States volleyball. The All-Army's success spread to the other branches and an Armed Forces Division was formed as part of the USVBA Nationals beginning in 1952.

"Who's playing defense?. . ."

During the first 50 years of volleyball, one of the overriding constants was that offense, individually and moreso on the team level, developed more quickly than defense. Defense was always trying to catch up—the perpetual bete noire of the sport's caretakers. As in most sports, offense in volleyball was much more fun. From the first time a guy or girl laid into that leather target with all their might, it was discovered that smacking the ball renders the greatest satisfaction. And so today on the beach and in gyms everywhere, what players most pant for is the opportunity to drill one straight down.

Spiking got so good after the war that points were becoming continuously more scarce. Even the two-man block rule of the late '30s was not keeping up with the new angles and speed of hitters. The rules would have to change. Murray Koorhan, a dentist from Detroit who got in volleyball for "relaxation," and stayed on as a player, official, and administrator for over 50 years can still vividly summon the image of

"Harry Wilson arriving with books in arms for late evening rules meetings. Arguing about rules, such as fists versus fingers, until three in the morning to be presented to the board at nine o'clock." In 1949 a third blocker was allowed to try and deflect the oncoming missiles even though blocking over the net was still prohibited.

Defense in the backcourt stayed farther behind in development. The two-handed dig was still unperfected since it wasn't used for serve reception, so digging the ball was largely overhand or performed by one-arm saves with the back of the hand. The players with most renown for getting hard-driven balls up were not surprisingly the same guys who excelled on the beach. An article in a 1949 Review written by Herb Wilcox of Minneapolis summarized the state of backcourt defense with a dose of foresight:

> Southern California players, of course, play volley ball on the beaches in the sand and develop terrific defensive ability to "dig" for balls, and until eastern, central and southern teams get to the point of playing outdoors on beaches or the equivalent it is my impression that a cycle of domination in volleyball by Southern California will be with us for some time to come.

In 1950, the beach doubles game had begun its slow spread from Santa Monica. Pockets of interest were forming on public beaches and even in such private domains as "Shattucks" in Hermosa Beach. In Dave Shattuck's front yard, the sand court would become famous for its fierce doubles battles. . . and the weekend beer fests Shattuck threw as well. There Jim Ward got his baptism into volleyball. Later such greats as Mike Bright and other South Bay locals would cut their sand teeth in Shattuck's yard. As for tournaments, they had spread to Santa Barbara, Laguna Beach and La Jolla. Yet as far as who ruled the growing game, it was still the same two guys: Saenz and Holtzman. That year the 35-year old Saenz

knew his domination was fading. At his age and height, he was getting most of the serves and it was wearing on his strong legs. Besides there were more guys now, younger and hungrier, who wanted his spot. They weren't going to get it without a price. Saenz would play his personal best tournament in the 1950 Santa Barbara tournament:

> The sand was hard up there. They kept serving me and I kept hitting it down. I remember Don McMahon kept moving up; I still kept hitting inside him. Finally on one of the last plays he just threw his hands up. It was the best I ever played.

"Tragedy. . . "

"I have seen the best minds of my generation destroyed by madness. . ." was the opening line of Alan Ginzberg's 1954 poem, "Howl." " A seminal work which served as the anthem of the "beatniks:" those cats in goatees, dark shades sitting in San Francisco coffee houses like City Lights and listening to Jack Kerouac gurgle wine and spew amphetamined passages of "On the Road." On the other coast in New York, Miles Davis and Charlie Parker were playing this new, weird instrumental sound which departed from American music while strange things were appearing on canvas by Jackson Pollock and Willem DeKooning. The public cried. . . or decried. . . what does it mean? The artists stayed mum. "When you're looking down the barrel of a hydrogen bomb silo, what did it matter what it meant?" they implied. The nuclear age was here.

It shouldn't have been that way it seemed. Victorious, prosperous and leader of the free world, how could there be these subtle murmurings that all wasn't right? That must have been the thinking of General Douglas McArthur after he crossed the 38th Parallel and the so-called "Korean conflict" began. By the end of the conflict, Americans realized that the menace of war had only taken a brief respite and returned with a new danger only hinted at in World War II—the "bomb" was now in the hands of East and West. The Korean War took a heavy toll of human life on both sides and Buddy Montague was one of them in August of 1951. The last Review of 1951 was named the "Buddy Montague Memorial Number" and an excerpt of the dedication read:

If you knew him, you instinctively liked him and if you ever saw him play volleyball, you never forgot him. A left-handed spiker with the fastest wrist action in the game's history, an All-American in every respect, including a top selection on last year's volleyball team—his brilliant play, tremendous power from an almost slight frame helped his Long Beach team to win the 1950 National Championship.

The official report was that a direct hit by a mortal shell killed eight out of ten men in Montague's squad. He was 21. Buddy was not the only player from that famed Long Beach six victimized by the war—All-American setter Bernie Specht was a gunner when he had both eyes injured by shrapnel, losing sight in one completely. In 1951 no team from Long Beach entered the Nationals. . . the absence of Buddy Montague would be felt for many years.

*The fun kids. Led by the grin-
ning, teenage Montague
brothers, Long Beach Y was
the crowd pleaser of the '47
Nationals. Back row: (from
left to right) Don Miller,
Frank Riordan, Al Lippincott,
Jimmy Montague. Front row:
Bob Reed, Buddy Montague,
Bernie Specht. (Courtesy of
Jimmy Montague)*

*The Hollywood Y dynasty
begins in 1948. After several
years, Harry Wilson finally
wins his first National Cham-
pionship—speed, defense
and one giant, Jack
Stetson.Front row (from left
to right): Manny Saenz, Carl
Olson (Physical Director),
Les Meisenheimer. Second
row: David Davis, Al Harris,
Elmer Doumont, Bernie
Holtzman, Harry Wilson
(Coach),. Back row: Fred
Warren, Henry Cardona,
Harold Heller, Jack Stetson.*

The USA All-Stars, our first international team, tours Europe in 1948. Undedeated in Western Europe...then falling to the powerful Czechs. Action in Prague, Americans are in the foreground. Front court (from left to right): Stratton (15), Johnson, Collis. Back court:Specht (5), Wendt, Alton.

Women can play! In 1949, the USVBA Nationals in Los Angeles create a women's division. This team from Santa Monica finishes third...the tannest team in the tournament.

Triple block...in retreating formation. The same Santa Monica ladies at State Beach.

Hard-hitting Sid Nachlas. The Houston Y great was captain of the USA Team in the first Pan-American Games, 1955.

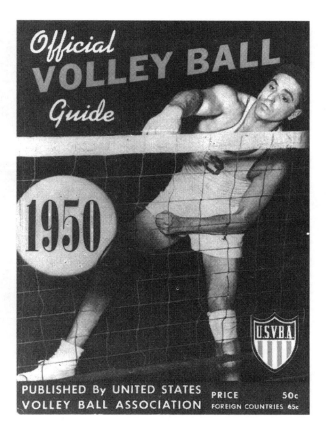

Official VOLLEY BALL *Guide*

1950

PUBLISHED By UNITED STATES VOLLEY BALL ASSOCIATION

USVBA

PRICE 50c
FOREIGN COUNTRIES 65c

Gene Selznick's first team, '51 National Champions. The first year All-American and coach Harry Wilson began as allies. Soon the most bitter rivalry in the sport's history would begin. Top row (from left to right): Norton, Warren, Heller. Middle row: Selznick, Wilson, Howlett, Holtzman. Bottom row: Morgan, Saenz, Harris.

Buddy Montague. "The most colorful player I ever saw," according to Bernie Holtzman. Spiking here in 1950, the spectacular lefty died in military action a year later in the Korean War. (Courtesy of Jimmy Montague)

Chapter 6
1951-1955

"Enfant terrible is born..."

The earth rumbled and the mighty heavens groaned when the grinning satyr arrived from the demiworld, flute in hand. Only 20 years old in 1950, splay-footed and long-armed, boundless talent would in time take a back seat to persona in Gene Selznick, and the game of volleyball would never be the same. One other player had reached comparable playing dominance, Jimmy Wortham, and one other who followed would even surpass it—the incomparable Karch Kiraly. But no one in the game's century would surface as such a touchstone. Visionary, the game's genius, maverick, flimflam man, or persona non grata? Irrefutably the sport's litmus test: touch Selznick and you'd have to go red or blue—there was no neutral position.

"Boletos! Boletos para el voleibol aqui!" the hawkers were out in force in Mexico City in 1955 for the first Pan-American games ever held. Surprisingly, one of the most popular events was volleyball. The small gymnasium which seated 2,000 fans was stretched to hold 4,000 people every night but the night of the finals for the men and women was even more crowded. It was the USA versus Mexico. People were crawling outside, it was rumored that the Mexican guards even considered bribes to let spectators inside!

The first taste of official international competition for American volleyball was a thriller. Exciting from the beginning. Rolf Engen, being the smallest on the team, unwisely was the last to march in and got waylaid by a couple of banditos who used his body as a bribe to get in. When the setter finally got past the door, his team had already followed the military escort up the steps to a small meeting room. It took Engen ten minutes to thread his way through the aisle to join them.

Things were going well...too well...for the first two games. Up two, the shrillness of the whistling and flying debris seemed to have gotten to the referee. The Yanquis, except for two receivers, all of a sudden developed a bad case of the shakes in the third—their palsied overhand receptions invited point after point. Never had Pancho Villa or Emiliano Zapata robbed with such daring and bravado—the din of the crowd deafened every ear. Surprise changed to rage and subsided to fear when the fourth game went to the Mexicans. Before the fifth game, the Americans huddled in confusion. Selznick grabbed Engen to get his attention and screamed to the rest. "Alright, this is how we play it! Rolf and I take every ball in the yellow—everybody else bail out of the court when the ball's served!"

Two guys take every serve! The roar prevented debate...and besides, Selznick and Engen had impeccable receiving technique...neither had been whistled all night. The first Mexican serve sent most of the receivers scrambling as if the yellow court marked a nuclear dump. Selznick flicked the ball with such delicacy, the ball rode on the wings of a butterfly. They stared in unison at the referee. No whistle. How could he? The valve hadn't moved an inch! They served away from the hands of Selznick and in stepped the little Engen with even more precise hands, a surgeon with the cold confidence of an assassin.

Doubles in the yellow—the USA won the fifth game and the gold medal. A forgotten triumph...but the first. In 1984, Doug Beal surprised the volleyball world, then won its praise by using only two receivers to take every serve on the way to winning America's first Olympic gold medal. Another Selznick story? For those doubting Thomases—oh ye of little faith—just ask Rolf Engen.

In 1950, Selznick had already teamed with Everett Keller, by then in his late 30s, and dethroned Saenz and Holtzman in a single Open beach tournament to begin a meteoric rise to the stars. Never playing high school sports—a roller-skating fall as a kid left him without several inches of bone in one forearm—his mother forbade him to compete. "That didn't keep me from playing volleyball with the girls in P.E.," he impishly adds,. "Well, I had an ulterior motive!" After high school graduation, he ended up one day at Hermosa Beach and as so many other volleyball novices, after getting his clock cleaned kept coming back for more until the embarrassment was tolerable. That was in 1949 and after only one year, reports about the cocky, brash kid were carried by Holtzman and Saenz to Hollywood Y and coach Harry Wilson. His indoor debut in the fall of 1950 was interrupted by the military draft, but Wilson, ever resourceful, pulled the proper strings to get him time off for the 1951 Nationals in Springfield, Massachusetts—where the game was christened. Selznick's later admission that he and Wilson were initially "the best of friends" seems borne out in an early example of Wilson's commentary in a 1951 International Review about the finals:

> As we were warming up something seemed wrong—one man missing—it was Selznick—a search found him sound asleep on one of the players cots, and I thought this first year man might be nervous!...

Selznick as a first year man makes the small errors of a green man but is a fine fielder and ferocious killer—and never tires—one of the best first year men in the game's history.

Another "ferocious killer" was the Texan, Sid Nachlas. Trying to fill the boots of Jimmy Wortham was no mean chore but Nachlas "hit the ball as hard as anyone I've ever seen," reports Murray Koorhan who has seen over 50 Nationals. Alas brute power alone was not enough as Houston went down against Hollywood late in the tournament—the reigning team of the '30s was glimpsing its last sunset.

Hollywood's victory over Chicago North Avenue in the finals was attributed to a rarity in the game of that epoch—backcourt defense. The team was made up of some of the greatest defenders of the game up to that time: Saenz, Holtzman, Harris, Fred Warren, Len Morgan and Selznick. The team would dig and run down balls until the last point came at two o'clock in the morning. Holtzman still reveres that Hollywood group above all others: "our defense was so good that we only used one blocker in the finals and sometimes none at all!"

As for the rookie Selznick, he flew back to the army and soon to Okinawa where even the long arm of Wilson could not pry him loose for the 1952 Nationals. He returned in 1953 to help Hollywood Y win its third straight USVBA National Championship. Up until that time, Selznick had relied on pure talent. Now he began to assume his acknowledged great savvy of the game. His first major assimilation came from new teammate Bill Stratton. Selznick studied the former Chicago great's gift of rotating the shoulder and wrist to cut the ball inside the block. Selznick quickly borrowed Stratton's notorious angle shot—he could now power or finesse the ball.

"The Colonel comes home..."

The year of 1952 saw the USVBA include a Military Division in the National Championships. The efforts of Colonel DeGroot had borne fruit and the first competition was taken by the Los Alamitos Naval Air Station. Able and dependable, DeGroot was asked to fill the position of one of the USVBA vice-presidents with the task of reorganizing the 12 regions of the USVBA upon his return to the United States. It was no mean task. The regions were just that...regions and little more. An operating function was as hard to find as an active functionary. DeGroot set about to shake things up through the U.S. Postal Service. He wanted to redefine the regional raison d'etre, find some new, enthusiastic individuals and create some type of communication between them all—something never before done. Apparently the wake-up call was a bit too much too soon—even for a go-by-the-book guy like DeGroot—as his labors elicited a warning response by USVBA President Fisher and his soon-to-be successor, Vice-President Bill Friermood. The two men took great pains to remind DeGroot that the present regional representatives were volunteers and no drastic changes should be made but "to go slowly with the reorganization." Some 75 years of inch-worming along and then to be told to go slowly! The Colonel, like a good military man, could only follow orders.

"Play it again...All-Stars..."

In 1953, Harry Wilson led another group of All-Stars abroad. Paying their own way again, Wilson recruited Selznick and new-found court general, Rolf Engen, and they began the trip in North Africa. It was foamy times in that part of the world; revolution was beginning to boil and by the end of the decade the French yoke of colonialism would be thrown off in a bloody struggle. Americans weren't liked much either. Adventures in mysterious places like the Casbah of Algiers were good for stories but still it wasn't quite like Bogie and Bacall in Casablanca and they were glad to soon be on the Continent. Aided by the thunderous smashes of 6'7" Al Kuhn of Chicago and 6'4", 250 pound Arlo Roberts of Des Moines, Wilson reported for the second time an impressive record of 9-2. But these were mostly club teams and West-

ern, not Eastern European teams, with the exception of an outdoor stadium match in Yugoslavia. Volleyball enthusiasts knew that power volleyball was truly found in the Communist Bloc. In 1949 at the first ever World Championships held in Prague, aficionados got a taste of what was to come: the USSR men and women triumphed—the Soviet men in a cliffhanger over the Czechs.

Once Harry Wilson got hold of a winning team in 1948, he held onto it as dearly as his extensive stamp collection. Transferring lessons from his vocation to his avocation, he won 12 USVBA National titles. The best strategy was to keep your aces. To do that, Hollywood's players received the best perks of any team: good uniforms, occasional meal money, and the comfort that the head man would always be organized to maximize conditions for winning. Harry got his players to the game...on time, fed and well-attired. For the more ambitious players, the knowledge that Wilson largely controlled the sport was a also boon. Daft as some of the "official" policies might seem to some, the coach of the winning team in the National Championships enjoyed having six automatic berths on the National Team. It made sense to an aspiring player to wear a Hollywood Y jersey...and keep it.

In turn, Harry kept his best horses close in the stable. One was the diminutive Rolf Engen. Only 5'8", Engen learned the game at Corona Del Mar during high school summers on the beach before going on a basketball scholarship to UCLA after starring two years at Santa Ana Junior College. Shin splints kept him off the team so he played volleyball at his fraternity house. Another player at the house was a tall, ungainly Mike O'Hara. In 1953, their intramural dominance took them to Athletic Director Wilbur Johns for donation of a set of old wool UCLA hoop jerseys and off to Omaha they drove for the Nationals. Who but Harry Wilson was asked to coach the team there and he wisely accepted. They knocked off Florida State for the gold and brought back the trophy to Johns who smilingly told the boys that "we're in the business of winning national championships" and gave them the highest earthly blessing. Volleyball became a full varsity sport at UCLA in 1954.

Engen had been closely eyed by Wilson— his touch and ball control were nonpareil despite his greenness. In 1954, he served double duty: after UCLA won its second title he was brought on to bolster the dominating player, Selznick, of Wilson's Hollywood Y team. Smart and a natural leader, Engen soon arose as the premier setter of the decade and was selected 10 straight times as a First Team Open All-American. O'Hara, also recruited in 1954 for Hollywood, took a little longer to ripen. His volleyball career interrupted by military service, O'Hara came back from Alaska in 1956 to earn seven First Team spots in eight years. Wilson made sure he kept both of them.

"The ball which bruised..."

The arrival of the famous rubber ball which was authorized by the USVBA in 1953 was acclaimed by some, particularly those who authorized it, as a boon to the game. Designed to be more durable, waterproof and economical at the same time, the smooth, rock-hard Voit CA4 was all of that and more. How many players in gym classes around the nation retained vivid memories of trying their best to avoid that stinging orb! Still, to the credit of its manufacturer and the USVBA, another version—the first synthetic—was softened and used in a test performance in the semi-finals of the 1954 Nationals in Tucson. A few remarks of praise are extant in historical records but the ball was never used again in National Championships; it seems the players' voice was heard. Meanwhile the CA4 would enjoy a long career as the ubiquitous ball in school and on playgrounds— and one of the best reasons why Americans weren't rushing to play more.

Voit became the earliest sports manufacturer to attach its name to a team in return for uniforms. In turn, the Voit women's team brought the first national title to Southern California, specifically to Santa Monica, in 1950 under the outstanding play of All-Americans Connie Armstrong, Anna Bauer and Johanna Cooper. The Voit women repeated the feat in 1952 and 1953 to seal the advent of Southen California dominance.

The first taint of professionalism appeared in that year when part of the players' expenses was subsidized to make the trip South to the first Pan-Ams. At the 1954 Nationals in Tucson, about $400 was gathered from contributions made at the tournament's barbecue as well as passing the hat at the final match. The USVBA deemed it worthy to kick in $500 more the following year. The proposed budget from the secretary-treasurer's report (Robert Morrison) printed in the 1955 Official Volleyball Guide rendered not only that transaction but gave a bird's-eye view of the organization's financial state of affairs.

PROPOSED BUDGET—MAY 1954 TO APRIL 1955

INCOME

Receipts from sale of Guide—	
10,000 at $.50	$5,000
Advertising	500
Incidentals	100
	5,600

DISBURSEMENTS

Contributions, volleyball team, Pan-American Games	$500
Annual Meeting	50
Midyear Meeting	25
Secretary-Treasurer Expenses	200
Mimeo-Stationery	250
Editors Expenses	150
Printing, Mailing of Guide	2,500
International Volleyball Review	150
Olympic Dues	10
International Federation Dues	50
President's Expenses	100
Incidentals	250
	4,235

A little ciphering reveals a projected surplus of $1365 for the year. To fatten the coffers a bit, the Guide reported the following "important decisions reached were: to raise the price of the Volleyball Guide; increase the prices on group purchases of the Guide and to make an all-out effort to sell additional advertising." The last item would have required looking in new directions since the four ads appearing in the Guide that year were all purchased by ball companies: MacGregor, Seamless Rubber, Voit and Spalding.

Ostensibly, no potential in product sponsorship was seen in other areas such as apparel. No standard uniform had been established in the sport, men looked more like basketball players than anything else and the ladies...well, it was the standard tasteless moderate blouse and short de rigueur for all sports. Shoes? The Jack Purcell tennis shoe was the basic model for men worn until the age of the low-cut Converse basketball shoe appeared in the late '50s.

Shoes. Typifying how far ahead was the rest of the world in volleyball, a Japanese company had invented a volleyball shoe in *1952!* In that year, ASICS founder, Kihachiro Onitsuka invented a light-weight shoe using vulcanized rubber on the outsole for the first time. With exceptional traction, the shoe became known as the Tiger. Why stop there? With characteristic thoroughness and ingenuity, ASICs took it to the limit in 1957 when the company came out with two models: *one for offense and one for defense!*

"The first Superwoman was a blonde..."

People just weren't used to it. Not that the early women players weren't competitive...nor void of talent. But by the mid-'50s when Jane Ward came into the sport, no one had ever seen a woman take the court not to compete...but to combat! With the same intensity as the fiercest male competitors, the short-cropped blonde turned heads.

As a transplanted college basketball player from New York, Ward somehow landed a job in a strange place, the Stockton YMCA in Central California. Still stranger was the fact that in Stockton an extraordinarily talented bevy of male players had assembled who would win two straight National Championships in 1954 and 1955. Leonard Gibson, or "Gibby" as he was fondly called, was the Harry Wilson of the Stockton program—organizing, sometimes coaching, keeping it all together. A young physical education instructor, Jane Ward, was impressed by this new sport and convinced Gibby and head coach Harold Peterson that she could play with these guys.

As odd woman out, she still found the volleyball rewarding while practicing with the men. Stockton however, came up short in her vision of California. Soon fate intervened and she moved to Hermosa Beach with a new teaching job that was more her style. In that epoch, centers of volleyball interest were still in the YMCAs and typically there was one man who took it upon himself, more often than not a former player, to nurture the game: in Detroit Northern it was Viggo Nelson, Walter Brown at Chicago North Avenue, Dewitt Sanders in the Houston YMCA, and at the Long Beach Y, there was Al Fish. All were dedicated pioneers.

Ward quickly gravitated south to Long Beach where Fish coached a team called the Westerners for a year. Her friendship with local star, ZoAnn Neff, led them both to Manny Saenz who was coaching the stronger Mariners of Santa Monica. Winning six straight national titles, 1955-60, the Mariners established the first female dynasty in volleyball and Jane Ward was the heart and soul of that team.

Like the USA Men's Team, a group of ladies paid their way to Mexico City for their historically first international competition. At the Pan-American Games of 1955, the American women lost to the host, Mexico, and if the refereeing didn't help, neither did the coaching. Under a coach from Texas, a frustrated Ward and other key players were saddled with the antiquated three-setter system instead of the 4-

2 style. The lack of informed coaching would be cited as the greatest problem of National Teams—men and women—for years on end. It was understandable; playing on a big island here, the only new ideas came from the occasional exposure to other foreign teams which were experimenting with systems as well as subsidizing their athletes. And more regrettably, an almost xenophobic attitude in the USVBA maintained that since the game was "invented in this country, we ought to play it our way." We did...and got killed in top international competition.

"Pass, set, hit...sex..."

Boring. That's what it was, plain and simple. Two out of three to 15 points, games went on and on...and on. An occasional dig and the interminable banter of guys like Holtzman and Selznick provided the real on-court entertainment. Local wags came just to sit and upstage the players with their wit—it was sarcasm...it was funny...it was live! Yet, Holtzman, Selznick and their ilk were purists at heart. They would rather play than entertain...well, arguable in the case of Selznick, but something was lacking to draw onlookers besides these wise-cracking jackdaws and girlfriends looking on in feigned interest.

Holtzman and Selznick decided upon a plan and decided upon a player, Jack Backer, to execute it. Backer agreed to unashamedly troll the beach, asking every handsome and curvaceous coed gracing a beach towel a simple question: "Would you be interested in having your photo appear in the newspaper as a contending beauty queen?" Vanity proved time and time again the best way to a woman's heart and soon there was a horde of Gidgets queued up for a shot. Prudently the players were prepared with a legitimate photographer, Dr. Leonard Stallcup, who had been shooting volleyball action for several years. No amateur, Stallcup had organized the Miss California pageant which only added fuel to the burning ambition of the contestants.

The formula was a resounding success. Girls came for a chance at fame, newspapers came for local color, guys came to see the girls. It didn't end there. Holtzman embellished the tournament board with players' photos and short bios; a roving microphone provided constant commentary, largely by Holtzman and Selznick. Question and answer sessions with the crowd reached the bawdy in this pre-Germaine Greer era: "Do you think the tournament queen is worthy?" rendered a typical response as: "I'll have to check her dimensions first!"

One year the tournament queen was actually Miss California who smilingly provided the traditional kiss to the winners. Perhaps the most memorable year was in 1954 when Greta Tyson, the star of a revue called Pajama Tops, assumed the crown of Volleyball Queen. Men played extra hard that year and it was none other than Holtzman and Selznick who came out on top. In fact, the two player-promoters didn't lose a tournament that year or the next in 1955. They continued that string until losing the last tournament in 1956. But for Holtzman the Pajama Top beauty was special. He chuckles at the poignant image in his memory: "At 38-19-36, you might say she 'stuck out' in the crowd!"

"The pipes of Pan...or Apollo's lyre?..."

Zeus bore them both. They were eternally at odds, condemned to be complements of one another. Dionysus, born of Zeus' loin: intuitive, visionary, in quest of ecstasy—the god of revelry, the grape, the flute, of music rhythmic and orgiastic. So different from his brother, Apollo: contemplative, intellectual, his music was the controlled numerical relationships on the strings of the lyre. Left-brained. In time, it was Apollo who gained dominance over his sibling by inventing the bow and arrow to steal the oracle of Delphi.

While Mike O'Hara studied, Gene Selznick danced. "I really was better known for my dancing," remarked Gene Selznick looking back at his long playing career. It's true. An insomniac, accounts still abound of his legendary dance prowess—trophies in top Los Angeles clubs vied in number with those of volleyball in his collection. A fever which raged in him every night, not just Saturday, and has continued into his 60s. A man who had to dance. Another dancer, Nate Parrish, recalls: "Selznick had the most incredible body language. We'd play this game where someone would just flip the station on the radio. It might come up ballet...or polka. It didn't matter. Selznick would grab a girl and dance to whatever the music was."

Not so Mike O'Hara. Early on, he prepared to win in sports and business at UCLA when he immersed himself in seminars to program his subconscious...for success and winning. Citing Napoleon Hill's, *Think and Grow Rich*, as an example of early influences, sports and business were interchangeable metaphors which would lead him into a career as sports impresario and promoter.

So when O'Hara joined the Hollywood YMCA team and Selznick in 1954, it was immediately oil and water. O'Hara served his apprenticeship without any nonsense and following a year in the service returned to become one of the stalwarts of the Hollywood Y dynasty until 1964. At 6'4" with a good jump, his corkscrew arm became a source of dread for opponents—it was hard to track. While in Hollywood he displayed another valuable asset: O'Hara excelled at hitting bad sets. When most spikers used control shots on sets deeper than ten feet, O'Hara had perfected a roundhouse attack which took broken plays and turned them into sideouts and points.

O'Hara also took to the beach but in a different fashion. There was no foolishness to be brooked; he worked, went to night school and played on the weekends. It was all business with him—a foreign element amongst the flippant crowd at State Beach. Eventually, O'Hara moved south to Sorrento with its coterie of UCLA students, nourishing themselves at the Sorrento Grill and disporting themselves in front of the wall, which was more to his liking. In some ways, O'Hara was an oddity at Sorrento

too. He played every game hard, often with Edie Conrad, the top woman of that era when the role of females was to stay at the net and set for the male spiker—not even dropping back to dig on defense. For O'Hara it was good training; he knew it would take time to beat the jocular pied piper up the beach who ran parking lots at night, danced late, then played and entertained during the day. O'Hara could wait. Mind would triumph over instinct—Apollo had proved it long ago.

"Hall of Fame...the first one..."

Created by Paul Helms and his bakery empire in Southern California, the Helms Hall of fame included a volleyball section at its building in Los Angeles in 1954. Four men were inducted into the Hall initially: William Morgan, George Fisher, Pop Idell and one player, Jimmy Wortham, "regarded as having been the greatest Volleyballer of all time." It was small, emblematic of the sport's growth despite a new awareness in Southern California since the war. Later that year, the Helm's Foundation honored "Southern California's all-time greatest athletes." Of the 19 honorees, two were selected for volleyball: Johanna Cooper and Manny Saenz. The Hall was later assumed by Great Western Bank in Los Angeles which in turn ran itself upon the shoals of bankruptcy, leaving the Hall to fall into desuetude. In 1985 the local citizens finally created their own Hall of Fame in Holyoke, Massachusetts, the birthplace of the sport.

The '50s marked the time of volleyball's modernization, the place was Southern California. Even the name of the sport took on a newer, more contemporary look. In 1951, for the first time "volleyball" as one word appeared on the cover of the USVBA Guide. Yet on the same cover, the older and stodgy two-word version was printed also. Was it an unconscious reminder of the perennial reluctance to change or just a misprint? At the bottom of the Guide appeared: Published by United States Volley Ball Association.

The Joker and the Penguin, 1954. Gene Selznick (left) and Bernie Holtzman (right) lost one tournament in three years (1954-1956). Tired of losing to the pair, some San Diego players dubbed the infamous nicknames. (courtesy of Bernie Holtzman)

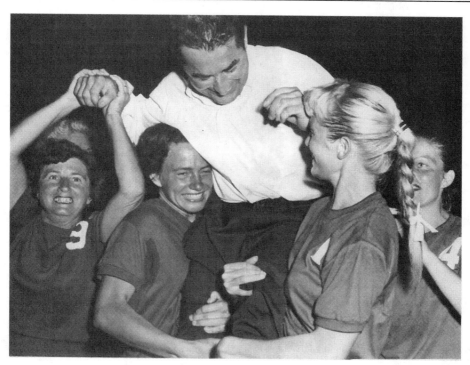

The house Manny built. In 1955, the Santa Monica Mariners celebrate the first of six national titles. Left to right: Grace La Duke, ZoAnn Neff, Manny Saenz, Patty Bearer, Marion McMahon.

First volleyball shoe, 1952. The founder of ASICs Tiger specialized footwear for Japan's booming game. (Courtesy of ASICs Tiger)

Six-man on the beach (above). Bernie Holtzman tools Bill Olsson and Hollywood Y team, 1955. (Courtesy of Bernie Holtzman).

Pajama Tops: Greta Tyson, tournament queen and Hollywood celeb, brings smiles to Holtzman and Selznick in 1954 (right). (Courtesy of Bernie Holtzman)

Chapter 7
1956-1960

"She walked the walk..."

The bleeding was already darkening her eyes; her nose was so far over to the side that she looked like one of those late Picasso portraits of Dora Maar—facial features abnormally aligned. The doctor spoke, "if you can take the pain, I can try to straighten it right here...without any surgery."

Pain! Was he kidding? "Go ahead," she commanded. Jean Brunicardi gripped the hospital bed with both hands as the emergency room physician pulled the broken nose back to its original position. Like chicken bones ripping apart, the thunderous cracking shot fierce bolts of pain up and out her skull. He held it firmly in place for ten minutes while her eyes sluiced water. The nose fused.

Pain was nothing new to her. As a nurse, she was around it daily. But pain was also a constant companion of her playing career. She played so hard and with such abandonment that for the first 20 years of women's beach doubles, she was the force. Even her notorious walk portrayed her hallmarks: speed and strength. Pulling her feet up high off the sand, quickly she flexed them back down, arching her toes at the ground. Powerful thighs then pushed her feet into the sand as if she was punishing it. Back perfectly erect and head tossed proudly back, Jean Brunicardi was a woman to be reckoned with. A broken shoulder, fractured toes, a shattered elbow, a reconstructed knee were some of the wages she paid for her fearless pursuits of a volleyball. Still she played on...and kept winning.

"Lower the net...but how?..."

It wasn't easy in the beginning for women. If allowed on the court at all, women would usually compete in the occasional six-women game or the more popular mixed doubles. Brunicardi paid her slow dues in six-women games with indoor players like Lila Shanley and Grace LaDuke as well as Edie Conrad of mixed doubles renown. Although occasional women's doubles tournaments were held in the early 50's, the first breakthrough for her occurred in Santa Barbara in 1957 when four women's doubles teams competed after the men were through playing on Sunday afternoon. They played on a men's net. The men were awarded trophies...the women ribbons.

Emboldened by even this short excursion into competition, Brunicardi and a few friends dared to organize a Women's Beach Doubles Open Tournament in the summer of 1958. Held at the Santa Monica Pier, the tournament was entered by a surprising 16 teams. Kenui Rochlen and Lila Shanley won that day, but their dominance was short-lived. Kenui, a fabulous surfer and volleyball player, returned to her home in Hawaii.

Once married to one of history's great surfers, Rabbit Kekai, Kenui Rochlen was a fearless soul. Out in the water one day while fully pregnant, she called over to a surfing buddy, Dave Heiser. "Heisuh, you bettuh help me in." The contractions were coming in quick succession so Heiser hooked his toes on the nose of her board and paddled for dear—and new—

life. They reached shore, and she had one of her four children within hours.

Two years of rushing to State Beach after work every afternoon to play until sundown, in 1960 Jean Brunicardi found the right partner in feisty Johnette Latreille. As tournaments were added in Laguna Beach, Hermosa Beach, Rosecrans and Mission Beach, so were the Brunicardi/Latreille victories—they won almost every tournament through 1966. Jean was almost invincible as she cut through the sand at a blinding speed, capable of reading opponents' shots like no one else. Her stamina was also a factor as the women continued to play on men's nets until the early '60s when the net was dropped to women's height at Manhattan Beach. Soon the others would follow. But a net of 7'10" made for long games for the shorter women in the early days.

Latreille was tough too. After a late night of revelry, she had to be awakened by her partner's frantic phone call to "Get down to the tournament!" Latreille bleary-eyed, jumped out of her car only to learn from her miffed partner that they had been unceremoniously bumped out of the event, top seed and all. After a little lobbying, the players voted to let them play if they started in the losers' bracket. Apparently the pallor of Johnette's skin and her drooping eyelids gave the others a new confidence. Even Jean was concerned: "Can you play?" Johnette nodded, then walked over to Sorrento Grill and asked the owner, Neeny, for a large beer. She downed it, marched out of the hallowed establishment and summarily charged through the losers' bracket undefeated.

"All-World Team...an American?..."

"Look at that! The hitter's already in the air when the ball is set," the player marveled, mouth agape, at the ingenuity of both teams using three spikers with the setter coming out of the back row. The crowd of 20,000 people almost startled him with their applause when a Czech digger, collapsing under a Soviet mortar, sent it 40 feet straight up. Thousands of heads snapped back with the ball's ascent, then bobbed a second time with the high set to the outside where a lanky Czech drilled the line and now a Russky popped it up! The crowd roared louder—and these were Parisians! "God, this is a great game," he whispered to himself.

He watched in awe, on his feet, for three hours while fabulous athletes toiled on both sides of the net—one organic being, 12-pointed, moving in choreographed precision, vying for that tiny white orb—all part of some larger biosphere. Fans screamed and applauded the entire time. The closing ceremonies came; flags, speeches and the Czech national anthem played for the winners. He kept redrawing all he'd seen and how he could take it back to where the sport was born...and use it!...when his name was called.

No! Unbelievable! Yes! "From the United States of America...Gene Selznick!" All-World Team—one of the best six players on the planet. That honor for an American wouldn't happen again for some 30 years. Selznick had done it with prowess, an unusual sense of intuition and an indecipherable gift of assimilation. He was also the United States' best diplomat. Rolf Engen recalls the delightful sight of the Soviets and Eastern Europeans trying to chew bubble gum for the first time in their lives. "Of course, Selznick brought it over. Before long, he had a whole roomful of these guys trying to chew this stuff. They kept trying to swallow it. Then imagine trying to teach them to *blow bubbles*!..." After a few nights of chasing the belle filles of Paris, the new star decided on the plane home that he was the chosen one to impart this sacred knowledge—this new offense with three attackers instead of two—to the USA National Team which would soon make for world greatness. That's the moment the long, white-knuckle rollercoaster ride took off.

At those first World Championships of 1956, the Americans received a bitter taste of truth. Under the coaching of Harry Wilson and his assistant, Harold Peterson, it was basically the combined Hollywood Y team sprinkled with some Stockton players which marched in wearing red, white and blue. Cool and smug—after all, they were from Southern California. Their first glance at those burly, unsmiling and *tall* Slavs and Cossacks provided a sudden clue that this wasn't going to be a waltz through the USVBA Nationals or even Mexico. How right they were.

Although they finished sixth, the men did make it to the final winner's pool where they were stacked up against the world's best teams. It is certain that there were periods when they felt outclassed; they had never seen the 6-2 offense with three hitters...much less tried to follow and block their lashing attacks of quick, low sets to the net. But there were also those instances when brute talent prevailed, some of the Americans could jump and hit as hard as anyone. To the amazement of the Europeans, Selznick could do *everything* as well as their best players. Not many setters anywhere in the world put up a better ball than Engen. It was just that over the course of a match, their outdated system and technical errors added up to a lot of points for the guys across the net. Frustration finally...but new hope too.

The women fared worse, finishing ninth out of 17 teams. It was obvious that these powerful women of Eastern Europe were much more concerned about pounding the ball and blocking than looking good in a bikini. An improvement in coaching at least occurred when Al Fish took over the team and incorporated a 4-2 attack with almost no training before departure. Yet even Jane Ward admitted that the women given free rein were "more into fun than competition." Well, why not? After all, they had paid their own way and this was Paris...all those boutiques on Rue St. Honore and that famed Gaullic charm found nowhere else but in French males. Harry Wilson subsequently commented on the feminine competition: "the fact that volleyball in Europe started probably ten years prior to our national championships in 1949 was important and it showed...I feel sure that the girls from the Iron Curtain country teams are trained starting at a very young age..." Understatement was the prescribed protocol during the Cold War.

"Hollywood here we come...again..."

1956 meant a lot to Harry Wilson. Having finished second the past two Nationals to Stockton Y was bad enough, but the World Championships in Paris meant that someone was going to establish a beachhead in that international arena and he had been diligently preparing himself for a long while to capture that grand domain. Still, there was a fly in the ointment. Official policy dictated that the coach and six playing positions would go to the winning team in the USVBA Nationals. He must win it! To knock off the cohesive Stockton team, Wilson knew he needed more muscle. Luck would have it that Mike O'Hara returned from his military obligation, frothing to improve his game and compete. But a greater coup perhaps was the arrival of a tall, flat-topped bomber: Bill Olsson.

In 1953, this pro baseball pitcher was done trying to make the Majors and stuck in his hometown of Long Beach. Only 23, he was looking around for some exercise and happened into the Long Beach YMCA. He discovered volleyball, got hooked, and made his first trip to the Nationals that same year. He was chosen All-American Honorable Mention which bespoke something of his talent—not quite 6'6" with an awesome vertical leap and an arm used to throwing bullets. What more could Coach Al Fish ask for? Maybe one other thing, a burning intensity which at times boiled over at his teammates but it also served to make him one of the most dominating hitters to ever take the court in this country. Jimmy Montague, known for his scrappy and fearless defense, admitted that "Olsson was the one guy I wouldn't stay in and try to dig at point blank range." But it was Olsson's dislike of losing which finally led him to leave the declining Long Beach Y team and join the powerful Hollywood Y in 1956. Coach Harry Wilson was already emerging as the czar of the sport, which was an anomaly in volleyball coaching. He had a vision, a program to realize it, and organized practices. With a clipboard and drills! All that Olsson was looking for; Harry in turn was ecstatic and rightly so. With that early core of Engen, O'Hara and Olsson, Hollywood Y won the '56 Nationals in Seattle and eight out of the next nine National Championships!

"Hawaiian style..."

The Outrigger Canoe Club is an institution in the Hawaiian Islands. Anyone who has ever sat on the wall watching a tropical sunset explode and melt into the passion fruit of their Henry Special (an exotic cocktail) could testify that it doesn't get much better. Outrigger canoes and iridescent triangles slice the horizon, from behind one can hear volleyballs like falling coconuts thud the sand in the caged courts...something which has been going on since the late '30s when Pan-Am pilots who picked up the game in Santa Monica brought it over on their twin-engined DCs.

As most things in the lush environment, the game spread and enough interest inspired the Honolulu Y to send a team to the 1956 USVBA Nationals in Seattle. One of the athletes was a young, barrel-chested Tommy Haine. A man of enormous strength, his vitality both physical and social made for a Hemingway-like figure who would later captain the 1968 Olympic Team in Mexico City. If any of the young lions (and occasionally some older ones) of the Outrigger teams got into trouble in the islands, Haine's number was the 911. His helpfulness later earned him the moniker "Daddy" although his gracious wife, Marilyn, claimed she donated that nickname by using it anytime she found her gregarious husband conversing with a group of good-looking Wahines.

The Coppertone boys of 1956 caused quite a sensation by taking third place. Besides Haine, one other player caught the attention of observers—in fact, more than the hard-hitting Tommy. A professional beachboy from Honolulu, Ed "Blackout" Whaley, was the man to watch in rain-soaked Seattle. Named for his dark Hawaiian tan, he offset his muscled thighs with pearl-white knee braces, but what got everybody buzzing was that he played barefoot! It seems Blackout's acting skills practiced on the many Gidgets back on Waikiki had become part of his playing routine as well. Anytime he fell to the floor in a defensive effort Blackout in-

variably would lay there in a silent heap, moaning, then abruptly take to flapping like a fresh marlin on deck; the girls in the stands gasping at the mangled star. He would remain on the floor until the mean-tempered and tough setter, Bill Cross, would come over and grumble at the shoeless marvel: "Alright Ed, get your ass off the floor!" Still Blackout impressed most others; both he and Haine were selected as First Team All-Americans—as rookies.

"Blood on the court..."

If a little knowledge is a dangerous thing, a lot can be lethal...at least in the case of Gene Selznick. Now recognized as one of the world's premier players, he quickly assumed his cause celebre of revolutionizing the American game which would split the sport right down the middle for years to come. The line was quickly drawn: it was Selznick and part of the playing populace (mostly Californian) on one side, Harry Wilson and the USVBA establishment on the other. Not that Selznick didn't try to wage his campaign firstly on the inside. His first attempt was a direct one with his soon-to-be nemesis, the coach...the same man "who did a lot for me." Selznick pleaded with Wilson to adopt the 6-2 system for the Hollywood Y team; join the best of the world and play this new exciting brand of volleyball. There was no way in Wilson's mind—a mind when it shut, closed with all the force of a steel vault. But there was more to the question than these rules—this was a wrangle for power and if this mad youth was allowed to have his way once, where would it end? Surely a monster would be set afoot in the land of volleyball. Best to uproot it quickly and cleanly, like an onion in a petunia patch.

The crusader persisted: "If you won't change to a 6-2, then at least drop the four-blocker rule I argued." Unmoved, the czar slowly shook his head no. "We invented the game. Why are their rules any better than ours?"

Selznick promptly reeled off a thousand reasons. What irked him most was that in Paris the international rules had forced big men to play defense in the backcourt, setters to block at the net. It made for a better game, and more to the point, if we didn't change to the rest of the world's ways of playing, we could only get further behind with time. Harry responded with the argument that the little man would be legislated out of the game. In fact, he stated that he had discussed the issue with the Japanese and they stood on common ground: slighter and shorter than the rest of the world, ostensibly they would support the adoption of the American rules to save their small men.

"Nonsense!" countered Selznick. Why, even the mighty Russians had a setter no bigger than the Americans' own Engen. Besides, "...a good little guy can more than make up for his lack of height by backcourt defense"—what hurt far more were our lumbering giants who couldn't handle the ball because they never played in the backcourt under American rules. All they ever did was hit and block. That was mostly true; since 1952, the USVBA rules had adopted the rule that any number of players could block at the net—even six if desired! Therefore, in the States when a big stick arrived in the back row, after the serve he stepped to the net to block and the smaller setter stepped back to defend. Specialization was, well, boring. Impassive and mute, Harry coldly wagged his head from side to side for the last time. Finally, immovable as the Sphinx.

Oh persistence! Next Selznick took his plea to the other power brokers in the game. After all, everyone liked or at least admitted the charisma of the game's best player. Many of their wives had enjoyed the evenings at the Nationals when a large group would go out on the town. They would watch Selznick take control of the dance floor and then tirelessly dance in turn with every woman present. He now pleaded for the officers' reason. How would the USA ever become the best if it played with archaic systems...and worse, different rules! A few shrugged to acknowledge that at least it was a good question. However, Wilson held sway in the game, and face it, he was one of them. He had sacrificed his services unselfishly for years, written and published the International Review, and gone to endless meetings—some of them overseas at his own expense. Viggo Nelson,

incoming USVBA president who replaced Bill Friermood (1952-1955), was no more sympathetic.

Murray Koorhan was another of the sport's shepards having his ear bent by Selznick the provocateur's idea. Koorhan could readily give an example of his own commitment to the development of the game. In the '57 Nationals in Memphis he played and officiated according to his count for 27 games in one day! With only six guys on his Detroit Northern team, there was no relief from playing and he was committed to officiate as well. Finally, on the referee's stand that night both legs went. Ping! Doubled over in cramps. So he didn't want to hear Selznick talk about time and sacrifice!

"Time?" retorted the star. "How much time do you think the players put into this game? A lot more than the week back here! Some of us play more than 300 days a year...driving all over Los Angeles for free...then pay our way to the Nationals and USA Team trips! That's sacrifice!" The debate began to heat up. The administrators insisted that Harry was the coach and had established himself as the link to the FIVB. Selznick was just a player...admittedly a great one, but he should stick to that. Silence suddenly reigned. The recalcitrant got up slowly and retreated to the door. The genuflecting over, Selznick's righteous indignation now swooped in. Those final words have not been left to posterity...certainly not to children. Yet walking down the hall of that hotel, Gene Selznick was heard talking to himself. "Okay, if that's the way you want it...I'll just get my own team and beat your asses with modern volleyball. Then you'll have to change!" In 1957, Gene Selznick dropped off the championship Hollywood Y and formed his own renegade band with the Westside Jewish Community Center. War was declared. The controversy would last for many years and take many casualties.

"Bowling for dollars...or just to get better..."

When the dust and smoke finally settled, Selznick was now in command of his own movement had a lot on his hands. He had to raise the insurgent army, indoctrinate, feed, clothe, and train them for the conflict which would take place in May, 1957 in Memphis. He had a year but where to find the troops? Where were the players that would rally to his campaign, storm the barricades, and throw themselves in fury at the enemy's fire? Well, he quickly saw it would be confined to a small place. No one outside the state of California was going to buck Harry Wilson, and inside Los Angeles it was a daunting thought for a serious player who had any aspiration to ever don a USA jersey. There was only one sure place, at least to start handing out inflaming pamphlets and preaching revolution. State Beach!

Quickly he went to his old comrades. The two guys who taught him the most—"never let me do anything wrong"—even though one of them was already let out to pasture, coaching women and reveling in past glories at State Beach: Manny Saenz and Bernie Holtzman. But would they take up arms against what they knew would be a sea of troubles? In fact, both Saenz and Holtzman admired Harry Wilson's past efforts—at least he had provided *structure*! But Selznick persisted: "the game must change and only we can do it!" Saenz at 43 and Holtzman at 35 caved in and from old trunks pulled their musty uniforms and oiled their tired, rusting muskets. Besides, how could they spend an entire year rebuffing the young firebrand's entreaties? And there was a clincher: with the Westside Jewish Community Center procured as their sponsor, an ethnic flavor was added to the team—many of the players were Jewish as well. Selznick promised them all lox and bagels every time they played.

Ultimately, it was a rag-tag militia assembled: a couple long-in-the-tooth but crafty generals, another 35-year old setter in the colorful Jack Backer, an intense but limited 30-year old Harry Cohen, and Holtzman's long-time crony, universally known as "The Crow." Could he really go to war with this bunch? Well...maybe a year or two of subversive activity, some sniping and guerilla warfare while the search for younger recruits continued; some young talent was needed tospend thousands of hours in the gym to carry the 6-2 system into battle. Most of all, he needed a young Turk, a lieutenant to form and give the campaign the irrepressible flair of youth. This was revolution, wasn't it! Fate would have it that his Crazy Horse, his Che Guevarra, was already there running over the State Beach sand. Practically living there! From eight in the morning until five in the afternoon everyday, then home for a sandwich and off to a gym for four hours of indoor doubles—short court version at the Hollywood YMCA, John Adams Junior High in Santa Monica or Robertson Gym in El Segundo. The same kid who in high school after getting the bug to bowl, would bowl a minimum of 40 games a week: Ron Lang.

Perhaps the fiercest of all competitors in the sport, Lang took no prisoners...ever. "If two guys came down the beach who I'd never seen before and got in a game, I'd beat their brains in! I made sure they walked away knowing there wasn't a chance in hell they could ever beat me." That terminator view extended to players he knew and friends. When an unsuspecting Smitty Duke—an indoor great from Dallas who was training in Los Angeles for the USA team—happened to stroll down to the beach for a relaxing game at Marine Street, Lang gave up a total of five points in two games to 15, then greeted his out-of-state friend. "If I played a guy five days a week and gave him no more than ten points everytime, then I knew that when I met him Saturday or Sunday in a tournament the match was half won." In an era when partying eclipsed playing for many, Lang was abnormal. Not that he didn't enjoy socializing as much as the next player, quite the contrary, he was a first-rate raconteur. He simply decided that if he drank beer and schmoozed with an amicable opponent Saturday night, it might blunt the edge, even ever so lightly, of the huge gleaming scimitar he planned to bring down on the guy's unsuspecting head the next morning.

"Money, marble, or chalk...I wanted to win...even if it was flipping coins," said it all about Lang. His looks belied his raison d'etre.

Not quite chubby, he was powerful, compact and rounded—far from the typical cut and chiseled beach warrior of the sand. But Selznick, always an able connoisseur of talent, saw an assassin in the 19-year old. He also learned things about the kid's character from Harry Cohen who had drilled him when he was 17, both on the beach and at the Hollywood Y gym. "I hated Cohen. He was merciless...but I learned," Lang admitted later.

In 1956 Lang teamed with Dick Davis to play in Open beach tournaments; when he and Davis put Holtzman and Selznick in the losers' bracket then lost to O'Hara and McMahon in the finals of the winners' bracket (9-11, 11-9, 9-11), Lang knew he had a future, despite the caning Holtzman and Selznick gave them late Sunday afternoon in the finals of the losers' bracket. Later that summer, his dream to play with Selznick on the beach got closer when the legend asked him to sign on with the new Westside team. Wow! It was kind of like being asked to join the band of Robin Hood, or Jesse James—Lang was riding with the best and baddest desperados ever, blazing new trails never seen, riding right behind that daring and dancing black-boleroed leader. Following Selznick was like following Errol Flynn.

Then there was reality. Six guys staying in one motel room in Memphis. The team with a cause, Richard the Lionhearted and his noble charges finally reached the Holy Land—to drop into the losers' bracket in their second match by an unknown Midwestern team—tantamount to the twelfth century sainted king and his army being scattered by a band of goatherders with sticks. There was a reason. Holtzman had demanded on the first night that Selznick stay confined to the room for rest...the other five supported the elder spokesman and the door was chained. But the steed was restless in his stall all night. But he would not be the next; the cobbled stallion announced, "Screw you, Bernie! I'm going out." Out all night tripping the light fantastic, Selznick's feet set fire to Beale Street and that's all the team needed the next day. Their game elevated and they roared through the losers to capture a representative

third place. Harry Wilson could gloat freely as his Hollywood team steamrolled through everyone but a few tremors of fear must have infiltrated his aplomb, particularly when the evil genius unwrapped a new serve which set tongues wagging. From a high toss, Selznick's fiery roundhouse wreaked havoc with the receivers. It was simply too fast and had too much drop on it to take overhand unless a receiver happened to be starting in the right spot. "Well...it was only served by one guy!" opponents claimed.

On the female slate in the Memphis nationals, the shocker was a fifth place finish by a high school team! Yes, a high school squad from Big Springs, Texas—the "Steerettes"—was the most popular team in the tournament and returned to a ticker-tape parade down Main Street in their home town. And although widely talked about in the volleyball world the rest of the year, the girls on that team soon sadly dropped into a historical footnote. It was a latent spark which caught fire two decades later when the revolution in junior girls' volleyball hit the nation. Even Big Springs—with its cool, clear water—would replenish its long-gone tradition by developing a local girl, Rose Magers, for the 1984 Olympic team.

Soon the first summer Open came knocking and Lang's dream of playing with Selznick didn't work out. The young protege had to wait until 1958 when the great Holtzman would finally give up the competitive ghost. What a team that new one made! Although a student at USC, Lang had loved it every time Selznick had called him the previous year to go down to the Westside gym and work out—just the two of them. Hitting at chairs until they were too tired to continue, then serving until they were rested enough to work on hitting the new shoot and "one" sets brought back from Paris. "Selznick was so innovative that he wanted to take the first pass and make it a set, then the second contact would be a hitter jumping at the net. That guy had the option to attack or set again depending on the block. Gene and I had the control to do that—the rest of the team didn't, nor did they have the time to work on it.

I consider Selznick the architect of today's game; he had all those ideas before anyone else even dreamed of them. Of course, he never got that recognition because of his political enemies."

On the beach, they were brilliant as well...at least after the first few tilts. In the first Santa Barbara Open, gale winds didn't seem to unsettle Mike O'Hara and hard-hitting Barry Brown from Stanford who easily walked away winners. In the next tournament at Laguna, Selznick-Lang found themselves in the losers early Saturday, knocked out by "two local nobodies" before wending their way slowly back to win the tournament. From that point on, it was smooth sailing the rest of the summer. My how they could take so many crushing balls off their fingers! Lang recalls, "playing defense with Gene was like no one else." The new dynasty was short-lived, however. Lang's duty in the National Guard allowed him to play only one tournament in the summers of '59 and '60.

In 1961 Lang returned with a vengeance to play. But there was a feeling, impalpable, about his partner which Lang had sensed all along and became a subtle bother. Lang noticed a certain delineation in the indoor-outdoor attitude in Selznick. While Lang sat on the sand and studied every player's hitting tendencies in warm-ups, Selznick was busy holding court with his sizeable entourage. Where was the party? Where to dance that night? "Gene played hard everytime he played indoors. But on the beach he didn't have any strategy. He just expected to walk out and win." Most of the time, they did. In fact, the duo's dominance was so great even at State Beach that Selznick began passing the serve into the net one day. "He would make me run in and play it out of the net...to get some competition," Lang remembers. Years later Selznick confessed: "I didn't care that much about the beach; it was just fun. The whole thing was six-man...and international."

Not so for Lang. On the court he was an instant killer, but he had a practical streak in him. The game didn't consume his personal life quite like it did Selznick's. Marriage, jobs,

things of that nature caused him to pass on every USA trip except one—the 1964 Tokyo Olympics. "Gene's main goal was to win with a US Team internationally. I just wanted to play—indoors, beach, it didn't matter. In fact, thinking back about our indoor experience it seems kind of stupid. The goal was to win. But we played more for Gene's campaign," Lang laughingly observes.

International victory was a raging fire in Selznick and he refused to relent. He phoned and lobbied incessantly to get the sport's rules internationalized. His persistence only steeled Wilson's resolve. Ultimately, there was only one answer: he must win the USVBA Nationals with the new system. Experimentation was called for; they needed more work and better personnel. In 1958, Jimmy Montague was a great addition and Don McMahon came on board as a setter. Coach Selznick also decided to make Lang the other setter...sweet hands and a good head were paramount for the 6-2. Their team was a runner-up in 1958—more tinkering was required. The versatile Selznick decided to play as the other setter. Now he and Lang could both hammer away, and who else in the country could better put up the exacting sets needed for the system? Nobody. The recruitment of the high-flying Hawaiian, Alika Smith, made things look hopeful for the toppling of Hollywood in 1959. But a stellar spiking demonstration by Bill Olsson and crew foiled the Westside dream again.

Time for despair? Not yet, but the basic Hollywood team plus Selznick and a few others conformed to Harry's simple offense and manhandled all comers in the Pan-American Games held in Chicago in 1959. Wilson was taking on a glow of invincibility when disaster struck in the Dallas Nationals of 1960. Powerful 6'4" Jim Kaufman led Westside's onslaught with fearless banging away and got some help from the stratospheric leaper, Alika Smith. The two-man block which Selznick had engineered and perfected for four years paid dividends; they dug a million balls in Dallas. Down to the wire in a double finals, Westside and Hollywood provided the volleyball world with a sense that they were watching history. They were. Playing under eight-minute, ball-in-play, timed games, despite the gravity of a National Championship, the final game was ticking away. With an early lead by Westside, sideout after sideout was making things look shakier and shakier for the defending champs. Selznick and crew even began serving looping balls to kill time. One player, Olsson, was finally unnerved and went to Engen during Hollywood's final timeout. He demanded that the setter step in and start setting the serve directly to Olsson for a kill thereby saving precious seconds to score points. With Engen and Walt Schiller's deft hands, they'd done it many times in the past. Engen went to Wilson for his counsel. Negative. "That's when I knew that the game had passed Harry up. And eventually I would leave Hollywood because of it."

The clock ran off in agonizing speed for Hollywood; Selznick lobbed his last serve with a Cheshire grin that stretched from ear to ear. Westside had done it. The bells pealed in Dallas, peasants took to the streets, the long struggle had ended. Sure...for about a day!

"And I think I've seen the last of you...Rio de Janeiro blues..." (Randy Crawford)

"Periscope down!" Gene Selznick smiled as the long, sleek vessel slipped out away from the dock to cross the harbor at the scatter of diamonds twinkling in the blackness which was Rio de Janeiro. A submarine was an unorthodox and expensive way to get to the fun capital but there was no other choice to get off the little island where the Americans and other teams were housed—a ferry strike had shut down all transport except for the official boats to and from matches for the World Championships of 1960. Not what he had in mind. What was in his head was a one-note Jobim samba...and all those "soft and tan and young and lovelies..."

How did he pull this one off? Easy. The brother of a Brazilian player was the admiral who commandeered the submarine for the Brazilian Navy and volunteered its service. Selznick had a charm which cut across borders—players like this Brazilian remembered the bon vivant from Paris in 1956—from then on it would

be like this at these international competitions. "Where's Selznick?" asked Russians, Hungarians, Cubans and French players. He had All-World talent laced with that New World irreverence, the breezy insouciance of "Let's-squeeze-every-moment-for-its-fun-juice-because-we-may-not-be-here-mañana."

And his teammates? He was a line of demarcation. For Mike O'Hara it was: "You had to be a minion to get along with Selznick. But he had people who would die for him." What was different on this trip was that he was in effect the coach too! Hadn't his team won the preceding nationals? The spoils went to the victor according to official party-line. Still, the USVBA couldn't send off their ambassadors with Genghis Khan in total command so Doc Burroughs went to ensure respectability and was the coach in name. Besides to both play and coach was too much for any mortal—even Selznick. Especially when the honorary Vice-Admiral of the submarine arrived in the morning at the humble barracks after dancing all night to rouse his troops. Some didn't care, as long as he played well...but some were furious. Yet this captain would never answer to any code of conduct but his own: "Some of the guys were pissed off...but that's the way it goes," he would chortle many years later.

Despite the less than traditional situation, the American men again had moments of brilliance. Against the world beating Russians, it was tooth and nail for the first two games: 15-13 and 16-14 before they succumbed in the third game. Olsson and O'Hara were on fire as Olsson brought out a serve which marked four aces in one game. Always a good server, Olsson admitted that perhaps the ball itself was a factor: "the thing was harder than a rock and out of round, shaped like a cube!"

Yet the team was faced with continual problems—internal ones as well as some with a foreign flavor. Painful lessons were learned about playing abroad. During the first few days an inconsistent diet induced Mike O'Hara to quaff a delicious quart of milk. Before long, his teammates had to carry him to the commode as his strength ran out of him. Olsson soon followed with his own case of dysentery, but somehow they hung on for the final pool. What hurt worse was the lack of a second setter. The dream-merchant coach couldn't run his 6-2 as planned; Engen could have adapted to the system had new job opportunities not waylaid him. But Lang's absence, due to a new job, was what hurt the most. He and Selznick were the architects and builders of the new modus operandi, and one of the cogs in the machine was missing. So Dick Hammer, a good hitter, was utilized instead to set the ball.

Lack of money was a permanent and formidable obstacle to international success but it was just another battle in the coach's mind. Prior to the trip, Selznick canvassed his many friends and acquaintances for ideas. One friend owned an oil company. "No money but he had plenty cans of oil," reports Selznick. "So we called up gas stations all over LA and sold cases of the stuff. Some of them thought it was hot but that didn't matter. We made money." It helped get some of the more needy players to play but it wasn't enough to justify endangering a good job—the factor preventing Lang's participation in 1960 and Olsson's refusal to go to Paris in 1956. Olsson, who did go in 1960, remembered that the players even had to buy the "cubed" balls to practice with during their month long training camp of four nights a week. The average age of the team was about 30 and most were working so the purchase wasn't too painful. Good idea, too! Although it was customary to be met with surprises upon arriving at international tournaments in those days, the less than round ball, sight unseen, in Rio could have presented big problems.

Ron Lang, ever the pragmatist, commented on that epoch, "Nobody here cared about the international game—no one knew if the USA Team even played! At least on the beach it was a great environment and a lot of people to watch. And you didn't have to sacrifice your livelihood. For what? That was absolute insanity!"

For the women players, fortunes continued on their sad, uneventful path. Beating countries which were smaller than the smallest state at home provided no real sense of accomplishment and getting annihilated by the better teams was bitter gall. Although Manny Saenz was coach of the team, a couple weeks of practice couldn't cut it. If there was a lesson in it all, besides learning to cope with frustration, it was found in the first time the Americans saw the Japanese women play. The famed coach, Hirofumi Daimatsu, had the slight female samurais flying, rolling, diving and digging spikes that the rest of the world's defenders would run from, or shy away from at best. "Can we do that?" the mostly-Californian women asked themselves. Yes, they could...in about 20 years.

Uncle Sam's men not only enjoyed greater success than the women's team, but they also caused some fireworks on a few occasions. Playing in the first round of pool play in Belo Horizonte, some of the guys learned the international lesson that the shrill whistling they provoked was not praise but rather a derisive signal. Understandably too, as this city was a Communist stronghold in a hotbed of social change. A bevy of Brazilian fans can shame a thousand supporters of most other ilk. Ten thousand rabid, imperialist-baiting howlers can unravel any six guys down on the floor.

France, a team that should have been cakewalked by the USA Men, suddenly had several early points and the red, white and blue showed null on the board. Worse, two or three of the first nervous American servers had put the ball in the net or out. What a perfect cue for the irascible captain on the floor to go bigger-than-life once again. Taking his sweet time, he scanned and grinned at the crowd in a silent challenge. They saw the gauntlet and roared; guards contained a small cell of enraged Bolsheviks who seemed intent on martyrdom...after murder. Selznick tossed the ball high and caught it. "The nerve of the scoundrel!" resounded the great wall of sound. He grinned and did it again. Ears splitting now, he held up his index finger of one hand—his teammates thanking dear God it was *that* particular digit—in a loan from Babe Ruth. He launched a roundhouse. Point. Another and a third. Each point dropped the sound and rancor a notch and the USA strolled to victory with eardrums intact—except during those moments when Selznick went back to serve.

Viva America! The first USA Women's Team won a silver medal in the 1955 Pan-American Games in Mexico City. Pictured, from left to right, lower row: Pat Witherel, Bonnie Pride, Polly Lowry and Verne Stevenson. Standing: Gladys Petter, Rita McMichael, Lillian Novosad, Jane Ward, Joyce Posey, Pat Bearer, Scottie Bailess and Coach E. A. Snapp. (Photo by Dr. Leonard B. Stallcup)

USA Men—1956 World Championship, Paris. First Row (left to right): Rolf Engen, Lou Wentzel, Jack Woods, Leo Morgan, Walt Schiller and Bud Klein. Second Row: Coach Harold Peterson, Don Hall, Dick Williams, Bob Klinger, Gene Selznick, Art Alper and Marvin Wigley.

Surfin' at Malibu or volleyball at Sorrento? Ross McCullum and Jerry Hill try to decide while sitting on McCullum's '32 Ford parked in front of the Sorrento Grill. (Courtesy of Dave Heiser)

Volleyball's first ambassador...unofficial. The original caption read, "Gene Selznick of the United States Team amazed two players from Russia and one from Yugoslavia with his skill in manipulating 'Bubble Gum.' They had never seen it before."

Lang to Selznick, indoor or beach. Selznick shows the form which made him All-World in Paris, 1956. (Courtesy of Bernie Holtzman)

Hollywood Y...volleyball's greatest dynasty. 1956, another of a dozen National Championship teams. Front Row (left to right): Bill Stratton, Art Alper, Bill Olsson, John Brame, Gene Selznick. Back Row: Bernie Holtzman, Walt Schiller, Richard Cooper, Rolf Engen, Coach Harry Wilson. (Courtesy of Bud Fields)

Island boys, 1956. The Honolulu Y drew the largest crowds: especially Tommy Haine (back row, second from right), and "Blackout" Whaley (left, second row). Blackout's barefoot style was copied by at least one other player...(second from left, bottom row). (Courtesy of Bud Fields)

Apollo vs. Dionysus at State Beach, 1956. Mike O'Hara drives one down against his famous nemesis, Gene Selznick, and his partner Bernie Holtzman. (Courtesy of Bud Fields)

"Just get there! It'll be on the net." Lang sets Dick Davis in first ever Sorrento Open, 1956.
(Courtesy of Dave Heiser)

Mixed pleasure. Edie Conrad sets Mike O'Hara, a routine which made them a dominating team for a decade. (Courtesy of Dave Heiser)

"The one guy I wouldn't stand in against," claims Jimmy Montague. At 6'5, Bill Olsson was also springloaded and a key to Hollywood Y's dominance. (Courtesy of Bud Fields)

Selznick's raiders. Small, over the hill, but they knew how to win...and had the one young lieutenant, Ron Lang. Westside JCC, third place, 1957. Front row (from left to right): Manny Saenz, Bernie Holtzman, Jack Backer. Back row: Ronnie Lang, Gene Selznick, Harry Cohen, "The Crow".(Courtesy of Bud Fields)

Too easy. The Mariners keep rolling..now with the talented Jeanie Gaertner. National champs, 1957. Front row (from left to right): ZoAnn Neff, Edith Conrad, Lois Haraughty, Lila Shanley. Back row: Manny Saenz, Pattie Bearer, Jean Gaertner, Jane Ward, Marion McMahon (Courtesy of Bud Fields)

The dream comes true! Westside JCC wins it all in Dallas, 1960. Front row (from left to right): Selznick, Montague, Scott, Smith, Kraushaar. Back row: Kaufman, Bena, Hammer, Apel, Lang. (Courtesy of Bud Fields)

Chapter 8
1961-1964

"26 miles across the sea..."

Mike Bright swore at the boat of photographers. Trying to get too close for shots, once again they had cut in front of his board creating a small, cross-wise wake—big enough to knock him off his 18-foot paddle board or at least cost him valuable time. However, he knew his lead was big enough. Arching back, he couldn't see anyone and after five hours the Manhattan Pier was about an hour away...a mere six more miles. He just didn't need that damn boat cutting in and out.

"Nice goin,' Bones!" the South Bay locals cheered when he sprinted out of the water to claim another first-place trophy of the Catalina-Palos Verdes-Manhattan Beach race; most of his friends in the crowd were local surfers and boardmakers who, in time, would become household names in the surfing world. In 1961, Bright was already a water-man legend. He'd represented the USA in the '56 Melbourne Olympics as a paddleboarder and at the same time introduced surfing to Australia with a handful of other guys—"Da Bull" (Greg Noll), the most famous big wave rider of all time, being one of them. It was a regrettable act of goodwill as the Aussies would later dominate world surfing.

The 6'4", 165-pounder took all the congratulations with few words. After 32 miles...a bite and a siesta? Maybe a beer with his buddies? Are you kidding! Bright immediately joined the Hollywood Y crew warming up on the main court. With an understandable show of clemency, they let him miss the first game,

afterwards he played all day to help them win the popular Manhattan Six-Man Tournament. Crazy? A fluke? Not at all; he did the combined feats several times...winning them both. Dave Heiser, an avid surfer and beach volleyballer himself, claims the double victories unparalleled in beach sports.

Bright also won the first Manhattan Beach Doubles Open in 1960—and the first five in succession (1960-1964). The year of 1960 was a big beginning. Earlier that summer he won the State Open with Mike O'Hara, a contest which would signal the most fierce and enduring rivalry in beach volleyball history for a long time. Lang-Selznick versus Bright-O'Hara. A huge first year for the skinny kid, but only the first of a dozen years of greatness.

"Shattuck's...memories of Sand Acre..."

It would be hard to relocate Sand Acre today. Real estate booms beginning in the '60s transformed sleepy beach towns into congested neighborhood communities for the aerospace denizens who could afford to pay the high rents and mortgages. Pre-war dwellings were torn down and the word "condo" sneaked into LA speak. Dave Shattuck held on through the '50s and offered his sandy front yard as the coolest place to play in the South Bay. Heated doubles games attracted interest, but on Sundays the standard fare was six-man. The suds flowed freely from the keg, Jerry Lee Lewis and Chuck Berry rattled the windows after the sun went down. On one of those hot Sundays, the lanky Bright strolled into his first six-man game. The last thing he needed was another sport. Surfing and paddling should have been plenty; catching the sun-up and sunset glass-offs up and down the coast was already a full-time vocation for some of his buddies. Bright's time as a celebrated basketball player at nearby El Camino was enough for most athletes as well. It was different for Bright. If you loved something enough, do it while you can...and as much as you can.

All the while Mike O'Hara had been on track for his calculated ascent to glory. Since 1956, he had served as a First Team All-American cornerstone of the Hollywood Y. Let that wild-eyed renegade rant and rave and carry on with his shenanigans—who had the most gold? Hollywood had won four out of the last five years. On the beach it had been a trifle slower. The maddening cavalier behavior of his rival was harder to stomach in such close quarters—and while O'Hara's partner, Don McMahon was giving up the game, Selznick had replaced the fabulous Holtzman with the fabulous Lang.

In 1959 when O'Hara saw the rightsider Bright banging balls at will, he was interested then and there. Further observation showed him the guy had a good set of hands, and he didn't tire. How could he? Doing what he did day in and day out. In 1960 there was an immediate adrenalizing element in the staid beach game. Bright allowed the O'Hara-Selznick indoor rivalry to hit the sand. It never came to fisticuffs between the two but it was truculent; the poor guy on the referee's stand often suffered most. Squeezed between two great competitive pincers, the seat of the referee sitting up on the pole got hotter than a torrid Santa Ana. And not a penny for the abuse!

At least O'Hara was more diplomatic. Business negotiating perhaps had taught him when to hector, when to coo. Selznick leveled broadsides every time, threatening life-long banishment, not just from calling games, but from ever stepping on State Beach! Bright stayed

out of it hoping that the two guys barking at the poor soul would settle it quickly.

Bloody affairs they were. Great playing, endless playing...usually into darkness. Tournaments in those days were two days of many hours laboring under a July sun for two guys covering 30 feet by 30 feet of hot, deep sand. Sweating, lunging, jumping and more sweating, always sweating. Cramps were often a result. No matter how much liquid, salt and electrolytes were absorbed, a few players simply couldn't stave off the rapid dehydration and if any player ever witnessed a guy with full body cramps, he'd never forget it. Starting at the calf, up the hamstrings, then up to the quads, cramps would fold the legs up like a jackknife. Next the arms, neck and abdominals contracted a man into a human cannonball. Finally the fingers and toes curled tight, but at that point it didn't matter—it was all one giant, wrenching agony. Frantic massages by friends were worthless; the poor soul had to suffer until a physician's injection of a muscle relaxant unbound his body.

In those mighty standoffs, some new strategies emerged with Bright and O'Hara. They decided to use the blocking skills which they had honed indoors even though they carried their own danger. A fingernail traversing the plane of the net was a violation. Still they threw up blocks or faked only to drop back at the last second: "I couldn't believe how fast O'Hara was in the sand for a guy his size," remembers Bright. Sometimes it worked; against Selznick and Lang, usually it didn't. It was sideout ad infinitum with both teams. The only points of vulnerability, however slight, both sides plied over and over. O'Hara and Bright served Lang deep into his corner thereby making him hurry 30 feet to the net to attack. The shortest of the four and not gifted with great spring, his impeccable timing and snap might suffer after enough long-distance approaches. Better yet, serve Selznick short and to his left. He had developed a problem in his left knee so repeated leaning and bending could take a toll.

Against the taller team of O'Hara and Bright, both 6' 4" and good jumpers, there was less strategy simply because of the more impetuous nature of Selznick. The carnivorous Lang was the master predator, uncannily capable of identifying a weakness and attacking it, but when he played with Selznick he uncharacteristically deferred to his older mentor. Selznick wanted to beat O'Hara by serving and digging him. Then it would be so much sweeter to win. But O'Hara was a nut almost uncrackable. Lang would name him as one of the four players in his two decades of playing who would "die before giving up a point:" Holtzman, O'Hara, his later partner, Ron Von Hagen and the fourth...himself.

For five summers, the rivalry raged on until the Tokyo Olympics changed a lot of things. Back and forth the battling went and a slight edge finally went to O'Hara and Bright, particularly when the ever-growing Manhattan Beach Open went to them five successive times between 1960-64. For Mike Bright, the prospect of going to another Olympics was a needed stimulation. He claimed to be bored both with Wilson's monotonous brand of indoor ball and the beach as well. "Pass, set and hit until one guy cramped," had made him look over the sand and out to those silent waves peaking. Alone, no competition, no hassles. But the inclusion of volleyball into the Olympics had everybody abuzz and gave the indoor game a brand new status in its hotbed of California.

Prior to 1964, the American version of volleyball was headed down a path which was progressively diverging from the brand of play and rules the rest of the world was following. As Mike Bright observed, the American game was slow and dull with its four blockers and in some ways bizarre. With the elimination of the two 'xs' on the court in the late '50s, the practice of screening became part of the game. Five players could now bunch together at the net and in time raise their arms before the serve— quite a wall to get around. If that alone didn't make it tough on a receiver, the increasingly tight calls of the overhand reception made it an art few players could master. In fact, referees

came to even use sound as a criterion for a flawless touch. So by the early '60s, the five players not receiving the ball would simultaneously clap their hands to drown out any audible trace of mishandling.

Geography had much to do with the diversion of the two games but a greater factor was undeniably the stubborn refusal to adopt international rules by the USVBA—and, of course, by its most powerful man, Harry Wilson. In a lengthy article from a 1959 Review published shortly before the Pan American games, Wilson justified his philosophy. The following are excerpts from the article, "International Volleyball."

If you do as some of the others have done who have been to Europe, you may go away saying, "I love those International Rules, why don't we adopt them." To you I think we should prepare our answers in advance and say, "No, these things are not allowed by International Rules." The International Rules say very clearly that the ball must be clearly batted, must not be held or thrown or may not visibly come to rest. What you may be seeing is the European interpretation. Some of our Latin friends have found this acceptable and have even declared that it is official because they have seen it done at the Worlds championships held in Paris where our international officials live and where the Italian head of the International Arbiters Committee condones and looks with favor upon this interpretation of the rules...

...The truth of the matter is simple. The only place in the world in which the game is played according to the rules is in the United States. Why do these other countries play contrary to the rules? Probably for the same reason that they allow players to go over the net. It is another skill, difficult to learn and the players and coaches that have not taught this to their players have prevailed on first their own national officials and then on the international officials to allow these crutches to be placed under their play. If this is not true, why are not the rules themselves changed?

Maybe the coaches are not the ones to blame—maybe it is the players themselves. Learning to stay on your own side of the net for blocking and spiking is not difficult to learn. Clean ball handling takes longer, but we do it—it can be done if officials call by the book as they should and players and coaches stop fighting it and learn what they must. To those of you who might suggest that we adopt International Rules without reservation, you must consider that;

1. We would have to scrap the finest, most able and experienced Rules Committee in USVBA history. All are students of the game, with no political entanglements, they have proven themselves by making fewer bad mistakes than any other sport (look at the jumping around the football and basketball Rules Committee have done in recent years.) Their knowledge of volleyball itself is much greater than most members of the International Rules Committee. No axes to grind, no one to account to, they vote their conscience.

2. We would be at the mercy of the International Rules Committee...

6. The official ball can be a first cousin to soccer. Probably a concession to poor people that had a soccer ball and no money for a real volleyball—only official change is its been made smaller— "All the better to catch and push, my dear."...

"The Tao of volleyball..."

Strange, wasn't it? Take this softball. If it were infinitesimally shrunk to a subatomic particle and you measured its position, you inescapably changed its velocity...forever! The reverse is true as well: your act of measuring its velocity just changed its nuclear address for eternity. Eternity? Hmmm...better not get into time flow right now. Back to the tiniest softball and the admission that it all came down to prob-

abilities—nothing was stable and immutable at the most basic level of matter. Einstein was wrong about God not playing dice with the universe. It was more like one huge Las Vegas out there where limitless games of chance decided different realities: spinning roulette wheels, video poker and slots operating under what Heisenberg called the Principle of Uncertainty. So the more we know, the more we don't know. Funny. She seemed to have always sensed that...always chafed at so-called experts telling her the only way it was.

Mary Jo Peppler dropped metaphysics from her mind and picked up the softball. "That camera's too close I think," she admonished the network crew and motioned out at the television camera planted on a chalked semi-circle at the end of the field in Houston's Astrodrome. Most of the women in that first Women's Super Stars event in 1975 were throwing it some 50 feet short of the line so they chuckled at her comment—it was pleasant to see a sense of humor in athletes. She warned again; she was less funny this time. The cameraman replied, "Please, just throw it. We're behind schedule as it is."

As she stepped up caressing the 12-inch ball, the crew admitted that the leader in the competition had impressive physical traits. At 6'0" and 150 pounds, she had a well-defined musculature which bespoke power. Wasn't she the one who almost went to the Tokyo Olympics as a shotputter and javelin thrower? She elected to instead go as a volleyball player. "You should see her play basketball!" one guy exclaimed. The chatter subsided when the southpaw Peppler unleased a moon shot. Up, up, up, the object finally dropped on its parabolic path— right at the uptilted camera. Like a heat-seeking missile, the ball homed in on the apparatus then blasted the target and ricocheted off. To the glee of the astonished crew, the camera man bailed out for cover at the last second, only to trip and land unceremoniously on his butt.

To no one's surprise, Mary Jo continued to run, row and throw to win it all in Houston. For a decade she had displayed a natural athleticism that few women in the world possessed. A searing desire, some said obsession, matched her corporeal abilities. "With my same talent, any man would have been a millionaire." But she wasn't a man...nor did she want to be. Rather than spending her time bemoaning male dominance in the world of sports, she took up the mantle of women's volleyball in the United States. How to change it? How to get a training program so our women were no longer the raw material to be ground up by Japanese and Communist teams. She was also interested in how to tap into the burgeoning fields of research: particle physics, astronomy, sports psychology and all the inter-related disciplines. Neuro-linguistics programming for example. This was the New Age, wasn't it? Human potential was waiting to burst from its mummified wraps. Every new idea was worth examining and empirically tried, a priori and a posteriori logic combined. Just don't try and tell Peppler it couldn't be done! Ah, and you thought Gene Selznick took on a big job...

At the GAA (Girls' Athletic Association) sports awards ceremony in 1962, there were a half-dozen outstanding athlete awards for girls—Mary Jo Peppler got all of them except one. Pure physical talent packaged like this didn't come around often. A full six feet tall, she was also fast, strong, agile and smart. But what was such an example of physical talent to do in 1962...as a *girl*! One of the activities she picked up to occupy all those extraordinary gifts was volleyball—her introduction was an outdoor mixed-six league between local parks. Still in high school, she might have done worse for the two rec directors of her parks: Leo Apel and All-American Dick Hammer drove them to the games and gave them some sage advice as well.

At the bidding of another rec director who was taken by the youngster's play, Jo Rae Zuckerman soon arranged that Mary Jo practice once a week with her own team, the national champion Shamrocks. "I lived for that one night in the week," she confessed. Working with "the only coach I ever played for who I respected," Gene Selznick worked her as hard as the other women on the team. And he liked

her. "If he didn't buy into you, it was a nightmare. I attribute a lot of my early success and attitude to him. He made me better." In the midst of the many volleyball stars at those practices including Jane Ward, the brightest was the other physical phenom of the game, Jeanie Gaertner. "She had such a pretty style of playing. So fluid...I respected her. She had so much talent." Indeed it was a rare occurrence when Peppler was impressed with another's prowess but long-limbed and graceful Gaertner merited it—she was an Olympic high jumper in 1960.

In 1963 Peppler played in her first Nationals and although her raw talent piqued a lot of interest, the system for choosing the National Team at the time effectively took the winning team and whoever else the winning coach fancied. The rookie on the second place team, Spartans, wasn't invited on the Pan-American Team. When the women lost in São Paolo to Brazil, the spot to go to the Tokyo Olympics was lost as well—there would be no American women playing volleyball in Tokyo. This was no reason to foil Peppler's dream. She and teammate Mary Perry decided to try another sport so they trained for about six months under a Hungarian Olympian javelin thrower, Bela Farkas. The abundance of ability in Mary Jo persuaded Farkas to groom her for the pentathlon but ultimately she scaled down to training as a shotputter and javelin thrower. She came very close to making the team, but she didn't make the cut. What fortune when the political problems in Brazil waylaid their volleyballers and the Americans were next in line; Peppler marched into the opening ceremonies in Tokyo as a volleyball player.

At 19 years old, the Olympics had a great impact on Mary Jo, "It shaped my whole life." It was also the initiation into a concatenation of achievement, frustration, challenge, struggle and achievement—over and over and over again—for the next 30 years. Never without a campaign, with bulldog determination, like a female Don Quixote tilting at windmills in a man's world of sports...and sometimes pushing one over!

In the early '60s, the Shamrocks had assumed the Mariners prominence in women's volleyball and some of the their younger players as well. Jane Ward, Jeannie Gaertner, Johnette Latreille, Mary Perry, and the 6'3" Linda Murphy supplied enough talent for two championship teams.

Overloaded with good players, a faction split off in 1964 and formed the aptly named Renegades. Gaertner, Perry and Ninja Jorgensen added two future titans of the sport: a young Kathy Gregory and the all-time "renegade" herself—Mary Jo Peppler. Part of the reason for the split was that this progressive contingent wanted to try new, innovative techniques. For example, the Japanese roll. Mary Jo laughs, remembering, "In 1964 the standard thinking on defense was that if you had to hit the floor, you were out of position." The Renegades lost to the Shamrocks in the '64 finals despite their new style of play. Still the split made for new playing opportunities.

A cute pixie blonde, Patti Lucas, arrived in 1963 to take on some of the setting duties for the Shamrocks. The year before, Lucas had finished her year at DePaul in hometown Chicago and convinced her mother to let her come out for the summer to play beach ball...and have a good time. She did both and in two weeks had enrolled at USC. Why go back to the Windy City when you could go down to State Beach and play mixed doubles everyday, which was all a girl could play at the tradition-bound beach except on rare occasions. Her mother, Bertha Lucas, had been a tireless supporter of volleyball for years in the Chicago area whose playing career reached back to the days when a woman was allowed *two hits* per player—ostensibly females weren't skilled enough in the early days to perform with one touch on the ball. So she understood Patti's desire to play but change was still slow for women, indoor and out. However the social aspect was strong as ever: good-looking, healthy people met each other. Patti Lucas met one and married him in 1964: Mike Bright.

The Shamrocks also had a huge advantage over other teams in their coach, and dance teacher to boot, Gene Selznick. He danced hard and he worked his players hard—even females—an anomaly in those days. The assiduous Jane Ward numbered among many of the women who praised the heretic's taxing workouts. Ironically his success as a coach ultimately figured as another kink in the inextricable Selznick knot which always seem to land in the lap of the USVBA. Now with the Tokyo Olympics around the corner, he was an unwelcome burr under the saddle of both men's and women's games.

When the 1963 Pan-American games arrived, it was with some trepidation that Harry Wilson pondered Selznick's role. A sigh of relief was heard around the volleyball world when the incorrigible Selznick refused to play with the men. "Why play that same old system again?" he rhetorically asked. The fear and trembling returned to the USVBA when, according their own rules, Selznick as the *winning coach* had the right to coach the USA women in São Paolo. He took it.

The Pan-Ams in Brazil took on an added dimension in 1963—the winner and runner-up for the men were awarded berths in the Tokyo Olympics. The men played once again without their best setting talents: Lang, Selznick and Rolf Engen, who had been operated on for a damaged Achilles, were not there. Against Brazil for the championship, the USA team played once again under some unusual circumstances. Early on in the match, the men seemed befuddled as to why so many of their serves were floating out. Not so for the Brazilians. Eventually one of the players on the bench noticed that just before an American served, a large door behind the court was opened. The onrushing wind had been blowing out serve after serve. Unable to persuade the official to keep it closed—he pleaded confusion—prior to serving the rest of the match, a quick glance over the shoulder determined if the velocity needed adjustment. It wasn't enough. For the first time, they failed to win the gold at the Pan-Ams but, far more importantly, they still qualified for Tokyo.

The women were lest fortunate. They had a door problem as well but their's was simply a matter of the overflow crowd busting the door down from too many people outside leaning on it! However, things started well for the Americans. Up two games, the wily coach knew that putting the match away would not be easy. Not in front of 8,000 crazed Brazilians and a lone mortal on the stand as referee. He was right. Like a bad dream, the first Pan-American final in Mexico City came back when the referee started calling their overhand serve reception. But this time neither he nor a female version of Rolf Engen was there to provide such a flawless touch; in any case this ref was ready to whistle even Mother Teresa for bad hands.

In the fifth game, the girls were beside themselves and getting worse with the growing roar of the crowd. "I had to do something, so on his next bad call I went over and shook his stand...hard," said Selznick. Unperturbed, the official continued his unseemly ways, and Selznick decided he had one last chance—so better make it grandiose. He rushed to the stand again, this time pulling it so hard that although the referee barely hung on, the net collapsed! Chaos. As the crowd bellowed, from the scorer's table sprinted Brazilian officials supporting the referee's screaming decision to oust the coach from the game...and the gym...and probably the country. Endless spewing of Brazilian obscenities did nothing to improve Selznick's understanding; he wisely realized that none of his opponents spoke English so he simply kept repeating one line: "I don't speak Portuguese!" and refused to leave. Finally they gave up. The net was restored and the Brazilians won the fifth game. It was a heartbreaking but when the country broke out in civil rebellion the next year, the Brazilian women were replaced by the Americans in Tokyo. With a new coach!

"Locals only..."

You could have pulled into the parking lot at East Beach in 1964, in front of the stately Bath House, a shining white jewel topped with red Mexican tile whispering of quiet opulence and pleasure, and parked in any space...with no meter. When Bobby Garcia arrived with Rich Riffero one Saturday morning—top down in Riffero's red '62 Bonneville convertible—rolling up to the curb required a double-take. There glistening in gold offset by shiny black paint, about a dozen names appeared on the curbs of the most primo parking spots: Garcia, Riffero, Martin, Doo-Doo, and Conway ("mayor-in-residence"). After careful deliberation they figured it out; it had to be Tom Smusz. Smusz was one of the guys in their group of players and as an employee of the City of Santa Barbara he'd decided to do a little overtime painting.

Every beach had its own crew and character. Santa Barbara at the northern extreme of the beach volleyball kingdom was one of the more hedonistic...well, less serious. How could you get serious about competition when you lived in paradise? For that matter, why ever leave East Beach to play a game? For the few who did, it was for competition and a new set of girls, friends, and parties. With the ruggedly handsome 6'5" Riffero behind the wheel and the dynamic 5' 8" Garcia riding shotgun, only the reticent Henry Bergmann in the backseat dented their reputation for loving good times. Cruising south down Pacific Coast Highway sporting ebony Wayfarers, there was more physical ability in that cherry red Pontiac than in a busload of normal players. But with the exception of Henry, Saturday night's festivities were just as important as Sunday morning's first game.

Garcia recalled one State Beach Sunday morning that came too soon. After only two hours of sleep and way too much beer and red bulk wine, he now found himself preparing for his first match... by emptying his insides. Retching away on his knees, he overheard the same familiar sound in the next stall. Could it be? "Rich is that you?"

"Bobby? Is that you!"

Journeying south along the coast in the Bonneville with James Brown pushing the envelope of the quadraphonic sound of the speakers in pleading "Please, Please Me" or announcing "Night Train," a glance at the matchless point of Malibu might offer a glimpse of another outlaw, Mickey Dora, on the nose of his surfboard...in a soul-stance on one of those endless, perfectly reeling rights. Ten more miles and off to the right was the broad white sand of State Beach. Stop for a few games? Nah, too serious. How about Sorrento? Well...better, that line-up of luscious trollops along the wall but...let's keep goin'! Muscle Beach? Too hard to park; besides, rather go to the zoo. Now the great middling—the South Bay: Manhattan, Hermosa? Hmmm...tempting; beautiful but too clean, too conservative...boring. We got the whole weekend! Alright, Laguna!

It seems that the sun got hotter, or at least affected the players more, as one moved farther south. In Laguna Beach with its deep sand feeling like quicksand to visitors, Peter Ott, Woody Brooks and Dave Andersen were always a show. Ott, hirsute body and full beard, was rumored to live in the hills of Laguna. Strangely enough, Ott rarely traveled out of Laguna Beach to play. But when the cool winter months came, like a migratory bird he was known to descend to the tropical jungles of South America—in search of exotic reptiles!

How Ott jumped so high out of that loose sand was a wonder...and could he hit! He was the guy to watch at Main Beach because you never knew what he might do. When he needed a timeout and was out of regulation timeouts, he simply took a swing at a ball and hit it a couple hundred feet up into the heavy traffic of the Pacific Coast Highway. That took some *time* to get the ball back—it became known as the "three-minute serve." Another moment which lived on in the game's annals was the time when he and Ron Lang were flipping for the serve in the Laguna Beach finals. Lang in a surly mood

claimed not to have clear view of the coin. He snapped, "flip again!" Ott dipped his knees and launched himself out of the sand into a perfect backflip.

Still, Ott was mostly a player in the final analysis. Clyde Hyatt was the guy to watch for entertainment. As a stunt man in the movies, he was predisposed for bizarre acts but he took his work far beyond. Stories of him abounded—like standing on the hoods of speeding cars down the PCH. He lived on the edge. Mike Bright and Butch May remember walking into a hotel room in 1963 to see Hyatt on the small balcony looking out on the lights of San Antonio. They asked Hyatt where his roommate Hogan was. Smilingly he nodded down to the concrete ledge of the overhanging balcony where the two visitors saw a pair of bloodless human hands! Peering over the thin guard rail, they saw Hogan's arms in a full quiver trying to pull his head up even to his hands. "Seventeen!" he growled clenching his teeth. "What the hell?" they gasped and snatched hold of the dangling Hogan to pull him to safety. On a bet, he had to do 20 pull-ups to get the five dollars. Hyatt had already completed the feat and seemed quite miffed at his two friends for interrupting the wager. They were 19 floors up, and there was absolutely nothing between the ground and the bottom of Hogan's bare feet.

As Laguna Beach had Hyatt, San Diego had Nate Parrish as their champion. He was a great beach player but far greater character. Thirty years later, a player from the group, Jack Henn, tried to analyze it. "It kind of came down to: Can you top this? We would hear about what the guys did in LA, so it was try and go one better. Years later when we finally met the guys who were supposed to be committing those outrageous things up there, we found out our stuff was just as good."

The Goss brothers, Al Woerner, Royal Clarke, Judd Millard, Ron Lapolice: an All-Star team more bent on adventurous fun would be hard to find...in any epoch. One of the less criminal activities was permanantly placing a huge sling of surgical tubing in the humble haunt of Royal Clarke in South Mission Beach to fire water missiles several blocks into ocean front windows, occasionally shattering one. However, Parrish was the eminent trickster: he once entered a 32-team men's indoor doubles tournament with a woman and they won—with Parrish playing the whole time in black leotard, black cape, black mask and shoes. His famous "Flexi" (a little toboggan on rubber wheels) race down a *steep* couple of miles of Mount Soledad in LaJolla reaching estimated speeds of 50 miles an hour and avoiding instant death from the approaching cars by mere inches still lives in infamy. His exploits reached to the court as well. Parrish invented the "cobra"—a placement shot made by extended fingers jabbing the ball. After further experimentation, he broke out the ultimate weapon: the two-handed "double cobra."

Apparently, Parrish's upbringing was conducive to such adventure. His parents managed a famous bath house in South Mission Beach; where the OMBAC (Old Mission Beach Athletic Club) was soon formed and where stood the first beach volleyball courts in San Diego. Converting the bath house to three bowling lanes and beach equipment rental, the white-haired kid was raised on good, clean mischief—'50s beach style. As he got older, his sense of the outrageous grew in sophistication as well. "Chester Goss and I used to buy these old cars for a hundred bucks. We'd each have one and then stage accidents in front of The Pennant (a local renown bar still extant). Sometimes we'd leave one empty in the street, then plow into it with the other one. Or we'd lock front bumpers, throw them into reverse and jam on the accelerator."

"You couldn't do that on the beach today!" Indeed, Parish was talking about a virtual impossibility in 1994. It happened in the late '50s after a tournament in La Jolla. Parrish grabbed another first place and subsequently healthy rounds from the omnipresent keg of beer with his partner, Mike Moore. Driving back south to their home turf, Parrish decided to pull off in Pacific Beach and drive all the way to South

Mission on the beach—some five miles! "People at keg parties all the way down were cheering us on. When we got to OMBAC, I just took a right turn...straight into the ocean. When the water got about windshield high, the engine died. The water kinda sobered us up." Amidst the uncontrolled applause of their local group—this was a topper even for Nate!—Steve Goss and Gordie Evans ran out into the surf. Parrish with a clearer head was struck with a sudden fear he might get arrested for this, "So I told Steve Goss that if he could get the car out of the water, he could have it." Goss and his friend agreed, pushed the wet hunk of metal back onto the wet sand...and it started! Parrish signed over the pink slip at the party. "I was very honest and pleased about it; a deal was a deal. But later that night, our psychotic side came out like it always would," Parrish's glimmering eyes speak. "So, we snuck over in the middle of the night to find Steve's car, and torched it!"

Ah Nate Parrish! He hailed from the same stock whom chronicler Tom Wolfe memorialized in the summer of 1965 in "The Pump House Gang." They didn't come any crazier. Many of his former cronies still relish the time he prepared for the Halloween bash by sitting in a bathtub of green dye for three hours prior to the party. He strolled into the assembly of 300, cutting through the crowd, on either side a double wake of astonished costumed revelers—Parrish was a brilliant glistening green, goggled and finned in emerald...wearing nothing else!

Perhaps the most notorious party of beach volleyball lore took place in Corona Del Mar of all places—a rare beach where no drinking was allowed. So after Saturday's play, most of the players assembled at some unfortunate's two-bedroom apartment for a little get-together. Easily exceeding 100 people who were freely imbibing, the party was soon spilling out people on the terrace. When one of the inconsiderate neighbors began to complain of the noise, a couple of the guys responded by hurling empty beer cans from the terrace down into the uncovered seats of his new convertible. Other neighbors joined in the complaints. The nerve! Next, a hurtling floor lamp in glittering sparks pierced the hood of a new Porsche. Then an entire sofa was pitched from the cheering crowd. There was free entertainment inside as well. Danny Patterson recalls, "Nate Parrish and the Goss Brothers in a nude wrestling match on the kitchen floor, a full inch of red wine flowing on the linoleum." They were still grappling when the police came, and in a clear demonstration of what it means to be in the wrong place at the wrong time, Ron Lapolice had just arrived at the party when he was promptly arrested for disturbing the peace. "But..."

In the drunk tank until noon the next day, Lapolice was probably wishing he had stayed with the Over-the-Line crowd of Mission Beach—the famous tournament he had already created with OMBAC. He wasn't alone. When they called up one of the Derwin brothers Sunday morning to play his first match, his friends shouted, "He's in jail." The crowd responded, "Good! Forfeit him!" Meanwhile, the San Diego contingent spent the morning at the tournament asking for contributions to free the wronged Lapolice. The fine was a hefty $60. "We raised $53. Then we figured we'd just go and somehow get the other seven bucks on the way," Henn recalls. Having tapped all sympathizers, they took off for the jail with Parrish driving and holding the cash. Before long the notion hit home that they really weren't going to find the remaining amount. Where? From the cops? Parrish pulled off at the nearest handsome food establishment to use the phone. One of them gave Lapolice a call of condolence and promised they'd kill themselves to get him out by Monday...no later than Tuesday. Five guys could eat and drink quite well in those days for $53.

"Mean Streets..."

The setting is 136th Street in the Bronx, just south of Yankee Stadium—Martin Scorsese territory. Had you had been bustling along to the subway on a wintry day in 1960, cursing the sludge and dirty snow, you might have looked up at number 50, a typical brownstone. Up on the second floor, or parlor room, the silhouettes would have provided a baroque scene—two figures playing catch or something with a basketball? Why? Well, they were really playing pepper—surely the only ones doing so in the five surrounding boroughs of New York—and it was the teenage brothers, Rudy and Ernie Suwara. Getting in some practice in the cold room under a 16-foot high ceiling.

Rudy the older would meet his dad, a cop whose beat was Times Square, twice a week at the Westside Y in Manhattan where a rare tradition of volleyball had reigned. For Rudy it was just fun until he saw a bonafide international star in action at a tournament at the Brooklyn Y. Just arrived from Yugoslavia, Gabriel Budishin was a remarkable athlete. While a leading player in the world on the Yugoslav National Team, he defected to the west. Neither Rudy nor anyone else had ever seen a player like this: a one-man show with the physique of a body-builder, he hit in every position, a tactic never used in this country. He even spiked out of the backrow (the attack line was placed at seven-and-a-half feet then), something US players wouldn't use for 20 more years.

Ernie remembers hitting the ball against the wall at one of his father's tournaments. At 12, no one wanted to play pepper with the little redhead...besides, the best teams were already showering and leaving. Out of nowhere Budishin walked up to him and asked, "you like volleyball, don't you?" Ernie, in awe, whispered "yes." The greatest athlete he'd ever seen now talking to him! From the self-assured man, dark virile chest hairs springing from his unbuttoned shirt, expounding freely in hardened vowels of deep masculine resonance, one final line never left Suwara: "To be good...you must be fanatic!" He apparently followed his own counsel. Using his good looks, aggressiveness and cocksure aura, the Yugo refined those traits to seek out the good life in the land of the free. The story goes that after finally landing an heiress of a shoe fortune in Chicago, he died in his 40s—a victim of his own dissipation.

In 1958, Rudy played his first USVBA Nationals at 16 with the Westside Y in Scranton. His team's participation was "Uno, dos, adios," as he recalls, so he had plenty of time to watch the older players. By 1962, the East could boast some real talent in the heavy artillery of the Suwara boys—but the Westside Y team of New York had too many weaknesses on the court to rise above their normal ninth place in the nationals. The West coast teams took the siblings seriously: both 6'3" and powerful jumpers, they could bounce the ball with anyone in the country. Whereas Rudy used his savvy relentlessly— he diligently studied the world's best blockers before becoming in his own era the best American at that skill—Ernie, with an exaggerated backswing of powerful arms was the personification of brute, primal force on the court.

"Money players..."

Joe Gold of the famed "Gold's Gym," progenitor of the original muscle factory at Venice Beach, stood and haggled with his good friend, Cy Rubin. Like two rug merchants in the street they chewed back and forth, cajoling then blustering for the extra point which might ensure a victory. Rubin was no mean adversary—a man whose livelihood was the horses—he knew talent when he saw it and he knew how to wage it. Finally arriving at the point of equally begrudging the other's better odds, they could begin.

Today it was Ernie Suwara and Gold teamed together, with a three-point handicap to surmount and $100 riding! Ernie had been on his game the last couple days and Gold was a shade better player even though Rubin claimed his opponent's rippling physique alone should have been worth a minimum of nine points! As both teams went to their corners, Ernie and Butch May had a little secret between them. Waking up that morning in their slovenly flat on the low-rent border between Santa Monica and Venice, they side-stepped through a few empty beer cans to find a not unusual sight. The cupboard was bare...*really bare*. No moldy bread

ends, no stray corn flakes, the peanut butter jar wiped perfectly clean. In the fridge, only an unappetizing plastic pitcher of tap water. Not an edible morsel in box, bottle or can!

Walking to the pier, pangs of hunger emphasized the need for a score today. The last two days proved feckless; splitting the first two games, the older gamesters were too tired to play the third rubber game. So no decision...no money! Because whenever one of the bettors won a completed match, they would graciously split the purse with the younger partner. Half of the normal $25 bet could keep two big guys in food and beer for a number of days if husbanded well. But today they were unusually low on fuel, and as hunger is a great inventor of ideas, they fell upon a new plan.

Play the first one hard and regardless of who wins, the same team must win the second game as well. The bet would now be completed every time they played, and one of them would pocket the winnings for their household needs. Ernie and Gold won the first 16-14 in a dogfight. Up 12-6 in the second and a little light-headed from low blood sugar, it struck Ernie as odd that suddenly Butch started digging everything on his side of the court—and banging away for points! At 13-12 in Butch's favor and changing sides, Suwara whispered in fury: "What the hell are 'ya doin'!" Butch's gritted a common and short expletive heard wherever angered men are found.

May scored two more fiercely fought points and predictably the gaming elders were too fatigued for the third and deciding game. "Unbelievable!" steamed Ernie the Red somehow biting his tongue. Dragging themselves home, not a word was spoken between the two enraged starvelings. Yet once inside. it seemed the reality of no food softened up May. "Sorry, Red," he continued to explain that an acute competitive urge overtook him in the second game. "That's great, Butch. Too bad you can't eat it!" Suddenly the 200 pounds of Hawaiian muscle leaped at the fridge. Grabbing a knife, he ripped open the door and began blindly chipping at the solid block of ice which had overgrown the freezer compartment. Sweating, he pried loose a single, frozen pineapple pie hidden in the furthest reaches. "I knew it was in there! I'll even cook it for us, Red!" Ernie lit up with a salivating grin.

As the pastry heated, redolent odors of processed pineapples filled the small room causing the famished men to swoon. They kept checking the browning crust. Ah, what sweet torture! Finally May pulled the small treat from its fiery oven and...dropped it! "No!" screamed Ernie. Alas, the heat conductivity of the thin tin was too much even for Butch May; the delicacy flipped over, plopped and flowed into a steaming lump. Both men wanted to cry. Instead, they looked at each other and instantly communicated the same unspoken thought. Butch grabbed the abode's only two forks lying unwashed in the sink and they both dropped to the floor...greedily, unashamedly scooping up the savory pineapple tart.

Junior colleges were something practically indigenous to California in the '50s. The two-year colleges first sprouted in the bigger cities then exploded in the early 60s, setting the trend for future American education and becoming known as community colleges. In 1960 Colonel Burt DeGroot had retired from volleyball—well, at least from the most time-consuming activity of any sport—coaching. "Enough's enough," finally declaimed a member of that forgotten species...wives of male volleyball coaches. Long-suffering, understanding, even Ruth DeGroot had her limit. After an itinerant career and establishing military volleyball in this country, as a counselor and teacher at Santa Monica City College, the Colonel could at last breathe a little and devote more time to his sons. That he did...for about 30 days—until a cadre of beach bums walked into his office one day and asked him to attend a few practices and make some observations. No big deal. A club team...maybe play in a couple local USVBA tournaments. Fat chance! Young guys with talent and desire to learn and a man who knew the game as well as anybody in the country: the combination was lethal. Ruth put up a brief

resistance and then sighed in resignation. Why try?

The sport owes her a debt. Colonel DeGroot took the team and won the Collegiate Nationals that year and three more in a row. With the help of Bob Newcomb at U.C. Santa Barbara, he also formed the first inter-collegiate league in Southern California. Success breeding success, every frustrated basketball player or dropout surfer with athletic ability looking for an alternative, cool sport could play volleyball at City College. City had it all—babes, parties, and Malibu was nearby. And you were eligible to play merely by being enrolled in 12 units...which cost about ten dollars. That was worth the ticket to walk around and check out the girls!

Word got out. Talent poured in from all over the Los Angeles basin. In 1962, Steve Kiel, Bob Hogan and Butch Friedman showed up to make easy work of the four-year schools. UCLA, USC, Stanford...who cares? SMCC had the talent, the Colonel and the magnet grew stronger, drawing iron shavings from beyond LA. The other place where volleyball boomed was at El Camino Junior College in El Segundo. It was the South Bay counterpart to City College; volleyball classes were overflowing and the gym's doubles and mixed competition formed some future great players: Spike Boartz, Tom Sonichsen, Larry McCullough, Mitch Malpee, Christy Hahn, Linda Phillips and Sharon Peterson.

"Midnight Cowboys..in reverse..."

In the summer of 1963 after five days of hitchhiking and precisely 83 rides, 18-year old Ernie Suwara and his friend from New York who came "just to party," got out of their last car and stretched their legs overlooking the Santa Monica pier. Each lugged his one suitcase to a phone booth where Ernie called the only soul he knew in Los Angeles. Soon the Colonel picked the two up and descended directly to Muscle Beach for a beach doubles introduction. The alabaster-skinned carrot top, who within a year could hit the ball harder than anybody in the country, lost a doubles match to Colonel DeGroot and another colleague on the other side of 50. Crawling off the court, Suwara seriously pondered going home. Another 83 rides? No way!

Good thing. Within a few months everybody was talking about the hard-pounding redhead with a Brooklyn accent. One story of his first months there has survived for posterity. In one of the popular mixed doubles contests held during hot summer nights at SMCC, Ernie found himself in the finals. The woman's primary job was to put the set right on top of the net—no blocking over in those days—and the guy simply tried to crank it as hard as he could. A pound-out between two men. Points came hard and usually from missed serve receptions. As the ball cannonaded off the floor approaching 80 miles per hour, most of the poor women were cringing and turning away in the primal instinct of flight from danger. No reproof from the guys since they were usually bailing out too!

However, on this particular night a six-foot All-American, Connie Keller, tried the unimaginable. Sneaking up to the net, she jumped and stretched her hands up as high as she could. The ball splatted off one stinging palm and back for a point! The gym erupted. Ernie who hadn't even seen her execute the block now went into the modus operandi he would become famous for. If you blocked him, get ready again! He was coming right back at you with double fury. Not to hit by you but simply to beat the ball off or through your pitiable hands, his ruddy face now crimson. But Keller had a way out—she was a woman—and to block Ernie Suwara just once was a lifetime memory. She could slink away in pride. The audience gushed when Keller went up again; this time Ernie knew it. Kaboom! The blast rattled every joint of her upper torso...but she got him again!

Upon landing the big redhead nodded and turned slowly for the next serve as his face went purple. No greater valor had even been seen in the sport's 70 years when Connie tried it a third time. Veins pulsating in his plum-colored vis-

age, Suwara unleashed a bazooka, which this time shattered the bone in the forearm of Keller before she slumped to the floor.

His roommate had people chattering too. Known as the Hawaiian Cowboy, Butch May sold his only possessions at 16—two surfboards—and came to seek a new life on the mainland. A son of part-Hawaiian parents, Butch grew up in the "Jungle" of Honolulu with the other poor, brown kids looking through the fence of the old Outrigger Club next to the Royal Hawaiian. It was an unattainable world. Watching them play volleyball on the sand, Butch would see the rich haolies sipping their cocktails, admiring the competition and waiting for the iridescent sunset to appear.

Teenaged May found himself in a lumbermill near Tahoe and in the company of some genuine rednecks he was introduced into the honky-tonk life. He'd fought enough humans as a kid, so why not try something more challenging...like a Brahma bull! Soon he was riding the monsters and playing rugby for the Olympic Club in the off-season. It could be said that he was a man who *enjoyed* contact. When a 1000-pound snorting Brahma landed on his leg to sever an artery, the surgeon after almost amputating suggested that he change his choice of sports. Remembering those graceful hoalies at the Outrigger, May gravitated from the ruggers of the Olympic Club to the volleyballers. A natural athlete, he was quickly hooked and heard of SMCC and the Colonel. Within a short time he was established in Santa Monica with a roommate—another poor kid— a redhead from the Bronx! They resided in a $60 a month apartment with an invalid landlord who had a pet monkey as his constant companion. That was fine, but after a few months they figured out that instead of the other guy drinking more than his share of beer, it was the *landlord* with a key who entered during the day to help himself to their primary source of nutrition. They suspected the monkey did too!

Over 20 guys showed up for tryouts that spring of 1964. With Bill Clemo, Bobby

Conrad, Larry Falcinella and others, the team was loaded except for one setting spot. Amongst other things, war had taught the Colonel that you go with what you got. To round out the two 18-year olds on his squad, he took a 43-year old Art Grossman and they began to roll through opponents like Sherman through the South. "We wanna do what Selznick's team is doing!" was a continual cry from his troops, however. Sorry, fundamentals first for the tough coach. "It was a battle but he was right. We had the best fundamentals of any team," recalled Suwara. May added, "Besides, he had some leverage. One time in Fresno, he threatened to hold back our meal money if we didn't straighten up and win the tournament. For me and Ernie, there was no greater motivation!"

Harry Wilson whose nose was incessantly to the wind quickly snatched up the two wonders. After all, they were finishing second in Open tournaments and even beat the Hollywood Stars on occasion. Butch was put with a younger, green team under the able leadership of setter Walt Schiller—the Hollywood Comets. Wilson took a gamble on the Easterner. He needed some fire power. Because Mike Bright and Bill Olsson had defected in 1963, there was a serious chink in the Hollywood Stars' armor. It turned out to be one of the most important recruits Wilson ever made as Ernie hammered away to win the MVP at the '64 USVBA Nationals in his hometown New York City—at 19! Never done before...never since. More importantly, it put Hollywood's players and Wilson in a propitious position for the Olympic Team selection which would culminate in an all-day tryout the following day.

"And the envelope, please..."

A sudden hush reigned in the lobby of the Roosevelt Hotel in Manhattan when David Stubbs held up the piece of paper, clearing his voice. It was already after midnight but every eye was peeled with alertness. At a table gathered the selection committee of the 1964 Men's Olympic Team, which included Emil Breitkreutz, Jim Coleman and, of course, the head coach, Harry Wilson and his assistant,

Burt DeGroot. The forty or so guys were sprawled in the plush armchairs or milled in small groups in light chatter until Stubbs spoke. Every head inclined toward the chairman of the selection committee, Stubbs dutifully thanked the men for attending the one-day tryout which had started that morning at nine and ended some 12 hours later. The grim faces of the committee and his own nervousness bespoke something foreboding about to happen. He made it quick, down and dirty. Twelve names were read: the lucky dozen who would go to Tokyo. Halfway through the dozen names an audible murmur spiked with groans filled the room requiring Stubbs to raise his voice just to complete the list and the six alternates.

The entire room became animated...some went animal. As questions were beginning to be voiced from the boisterous floor the committee briskly marched out. Only Jim Coleman stayed to face the music. And it played until the wee hours of the morning—strident, virulent, a four-act Italian opera spilling over with pathos, mostly rage. Coleman who remembers that his first daughter was unexpectedly being born that night, regretted not being by his wife's side...although he would have rather been any other place than where he was that night! Never had he undergone such a grilling. After the first few hours, the less vehement surrendered to fatigue and slid away to bed. Leaving behind three relentless men who kept it up until dawn...finally, the discussions approached the abusive. Coleman stayed on because he believed that the men deserved an explanation behind the decision—even though he and the committee knew it would never go down with some of them. He tried his best. The one question kept coming back from Dick Hammer, Ron Lang and Gene Selznick: "How could you do it!"

How could they do it? Leave arguably the best...undeniably the most experienced player off the team? Could Coleman tell the real reason behind the official decision? The one that everybody knew...even Selznick himself? That there was no way in hell that the coach, Harry Wilson, was going to take the infidel...no matter how good he was! Of course not. It was only protocol—that dubious glue of society and civilizations—which dictated the absolute truth go unuttered.

Fortunately for the committee, there was some sound reasoning to hang the decision on—at least in their minds—which of course only appeared as careful subterfuge in their adversaries' thinking. "Why it was all based on the players' tryout," the committee contended. And that all started in the Nationals four days before, which was uncharacteristically held in September. That way apparently, our first Olympic athletes would be extraordinarily trained for the pinnacle of competition in the following month in Tokyo. Although the USVBA had decided to revamp their National Team selection process by dropping the automatic six berths from the winning team (could it have been partly out of fear of a Selznick and company victory which rained on their parade as in the 1960 Dallas Nationals?), certainly a first-place finish would carry a lot of weight. Ah, the stars wreak havoc on us all...and they certainly did on Gene Selznick's best-laid plans.

"Altius, Fortius...Politicus..."

The Long Beach Century Club started play at Queens College with disappointing news. Big Jim Kaufman hadn't made the trip. As a student in dental school, he decided to do his hard drilling there rather than on the court, knowing the Olympics weren't a possibility for him. Still, things were going alright until the semi-finals when Long Beach was upset by the tyros of Hollywood Comets who were improving with every match. The Stars barely escaped the same fate against the youthful Comets in the finals of the winners. Long Beach roared back in the losers only to find a stubborn Comet team once again. However, Selznick and company prevailed the second time to set the stage for what volleyball had been evolving to for the past 10 years.

Every player in the tournament crowded in to watch. Every soul was a partisan: who do you take? The guys in white, Harry Wilson's knights of the USVBA...or that dark, marauding band led by the infamous blackguard, Gene Selznick. The outsiders were mad with joy! Long Beach handily snuffed out their arch-rivals, 15-5 and 15-10. Was it planned? Because now the game of the first 75 years of volleyball would take place. One to 15.

It looked like the old Selznick magic would work again; up 10-4, it was close to being put in the bag. Five easy points...not so easy. Harry's frantic praying and the decade-old rancor between the two camps surfaced—O'Hara and Engen might go down but it was gonna take some time, flesh and blood. As the vets raised their perpetual contention to an uproarious tempo, it was two big fledglings on the court who really decided the fate of their masters: Suwara versus Erickson. The sandy-haired hometowner grew beet-redder with every hand-breaking smash and inched Hollywood back into the game. UCLA basketball player Keith Ericson, the gifted athlete sent from the pantheon of the gods—John Wooden called him "the best athlete I ever coached"—hit at will, line or cross-court and hard! Players and the few fans had never seen anything like it; their own breed battling in such ferocity.

Then lightning struck twice. At 13-13, a ball was hit long by Long Beach which broke a deadlock. Hollywood went up 14-13, and one single point away from the dream. Sideout. Long Beach served and it was Hollywood's turn to feel the pressure—a high set was drilled deep and barely out. Duece at 14-14. Barely perceptible, Dick Hammer, raised his hand. What! He was calling a touch on the block—on himself! "Dick!" they screamed. "This is the '60s! Do you think *they* would call it?" Today the man who committed the honorable anachronism is troubled by his critical call. "It was mostly reflex. Later after thinking about it, I'm not sure I did the right thing." Unlike that famous 1924 thriller, the admission didn't garner any national attention but like it, the outcome was changed. It also inalterably impacted American volleyball by nudging the fine equilibrium towards Wilson in the decade-old feud.

Soon after, the victors were on the New York subway at midnight. Go down to the Village and have a beer to celebrate or not? No, the champions decided. This was the Olympics they were talking about! Must get up and be ready to play at 9:00 AM the next morning—and all day as well.

When the morning came around too soon, the Achilles tendon of Rolf Engen was speaking to him. Wilson agreed to let him only set the first game of each match—they won every one he recalls—but he had to be called back in to set the third every time. The Hollywood Stars won the Olympic tryout tournament as well which for the selection committee put the final nail of rationalization into the coffin of Gene Selznick. It seems that the unlucky star which had visited the renegade had not left him overnight. Crazy things kept happening.

For example, how could it be that the guy who was always first at a match didn't show up until the second game against the Stars in the round-robin tournament...the most important tournament of their combined careers? Not to see Mike Bright waiting for everybody. Not to see him for the start of the match. Not to see him until he sprinted into the gym during the second game was unthinkable. It couldn't happen. Would Lou Gehrig miss a game? Worse, a game in the World Series? "I got lost," was all he could mutter. It seems that the guy out of the lifeguard towers of Hermosa Beach suddenly trying to catch the A train...or the B or the D, goin' Uptown or Downtown, Brooklyn, the Bronx, Queens, Jersey, Flatbush, Sheepshead Meadow, Jamaica Station, Harlem, Staten Island had a hard time of it. "Come on, buddy! Where do ya wanna go? I ain't got all day!" It happened. They lost to the Stars. Even worse for Selznick, the Hollywood Comets took second in the six-team round-robin.

At the end of the marathon, Engen, who was definitely a mature horse, had arguably been run to the paddock for retirement. The little general had played hard for several matches in three straight days—then had played five straight throat-ripping matches on the fourth day! He could barely jump "and I wasn't sure how I could play in Tokyo," he recalled. "Still, I thought I'd be on the team."

Harry Wilson, one of three vice-presidents of the USVBA, and the committee members needed a kind of quid pro quo—a way to ease the path out of the huge pickle they were in, which of course centered on Selznick. Should they put the loosest cannon who ever played volleyball on the Olympic Team or not? There was no question that he was good enough; he could hit or set, and had more international experience than anyone in the game. He could lead...or he could divide. If the leopard could change its spots in a few minds of the committee, it didn't in Wilson's, who everyone knew would ultimately decide this issue. He'd battled with the recalcitrant for eight years and if there was a glimpse of hope it had been dashed several months before—at least according to Selznick. He claims that his adversary came to him at the Far Western Championships in April, olive branch in hand. "Gene, drop this rule change campaign and you've got a spot in Tokyo."

"No." Selznick predictably resisted: "It wasn't so much because it was a stupid idea but it was making us bad players. I could see we wouldn't have a good team in Tokyo if it stayed the same. I'd fought almost ten years, too long to give it up." Better to try his same old strategy—beat them in the Nationals—like in Dallas in 1960. But not this time.

Now how to justify it to the ranks? Wilson thanked his lucky stars that Selznick's plan had backfired. He was thankful for the honor system...even more for an anachronism like Hammer who had honored it...and, above all, for the criss-crossed network of confusing subway lines which ensnared Mike Bright. Still, after the Hollywood pillars had been selected, the next choices would be topical and require defending. Debate raged between the men on who to take: young or old, big or small, Easterner or Westerner, collegian or military, pro-Selznick or anti-Selznick? A cushion would help things; the committee knew it would get hot in the kitchen. Well, there was one thing which might cool the oven being fired. If Engen wasn't going to grow anymore, and there was good reason to believe that a man in his young 30s wouldn't, leaving him off could dampen the certain outrage of Selznick's ousting. And as Jim Coleman later added, some on the committee indeed thought Engen was too short for international play anyway—or at least they said that—another ironic twist in view of Wilson's past coaching history which built his teams around Engen.

Finally, it looked to many like a sop. It was the stuff of politics, of power, of backroom give-and-take—and for the uninitiated—the stuff of amateur sports too! Engen, loyal and stoical held his peace; yet he would carry an uncomfortable feeling that he'd been a pawn in a deal of a smoke-filled room. Dropping quickly out of the game, he surfaced a decade later to coach several Laguna Beach CIF championship players including Dusty Dvorak. His Olympic dream was realized in a different guise when he became the Commissioner of Volleyball for the 1984 Olympics—not a player but still a general.

Selznick, the reprobate was selected as an alternate—the seeming wisdom of which must have been mightily questioned. Do you invite a rabid, starving dog into your barbecue? He showed up for the two and one-half week training period in Los Angeles, his brilliant needling skills concentrated to laser-beam sharpness. He immediately went to Wilson and asked him where his services might be employed should an injury occur: setter, hitter, server, backcourt specialist? All roles he could fill...better in every one in fact, than most of the players on the team. Harry stumbled to avoid a commitment. When it became apparent that he wasn't going to be seriously considered as a candidate to make the team—no matter how he played—he assumed the role at which he had no equal...irritant.

Not that the chances of an injury were great. Rudy Suwara, always arduous, recalls guys showing up late and strolling into the gym without concern. Even his brother who at 19 was the game's new star, and Harry's brightest, was not worried. A few warm-up laps—some guys even evaded that exercise—and they were ready to scrimmage...by far the greatest training activity during the camp. Another alternate, Jack Henn, smilingly remembers arriving one

evening when an impetuous Keith Erickson had donned a complete Santa Monica City football uniform—pads, helmet, everything except shoes—and was bounding on the trampoline! Harry went to trembling, then gathered enough presence of mind to command his descent...sans dismount.

With Selznick there, the division between the two camps exacerbated. Long a Selznick loyalist, Lang was still clearly a starting setter and a strong personality. Still, it shocked him at the first practice when Wilson came up to him for a confidential chat. Showing him the six guys he had chosen to start he added, "you put them in the order you want." Lang shook his head. "No. That's not my job."

Bad went to worse. A petition went around in support of putting Selznick on the team: many of the players signed it. Mike O'Hara wasn't one. Ernie Suwara was a signatory and summarily received his chiding by Wilson. That was nothing. Journalists were snooping around for stories to support the wronged player; finally, Selznick had a lawsuit filed against the USVBA. Still, what could happen in two weeks?

Selznick must have known the ending all along; it culminated in one night in a scrimmage not too surprisingly. It was the old guys against the young. Youthful Jack Henn was serving and firing BBs down the line at a veteran adversary of Selznick who now was playing on the same team. Things got worse for the undone receiver with every ball, mishandling every bullet serve in the back left position. Selznick who was in front left did not step in to help out—which wouldn't have been welcome anyway—but instead inched towards the sideline to give the guy even *more* unwanted territory. After four points, Selznick stood with his toes on it. Just before the next serve Selznick dropped to the floor, rolled to his side and rested his beaming mug in the hand of his propped elbow. He softly patted his mouth and yawned as Henn drilled the next serve for another point. Some snickered, a few like Wilson almost cried. Selznick was gone the next day.

Ronnie Lang. The consummate killer, he ruled the beach in the '60s. (Courtesy of Volleyball Magazine)

"Von Muscle." A young Ron Von Hagen cranks a 50-50 set in the face of a courageous Dave Heiser. (Courtesy of Dave Heiser)

The craziest of the crazy decade, Nate Parrish. Pictured left to right, Walt Schiller, tournament queen, Nate Parrish.(Courtesy of Nate Parrish)

Nate could party...and play. Drilling a Schiller set in front of the Sorrento wall c. 1962. (Courtesy of Nate Parrish)

Vogie, a young version, in a rare moment of seriousness. Alika Smith (r) is partner of the Court Jester. (Courtesy of Dave Heiser)

Ernie Suwara could break bones. At 19, MVP of the Nationals in 1964 and first UCLA volleyballer to receive a scholarship. (Courtesy of Bud Fields)

"To be good...you must be fanatic!" He was. All-World player, Gabriel Budishin (left), came from Yugoslavia to electrify American players including the Suwara brothers. 1960 action. (Courtesy of Bud Fields)

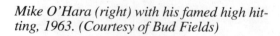

Mike O'Hara (right) with his famed high hitting, 1963. (Courtesy of Bud Fields)

"He would have been the best ever!" says Gene Selznick. Keith Erickson instead went to the Lakers to play pro basketball...after starring on the '64 Olympic volleyball team. (Courtesy of Bud Fields)

Sorrento mixed, 1962. All-time players...and characters. From left to right: Joan Dempsey-Klein, Butch Friedman, Tournament Queen Susan Busch, Steno Brunicardi, Jean Brunicardi, Dave Heiser, Patti Barrett

Bigger and better. The Shamrocks of Long Beach grab eight national titles between 1962-1970. Here they are in 1963. Back row (from left to right): Johnette Latreille, Jane Russell, Nancy Owen, Patti Bright. Front row: Jane Zerwig, Jo Rae Zuckerman, Linda Murphy, Jean Gaertner, Jane Ward. (Courtesy of Bud Fields)

The great Pedro Velasco (right). He could do it all...with both hands. (Courtesy of Bud Fields)

The overhand reception. No one could do it better than Ronnie Lang, 1961. Unfortunately, the rest of the world was bumping. (Courtesy of Bud Fields)

Iron man . Mike Bright arrives first as usual...another paddling victory in the Catalina—Palos Verdes—Manhattan Beach race, some 32 miles. Then off to win the Manhattan 6-man. (Courtesy of Dave Heiser)

Bright on the beach, winner of the Manhattan Open (1960-1964).

East meets West...almost. An improving West Side Y team dominates the Atlantic Coast with the young Suwara brothers. Back Row (left to right): Scottie Mose, George Fetz, Rudy Suwara, Ernest Suwara, John Suwara, Joe Widmer. Front Row: Identity unknown, Logan Mudt, Alex Valow, Heinz Schaal, Henry Schael, Fred Kuhr, Jr., Fred Kuhr, Sr.(Courtesy of Bud Fields)

Chapter 9
1964 Tokyo Olympics

"Tokyo...and sayonara..."

A scatter of primary colors were winking in the sunlight; suddenly, thousands of doves were released to soar with the heart of every athlete. Flapping white messengers of national pride, brotherhood and sport took the thoughts of those present past all earthly subjects. Every past scrape and peccadillo, every drop of sweat, trickle of blood, each victory and defeat great or small, shrunk to a meaningless shadow of a memory. A few tears rose in the eyes of the USA women: Ward, Murphy, Gaertner, Perry, Owen and Peppler. Nearby stood the American guys, rarely seen in ties: Bright, O'Hara, Velasco, Suwara, Ericson, Hammer and Lang. For one man standing there, it was the beautiful end of a long road. Dreams rarely take earthly form in one's life, but at this moment,this dream had for Harry Wilson. His eyes glazed over in rapture, to have arrived here from Evanston, Illinois was surely enough for any one mortal. Now if the USA Men could do well, how sweet the red, white and blue frosting would taste on that hard-fought cake. Indeed it was a glorious moment for American volleyball...for volleyball everywhere. As their glistening eyes trailed the flight of the colorless specks flying out of the Tokyo stadium, it was the hopes of the athletes which climbed. But the cruel descent would soon begin and as it dipped, no one could have foreseen the force with which their plummeting aspirations would hit the hard, unforgiving earth.

"And for your distinguished service...you're coach of the Olympic Team!..."

It would have been hard to find someone who didn't think Doc Burroughs was a nice guy. A kind, gentle soul, he'd been around Los Angeles and the USVBA Nationals giving freely of his time on committees for over 20 years. On the other hand, it would be just as hard to find someone—certainly any of the women who played on the '64 Olympic Team—to articulate a compliment on his coaching abilities. How could they? In a time when the coaching knowledge of volleyball could have maybe filled up a dozen full pages in this country, finding anyone to teach the game was admittedly tough...but Burroughs was basically an administrator! He had served as a coach many times in the past, but there was more to coaching the U.S. Women's Volleyball Team than calling timeouts. Symptomatic of the sport in those days—and most amateur sports—those who gave their time were given recognition. Some wanted that reward in the form of a coaching position, some didn't. A few actually were capable coaches, some weren't. It was a dilemma which would improve over time, but it was only with the advent of money in the game that qualified coaches begin to appear courtside to cultivate the wealth of talent that had always been there. "It was just a payback for his time in the USVBA," believes Mary Jo Peppler, "besides, it was always obvious that the USVBA didn't care about the Women's Team."

Well, they did have a two-week training camp before departure. "I remember two things said to me at that camp," Peppler chortles, "'Circle out!' which meant get in hitting position, and 'Bend your knees more, honey.'" As far as an actual drill to improve skills, the only one she recalls was serving at towels dropped on the floor. Team strategy and team drills? Didn't happen. "We had no defense," added Jane Ward. That became evident before the tournament started when the team was defeated by a *high school team* in a scrimmage. "That was the low point for me," Ward confessed. Not a good omen, knowing that in a few short days they would get a hands-on experience with the world-famous Japanese women. Coach Daimatsu's rolling, diving acrobats making impossible saves were such a national sensation that "they were always on Japanese TV," recalled Patti Bright. A few days later they made mincemeat of the American women.

"Whadda 'ya mean that's a throw!..."

The USA Men received their own harbinger of things to come in a scrimmage with another Olympic team...officiated by a Japanese. Ernie Suwara remembers the questioning look spreading on everyone's face when the ref blew the first serve as a mishandled ball—a perfectly passed overhand one! The second whistle brought scowls. The third had guys charging the stand for an explanation.

It was then, *the day before* the Olympics began, that both USA Teams got their introduction to what would be their biggest nightmare. The rest of the world was bumping the ball on serve reception! Oh my God! Harry Wilson uttered his famous cry once again: "But volleyball was invented in our country!" So what? Pizza was invented in Italy, champagne in France, the printing press in Germany. Does that mean it should stay there...in its primitive state in a museum? To Harry's great chagrin, the referees didn't care what the players in the U.S. were doing. Point after point was given away like hundred dollar bills to the greedy opponents. "Robbed!" our players cried. Perfect passes, with no spin were whistled. Finally a few of the Westside players who had practiced it under Selznick, and a couple beach players like Bright and Lang who had been bumping the ball partly on the sand, tried to perfect it indoors...overnight with a new 12-panel, aerodynamic light Japanese ball. It was another problem. The ball was introduced in the States only months before in an arrangement between the ball manufacturer, Tachikara, and an exclusive American distrbutor—Harry Wilson.

"How could it be!" the players screamed. How could we not have known? True, communication was not good in that era and the FIVB was not the animal it is today...but Harry Wilson himself was the man who attended those yearly meetings in Europe! Could he have not known how the rest of the world was playing? How the rules were being interpreted? Of course he knew. He often stated it in his Review, but...he disagreed. In his mind, their interpretation was simply faulty and formed through the ganging up of Soviet Bloc countries. It was best to stick out their chin and persevere.

"Harry was just blown away by the fact of the Olympics," remarked Ernie Suwara. "He was completely lost." Other players concurred, adding that his limited coaching abilities were further hampered by his bedazzled state. Many of the grumbling players wanted his assistant, Colonel DeGroot to take over. However, he was the wrong man to ask—DeGroot would never break the chain of command, distraught as he might be himself.

The rules killed them, but their on-the-court problems were worse. "We never had a scouting report on what the other teams would do," said Bright. "Harry just put six guys out there to play." Setting was a shambles. "We left the setters home who had international experience: Selznick, Schiller and Engen," Lang lamented. "It was my first international trip too!" The other setter was the fabulously talented Pete Velasco, but he was also a woefully inexperienced setter at the time. "It soon became set the ball high to me and Erickson...until Keith couldn't lift his arm to comb his hair," remembers Suwara.

Using a 4-2 system which most other teams had discarded over a decade ago, the men relied on raw physical ability to make a reasonably good showing. Winning their first two matches against the Netherlands and Korea, things changed immediately against the tougher teams. They lost to Hungary and Czechoslovakia 3-0, but in close game scores. Another good effort against Japan ended in a 3-1 loss, likewise with tight scores. A loss to Bulgaria and a thrashing by the gold-medalists Soviets (15-6, 15-5, 15-4) all but prevented them from entering the medal round. Falling into disarray by the end of the competition, a 3-2 loss to Brazil ended the frustrating tournament.

The American women fared worse. With only six teams in the competition, they lost 3-0, and badly, to every team except Korea. They did manage to put away the Koreans 3-0 (15-7, 15-13, 15-13) to escape the cellar in the first Olympics.

"Disastrous," echoed Mike O'Hara on the whole experience. In essence, our players ran amuck without direction until the end of the tournament when it all came down to a final tell-tale point. Lang took a short serve on match point and flicked it perfectly to his nearby hitter. Whistle: point, game, match. The ball never touched the floor. The fiery setter doubled his fist and launched the light object some 50 rows up...to the quiet surprise of the polite Japanese spectators. They had never seen anything like it.

The 1965 Guide printed the following comments:

Our United States Men's and Women's Olympic Volleyball teams left this country with high hopes and returned with mixed emotions. No one could deny that most of our players did their level best. (Unfortunately some seemingly lacked certain qualities including self-discipline and did not perform at their peak. This was a disappointment to many persons). It is no dishonor to be defeated by superior play by sportsmen of high standards who have trained hard and successfully. There are some regrets when the above does not hold and our teams might have done better! ...Other nations have learned volleyball from us. We should learn something from them!

1964 Tokyo Olympics are announced...and Olympic volleyball too! (Courtesy of Holyoke Volleyball Hall of Fame)

Getting ready for Tokyo. Mike O'Hara and Bill Griebenow flank assistant coach and manager, Colonel Burt DeGroot.(Courtesy of Bud Fields)

Mary Jo Peppler, at 19, a star on the '64 Olympic team. (Courtesy of Bud Fields)

1964 Women's Olympic Team. A lesson in unpreparedness. Front row (left to right): Coach W.P. Burroughs, Patti Bright, Sharon Peterson, Gail O'Rourke, Mary Perry and Manager Ida Litschauer. Back Row: Jean Gaertner, Lou Sara Galloway, Jane Ward, Linda Murphy, Barbara Harwerth, Verneda Thomas, Nancy Owen and Mary Jo Peppler. (Courtesy of Bud Fields)

1964 Men's Olympic Team. Talent amidst confusion. From left to right: Coach Harry Wilson, Pete Valasco, Chuck Nelson, Jake Highland, Dick Hammer, Mike Bright, Keith Erickson, Barry Brown, Bill Griebenow, Mike O'Hara, John Taylor, Ernie Suwara, Ron Lang and Manager Col. E.B. DeGroot, Jr. (Courtesy of Bud Fields)

Chapter 10
1965-1968

"Down at the Sorrento Grill..."

It was 1965. The Mustang had just rolled out of Detroit. Could things be better? Not in California! There were shades of something going on...something about Vietnam on the news and guys 18 and over having to register for the draft, but even if you watched the news that seemed like a world away. Wasn't the music great? The British invasion had hit,only enriching the Beach Boys, Righteous Brothers and the Motown sound: Temptations, Miracles, Supremes, Marvin Gaye. There was that folky stuff up in San Francisco too: Joan Baez, Pete Seger and the others, but you never heard it on the radio. Only college students listened to it. The "Beatles 65" album was surely new and good but good times, girls, and broken love were the same old themes. Just that one song, over six minutes long, was like nothing else on the radio: "Like a Rolling Stone." Bob Dylan. Suddenly, the wispy, harmonica-slung kid was a sensation. Soon other Dylan songs were heard in the Byrds' electronic sound, giving new power to the lyrics of the Jewish rebel from Duluth. "Mr. Tambourine Man" swept national radio waves. If you lived in a beach town of Southern California, life couldn't be easier and for that matter, never would be that easy again. Never.

On a typical summer morning at Sorrento, the clean white sand was warming up when Ronnie Lang arrived at the beach with a demure tint to his expression. Selznick was nowhere to be found. Not too surprising...he could still be doing "the Jerk" in some darkened "Go-Go" club. To the guys already on the court as well as those lazing near the wall, it seemed just another day of 80 degree tanning weather and 70 degree water to cool off in. But for beach volleyball, it would figure as a day of destiny. Lang scouted the talent then cut to the chase. Approaching the chosen one, he quietly settled down next to him. Behind black Ray-Bans, Lang stared straight out at the small waves humping and pitching. In time he uttered the three memorable words which Ron Von Hagen would never forget: "You wanna play?"

> "I've never seen an exhibition of beach volleyball like that day. We played for three straight hours, running through some teams without giving up a point. They mostly served Lang, and I couldn't believe how he was hitting that day. Lang was the guy I'd always wanted to play with—and here it was."

In fact, the two Ronnies would have to wait a year before the formidable team would pair up to strike fear in every opponent who ever looked up on the board and saw their names in the same bracket. Lang had to finish the season with a flagging Selznick, who at 35 could still play with anyone but was losing the mental edge. Still good enough for Lang and Selznick to play the first tournament of 1966 and in a heroic struggle back through the losers' bracket, win it—a fitting way to dissolve the famous duo.

In '66, Lang was free but there still remained another problem. The year before, Von Hagen had committed to his old partner, Randy Carter. Admittedly dying to play with Lang, his better instincts wouldn't let him drop Carter for the top player on the sand and the self-effacing Von Hagen still harbored some fears as to whether he could live up to Lang's reputation. Fate again. Carter decided not to play that summer, and Von Hagen indulged himself in a rare beer, thanking his lucky stars.

Yet, it was all the more curious that Lang, through friends, had made overtures to Von Hagen that he was the preferred successor to Selznick. Frequently it was like this—a strange type of courting game. Players wooed desired partners and depending on their own designs and ambition, could just as quickly drop them if a more fitting one came by. The sport had a queer social facet to it. Like looking for the prettiest girl on the beach, players sought out the best partners. Next marriage, and then it became a decision of marital behavior: the monogamous stayed faithful to one partner...others preferred polygamy. It was a big part of beach volleyball.

"Von Muscle..."

For 18 years (1961-1978) if an unsuspecting stroller with a curious mind should happen upon an Open beach tournament, one player would have demanded attention far more than any other. The physical presence of Ron Von Hagen was simply too imposing. Stark dimensions of 6'1", 190 pounds, beggared description of the man's body. Here was the paragon, the steel-flanged Aryan issue of the Third Reich. Equalling the chiseled power of his torso was that irrepressible march through the sand after a point or sideout. Striding without a trace of fatigue, ball in hand, a quick turn at the back rope, snapping his head to attention. Total concentration. The Greek ideal of mind and body going in one direction: to win. In humble beach chairs, men watched slack-jawed, young women witheld secret fantasies.

Beach volleyball was a game waiting to happen for Von Hagen, but it came quite by accident. Richard Von Hagen, his father, had been a UCLA basketball star before turning his talents to law. Sending his son to a military school in the San Fernando Valley, Richard was aware that his promising son was immersed in all sports but as a 15-year old high school senior, the rules wouldn't allow him to play his first love—football. Following graduation, he and a friend set the record on the physical test of UCLA football, but his father still thought him too young to go out for the team that freshman year. His dreams somehow kept getting stymied. He made the UCLA frosh team in basketball but decided to quit before the season ended. Next as a 177-pound wrestler for UCLA, he became one of the best in the conference before injuring his back in a match and was grounded in the summer of 1959. So he went to the beach to sit and heal, at Sorrento of course since "it was neat to watch the girls around the Sorrento Grill." The girls were captivating and that game out there on the sand looked kind of interesting too.

Sitting against the famous wall, with his Germanic mind given to analysis, Von Hagen pondered hour upon hour his future. "All I ever wanted to do was play a sport." But what? He loved running that marvelous physical machine that was his body...from childhood he was continually doing chin-ups, push-ups and actually used the set of weights in his room. His mother, an early advocate of health food, campaigned in the home for dishes of only fresh, raw and uncooked foods—a regimen he would later take to its outer limits. But why all this if there wasn't a sport to devote it to? He knew, or rather intuited that the sport for him wasn't wrestling...just like it wasn't basketball. Strangely he found his ruminations following his eyes to that Spalding ball on the beach. Although the guys were laughing as much as playing, he had glimpses of a sport which required athletic prowess and training, and look at the environment! Compared to a sweatbox, rolling around with your nose pushed into some guy's armpit and worse, with cauliflower ear and spitting all day long to make weight? Come on!

Like a message from above for the troubled youth, the decision to play volleyball descended at a UCLA workout. Russ Hodge, a world-class decathlon and his weightlifting partner, one day pronounced: "Pick what you're made for..." Beach volleyball! "That's all I did for the next 18 years."

His back healed, he quit wrestling and soon began knocking the ball around on the second court at Sorrento with Bill Leeka, his best friend and a gargantuan All-American tackle for UCLA. Disappointedly, his new-found sport was interrupted by a six-month stint in the US Army. In the spring of 1961, he returned to pick up the game for good with Leeka. One day, an older player "with an untouchable dink" asked him to play on the center court. It was Jim Smith, the father of Sinjin who one day would be the man to break Von Hagen's all-time record of 62 Open victories—then a scrawny urchin chasing down errant balls for his dad—and watching. "I was so in awe of Von Hagen. I concentrated so hard on throwing the ball back without making a mistake."

Von Hagen took the court with much trepidation. He'd already heard the sarcastic asides, seen the stares and mock-flexing of the frat boys. "The guy has the wrong beach, man! Muscle's a few blocks south!" What few people suspected was that underneath the finely-tuned frame was a very unassuming person—a guy much too humble for that body. Yet, he was tough too...and determined. He played hour after hour, analyzing and asking questions from any player who might help him. He got better.

A body cut and shaped like that, coupled with a genuine sincerity not given to sarcasm and wit, was a double oddity for the cool flippancy of the beach crowd at Sorrento: "Wait until Von Hagen went up to State Beach for a better game!" Those grinders would take a hunk of Teutonic flesh like this and in an hour, all that would be left would be a string of German frankfurters! And they did. Weightlifting at that time was no part of a sport based on speed and coordination—it was just bodybuilding. Gene Selznick, Ron Lang...touch a barbell? "Oh sure! Right after windsprints!" And how about the nuts, seeds, herbs, fresh fruit, and that bag of vitamins Von Hagen always carried with him! It was always a kick for a guy on the way to the Grill to ask: "Hey Von Yogurt! Want me to bring 'ya back somethin'? Hamburger, coke, grilled cheese, bologna on white, Milk Duds, Abba-Zabba?"

Still, this anomaly had a tenacity which fended off the subtle heckling, and they knew he was too nice a guy to put one of their witty skulls in the crushing vice-grip of his forearms. By 1962 he snagged a third place finish with Randy Carter in the State Beach Open. But like many serious beach players, he was pulled to the bigger arena of international volleyball and the possibility of donning a USA jersey, which was indoor. In 1961, a UCLA professor invited him out for a varsity practice even though he no longer had eligibility. The educator had heard of his promise on the beach and his real agenda was to have Harry Wilson drop by to see if here was a prospect for Hollywood Y. Wilson walked in and glanced at the leaping receptacle of muscle and sinew, then quickly told the 21-year old: "We really don't want any muscle-bound guys playing volleyball." It was a devastating blow. "All my early experiences with the USVBA were bad," remembers Von Hagen.

No player would ever more typify the California beach player image than Von Hagen, and appearances many times count for more than truth. Regrettably, appearances and suspected alliances increasingly took on more and more importance in American volleyball in the '60s. It had quietly begun in the '30s when the LA teams began their eventual rise to dominance—in a sport which was controlled by men not from California. Although Californians like Burroughs, Prugh, Fish and Gibson eventually would integrate the bureaucracy, most of them like their Eastern and Midwestern colleagues were of YMCA background and that philosophy would not be seriously challenged. The eventual czar of the game, Harry Wilson, although transplanted in Los Angeles, would continually have his most serious and vocal criticism from Californian players. Of course, that the less than diplomatic firebrand Selznick—not only the best player of his generation but a restless and ruthless campaigner for innovation—became Wilson's arch-rival only widened the rift between East and West, administrators and players. By the '50s, the vast majority of the best players, men and women, came from California and that gap only kept growing, particularly with the expanding pool of good California players.

Unfortunately, the schism of feeling between players and administrators was ironically increasing with the new opportunity for international competition. Players were getting better and wanted improved conditions to compete—financial support and better coaching was called for. Not only was the governing body unprepared to deliver, but much of the players' plea entrained ideas which flew in the face of the YMCA credo and that slow, plodding tempo: volleyball, and all sport, should be firstly for the many and money has no place in an amateur sport. In the minds of the administrators, the USVBA Nationals were the apex of the game and regional competition came next, left to like-minded administrators in the regions. Whoever gave of their time, ran things. That was fair enough, and it is a truism that players in any sport are always eager to grouse. Yet it seems that there was a real hesitancy to go outside the established bureaucracy for expertise—to seek outside help to raise needed funding to nurture the sport, or at least, to find ideas on how to do it without money.

Regardless of his opinion on international rules vis-a-vis the rest of the world, it must be stated that Harry Wilson attached great importance to USA competition in international volleyball. Considering that it was openly known that other national teams were subsidized, trained full-time and traveled year-round for top competition, it was presumably not a major concern of most of the other USVBA offic-

ers. In 1964, Wilson made this revealing report:

> At the present time the membership of the USVBA is about 2,000, where Holland has 20,000, Czechoslovakia has 27,000 and Hungary has 22,000. The story is the same throughout the world...money raised by membership finances teams to foreign countries and to the Olympics. I suggested in 1957 the advisability of hiring an executive secretary who would devote full time to the affairs of the USVBA and who would justify his expense but the Board of Directors voted it down.

Small wonder players felt alienated from their governing body. It can only be guessed that growth in some aspects sadly posed a danger and threat to the stewards of the game. It also seems that Wilson's assertion that other countries financed their national team programs exclusively through membership dues was naive. That effort required much greater governmental subsidization, which admittedly was not feasible in American amateur sport at the time.

Since proponents of change were largely contesting YMCA thinking, amateurism was the sacred cow which most raised the blood pressure of the sport's guardians. The best example of that posture, and the most astounding, was the ruling which disallowed coaches and YMCA employees to compete in volleyball since they were considered professionals. A good number of the best players were coaches! Was an aspiring young player who loved the game, longed to play on the USA National Team one day, and very likely dreamed of coaching it later, to sacrifice his or her goal of becoming an instructor or coach...as the price of playing the sport?

When Al Scates, as a grad student in 1963, took the UCLA coaching job he was paid $100 per year—expenses in lieu of salary. "I could have made more money but I would have had to forfeit my chance of going to the '64 Olympics. I wanted to play so I took the $100," Scates remembers. It was a philosophy of sport heavily subscribed to by the President of the US Olympic Committee, Avery Brundage.

It took years to sweep this ruling away. How could the mounting frustration ever level off, much less go down? Thus, the confrontational stance of players—and particularly California players—versus the USVBA had taken hold early on...and would stay.

So, Von Hagen stayed where there were less politics. You could be captain of your own soul on the sand. He stayed largely with Carter, a college quarterback, and won his first Open at Laguna Beach in 1964. On a steady incline, they improved their consistency and won the same tournament in 1965. With more confidence, they looked forward to the Manhattan Beach Open, which had far eclipsed the stature of any other beach tournament since its beginning in 1960. Hordes of beach revelers came to the pier for the weekend. In 1965, Von Hagen and Carter swimmingly found themselves in the finals, having won the winner's bracket. The huge crowd assembled to see the finals and, always the show of shows, Selznick. At 35, his concentration ebbed and flowed but the master entertainer never let a crowd down...especially the couple thousand flocked around the main court. His cohort, Ronnie Lang, was no shrinking violet either. Show time!

It was a scorching weekend. The heat taxed many of the players; those who recieved most of their opponent's serves were praying their twinging hamstrings wouldn't fold up. Many did. That was Lang and Selznick's biggest fear. The older Selznick had been targeted all weekend: in 90 degree heat in the loser's bracket of a 64-team tournament, a man will lose a lot of water. The elder statesman had. Thank god he didn't drink!

But it happened, and soon, in the two-out-of-three to 11 winner's finals. It had been just a matter of time. No different from a deer, an elk who has been singled out by the pack and maimed. A broken leg, a bleeding wound, bounding away just enough to escape the snarling nips of the predators. Not for long. The cramps started in the first game; he tried to hide them but soon there was no hiding them. He could jump and hit but every time he landed, the hamstrings grabbed and both legs doubled up. How could he let the crowd down? Give Lang more court? They tried it. Von Hagen and Carter still zeroed in on him. Well, he'd make as many shots as he could and hope for a miracle.

They were going down fast when in the second game, by painful accident, Selznick realized that if he jumped and landed directly on his knees rather than his feet, he wouldn't cramp every time. So he did. And after the many times he did cramp, fans and cronies from State Beach would jump onto the court, massage the contracted muscles and get him to his feet. They held on to win the second game. Now the crowd, abetted by cold beer in the hot sun, was crazed. His retinue responded as well, a few times carrying the grinning hero back to serve. The crowd howled for more. Von Hagen and Carter alone in a sea of incited maniacs, had little refuge. But...after two timeouts according to the rules, a team couldn't take more than reasonable time to play. Not this nonsense Selznick was employing to get more valuable rest and turn the momentum. The ref agreed with them and immediately risked his being strung up from a light post on the pier.

"Ah-hah!" responded the cramping man, "Sand timeout!" Now he was right; excessive sand on your body constituted a quick break to rid the sand, usually walking to a towel off the court to brush it off. So he used it...and used it...and used it. Landing on his knees in the double final, now cramping more than not, the State Beach loyalists rushed to the man on all fours and scooped up sand to pour it on his sweating body. "Sand timeout!" The ref smiled and nodded okay, the crowd screamed. Von Hagen and Carter thought at least once about protesting but after looking at the frenzied mass, used their better judgment. After the last point, Von Hagen sunk down to the sand in dejection. It was a bitter loss. Every hoot and holler of the throng carrying away their wounded warrior to the bars above the pier was a poignant reminder.

Dinner done, the exhausted victors and their wives walked out of the restaurant, Selznick and Lang hobbling slowly—especially Selznick who had to jump to his feet several times at dinner to stave off the returning cramps. Walking to their cars, Johnette exclaimed, "Let's go dancing!" They went. At two in the morning, Selznick's extreme cramping kept locking up his legs with every repeated attempt to get in the car. Impossible to ride in it. Finally, Lang and the two ladies drove him home...lying on the hood of the car.

"Undefeated..."

From that first day in 1965 Von Hagen and Lang teamed up, they played together almost daily...summer, fall, winter and spring. Lang, a stockbroker, would finish his calls to New York and beat the final bell on the floor to normally arrive at State Beach about 11:00. After the Tokyo disappointment, he decided to concentrate his energies on the sand. Von Hagen was usually there waiting, his golden labrador in tow. How could he do it everyday? He worked part-time as a Hollywood extra but there was another factor in the equation; his mother came from a family whose wealth could support an entire colony of volleyballers. Alas, it wouldn't arrive in Ron's hands for a long time—in fact, his beach volleyball estranged his hard-working, successful father—but still there was the cushion of future ease. When offered a major role in the TV series, Rat Patrol, he turned it down to stay in his modest Santa Monica apartment and pound volleyballs.

So they played, on through the afternoons, through wind and cold. Taking all comers. "During the week, we did not lose a game in a year and a half," Lang recalled. Including Open tournaments over two summers, they lost less than 18 games in two years...day in and day out against the best players around. In 1966, after Lang won the first tournament with Selznick, he and Von Hagen won every remaining tournament. Lang would be the only player in beach volleyball history to win every Open in one season...Von Hagen missed it by one!

"We were so good because we practiced so much—more than the pros today. I'd learned from John Wooden that you play how you practice, and I loved playing with Lang." It is finally a futile exercise to try and determine the best players of all time in any sport...nonetheless, sports lovers continue to do it. Von Hagen, who would be named by many successors as the greatest beach player of all time, singled out Lang as the best. "He was the strongest mental player who ever played. He had the best flat serve in the game, the best cut shot I've ever seen, an incredible line shot and maybe the best digger." That's quite a package! When asked who was the best beach player he ever played against, Gene Selznick touted the same athlete, "Lang."

"What I most liked about Von Hagen is that the first game on Saturday morning, we might be playing a guy with one-arm but for him it was just as important as the finals," said Lang. "We played more games together than anyone—thousands. And we worked on things continually. You develop a sense of what's gonna happen on the court. For example, I would watch where he was served and adjust to it. If he was served to his outside, I'd release right away and get more toward his line. He knew where I'd be...so the pass, set and hit would all be adjusted according to where the serve was. Nobody else even thought of those things." The two were sideout machines but what gave them the deciding edge was defense. Each had his strength and with the two bodies combined, strength accounted for point after point in tough matches. Lang with his unparalleled ability to read hitters and lightning reflexes dug a million balls...and no one, with the exception of today's Karch Kiraly, could get out of the sand and run down balls like Von Hagen. Pure strength.

For beach volleyball, 1966 was a watershed year. The game's most dominant team in history would move their training venue from State Beach to Sorrento. This proved to be a major power shift. Sorrento had a younger, hip crowd with a more liberal outlook—the good-looking guys and gorgeous girls lined up and down the wall included a lot of UCLA students. A woman who was aggressive enough had a better chance to get in a women's doubles game there than at State.

The famous wall and the more famous Sorrento Grill had already become the Valhalla of beach volleyball. Getting your picture on the wall of the Grill meant instant deification: Holtzman, Selznick, O'Hara, Lang, Bright, Brunicardi and Latreille were part of the panoply of the gods. But the first step to apotheosis was normally the more mundane honor of getting your name graffitied on the wall...which often meant first earning a nickname. Jean Brunicardi was the "Gazelle," and one of the Smith sisters was affectionately christened "Peaches." No surprise that the new star had more than one: "Von Muscle" and "Von Steel" included. Yet another rite of passage for the males was to pound the ball hard enough so it bounced over the wall and into the pool of the big house adjoining the court. It was the home of Barron Hilton in fact; the Hiltons would graciously throw the ball back and at times drop by the luau that was thrown every weekend by the short-order grill's owner, "Neeny" Neinherhauser, a German immigrant. Cold beer, good food and a good time.

At Sorrento, Wally Busby was known by all as the "mayor," settling all disputes and issuing edicts of fairness which all respected. Another major protagonist in the Sorrento story was the man who carefully oversaw the courts and ran the tournaments, Dave Heiser. A gentlemanly man, he would organize the "draw" tournaments on weekends and in a distinctive conciliatory fashion hoped to one day have Selznick and O'Hara draw each other as partners! One blanches at the notion...it never happened. Heiser was important in other ways. Going over to ride the big waves of Hawaii in 1948, he introduced volleyball to the prestigious Kamehameha School. Soon students were clamoring to play on the eight nets stretched over the giant grass field. Later as vice-principal of John Adams Junior High School in Santa Monica, he probably coached and encouraged more adolescent All-Americans than anyone in the sport's history: Rundle, Milliken, Templeman, the Griebenows, and the Satos included.

"Too short...not pretty hands...for 10 years..."

Growing up in Los Angeles in the 1950s was an experience many Americans fantasized about. The Mickey Mouse Club and American Bandstand was the standard fare of America's youth, so innocent and naive about the rest of the world. On his Hollywood Hills street, Danny Patterson was a frequent babysitter for the kids of one of his neighbors down the street: Paul Newman and Joanne Woodward. On Saturday afternoons, he and a friend would stop and watch a young blond actor work on his Porsche which he would later put through some fast paces on Mulholland Drive. While under the hood, Steve McQueen would answer their questions.

Less than ten miles away, the diminutive Patterson spent his summers at the Hollywood YMCA. There he mastered all those Y games from ping-pong, pool, and badminton to swimming and gymnastics. An exceptional quickness was only eclipsed by a searing desire to compete; he became convinced early on that tenacity in the end could overcome a bigger, stronger opponent. In 1961, a neighborhood friend and Patterson were offered jobs in the "Hot Dog on a Stick" at Muscle Beach. All you could eat, great money for a 14-year old and a non-stop human spectacle. The body builders in scanty bunhuggers were joined by acrobats, some of them professionals, who lined up for the lemonade, hotdogs and cheesedogs for the less health conscious.

These same acrobats flexing in the sun and swinging through bar exercises would take to the sand courts for a little volleyball. Sometimes a springboard and small teeter-totter catapulted a spiker to well over ten feet. But the best came in actual games when a lithe gymnast sprinted to be hoisted off the uplifting hands of some giant, all in perfect timing so that the sky-bound spiker could drill the ball from a height only birds frequented. At 4'11", Patterson was soon included in the creative contests and would also begin to play serious doubles when the court was free.

The next high school summers were passed in the same manner except he, as every other aspiring volleyball player, went from Muscle to play night doubles at Santa Monica City College. Walking in, the sound of booming balls on the four courts told you this was special; sun-tanned males and females propped against the wall waiting to get on a court...and not lose! If you lost, it was a long wait. A consolation was to watch the main court. Some nights Ronnie Lang could be watched for free. Erickson, Pfluger, Friedman, Vogelsang, Suwara and May were some of the heavyweights who freely punished the challenging upstarts: Patterson, Rundle, Milliken and Templeman to name a few.

It all paid off for Patterson when he got his AAA with Scott Carter his junior year of high school and while playing noon ball with businessmen at the Hollywood Y. One summer day the powerful coach, Harry Wilson, asked him to come out and practice with the Open team. The invitation was almost too much for the compact bundle of energy: "I remember being so nervous for the first practice that I drove right into John Taylor's car in the parking lot. I almost went home."

Out of high school he headed straight for Aspen to spend a year doing the other thing he loved—skiing. In 1965 and barely 19, a phone call from Gene Selznick convinced him to join a throw-together team for the USVBA Nationals in Omaha. Talk about a rag-bag squad! Bernie Holtzman at 43, a little leaper Dave Boardwell, Gary Weiss, Jack Jansen, Harlen Cohen, and of course the indefatigable Selznick. It is doubtful if the team averaged six foot in an epoch when players had gotten much taller; they lost in the quarterfinals. Patterson replaced the venerable Holtzman who would now only

coach...well, sort of. Patterson remembers that immediately after Holtzman called time-outs to give instructions, Selznick would quickly regroup the six walking back on the court: "Okay, listen up! Forget what Bernie said. This is what we're gonna do!"

Being put in the snakepit early was not a good thing in the Nationals, but no one expected that team to finish higher than fifth anyway. They came back, crawling, stumbling, running, then flying—knocking down team after team— 22 games in three days! For the man who had lost his greatest battle the year before in 1964, this would be Selznick's finest moment. It was a dead-tired team which reached the finals against a fresh Los Angeles Tigers brimming with the stars of the game: Lang, Scates and Tom Ryan. Westside had already disposed of the other favorite: the Sand and Sea Club loaded with stallions like Erickson, Henn and Bright. Realistically, Westside had already far surpassed anyone's expectations; a lot of people were happy for Gene...but this was going to be some quick work and the partying would get an early start.

Selznick: he did it all—Cohen and USVBA Rookie of the Year Patterson put up set after set to the tireless 35-year old. Angle, line, dink, he was unstoppable. He blocked; his sixth sense was never sharper, time after time he was waiting in the right spot to pop up another dig. His fireball serving alone was worth a third of his team's points. "He was a one-man team," Danny Patterson remembers. The USVBA hierarchy must have collectively felt a wave of nausea when on the final point, Patterson gave the captain a backset and he drilled it off the outside blocker's hands. Never had a team with less talent risen to this height...and never in the game's history of USVBA Nationals would one player be so dominant in playing as well as leading a team. "That was the biggest win in my volleyball life," admits Selznick. Oh, what things must have been said amongst the harried minds of the All-American selection committee right after the finals! "The win was great. But the best moment in my career was walking over to find the guy who was the head of the All-American committee. I wasn't surprised what they'd done...they'd already kicked me out of the Olympics in '64. I just wanted to hear how they would justify this."

Safe to say that every player in the gym, jointly confused, had the same question. How could they give the MVP to a guy off the fourth-place team? Especially after seeing Selznick's performance? Had they watched the finals? Good questions. This was not a National Team selection. This was a competitive event, ostensibly built on a sense of fair play! The responsible person was hunted down and pinned. He stuttered through the rationale: "When you played Outrigger, we counted that Velasco had one less error than you."

Jaw on the floor, Selznick retorted. "First, why count errors in only one match? And two, did you count the number of chances to make errors? I touched the ball on probably every play!" The expert repeated, "No, we just counted errors and you had one more..."

"A new guard..."

Harry Wilson flew back a dejected man among the many dispirited athletes from the Tokyo Olympics. Tokyo had been a bitter pill to get down. To his credit, he didn't walk away from the debacle. He told Jim Coleman, "This can't happen again." To that end, he wisely recognized that it was his time to get out of coaching and remain in the administrative arena. Hand picking his own successor, Wilson selected Jim Coleman. Coleman was not an established coach by any means except in Midwestern circles. Known by Californians for his all-night vigil at the Roosevelt Hotel, he was part of the USVBA establishment and that caused immediate concern among players. To help matters, Wilson used his international contacts to provide his protege with a chance to bring something new to the game by arranging a two-month trip to Poland to study a different kind of volleyball. Also aware that the gold-medalist Soviet men were touring Canada,

Wilson set about arranging for the Americans to join the competition.

Jim Coleman arrived at Santa Monica City College with a great deal of apprehension. Most of the great players were already working out by themselves preparing for the Canada tour. In fact, he was pleased that his flight was a little delayed; now he could show up that first night an hour late just to observe what was going on. It wasn't going to be easy for anyone coaching this headstrong lot after the Tokyo disaster, and he was a Midwesterner painted by the unpopular brush of the USVBA.

Oh irony of ironies! When he walked into the gym, who was the first guy he saw, in charge, shouting orders, running drills and playing at the same time? Yes, it was Gene Selznick he saw. Like a cork on the ocean, the guy kept bobbing up. And for the new coach...talk about baptism by fire! Coleman made a wise decision: he went up to the rebel and asked him to help coach. "After the '64 tryouts, I remember being in the same car in Omaha the next year at the Nationals with Gene—he didn't say one word to me. Now he couldn't be nicer. I made him my roommate on the trip to Canada so I could pick his brain." It went beyond that. When Coleman learned that Selznick was working out his own guys during the day at the Westside gym, the new coach asked if he could attend. He did and observed the same man teaching who was considered by the USVBA the arch-enemy of the sport. "It was the first time I'd ever seen a one set hit in this country." Strange. Was it a case of too little too late?

"Look out! It's a Tasmanian Devil!..."

The New Yorker paced the net liked a caged carnivore, a beaming glare framed by a thick brow that invited attention. Was a grand mal about to overtake the man? For the Soviets across the net, he conjured an image of a formidable and dark personality of their own history—Rasputin! They'd never seen anything like it. On the bench the first night, Rudy Suwara had been intently studying the acute angle shots of the world's greatest hitter, Yuri Bougienkov. Wearing a headband years before it became a symbol of the anti-establishment in the West, he jumped 40 plus inches and transformed into a Nureyev when airborne. He was incredibly balanced and could pick any shot on the court he desired from his lofty perch, soft or hard.

Rudy, prepared for his first entry into competition as a USA Team player, subbed in the second night and showed "Bougie" a huge cross-court hole before sweeping his hands back as far as he could to close it off. It worked! God, he'd just blocked the best player in the world! Unable to contain himself he howled with joy and ran to every other player powerfully slapping their hands and screaming that they could beat these Commies! The Soviets, who even after winning the first Olympics, could only manage a slight smile before putting on their sweats and strolling away, looked on in quiet bemusement at the wild-eyed American. Bougie, experiencing something quite new in getting blocked, seemed to wake up a little; he decided to quiet the crazed rookie down. He shaved hard the next set which probably would have taken the foot off the cross court defender. Suwara swept in again and got him with his inside hand. This time Rudy lost it completely, glowered at the Soviet cannon before barking at him with such ferocity that the Russky must have feared he'd murdered the blocker's mother at one time or at least stolen his wife. Instantly the official pointed menacingly at the American blocker now foaming liberally from the mouth.

Coleman called a timeout to settle things down. The captain, Selznick, was called over to the referee's stand for a conference. Selznick returned to the huddle and grabbed Suwara's heated arm. "Look, Rudy! If you don't stop running around like a Tasmanian Devil, they're gonna throw you out of the game!" That was it! Perfect! Never had a player been so aptly named. From then on Rudy could thank the snarling animal from Down Under as his namesake...although it would soon be shorted just to "Taz."

Well, they won only two single games in six matches, but as the coach said, "We weren't embarrassed," and that was a vast improvement over the performance in Tokyo. It looked like there was some material to build on for '68. And there was a bridge, however tenuous, with Selznick which might appease the harsh feelings of California players still fresh from Tokyo.

Bridges with Selznick had a tendency to wash out with the first hard rain. And one by one the toll was adding up for the gadfly...the USVBA was keeping tabs and the blade would come down one day. One black mark occurred right before the Canadian tour when the bronze-medalist team from Tokyo, the Japanese, came through LA for two matches: one at Cerritos and one at UCLA, which drew the biggest crowd ever in this country. Democracy at work, it was an open tryout—for fifty bucks. Money to buy uniforms, but if you made the team, your money was returned. Twenty guys made the team! "We worked out a week before," recalls Butch May. Val Keller was asked to coach and since this was the team which had introduced deception into international offense, there was much anxiety on how to track, much less block, the lightning-quick Japanese crossing behind one another and snapping down short, quick sets.

Predictably, the first night was a Hitchcockian masterpiece. Of the 20 men who suited up, more than half played in a search for the right combination...not an ideal time for experimentation against this team. In a subsequent team meeting filled with despair, Keller asked for comments. Selznick fired away, pointing out that the only chance they had was to pick six guys and stay with them...besides, this was going to be UCLA with a lot of spectators. Do we want to be embarrassed? Keller snapped, "Okay, who would you put in?" Like a starving mongrel, Selznick leaped at the morsel of meat. In one breath, he had his six named: Bright, Montague, Hogan for starters, and of course, himself. Keller went with the lineup.

The first two balls jackhammered by the Japanese the next night befuddled the block to pass untouched. One popped off Hogan's neck and the other off Montague's shoulder, straight up 50 feet! The Japanese had never seen that style of defense (nor had the Americans for that matter), but it worked. Playing out of their minds, they won the first two before Keller went back to substituting. He left in Selznick but yanked him in the fourth when they had regained a big lead and victory looked secure...thanks to some unseemly and frequent help from the officials on "touched balls" off the Japanese block according to Butch May. The Japanese crept back to 11-8 and Selznick now brewing, bolted up and went straight to the referee and subbed himself back in! A stunned Coach Keller sat and watched as the Americans pulled off a remarkable upset, 3-1. Do you think Selznick gloated?

"This is the place..."

Had you gone two hours south to Moonlight Beach in Encinitas in 1961, there would have been a tall, ungainly kid playing on the single court all day long. Afterwards, Jon Stanley would go lift weights and play doubles in a local gym at night. His normal partner was a childhood friend, Dan Cooper, and they would beat all comers day in and day out. The only local threat was the gifted athlete Al Jansci, who would go on to star in basketball at San Jose State, but he was not around that summer.

Encinitas was then, as now, a heavy surfing town. The famous Swami's break and Cardiff Reef were a surfer's dream in the '50s when San Diego legends like Phil Edwards, JJ Richards and Mike Doyle created surfing lore on long, glassy rights. While waiting for the tide and a swell to form some waves at the public beach of Moonlight, kids would bat a volleyball around the single court. It was a curious brand of ball in those days: underhand serves which had to be alternately placed on the opponents. As the summer went on, a tournament was organized and somehow word got down to the competitive sands of Mission Beach. One of the top teams, Jim Callender

and George Stepanoff, traveled the half-hour up for a little tune-up since they were playing in Open tournaments.

Their experience made quick work of the locals, including Stanley, and set them straight on the rules—civility had no place in a serious game. You served to win, overhand and to the weakest opponent. Stanley, both shy and a late bloomer who played one year of high school basketball as a sub, blossomed at local Palomar Junior College as an all-state forward. In 1963 he left for BYU on a basketball scholarship. While shooting baskets in the gym that summer, he sauntered over to a net where some Hawaiians were playing volleyball. By now 6'7", the "brahs" thought it not a bad idea to get this "haolie" on the club team which had formed. First he would have to pass the muster of the coach, grad student John Lowell. A huge, stern man who had served as a linguist officer in Japan, Lowell had come back with the forearm passing, rolling and diving techniques which no one in this country had ever dreamed of.

On the day of truth, Lowell walked up to Stanley speaking only a few words of command. "Set this. Okay, now hit a few." In typical military fashion, Lowell taciturnly informed his new middle blocker that he had potential...but needed work. Lowell must have been living right in those days since another guy off the basketball team just as big, John Alstrom, was recruited as well. Before long, the bespectacled crew-cut coach sat the two down after practice one day in 1964 and revealed to them both a rare personal secret. Incredulous, they still were impressed by the gravity of the man's voice: "Stick with me. All three of us will go to the Olympics." Four years later, these two big sticks and Lowell, as assistant coach, were on their way to the Mexico City Olympics.

But the road to Mexico City was like a Baja dirt highway—filled with potholes and stray cattle. Playing in the collegiate nationals in 1964, the BYU team was considered to be merely the usual fodder for the cannon of the California teams. They showed up receiving the serve with their forearms and occasionally one of them performed a funny looking roll to get a ball up. Joined by Carl McGown, later coach of the USA Men's national team (1973-76) and Henry Peters who later served as Speaker of the House for the Hawaiian State Legislature, the BYU team took a fifth! McGown was selected as Second Team All-American and Stanley was added to the Honorable Mention list.

The following year they inched up to a third place finish in the collegiate division which was won by powerful UCLA, featuring the ex-Olympic attacking of Ernie Suwara and Keith Erickson. The respect they had gained the year before took a giant leap when they upset USC, who had the talents of star Dennis Duggan. Stanley and Alstrom, seemingly joined at their high hips, were chosen as Second Team All-Americans.

In 1966, John Lowell went to Poland under a USVBA coaching program and returned to find his predicted dream coming true. Both Stanley and Alstrom were selected to the USA Men's Team which would compete in Czechoslovakia at the World Championships. Lowell would make the trip only to observe. It was a seminal year, a changing of the guard, as a new crop of athletes including Larry Rundle, Rudy Suwara, Smitty Duke, Jack Henn, Danny Patterson, John Taylor and Dennis Duggan would join old-timers Bright and Velasco. The older players of Hollywood and Westside had their better days behind them and the few young, dominant holdovers from the '64 Olympic team had enough of the game. Erikson was headed for the NBA and Ernie Suwara would play three years at UCLA on a partial scholarship—the first one ever awarded, but his fire had been doused for international play. However, Suwara led UCLA to two Collegiate national titles (1965 and 1967) and won his last Open beach tournament in '67 with Mike Bright, knocking off Lang and Von Hagen in a rare loss for the two legends. There was nothing too different to spur him to continue with the game...surely not another Tokyo. He passed on the '66 National Team and on the '67 Pan-

Am team, got married and "replaced volleyball with business." In 1968, at 23, the youngest star to have ever shined in American volleyball was finished.

The new bunch, raw and inexperienced, had a lot of size and a lot of physical talent. There was not much time to prepare for the Mexico City Olympics only two years away, but change by osmosis had breathed new life into American volleyball. The old, stifling game had disappeared with Harry Wilson and the Hollywood Y in 1964; now everyone was playing with two attacking setters, there were legions of black and blued limbs and hips for the more intrepid who tried to get balls up with the Japanese roll, and hitters were swearing at setters in frustration not quite connecting on that new quick "one" set. Players even looked different. Gone was the old basketball look—black low-cut Converse and tank-top jerseys. Taking a cue from what the Eastern Europeans were wearing, some of the Californians at the '66 nationals wore long-sleeve jerseys and the new light, sleek, white-with-three-stripes Adidas.

The core of the USA Men's Team which had toured Canada in 1965 decided to stay together on a team expressly devoted to qualify for the next Olympics in 1968. Doug Badt, who owned the Sand and Sea Club and was a perennial supporter of the sport, had already sponsored an Open team of eminent players not in college at the '65 USVBA Nationals. To that team of Bright, Henn, Rudy Suwara and Duggan, Lang and Hogan were added the next year. When Badt asked the knowledgeable renegade Selznick to coach them, he obliged, and they blew through the '66 USVBA Nationals in Grand Rapids without losing a game.

"Beach or indoor...the first conflict..."

A sweeter disposition never came down the pike than that of Bob Hogan. But to Hogan, life appeared a little more mysterious than to most people and it seemed his duty to find out the answer. Not that he didn't have fun on the way. This guy had leapt off the screen of Easy Rider into real life. In his family's huge house close to UCLA, he and his brother, Pete, threw parties which were legendary. Yet mostly he was a seeker, an experimenter. What would appeal to him was stuff from writers William Burroughs, Ken Kesey, and Carlos Castaneda. One might run into him after weeks in the desert fasting, only drinking water and eating grapes. His eyes would be limpid as mountain pools as he told you about his insights. He kept it up the rest of his life until a crowded bus in Mexico rolled over a mountain ledge, killing him and many others. Surely on another search.

As a player, he could do a lot for his size; he could probably take a bullet overhand better than anyone in the game. "Great hands, smart, a great player," Jim Coleman observed. He won the MVP award in the '66 Nationals. But to no one's surprise he came down on the side of Selznick and that was murder for a volleyball player with international ambitions. On the Canada tour in '65, they were nightlife conspirators. In the summer of 1966, they were both invited to try out for the USA Men's Team which was headed for the World Championships in Czechoslovakia.

There was a showdown brewing for the last weekend of the tryouts—the Manhattan Open. The biggest event in American volleyball! Many of the contesting players pleaded for permission to play. Coleman had to think hard...he announced that they could play provided they arranged their games around the their scheduled tryout matches before the selection committee at City College. Fair enough. Saturday everyone showed, sunburnt and happy. On Sunday afternoon when the tournament had shrunk to one center court and several thousand spectators began to crowd and the excitement rose, there was one USA Team candidate left in the finals of the loser's bracket: the 36-year old Selznick. Could the monarch of the beach, the wise-cracking, fun-loving model of the game walk away? Would they let him walk away? The masses wanted bread and circuses and he was the circus. The sun burned to an orange-amber and spread itself over the tanned, swaying crowd. Leave this? No, he wasn't going anywhere and neither was Bob Hogan.

He stayed too, Selznick's vice-regent in the first row basking with a cold beer.

Coleman, sacrificing any hope of popularity in the beach volleyball crowd, cut them both. "Had it been only Selznick, maybe I would have reconsidered. But Hogan had already missed seven out of 14 practices during the week. It was heart-breaking for me, for everyone."

Selznick and sidekick remonstrated with vigor...to no avail. Next a petition was passed to the other guys trying out. A tough spot to be, between the claws of the game's liberating Simon Bolivar and USVBA incarnate, Coach Jim Coleman. Much debate and they passed the pen man to man. No one signed; the other two had made their choice. Selznick took it as a betrayal of the troops, a selling out of the revolution, and for the first time the miscreant found himself abandoned by players who were friends. Shakespeare explored it in *Henry IV*: Bolingbroke must reject the old, lovable rogue Falstaff—as well as the shared all-night, wine-sotted carousings—when he ascends to the throne. Alas, duty triumphs over fraternity when expedient, no matter how sad. For Selznick, it would soon get worse and like a raft cut adrift, he would float farther from his greatest source of strength—the players.

Jim Coleman and his troops descended in Wiesbaden, Germany to train two weeks before going to Czechoslovakia. There they continued to practice the dive which John Lowell had them doing at City College—on the floor rather than on mats. Even gone were the sponge rubber pads which some of the more cumbersome had taped to their bruised hips and elbows; yet, a new mark of distinction for many volleyballers arrived with the new technique. The split chin. Countless indoor players wear, even today, the stitched-scar from having allowed their chins to bang on a hard floor. But the men's mettle would be tested early in the World Championships as they were slated against the world-beating Soviets. Having taken their welts the year before in Canada, they were better prepared, and besides winning one game, they played close in the three they lost...finally succumbing to the ferocious Russian block. A memorable match occurred when the USA team met China, the first time the two adversarial countries had teams pitted against one another since the Communist regime took over in 1949. The Chinese won a close one: 3-2. Not making the final pool was disappointing, but there were many bright spots for the young soldiers— Smitty Duke was selected on the all-tournament team amongst teams in the second pool of play. The team finished in eleventh place...but strides had been made.

"Vogie..."

Through the deep sand of Laguna Beach, "Crazy Lenny" traipsed along with the long, dead body in tow, leaving a wide furrow behind. Lenny dropped the rope tethered to its neck on the center court and reached high to the cerulean sky with the 34-ounce Louisville Slugger and, in a fashion only a psychopath could do, let fly blow after brutal blow on the lifeless form. Each thud was echoed by howls of macabre delight, and the blood thirst of the crowd rose. Exhausted, Lenny in full lather gave up the lethal baton to another crazed spectator, then a teenage boy, then a robust, young woman! After enough disfigurement and a healthy swill of a charitable beer, Lenny retrieved the rope and drug the victim to its final destination. The lynch mob followed in an angry wake and with two quick hoists, the varmint was strung up.

"Vogie! Vogie!" they chanted in unison as the mutilated torso twisted in the late afternoon breeze...until the voice of reason came from the microphone. The message stunned the crowd, "After three straight years of being hung in effigy"...the gruesome ceremony was to be retired. Enough was enough. After all, this was a civilized society. Meanwhile the real Vogie had grabbed the microphone. In mock sincerity, he thanked the crowd for their perennial support and in the best Hollywood talk-show manner admitted that "I couldn't have done it without you!"

The crowd roared...some cursed...no one cried. It was a sad day at Main beach. But the ghost hadn't really died. The very next year the crazed mob hung one final player in effigy. It was a confused local Doug Dunlap—a big, tall player but an angel when put up against his playing partner.

"Why me?" Dunlap demanded. Finally, he accepted his crime of capital oversight as the announcer screamed: "For playing with Vogie!"

Ron Vogelsang. Clown Prince. Raconteur par excellence. The greatest instigator of 100 years. "I'd rather entertain than win." No disputing that one. A better line and what came closer to his modus vivendi was the infamous: "If you're not cheating, you're not trying!" A gifted all-around athlete who played basketball at Oregon State, he came home to Santa Monica to tweak and taunt players and fans for more than 30 years...and is still doing it!

There are too many stories about Vogie: once in Santa Barbara after an ongoing argument with his opponents about the ball he didn't like, he finally called a timeout and went to his bag near the sideline. Curiously. Hiding a sharp hunting knife, he returned to serve a sky ball. The ball flew high and wide, but when it was picked up by the opponents...flat! Banned from tournaments of yet another beach, the creator of the soon dubbed "dagger" serve could be seen carefully scaling the steep cliffs behind the court in Santa Cruz, and from a height of 30 feet blast a serve down into the court before sprinting down the precipice—then argue 20 minutes about its legality. One serious thing he did, although it was only construed as another Vogie lark for two decades, was develop the jump serve. In 1965, out of boredom in a one-on-one game with Art Diamond at Sorrento, he received the inspiration to try it. "How can that be legal?" protested Diamond, and the normal lengthy argument followed. Still, incontestably, Vogie was the popularizer, if not the "inventor of the jump serve" (in this country) as he claims. He was the only one who used it, to others delight, until it emerged as the most powerful offensive weapon in contemporary volleyball! Alas, no royalties...

For the State Beach and Sorrento crowd...sure, he was full of it!...but the guy was a cornucopia of stories and free entertainment. In their annual caravan south for the Mission Beach Open, the ritual was to go Saturday night to the all-you-can-eat place, the Chuck Wagon. Forty or more people filed in, the big men were hungry but no one could eat those barbecued ribs like Vogie. After some 25 trips and a side of beef gone, the manager informed Vogie he was 86ed from the joint. Vogie, still hungry, protested a technicality in the rules. Others in the group joined the fray. No solution—the owner stood firm—he'd take his losses for that day. "Just leave!" Abruptly the group's ringleader, Selznick, pulled out a referee's whistle and blew it full force as he began swaying both arms and weaving through the tables. Soon they were all right behind: the Brunicardis, Brian and Bobby Jones, Keith Erickson and the rest in a long Conga line which went up and down the eatery. As Selznick sashayed out the front door in the lead, Jean Brunicardi remembers the entire restaurant on their feet applauding the performance.

Vogie's exploits transcended national borders as well. In Rome in 1968, he was performing as a Washington General against the Harlem Globetrotters, until one of Meadowlark Lemon's favorite routines came around. Getting his defender to stupidly turn around, Meadowlark would cleverly slip the ball up the General's jersey; then when the buffoon turned around in surprise he was whistled for traveling. Great laughs but they had the wrong person playing the fall guy. Vogie instead slipped the ball from his backside, dribbled the length of the court and thunderously jammed the ball! Ten thousand Italians went ballistic; Meadowlark went off even further, and Vogie got his walking papers during the immediate timeout.

"Don't you want somebody to love..." (Jefferson Airplane)

The undercurrents of change had been moving in America for sometime, largely with the Civil Rights movement followed by the Viet-nam war backlash, but in 1967 it all hit and hit hard. The message was immediate, as Marshall McLuhan pointed out, and it was pop music which gave the clarion call to sex, drugs, rock and roll. In the summer of '67, the Beatles' Sergeant Pepper's album and their influence indeed would soon be felt as John Lennon said, by more people in the world than any one religion contained. Other prophets of the new generation in San Francisco—Carlos Santana, the Grateful Dead, the Jefferson Airplane—were joined at the Monterey Festival that same summer by more avatars: Jimi Hendrix, Janis Joplin, Otis Redding, the Who and Eric Burdon. The new California wavelength was finally strengthened in LA where the ultimate shaman, Jim Morrison, and the Doors held court. Elvis Presley, in his 18-inch rhinestone studded collars, was left to sit in Graceland waiting for the green light from J. Edgar Hoover. Sitting with a loaded .357 Magnum in front of a TV and enjoying Mama's homespun recipes, Elvis was ready to serve the nation in espionage activities to stanch the tide of evil ideas infiltrating our great country. Between gigs in Las Vegas. No king lasts forever.

It was the summer of peace and love. The terrible flipside of drug abuse would not be learned for a long time, and the violence factor wasn't put into the equation until a year later at the Chicago Democratic Convention. This liberated culture of youth was ready for a good time and volleyball was a sport made for good times...for both sexes. The women's doubles tournaments were adding teams, and crowd size grew steadily, although tiny in comparison to the men's. The highlight of Jean Brunicardi's dominant career came in the Laguna Beach Women's Open when she won the tournament with her daughter, Georgine. What could slow the woman down?

For the fellas, no surprise then that the '67 Manhattan Beach Open was the wildest ever. That Lang and Von Hagen were in the finals didn't surprised any of the drinking, cackling members of the crowd. They'd seen their act many times—too many in fact—these guys took it so *seriously*. How far out when they found out that Bill Leeka, the huge football player with a gamesome personality, and Vogie would play them! With no laws forbidding open containers on the beach, the warm wine and cold beer flowed.

The usual sideshows like entreacts took place: beer-spraying fights, sand-wrestling, the occasional girl who lost her top, but the main court was the show. It was reported that when Vogie and Leeka during the day had been offered liquids to replenish lost fluids—they gladly accepted the beer. Why not? Heightening their sense of the comic, they proceeded to make the match as farcical as they were capable of. Running dialogues with alcoholized fans, stalling tricks, bluffing, gimmick upon gimmick to infuriate their intense opponents. It was working, the serious two became incensed and the crowd was screaming for more. Finally Von Hagen had enough. He marched up to his 260-pound friend and asked him to knock it off. Leeka suddenly went serious; eyes widened, his fist doubled then cocked. No! Dropping his hand, he planted a big kiss on the shocked Aryan's cheek. The coup de grace.

The audience erupted; a single beer can was thrown out on the sand in the direction of Vogie. "Hey, good idea!" A dozen more followed. On the other side, a half-filled jug of a Gallo vintage red landed near the foot of Lang. He calmly picked it up and *tossed it back*! Von Hagen's eyes bulged in incredulity. A new barrage of new cans and bottles. Quickly Steno Brunicardi, a fearsome man, jumped up with a few friends and tried to restore order. More cans and bottles and the crowd roared. Finally the barrage stopped, and the court was covered with the objects; Steno and some friends cleared it. Lang served and Leeka sided out. Vogie went back to serve and promptly got into it with some hecklers who threatened to toss their containers on the court. Vogie *invited* them to do so. They did...in great plentitude. A few more times it rained aluminum and plastic before the crowd collectively decided to allow the furious Lang and Von Hagen to dismantle their

opponents before storming off the beach. Summer of love...

"Goldstrike in Winnipeg...the ladies too..."

Make the impossible possible... When I considered their play insufficient I made them try over and over again however late it might be... The severity of my training often made bystanders shut their eyes... It was not only once that we practiced till the eastern sky became bright...

—Hirofumi Daimatsu,
1964 Japanese Women's Coach
(excerpts from *Follow Me*)

In 1966, Harlan Cohen had a problem. A big problem. At 31, he was engaged to coach the American women. Neglected, helpless and hapless, the females deserved a better shake decided the USVBA—especially after Tokyo. Let's get them a real coach was the thinking, and leave Doc Burroughs and other administrators to do what they were better prepared for on the international level—heads of delegations or team managers—propose toasts and give speeches of appreciation at banquets...or figure out how to get the uniforms of 12 reeking men (or women!) clean in a foreign country. Cohen, who had already excelled as a setter and defensive player, was selected to the 1963 Pan-American team.

About the same time, he was asked to coach the South Bay Triumphs women's team—a perennial USVBA Open contender with '68 Olympians Gail O'Rourke and Sharon Peterson. Cohen was nothing if intense. Cracking his chewing gum at rapid-repeater, staccato tempo, he seemed the right man to start the long awaited fire under the ladies' patient expectations. The problem was how to make a silk purse out of a cow's ear so to speak—and fast.

Cohen, a special education teacher, knew that there are sources of expertise to be tapped if one doesn't know the answer. So he looked to the women who were the best in the world and decided he would simply copy their formula. Logical...it was already proven. Fortunately, he was able to observe first-hand the Japanese women at the Women's World Championships in Tokyo in early 1967. Cohen was mesmerized by the Japanese women, the "banzai" mindset, the several-hour-long practices where women broke down and cried from fatigue, unable to get to their feet. He button-holed Japanese coaches for their secret knowledge.

In fact, he had already applied his theory in the months before the competition. "I hold conditioning uppermost in my whole program." It paid dividends, even in Tokyo; although the USA Women lost to the Japanese, they did so with scores of 15-12, 15-0 and 15-8. The Japanese coach had boasted prior to the tournament that no team would score more than seven points in one game against his invincible women! With new enthusiasm, they came home to prepare for the Pan-American Games the following summer. A *Sports Illustrated* article in June profiled the team and its coach, Harlan Cohen. He explained how he had been teaching the women the Japanese roll: "how to fall without injury—and, as he says, 'how to sweat.'" Still a pillar of the team, Jane Ward looking back comments, "At least Harlan trained the team better." Another player, Ann Heck offers, "Let's say Harlan was a good defensive coach. He worked us hard."

If he wondered whether he was doing the right thing, the confirmation appeared in Winnipeg when the USA Women dominated the opposition and won the gold medal. With Mary Jo Peppler and 6'3" Linda Murphy leading the charge, the Americans had too much size and strength for the rest of the field. Hard to argue with winning. Cohen's reputation—who at 5'7" would have the nickname conferred upon him the "Little Napoleon,"— grew in stature. When the Japanese women visited in November to play the Americans and lost a game to them, it was the finest hour in women's volleyball. That game was only one of *seven games*—not matches—lost since 1960 when Daimatsu burst upon the scene! It seemed doable in Mexico City...a medal was possible! Oh, how fragile the stuff of dreams...

In the men's competition the stakes were high on the final night—for Brazil and Cuba that is. The USA was already qualified but the second berth to Mexico City swung on the outcome of the Americans' match against Brazil. The gold medal too...if the USA won two games they won top prize. The Brazilians ignited from the start and won the first game before the Yanks climbed out of the hole to snatch the next one and then the fourth, giving the USA Men their gold medal. The second slot would go to Brazil if they won that fifth game...or to Cuba if they lost. It was a rare sight; to see a covey of red-clad Cubans cheering frantically for the arch-rival Americans. To no avail. They were hoping the momentum of the fourth game would continue; instead the red, white and blue went flat...pre-celebrating.

"They must have believed that the CIA set it up...I wondered myself," laughed Tommy Haine. When the teams lined up at the closing ceremony, setter Jack Henn and big Jon Stanley were selected to the All-Tournament team. Had the Cold War been in the hands of the Cuban players that night, certainly it would have turned to a hot one. As gold and silver medals were awarded to jubilant players, Cuban eyes were glowing with vitriol and spite. They would remember...that was guaranteed.

The Cubans earlier in the tournament had found at least one American friend...Gene Selznick, who else? Going into exile the year before, he decided to go down and coach the Puerto Rican National Team. He showed up in Winnipeg and was immediately sought out for fun and dancing by old acquaintances and new. However, the small gulf between him and the American players expanded one day when the USA team walked in to find Selznick practicing with the Cubans. So what? "I was a good friend with the coach." The Americans took the court for practice; on the next court some of the Brazilians were warming up before their own practice. Carlos Feitosa, the captain and a friend of Selznick's as well, came over to invite the ex-patriot to hit the ball around. Playing pepper they chatted and decided to go over and suggest a practice match with the Americans. Nothing abnormal. But their idea was six against two...Selznick and Feitosa against the *USA team*! He'd finally gone too far...

"Yeah, that got reported, I guess...amongst other things," Selznick laughs. A Canadian journalist sniffing for a juicy story on the tournament also sought him out. He cooperated with pleasure as he lambasted the USVBA in full measure. Soon he received a letter from the USVBA informing him he was suspended from American volleyball for a year. A year later, it was followed by another letter. This time he was given the unique and dubious distinction of being *banned for life*. Now a restauranteur who was plenty busy with the Windjammer in Santa Monica, Selznick had finally tired of the battles. He walked away from the game...until a friend came in one night and told him that the reason he was banned was that he had thrown chairs at the USVBA members during his hearing. Says Selznick, "That pissed me off so a friend of mine called Melvin Belli."

Belli flew down from San Francisco to study the USVBA handbook of rules, and quickly filed a lawsuit on behalf of the wronged Selznick: there was nothing in the rules to warrant his banishment said Belli. Imagine what trepidations were set off with the opening of that letter! To go mano-a-mano against one of the most successful lawyers in the world was a little out of their league. After seeking legal counsel, Selznick was handed back his USVBA registration card in return for dropping the suit.

Apart from his four-man tour with Wilt Chamberlain, the legend appeared sporadically to entertain at events like the Manhattan Six-Man. Still, one of his last official escapades was the best. During his suspension, he had volunteered to coach his Windjammer women's team. However, there was a logistical problem which few other coaches had ever faced. According to the stipulations imposed by the USVBA, he was enjoined from sitting on the

bench...but worse, required to remain out of shouting distance: "I think it was 200 feet," he recalls.

At every tournament that year including the USVBA Nationals, a man was seen skulking behind pillars and bleachers, speaking into an apparatus with an antenna. On the receiving end of the walkie-talkie was colleague Butch May, who would relay instructions to the girls in time-outs and during play. In the Theater of the Absurd, once again Gene Selznick was starring...to the utter dismay of his enemies.

"1968...the year of the Rags..."

The year 1968 belonged to Larry Rundle. His ascent to the pinnacle of the game had been arduous and surprisingly quick. At John Adams Junior High, he had learned the basics but despite his coordination it was pretty obvious he wasn't going anywhere—he was 5'2" on his sixteenth birthday! Delayed growth hit the summer after graduation and within a year he was six feet tall. Determined to use that new height with knowledge of how to play the game, he transferred from City College to UCLA and began a relentless climb to the top. Although he was a key player on the '67 Pan-American team, by 1968 he was the dominant American player—a flawless passer with an across-the-body armswing which was almost unstoppable. The MVP at the Portland Nationals helped to confirm it. Garrulous and quick to laugh, his lack of concentration on dress matters such as matching colors and tucked in t-shirts earned him his other name, Rags.

How did he get that good that fast? There were at least a dozen guys with more physical talent in 1966...certainly bigger. "I had less playing time in Czechoslovakia than anyone else. It was apparent that the only way I could play internationally was to play the game higher above the net." Since he wasn't going past six feet—he was extremely grateful for even that height—only one way remained to achieve it. Jump higher. How? Despite the traditional view that weights put on bulk and conversely slowed down athletes, a lot was going on at

UCLA to disprove that. A strength coach assured him that if he did the right exercises to develop the right muscle groups, he could jump higher and hit harder. For two years he lifted religiously, arriving at sets of 505-pound squats on his 165-pound frame. Jump squats with 50 pounds in each hand were also part of his program.

Determined to be a world-class player in Mexico City, like most of the better indoor players from California, he played in beach tournaments in the summer. Still, after indoor practices from fall to the spring, the USVBA Nationals in May followed by National Team training camps in the summer and a trip abroad, few National Team players played diligently during the week even if they weren't working. In 1965 and 1966, he went to Sorrento everyday after class and during the summers because that's where the two kings reigned—Lang and Von Hagen. There he set another secret goal: beat those two guys!

How? Well, first keep lifting, study the game and get the right partner. The third was the hardest part but two hours north on East Beach was a local phenom who was drilling oil gushers on shore. Henry Bergmann, on approaching a set, evoked as much excitement from the crowd than any player who ever played...and spoke less. He was like some kind of Apache or Nez Pierce warrior. All muscle and sinew, long-limbed, his hand almost seemed unhinged at the wrist until he wrapped it around the ball. Often the crowd would start groaning together with the pass then raise their joined voices when he detonated another set. "Ahhhhh...boom!" Tales of his workout feats are still part of Santa Barbara mythology. He might run to Carpinteria and back—sometimes with other East Beach legendary journeymen in unusual sessions—sometimes alone. Mark Laney recalls one day when "Rudy Perez and I took Henry to run with us up Rattlesnake Canyon in the hills behind Santa Barbara. It's a steep climb but we had been running it a lot. After a couple miles we hit the wall and started to slow

down. When he saw we were finished, Henry just took off...bounding. Running barefoot!"

Rundle didn't play beachball in the summer of '67 because of the Pan-Ams, but the Mexico City Olympics were in the fall so the summer was open. He and Bergmann teamed up and the path of destiny leading to Lang and Von Hagen had to end where only it could...the Manhattan Open. In 1968 the forthcoming Olympics as usual added an extra luster to volleyball. Rundle and Bergmann had proven after two years that Lang and Von Hagen were not invincible; in fact, they had essentially split tournament victories up to that point. Blowing through everyone, both teams met on Sunday afternoon. The first game was 21-19 for Lang and Von Hagen. Seven games were played between them in the two days and the biggest margin of victory was three points. Lang and Von Hagen prevailed in the third game on Saturday after three hours. For anyone who saw it, it was as flawless as four mortals could play the game.

The '68 Manhattan tourney figures as the most famous pre-pro beach tournament in history for its greatest duel, and it was also the scene of its most famous story. Steno Brunicardi and his renown beach-playing wife, Jean, were sitting near the court as Rundle and Bergmann beat Mike Bright and Butch May in the finals of the losers' on Sunday afternoon. Son of immigrant stone workers from Northern Italy, his parents hadn't bore Steno, they chipped, sculpted and blew life into his marbled body and face of brusque, handsome features. Rock-ribbed and sanguine, Steno refined his extraordinary strength at Muscle Beach before becoming a local at Sorrento when he took up beach volleyball.

While enjoying watching his friends play, Steno was disturbed at some point by a happy, spifflicated fan with his cooler who tried to nab Jean's spot after she vacated it for a break. Steno duly informed him of his error and the guy took a seat behind the couple, but it started a back-and-forth dialogue. Butch May was still standing on the court when he saw, and heard, "a beer bottle shatter on someone's head." The culprit leaped in front of the victim and onto the court, sprinting in escape.

For a rugby player who was an expert at throwing calves, this was easy work. Butch May had that doggie roped and tied in seconds, the perpetrator's face ground into the sand in an unbreakable headlock. Meanwhile, several grown men were using all their might to keep the screaming Steno at bay, the veins almost popping out of his fibrous neck covered with blood. Someone wisely alerted the police as the fool was dragged to the parking lot. When the patrol car drove up, the horrified man pleaded with the cop to arrest him. Danny Patterson still recalls the awful sight of tired, courageous men taking turns to restrain Steno...still screaming: "Lemme go! I just wanna kill him!"

Order returned, the finals were like watching a rerun—only this time Rundle and Bergmann pulled out the win in another three-hour grinder. Now one to 15. How? The sun was already down! You could maybe see for 20 or 30 minutes but they were taking that long to score five points! The organizers of the tournament suggested a draw. Lang and Rundle, self-appointed spokesman for each team, instantly snapped "no!"

This was Lang's bailiwick. When it came to this, it was more mind than body. Gone past the physical...fatigue, energy conservation, technique, strategy had become irrelevant...it was now mental. In the throes of the greatest danger and challenge, it is the mind which dictates survival or success. Lang and Von Hagen were off to an early lead and holding it. At 8-3 it looked good for them when Lang whispered, "I can't see the ball." At 8:45, cars turned on their lights in the parking lot to shed precious light but it was negligible. It was now dark. Lang wasn't the only one with failing vision. A fan complainingly asked the referee Bernie Holtzman, "Wasn't that a throw?" He responded, "I don't know. I can't see!" So dark was it now that both teams began shooting the second ball rather than try to set and hit.

Von Hagen today claims that Lang's extra years and the accompanying loss of night vision was most responsible for what happened next. Rundle and Bergmann crawled back when Rundle thought of an infallible weapon. Like unseen bombs falling out of the sky, high skyball serves permitted quick points to be reeled off. One hit the sand untouched, another caromed off a darting forearm. Arguably the greatest contest in beach volleyball history...ever...was over.

"High altitude problems..."

First, it was Linda Murphy. She had a personal problem: a friend was sick and she needed some time off to deal with it. Harlan Cohen figured she wouldn't call his bluff so he hardballed it. If she was going through with it, "Don't pack your bags!" She didn't. Instead, she called his bluff and Cohen summarily lost his 6'3" best middle blocker. "Well, I thought I could handle that one."

Then three weeks before the Games began, Mary Jo Peppler walked out of practice...for good. "I didn't respect the coaching, the line-up, the system. I'd been to the Olympics already. If I went again, I wanted to win and I could see that wasn't going to happen." Still, Cohen kept the remaining women running, rolling and diving at the Lake Tahoe training site. In his mind, they would leave after that month resembling Japanese defensive wizards—only bigger—which would help them earn a medal in the high climes of Mexico City.

Today, Harlan Cohen is a changed man...a rarity in human beings advancing in age. Still coaching as an assistant at Pepperdine University, he has learned the joy of coaching young players and "using positive reinforcement." He openly laughs at himself and his mistakes— ones he suffered for deeply. It was a classic human dilemma—a soul wending his own way truly believing he is right when *he is wrong*— the material of Sophocles, Shakespeare and Ibsen. "We'd won the gold medal in Canada, I thought I was a good coach." Admittedly, Cohen would have problems beyond losing his two big sticks...but in the words of a Texan sage in its euphemistic form: "You can't make chicken salad out of chicken manure!"

For the men it was smoother sailing, a truly novel experience for American volleyball: they were living in one place together, getting room and board without paying for it, to practice volleyball! Yes! Just like the rest of the world's great teams which had done it for almost 20 years. In the words of Mike Bright, "You were playing, eating or playing. I loved the workouts!" Bright and Patterson had already trained diligently together in Los Angeles months before the camp. Patterson reported, "It was the first year when lack of conditioning could get a guy cut from the team."

Some of the other 18 guys enjoyed the regimen as well but the few times they could get into Tahoe to play the slots, another contingent welcomed the relief. "We tried to pre-live Mexico City conditions in Lake Tahoe, including playing schedules," said Coleman. Although

the unsmiling taskmaster Lowell was none too popular with the boys, he got them unavoidably into good shape. They played, lifted and ran...most of the time. Once on a several mile cross-country run, the visiting parents of Danny Patterson happened to be on a picnic in the area when all of a sudden, a familiar looking guy came running up. It was Smitty Duke...taking a secret short cut! The friendly Texan was asked to sit down and have a chicken leg and some potato salad. He hesitated then thought what the hell! Why not? After a lively chat, he inexplicably sprinkled some water on his face and jersey, thanked his gracious hosts and sprinted off.

Before long, they were on the plane, caparisoned in handsome Olympic gear, the average body fat at an all-time low. And this time, there would be no surprises. For four years, Americans had played under the same rules as the rest of the world.

Coach Al Scates (above) draws it out for UCLA stars, Ernie Suwara (l) and Larry Rundle (r), 1966. (Courtesy of Al Scates)

Hook 'em Smitty! Smitty Duke came out of the Lone Star State to star on the '68 Olympic Team. One of the new breed of spiking hitters—the pride of the Dallas YMCA. (Courtesy of Bud Fields)

Jack Henn of the Sand and Sea Club, 1966: effortless, great setter, complete player. Selected as MVP of the 1967 Pan-American Games with Jon Stanley. (Courtesy of Bud Fields)

Mary Jo Peppler, MVP, 1967. The greatest of her time...and a woman with her own mind. (Courtesy of Bud Fields)

Harlan Cohen, head coach of the '68 USA Women's Olympic team, uses his All-American setting skills in practice.

One of the games' great upsets. Fresno Y in 1967 surprised everyone by winning the title. From left to right: Don Davis, George Sorrentos, Rich Gunner, Ted Bozigian, Jon Stanley, John Alstrom, Len Kazmarek, David Fanning. (Courtesy of Bud Fields)

Pre-Olympic fever. In '68 Nationals, Jon Stanley of Outrigger Canoe Club riddles block of champion Westside JCC's Larry Rundle and Mike Bright. (Courtesy of Bud Fields)

Chapter 11
1968 Mexico City Olympics

"Lightning again...twice in the same day..."

"Did you see that!" No one answered but they all had seen it. Sitting in the bus inside the Olympic village, they were looking out over the surrounding hedge of plants which acted as a barrier to the crowded street of the Mexican capital. Citizens were scurrying in the light rain when the lightning bolt hit the ground and shook the bus in a blast of silvery, illuminated power. Two Mexican men toppled to the earth. Jim Coleman and the team trainer, Joe Abraham, sprinted to the unmoving heap inside a circle of stunned faces. Both were lifeless. Abraham immediately began working on one to revive him. After a few minutes of manual pressure, there was finally a pulse, then breathing. He was alive. The other had no vital signs even after 20 minutes of the trainer working furiously to bring him back to life. An ambulance arrived and they took the dead man away...Abraham forced open the ambulance door and demanded he go with the man and keep working. His adamancy not about to be denied.

It was an hour ride to the sports arena where the USA Men would play their first match of the Olympics...against the world's best team, the Soviet Union. Coleman couldn't believe their luck; talk about a bad omen! "Not a word was said on the bus or in the locker room. I'd never seen a team in this state." Stepping up to give his pre-game speech in the lugubrious air, Abraham burst into the room. "He's alive! He's gonna live." Somewhere in Mexico, if that man is still alive, he surely must be grateful to Joe. Conversely, American volleyball somehow owes that man a USA jersey or some other token of thanks. Because shortly after the resuscitated Americans took the floor, Zeus threw down another bolt! The USA Men performed the greatest upset in American volleyball history by dropping the powerful Russians, 3-1.

How did they do it? As far as style of play, the 6-4 system used until then was consigned to the junk yard and replaced by a real 6-2 system. Prior to that, when the setter was in the back left, the hitter in the right back position would penetrate to set the ball...he could simply get to the net easier but imagine some of the sets which flew out of the hands of those lumbering giants! Now only a player with qualified and registered hands, a setter, delivered the ball. The other big change was also to put the setter, normally their best defensive player, in the middle back position on defense rather than back right. Coleman had originally placed the middle blocker in the center systematically; the change meant that many more balls were dug.

They had a game strategy for the Soviets too. Go at the great Bougienkov. Serve him, throw their best blockers at him, keep free balls on him, set at him...stare at him, think about him...anything that might put more of a load on the man and finally fatigue him.

Tire Bougie? How about trying to tire Godzilla? With Rundle leading the charge, the Americans were siding out like they never had before; Suwara, Stanley and Alstrom were getting precious points blocking. Henn and Duke were putting up sweet sets and serving rockets, but Bougie wasn't tiring. In the third game during a timeout Coleman admitted it, "If you think you can serve somebody else with some luck, do it. If not, keep it on him." But in the fourth game, the impossible happened. Bougie—the demigod now in his mid-30s—crumpled with fatigue in the fourth game. A few points later they took him out!

With the Soviet leader panting on the bench, the Americans grabbed hold of a confidence never seen in American volleyball. A last timeout was called by the befuddled Russians, down 13-6. Meanwhile, in the excited American huddle Mike Bright wryly spoke his famous line: "God, we've worked so hard to get 'em here...now let's toy with 'em a little bit!" Suwara eyes went blank, the entire huddle went silent...suddenly it rippled with laughter. It broke the up greatest moment of tension in 73 years of American volleyball. But Coleman was little relieved. "I had this fear that the Russians might go back and serve 10 straight aces." He was wrong. His men scored two points and the impossible had happened.

They had been to the peak of the mountain—could they stay there? "For 12 hours we were the best team in the world," remembers Coleman. "We were so naive. We knew how to lose. We had no idea how to win." Instantly reporters and TV crews were jostling for interviews. A sport which nobody in America cared about other than a cult following in California, was suddenly hot.

It would be an error to say the honeymoon was short or even interrupted; it was more like an annulment. The next morning the ABC television crew was set up before the match against Czechoslovakia. *That* was a first for the Americans, suddenly jumping a little higher in warm-ups. When the first whistle blew for the Czech server, Henn had called the normal play: 4-1-5, they would probably throw it out to Rundle on the left.

What the hell was this! The Czech turned around with his back to the net, and with reverse spin served a sky ball at least 70 feet in the air—almost touching the top of the huge dome. They don't play on the beach in Czechoslovakia! Where did he get that serve? While they were wondering, the ball descended faster and faster to fly off the arm of the team's top passer, Larry Rundle. Rags aced? "Alright! Get outa the way!" he commanded, knowing this could never happen again. It did, four more times. Biting his pride, Rundle let the other excellent passer Jack Henn try his luck. Taking him out of the setting, Smitty Duke would set the ball at the net in a 4-2 until they got out of this jam. Watching that ball come down in a reverse spin it appeared to curve back into the net! It was almost dizzying. Henn tried to follow the dropping ball all the way down...his hands splatted on the floor as the ball ricocheted off the court. Eight straight points for the server!

The first timeout did little to help...nor the second. The Czechs won 15 to...zero! Many of the fans got up, searching for tickets to more exciting events. Worse, as the teams changed sides, the folded-up TV cameras were already going back into their cases. It wasn't yet the era of the Hollywood minute, but it was the time of Andy Warhol's allotted 15 minutes of fame. For the American men, it had come and gone overnight.

Still, the Americans rallied to win the second game; the skyball artist had lost his touch. The third was back and forth...then, talk about some back luck! While chasing an outside set in the third game, Larry Rundle landed on the referee's stand and severely sprained his ankle;he was out for rest of the Olympics. Without Rundle and his needed passing, spiking and intensity, the team was not the same. The third and fourth games were very close but the Czechs prevailed in both. But it didn't end there; a string of injuries and sickness followed. Jon Stanley, so crucial in the middle, was stricken with "Montezuma's Revenge" before the Russian match but made it through that one. He barely made it through the rest of the matches, losing 25 pounds during the competition. Many others suffered the same affliction. Coleman was astounded that the Olympic Committee had not taken proper medical precautions for it.

"The medical care was absolutely inadequate for the athletes." In a later match he could only name five starters, he didn't know until right before the serve who could play or not.

Beating Brazil 3-0, there was still a chance to get into the medal round if they beat Bulgaria. After winning the first game, it seemed the second was won as well, when a Bulgarian took the final point with an overhand reception, less than cleanly. The East German referee didn't whistle it. The Bulgarians sided out and won the second and third games. Going to the fifth game, the Americans were celebrating when the last ball was hit long by a big Bulgarian. It was not another famous American honor call—this time the referee called a touch. The outcome would reverse and the USA tied for sixth with the same Bulgaria but officially finished in seventh place on the basis of total games won and lost.

"Other kinds of interviews..."

Howard Cosell even wrote about it in one of his books. When trying to crack the television world as a sports announcer beyond boxing in the '68 Olympics, he was given the assignment of covering the Japanese women volleyballers. After the Japanese team annihilated the USA Women, he stopped Harlan Cohen and asked him for an interview which Cohen granted. "I'm here with the diminutive coach of the USA women, Harlan Cohen. Tell us, Harlan, are the Japanese women that good or are your girls that bad?" Not quite ready for that one, Cohen stumbled through an answer, anxious to escape the glare of the cameras and inner disappointment of the loss. Just before his last words, the tape broke. They had to do it again; Cohen was condemned to die twice for his sins. "I'm here with the diminutive coach..."

When thinking of the women's plight in the Mexico City Olympics, one is reminded of the joke where a friend consoling another said, "Cheer up, things could get worse," and sure enough, they got worse! They lost to teams for the first time ever. "Peru and Mexico went out and got foreign coaches for the Olympics. They were different teams we played this time," Ann

Heck remembers. Things kept unraveling, and without a win on the final night, the Americans would play the host Mexican women. There was a full house of partisan fans but surely our women would get it together for that one. They had crunched them in the Pan-Ams only a year ago. Not this time. The US Women lost, and miserably—3-0.

There's a fine line sometimes between tragedy and comedy. Right before the match, Cohen was notified that one of his players would be tested for drugs after the game. Numbers drawn out of a hat, it was a urinalysis simply to determine if any player had taken something to help her jump higher or hit harder. Cohen had other things on his mind after the final point was scored—like getting on the first plane out of there—when the same jury member approached him to announce which girl was to go with him. Cohen stopped, silently cursing the procedure but knowing he had to cooperate. "Mr. Cohen, don't worry about that drug test after all..."

"Never look a gift horse..."

If American play hadn't excelled to the top of the world, its officiating had. Glen Davies had officiated in the Tokyo Olympics and was asked to do the gold medal match of the 1968 Men's competition between Japan and the Soviet Union. Deservedly so. "I thought I was the best referee in the world at the time." He had what he considers the two major requirements: "good vision and quick decisions." Yet in 1968, Davies discovered another side to international sports which the athletes rarely see, if ever.

"About three in the afternoon, a big package came: full of radios, tape recorders, and silks. After two hours of wondering where it came from, I finally figured it out—it came from the Japanese. Somehow Vlaidimir Savin (President of the Soviet Volleyball Federation) later found out about it and confronted the Japanese. Thank god the Soviets won the match!" In a 3-1 contest, the Soviets won their second Olympic gold medal, the only loss in this competition coming in the first match against the USA. A memory which would last a lifetime for those who were a part of it.

1968 USA Women's Olympic Team: the Japanese system didn't work for the American women. Pictured (from left to right): Jane Ward (Captain), Ninja Jorgensen, Marilyn McReavy, Barbara Perry, Laurie Lewis, Mickie McFadden, Fanny Hopeau, Nancy Owen, Mary Perry, Ann Heck, Sharon Peterson, Patti Bright.

1968 USA Men's Olympic Team: USA 3, USSR 1: the greatest upset of 100 years of volleyball. Kneeling (from left to right): Smitty Duke, Larry Rundle, Danny Patterson, Butch May, Jack Henn. Standing: Asst. Coach John Lowell, Alternate Bill Clemo, John Alstrom, Rudy Suwara, Wink, Davenport, Tommy Haine, Jon Stanley, Pete Velasco, Mike Bright, Mgr. Bill Neville, Alternate Jim Vineyard, Trainer Joe Abraham, Coach Jim Coleman.

Chapter 12
1969-1972

"Cuba si, Yanqui no!..."

Peter Jennings got on the bus with the CBS and Sports Illustrated crews. In 1971, he wasn't exactly a cub reporter, but he was still far from the ABC nightly news. This was a big story for him and the biggest media coverage ever awarded an American volleyball event. The USA Men were the first American athletes to compete in Cuba since the 1959 revolution. The occasion was the NORCECA (North, Central American and Caribbean Zone) tournament which meant that the winner would qualify for the Munich Olympics the following year.

This morning the bus was taking them to the beach as well as a visit to Ernest Hemingway's finca...a welcome break in the week-long sojourn. It was practice or play, then back to the old Havana Hilton to be served the same quotidian fare of paella—day and night. The scratchy voices of Patti Page and Frank Sinatra in the frayed furniture of the lobby eerily transported its guests back in time...just as the pre-'59 Fords and Chevrolets outside in the streets.

At long last the final night arrived. Over 20,000 Cubans jammed into the huge pavilion where a gargantuan image of Che Guevarra decorated the ceiling. Closed circuit television showed live coverage of the match on screens outside the arena to thousands more. The USA Team had just arrived and was headed to a conference room when a sudden commotion and rustling of the guards bespoke something was going on. Fidel Castro was approaching with his green-fatigued retinue! The Americans stood in quiet awe as he passed; Bill Wardrop intrepidly stepped toward the premier. "Fidel," he handed him a pair of red, white and blue wristbands. The bearded man graciously accepted through an interpreter before finally breaking into perfect English explaining how he still practiced baseball with the Cuban national team. The charisma of the man cast a spellbinding aura around the lobby until Coach Al Scates announced it was time to go.

Six American players took the floor and grabbed the first game. The second was going to the visitors also until the Cubans caught up at 12-12. A critical call on the line went against the Yanks but ultimately it was the gravity-defying Diego Lapera and fine setting of Jorge Perez which prevailed. The momentum had changed and the roaring chant of the many thousands was increasingly a tsunami too strong to withstand. Fidel had a right to be proud of his boys.

"Medal '72"...another slogan...

For volleyball, the '70s were much like America...and much like the state of the world for that matter. Flurries of brilliance, great designs were begun but never completed. The nation sighed when the Vietnam war ended then quickly gagged on Watergate. Country rock was born but ended in a disco inferno. Ultimately the promise of the '60s was a bust and their disillusionment turned to self-reference...the "Me Decade" was upon us.

In volleyball, there were many triumphs. Title IX was the progenitor of the women's boom and even money arrived for players with the International Volleyball Association (IVA). An executive director of the USVBA was hired and a slick magazine was born. However, the beach game stayed largely on the same, steady course as in the 1960s. There were also disasters: the USA Men got agonizingly close to going to the '72 Munich Olympics but after that would enter its darkest age. The USA Women's support and performance were nothing less than miserable until a few strong-minded individuals took the National Team's plight in their own hands.

Particularly in the first part of the decade, ships set sail in great speed but too often there was either a Captain Ahab or a naive yeoman at the helm. The crew often mutinied or simply jumped overboard and swam for new shores. What seemed to happen in every case was that the vessels were rudderless so all the great energy and good intentions were feckless...the boats simply circled. In that nowhere zone—like Coleridge's "painted ship upon a painted sea"...volleyball was stuck in the Horse Latitudes.

Not that there weren't ideas. After 1968 and the particular impact of the Men's upset of the Soviets, the USVBA announced its "Medal '72" campaign. Leonard Gibson was to spearhead it. "The great tragedy is that we didn't keep that team together with a program. I think we could have won the World Championships in 1970," commented Jim Coleman. If there ever was more to "Medal '72" than words, it was hard to find. One of the only concrete changes was the blocking rule. Prior to Mexico City, players were allowed to follow through with their hands over the net, but the ball had to be contacted on the blocker's side. Now blockers could reach over as far as they wanted and stuff a ball—surely a great relief to referees. The new 18-panel ball that had been introduced in Mexico City by Tachikara was all the rage. Harry Wilson had arranged earlier to import the old 12-panel ball through his company and the new version earned him royalties on every one sold.

In 1969, the new NORCECA zone was formed which changed significantly the Olympic qualification parameters. Before that time the top two teams from the Pan-American Games were guaranteed berths. Now the USA and Cuba would battle it out for a sole Olympic spot. In 1969, the first NORCECA tournament was held in Mexico City. When the USVBA announced there was no money to send a team, Jim Coleman formed a team largely of Midwestern players who went to the competition—paying their own way. A flimsy opening act for "Medal '72."

However, there was a Men's Team sent to Uruguay to compete in an international tournament that same year. Coached by Val Keller, less than half the team were members of the '68 Olympic Team and the team's performance was less than consistent. Probably the most memorable moment of the tournament, although unfortunate, was the career-ending injury to setter Jack Henn. Kicking an upturned tile, Henn's knee was severely damaged but he continued to play the rest of the tournament. Since the accompanying American doctor was really a *dentist*, a local physician was consulted. The diagnosis was not serious...they simply drained it everyday.

The team procured "expert" treatment as well. Henn distinctly recalls the massive chrome lamp with coils looking like something out of Hollywood movies of the '30s. It seemed that the unusual rays from the lamp would improve circulation, while the baby powder routinely rubbed into the knee would provide the final healing touch. When the specialist arrived with the bill the final day, Henn took him to the team manager's room, Len Kazmarek. A wildly funny man from the Olympic Club of San Francisco, Kazmarek was also intimidating. Huge and with a booming basso voice, he perused the bill. Going over every line attentively and confirming it with the doctor, Kazmarek calmly asked if the 1800 total was in local currency.

"Oh no," replied the surprised physician, "that's American dollars!" Kazmarek looked up calmly and walked to the window where he dropped the note to sail away on the Montevidean breeze. He turned and shattered the air like a foghorn, "Get the (expletive) outa here!" Kazmarek chased the terrified man down the hall, meanwhile Henn doubled over in mirth. Still, the setter who had a touch like Pablo Casal's on the cello, would soon be under the surgeon's scalpel and lost to the game.

Joint injuries would take their toll on the '68 USA Men's team. Jon Stanley's tendinitis in his knees kept him from jumping for three years. Tommy Haine showed up in the 1969 Nationals ostensibly only to coach the Outrigger Canoe Club. A perennial favorite of the crowd, the carob-skinned boys bedecked in red and white tropical were struggling late in the tournament. Like an outrigger with no paddler to dip in the rudder, what the listless crew most missed was having their spiritual leader on the court. He was only a few feet away, spitting and swearing on the sideline, hobbling up and down in a full-length cast which was the result of a recent knee operation. Captain of the USA Olympic Team the year before in Mexico City, Tommy Haine usually provided more than his smart hitting and notorious roll dink. There was more esprit de corps in that single bear of a man than in a battalion of grunts.

When another tipped ball hit the floor behind the Outrigger block, that did it! The nonplussed official scorer never thought twice about the substitution...nor did the Outrigger team...nor the guy coming out! A fuming mountain of rage clumped to his receiving position "pissed at the back row," as he put it. The opposing team immediately served him. A perfect pass. Another one. Then a dink was sent over the net...right in front of the impaired substitute with the unbending leg. Hey, this was competition, wasn't it? the spiker rationalized to himself. The guy shouldn't have put himself in! When 220 pounds of muscle, bone and plaster hit the floor, a collective gasp like a winter Waimea Bay crusher swept the gym. My god,

there was freshly stitched flesh covering newly sewn tendons under that cast.

Somehow he got the ball up! While Outrigger put away the set for a point, both teams were watching the flattened Haine, ready for blood to spurt from the petrified leg. None was visible, but the two teams agreed to get him off the court. He refused. Only a timeout and ten pleading teammates finally seeped some sense into him. Their shared knowledge suggested that gentle persuasion would be the best way to remove Tommy Haine from the court that afternoon. They didn't want to try it physically...not even all ten of them together. A better bet was to try and come back against the other team; they managed that...easily.

By 1970 when the World Championships in Bulgaria came around, only one player from the '68 Olympic team remained on the team: Danny Patterson. For 10 straight years, Patterson played on the National Team...still more than any other player in the game's history. "I counted all the players I ever played with on National Teams and it was over 75. I remember looking out at the Poles once who finally became the best team in the world and they had the same eight players they began with 10 years before." Two different programs.

Not that Patterson personally didn't try to improve things. In 1970, he persuaded Ron Smith of the Chart House restaurant chain to sponsor a team that would be essentially the basis of a '72 Olympic team. Rundle, Suwara, May, Clem, Bright and Patterson would be joined by the new sensation from Japan, Toshi Toyoda, and two young prospects, Marty Jensen and Byron Shewman. That group would develop the first fast offense to be seen in American competition. The 31 set was added to the one set, and the Chart House team blew through the '70 USVBA Nationals in Hawaii. The 5'7" Toyoda, an exchange student who walked into a UCLA practice the year before for a tryout, would continue to stagger players and fans alike, indoor and beach, with his flying digs and 40-plus inch leap.

With style of play, cool uniforms and a new type of corporate sponsor which seemed more suited to the game's image, there was some new excitement in the game. Why not try and persuade the USVBA to assemble a real program for 1972? They already had the slogan! Under the hand of Jack Henn, a letter was sent to the governing body and signed by all the players on the Chart House team. Essentially a petition, the letter asked for a bonafide training regimen: immediate selection of National Team candidates and coach to begin serious year-round training. Realizing full-time subsidization was unrealistic, a monthly financial assistance of $300 per month was asked for each player.

The response came quickly and directly from the USVBA: "it is not our responsibility to field nor maintain National Teams..." Whose responsibility was it then? No one bothered to ask...the players simply shook their heads in resignation. "Medal '72" didn't hold much water.

In May, 1970, no coach had been selected by the USVBA to take the Men's Team for the World Championship. Getting desperate, Jim Coleman was asked to take over the team. Hesitant, he finally accepted. The tryouts at Santa Monica City College were largely an open affair. Over 40 guys gave it a go—some of them class A beach players with little indoor experience. Gradually the team was whittled down and the squad selected. Once again it was Patterson who was the only player from the year's previous '69 National Team which went to Uruguay.

There were a slew of green players to pick from which made it tough for the selection committee. But to many it was speculated that the excitement over the surprising third-place finish of the Kenneth Allen team of Chicago in the Hawaii Nationals carried a little too much weight. Some players were taken and others left behind in a controversial selection by the committee. Essentially, factions and losing combined to make the trip to Bulgaria a disastrous one. With morale breaking down, Coleman resorted to platoon substitution. Finally in a small gym in a town of Bulgaria, the Americans sunk to 18th place...a finish which would have dire consequences for later seedings.

"Sol Ross University...where's that?..."

After playing in Mexico City, Marilyn McReavey went back to West Texas to do graduate work at a little university in Alpine. Peppler decided to join her there to finish her bachelor's degree. "Well," they thought, "Why not get a team and enter the first National Championships for collegiate women...just for fun?" Women's collegiate volleyball was indeed small in those days and governed by the AIAW. They drove out to Long Beach State for the tournament; McReavy coached and Peppler played, and they beat the host school for the national title. Driving back they were met by the local police who radioed in to the town hall 20 miles away. When the girls pulled up in their van, both sides of the highway leading into the main square of the town were lined with cheering citizens.

So, why not go for the USVBA gold as well? It was in Hawaii that year...expensive! So a sympathetic disc jockey at the town's only radio station got on the air and pleaded for donations. The town came through, but after a week, they were still $500 short. The same guy took a page out of the manual of the local Bible-belt evangelists and went to work. He announced, "Brothers and sisters, we need your help. We're gonna play this song 'til these little 'ole gals have enough money to go to Hawawyah!" It didn't take long...it was a good choice: Tiny Tim's "Tiptoe Through the Tulips."

Peppler had decided to give the USA Women's team another shot in 1970. She returned to play and found the same frustrating circumstances. Typically taking things into her own hands, the coach, Val Keller, allowed her to set the lineup one match "and we won." But, the experience was mostly disastrous—an 11th place finish. When it was finished, Peppler was convinced finally that change would only come if they brought about change themselves. "I think I quit every year I ever played for the USVBA since 1964 in protest of something.

So I did it again but now with a plan to change things."

As luck would have it...or more realistically as Peppler would make it...things started to slowly evolve. After the first success at Long Beach State, "people just ran to us." In 1971, they did it again! This time beating UCLA for the national title. Of course, there were some undercurrents of disaffection from coaches who were putting their young women out there against a star who had played in the '64 Olympics. But those were the rules. At the '71 USVBA Nationals, the same team took second place in the Women's Open Division.

Alpine was great but Mary Jo and her band needed bigger pastures...and bigger challenges. Soon they were in Houston where Peppler and Carol Dewey started raising money for a program to fund the USA Women's National Team. "If the USVBA can't do it, we can!" was their attitude. Amazingly, they created a full-time training program for the first time in history— with the assistance of the city of Pasadena. Again, talent showed up: Jerrie McGahan, Lucy Courtney, Ruth Nelson and Patti Dowdell included. Later on, a 6'5" lanky black girl from Los Angeles showed up as well: Flo Hyman. The group adopted a good American name for the team: E Pluribus Unum ("out of many, one"). They rolled through two USVBA championships in 1972 and 1973, but their sights were set on the World Championships in 1974.

"South Bay heroes arrive..."

George Brakel was late again...for good reason. He had started in his trashed Nash Rambler with ample time but for some reason he had picked a certain street in Manhattan Beach with its sleepy houses and perfect lawns still damp with dew. One by one, he drove his car up on each misty green lawn then stomped his foot to the floor to dig a long, fresh divot. As the grass and sod flew from his spinning back tires, George howled in laughter. His 16-year old partner, Duncan McFarland, was patiently waiting on Manhattan Beach Boulevard when George rolled up. Here was a contrasting pair.

George well under six feet with a kind of polyp-shaped body was something found in a Hunter Thompson novel...outrageous, on the edge. McFarland, on the other hand, was a cherub-visaged kid who made the girls swoon: a 6'2" rock and not given to words.

McFarland got in and kicked the beer cans away to make room for his feet. Headed to a AA tournament at Sorrento, they were running late on the San Diego Freeway which had a fair amount of traffic that morning. Their luck got worse: a guy in the fast lane was going the speed limit of all things—same as a woman on the right—Brackel was boxed in. He flashed his lights then honked. The guy couldn't hear or just wouldn't speed up. Finally, the lady on the right gave Brakel the few feet of clearance he was waiting for and he darted out. Gunning his faithful steed, he whipped sharply in front of the cur in the fast lane ignoring the man's frantic honking. Now, George leaned back comfortably and let his foot on the pedal relax. He went from 60 to 50 to 40 to 30 to 20 miles an hour! The man was now screaming and gesturing out his window; a terrified McFarland looked back to see the traffic stacking up as far back as the Rosecrans exit. They were a little late to the tournament, but George talked his way out of a forfeit.

Brakel excelled on the court, as well. A guy his size who would have had trouble jumping over the ball; he had precision timing. But his greatest gift was his ability to unnerve opponents. A good defensive player, the first time Brakel dug a hitter he would scramble to the net, try his pathetic jump and place a little dink shot inches out of reach...bellowing "Boom!" in the guy's face. He kept it up, an arsenal of shots and digging mixed up with trenchant remarks which bordered on the insulting. Player after player finally melted down. His art was good enough that he earned his AAA...one of the best shows around at the same time.

Brakel's notoriety spread to the indoor game. In 1971, he drove from Manhattan Beach across the entire country via Phoenix where he took his draft physical. Knowing that exceedingly high blood pressure would get a young man into the "4F" category and free of the draft, Brakel made sure he got his blood pumping through various means, some not legal—so high the military doctors almost hospitalized him. Like Neal Cassady of Kerouac lore, Brakel flew across the States to arrive in Binghamton, New York to find that the manager of his team had not even put him on the roster! Let loose on that town, one evening he found himself in the dining room of the hotel where most of the players were staying...the same of the USVBA headquarters. Happening upon 50 or so Baptist high schoolers who were there for a youth convention, Brakel assumed the persona of a hardshell TV evangelist and edified the youngsters. Afterwards, he kindly picked up the tab for the group's dinner...and signed it to a leading USVBA administrator's room.

By 1969, Brakel was part of the growth of beach volleyball and the most spectacular growth was in the South Bay. Manhattan and Hermosa residents were stringing up courts everywhere, and the number of tournaments exploded. The old system of simply A and AA was gone. Now there was a B rating below and a AAA added to the very top level. A player had to reach a certain finish in one class to advance to the other. Up until the early '60s, the AA players were awarded their ratings by an arbitrary decision made by a small group of tournament directors including Dave Heiser and Tommy Howlett. The number hovered around 20 AAs but no one overly fretted about the rating; it was designed more to keep the tournament competition even. Now it took on a different meaning. You were not allowed to play on certain courts, could get socially snubbed and get accepted or turned down on a date according to your rating.

In Manhattan Beach, as in Santa Monica, different beaches formed large followings. At Rosecrans, Pete Fields hung out and ran the tournaments while at Marine Street it was Mike Cook who donated his time. Soon there were AAA players congregating on certain beaches regularly which gave them instant status. Buzz

Swartz, John Gonzalez, Mitch Malpee, Jim Smith, Larry McCullough, Ken Petersen, Kirk Kilgour, Bill Wardrop and Mike Carey all showed up at Marine Street, which quickly became the heaviest beach. Also at Marine Street, a contingent of young high school girls began playing: Nina Grouwinkel, Rosie Wegrich, Rose Duncan and Christy Hahn became top-ranking beach players and some excelled indoor as well. One local hero, Mitch Malpee, was an unusual inspiration to all of the South Bay. Returning from Vietnam in 1967 as a 90% casualty, he was not expected to walk again. Walk he would, then run, then A, AA and by 1969, he had regained his AAA status! A living testament to the power of human will.

But in 1969, the beach game still belonged to Von Hagen with a new partner. Ronnie Lang had gone to Europe with another friend and player, Ron Snyder, and when he came back the old flame had dimmed. "I just didn't want to be at the beach everyday anymore. I still played, especially enjoyed the few times I played again with Ronnie...but it was never the same." John Vallely was a suitable replacement. The recent UCLA basketball star from Newport Beach was a flawless beach player: "as good as any partner I ever played with," stated Von Hagen. They dominated the summer but bad knees and the fact that "he didn't love the game like I did," made it a one-year partnership.

Few loved the game as Von Hagen. No one played as much day in and day out, year in and year out. "I had more desire. I knew I was in better shape physically. At the end of the summer, I'd play my best...when everyone else was burnt out. I just loved the game so much." In 1970, he was scheduled to play in an early tournament in San Diego with Dane Holtzman. Dane had been schooled in volleyball by his famous father, Bernie, since he could walk, and it paid off. A few months earlier he was selected MVP on the college circuit as UCLA won the first NCAA Championship ever held. After riding down to San Diego with the other Bruin star, the left-handed machine-gunning Kirk Kilgour, Holtzman got out of the van in the Ocean Beach parking lot to drop a bomb on the volleyball world. He was going into Hari Krishna the next day! Completely flummoxed, Von Hagen was soon scouring the beach for a partner...and many players were tempted to break commitments. For Holtzman, it was no lark. The next day he was wearing saffron with a shaved head; today he is a high-ranking member of the organization.

Von Hagen, still at the summit of his game, commanded good partners. Soon he was dominating another summer of beach volleyball winning nine out of the eleven Opens with Henry Bergmann. Few players have ever played both sides with equal skill: Von Hagen was one and now found himself playing the right side as Bergmann stayed fusillading on the left.

"The other Wizard of Westwood..."

When volleyball went NCAA in 1970, it was no surprise that UCLA and West coast colleges had an early lock on the competition. Beach striplings were already playing, some in high school programs in Los Angeles—so why would an 18-year old Southern Californian go elsewhere to play college ball? UCLA, USC, UC Santa Barbara, Long Beach State and San Diego State were all tough to beat for warm weather, waves and attractive coeds.

In fact, the preceding years had already cemented the Southern Californian dominance. City College had its last hurrah in 1966. Led by Danny Patterson and Rick Duggan, they had upset seemingly invincible UCLA which featured Ernie Suwara, Larry Rundle and Mike Alio. The vengeful Bruins reclaimed the '67 title; in 1968 the championship under transfers Patterson, Duggan and basketballer Bob Clem went to San Diego State for the first time; and the last USVBA Collegiate Division champions were the '69 UC Santa Barbara Gauchos—a crew of long-hairs which included Jon Lee, Chris Roberts, Tim Bonynge and Dave Shoji.

Even in 1970, coach Al Scates at UCLA took his recruiting seriously. He found the motherlode in three AAA beach players: Dane Holtzman, Ed Becker and Kirk Kilgour. In 1971, Holtzman's departure hurt but Kilgour the fast-talking, faster-swinging lefty filled the void and more. At 6'4" and close to a 40-inch leap, the blond bomber was unstoppable if he was on his game. A flamboyant and cocky player, when his play became erratic, Scates knew how to rein him in. By 1972 Scates had a factory going: scholarships, prestige, and an already established tradition of winning kept attracting new players like moths to the flame. In 1972, behind Dick Irvin, he won his third straight NCAA title.

"Medal '72...begins in '71..."

"In '69 and '70 there was no plan," remarked Jim Coleman. Realizing that 1971 was around the corner, the USVBA took a bold new step and selected a coach for a two-year period. He was not to be paid for it, but still he would have the position: Al Scates accepted. By 1971, the international game had already appreciably changed since even 1968, for one single reason...the Japanese. Yasutaka Matsudaira had set about what to do with the men what the Daimatsu had done with the Japanese women. In similar fashion, it was a comprehensive, in-depth analysis of their opponents' style of play...and above all, a search to discover and maximize the strengths of his own personnel, both physical and mental. Which finally meant emphasis on digging as much as blocking for points, and perfecting an ultra-fast offense in which crossing and faking spikers confused the opposing blockers. They also had the brilliant floor general in 5'9" setter, Katsutoshi Nekoda, and an array of lethal attackers including Oko, Minami and Yokota. In 1972 in an awesome display, Matsudaira's fine-tuned machine systematically dismantled the world's best to win the Munich Olympics.

It seemed to be always the case that American players and coaches observing and playing occasionally against the best teams in the world would expropriate new techniques and systems and bring them back to try and use them on their club teams. Yet since they were actually performing the new skills, the players often learned and implemented them the fastest. Even the top coaches, now mostly gravitating to colleges, were a step behind the latest techniques. Al Scates was probably the most astute and inarguably the best game coach of the era. There might be better statistical analyzers, or practice coaches, but Scates had an all-too rare quality in American volleyball: leadership. He commanded respect of the players— he had been a great one himself.

The summer of '71 included over 40 days of travel and competition for the USA Men, after almost six weeks of training at City College. That wasn't even near what the other teams in the world were doing but it was a vast improvement for the American players. It was also the last year that players could realistically play both beach and for the USA National Team. More than half the players on the '71 team were former AAA beach players but the time commitment from that point on required the entire summer. A National Team player might sneak in the summer's last beach tournament but that was the extent of it. Volleyball's best had to decide...wear shoes to play or not.

Although Scates came in determined to change things, he saw right off it wouldn't be easy. "The USVBA gave me no help. I had to get a gym through Colonel DeGroot. Then I arranged an international trip through a Polish student, Tad Bugury, at UCLA. Thank god he was there; we did it all at my office." The summer began with a tournament in Poland, followed by the Pan-Ams in Cali, Columbia and the NORCECA tournament in Havana. Using a 6-2 with setters Patterson and Smitty Duke, Scates experimented with various hitters to find the right lineup. It appears he finally found a good one in Cali when the Americans broke out the 31 set to pick apart Brazil in a 3-0 whitewash. With Kilgour, Rudy Suwara, McFarland and Shewman on the court, "that was as good a match that any US Team has ever played," in the opinion of assistant coach, Jim Coleman. Since Brazil had run through Cuba, 3-0 the

night before, things were looking really good for the final night. They only had to win *one game* against Cuba and the gold went to the USA.

Scates, given to slyness, decided to make a deceptive move. Having seen the Cuban coaches in the stands observing the USA-Brazil match, he opted not to use the 31 set which was so effective—only employing the one set in the middle. Hmmm...but still they'd seen it before the Americans used it...surely against the Japanese...thought some of the players amongst themselves. But Scates wanted to save the 31 for Havana when the Olympic berth was on the line.

How much of a factor was the missing weapon? Never to be known but one certain influence on the final score was the officiating. The Americans bolted to a 12-3 lead in the first game despite several touches and foot fouls which no one could account for except the officials. It had an unsettling effect and the Yanks began slipping. They lost the game 15-12. Scates went to the bench but the Cubans were flying higher than ever. A 3-0 loss: gold to Cuba, silver to the USA, bronze to Brazil. In former times, that would have been good enough for a trip to Munich. Not this time. Now, Cuba had to be beaten...in Cuba. When Leonard Gibson, the USVBA representative who attended the meeting which determined that the NORCECA tournament would be held in Havana, was asked by some players: "Why Cuba?" He responded: "Well, they speak French in those meetings and it's not easy to understand what's going on. And I talked to the Cuban delegate before the vote. We agreed that I'd vote for Cuba and he'd vote for the US." Perhaps not understanding that logic, one player quipped, "I hope it wasn't a secret ballot vote, Gibby!"

Meanwhile, Scates was losing sleep over the loss in Cali. In a moment of inspiration, he decided to call for help. In the move he later admitted was a mistake, he called former Bruin and '68 Olympic star, Larry Rundle, to meet the team in Havana. Rundle was put into the lineup replacing the other quick hitter besides

McFarland. Rundle was a great player, but the move had ramifications on several levels...and changed the former quick style of play (including the new 31 set) even further since that wasn't Rundle's strength. The performance in Havana was better than in Cali but the USA was now the odd man out. On the flight to Miami there was some second-guessing. What if, what if... it was another case of eternal speculation.

The USA Women were coached by former great Jane Ward in Cali. With the all-around play of Terry Condon, Mickie McFadden, Roxanne Demik and teammates they had bright moments, but not many. The same problems seemed to plague the ladies, and they finished in a lowly sixth place in the Pan-Ams. In the NORCECAs, the women failed to qualify for Munich—a third-place finish sealed their Olympic fate.

One fiery setter on the team, Kathy Gregory, made her presence felt. Gregory began her long, illustrious career in 1964 with the Renegades while a student at Cal State Los Angeles. There she played basketball and tennis, and with a group of other top female athletes, formed a club volleyball team. One of the players on that team was "a pretty good jumper but could hit the ball out at times," remembers Gregory. That outside hitter was Billie Jean King! Even with the concentration of raw talent, they lost to Long Beach State. However, it should be remembered that many on the team were training more seriously for other sports, especially Billie Jean!

Gregory would go on to make her mark as an indoor setter, playing on the USA Women's Team in 1970 and 1971. But it was the beach where the loquacious dynamo would stake out her territory—and everyone knew it was there—not so much by sight, but by ear. A constant dialogue with fans was interrupted only by bursts of encouragement or critiques of her partner and verbal onslaughts at her opponents. "Is that the best you got!" she would growl at an opposing spiker while bringing up a dig. Women had never seen one of their kind talk and play like this. Many opponents came unglued. For Gregory, "it kept me loose; I enjoyed it."

Of course she received good training for her brand of play by watching the men play at Sorrento and State especially, where the word vied with the body in competition. Great defense and her notorious mastery of shots were learned on the men's nets there—"only Manhattan had women's nets up until 1970." Early on, playing with an array of partners, including Mickie McFadden, Nancy Cohen and the young Nina Grouwinkel, she exchanged victories with opposing teams like Edie Conrad and Patti Steer, Sharky Zartman and Nina Grouwinkel and of course the great Jean Brunicardi. But as Brunicardi entered the twilight of her 22-year career, the mantle of the first beach queen would be passed on to Kathy Gregory for a reign almost as long. Two very different queens with different styles. Brunicardi, tireless and tough as any French Legionnaire in the Sahara Desert, let her playing talk for her. Gregory, a consummated extrovert, played with an unabashed exuberance which has never been matched in the game. Fearless, competitive, screaming...she used the intimidation factor more than any player—man or woman—and backed it up.

"Marine Street..."

In 1971, the beach game was as if magnetic poles were changing. State Beach was looking more like a bleached desert, isolated. On those rare, foggy days, ghosts of the great players of the past could be seen tripping over the dull, silent sand. The local jokers were still there, their aging wits still strong, but the vital force of beach volleyball was gone. Of course, Sorrento stayed strong with some upstarts who would soon make history, but they were still journeymen. The hottest place getting hotter was the South Bay with the focus of the Manhattan Beach Open: Buzz Schwartz and other veterans were joined by newcomers Matt Gage, Bill

Imwalle, Fred Zuelich, Bob Jackson, Dennis Hare. They were all consistently top Open finishers and South Bay players, except for Hare who hailed from San Diego State. With the summer in flux, Bob Clem had given up the indoor game for the beach as well as Larry Rundle. They entered five tournaments, including the Manhattan Open, and won them all. "Something told me that this isn't right. I was working during the week and only played on weekends...not nearly in the shape I was in before...and I was winning tournaments!" Rundle declared. "The beach game for me was 'checkers'—indoors was 'chess'—faster, more strategy and more exciting. Back then, the beach game was so repetitive, it was more a battle of wills than anything else."

In 1972, Rundle and Clem were still playing "checkers" well enough to finish second in the Manhattan Open to Buzz Schwartz and Matt Gage—the first team of two South Bay locals to ever win it. Probably just as well for the game's image. Rundle, now a responsible citizen, might have been playing checkers but he looked more like Bobby Fisher. With his skin approaching the whiteness of his pressed, cotton button-downs, his weekend appearances— usually in a t-shirt—were disconcerting to some of the hard-core beachies. As tan in January as in July, Von Hagen still hovered near the top, looking the part, seeking the right partner and battling the new tendinitis which had set in those reportedly indestructible knees.

The true hybrid, mixed doubles, began to grow in this time of "free love"...well, for most at least "free like." There were really two versions of the game: the courtly, or polite, where the man and woman split the court as in a normal double's game. Women served to women, men to men. When it got down to competition, chivalry was thrown out and it was go for the jugular. Serve the girl every time you could, dink to her, take her face off if she charged in anticipation of an overset! Strategy followed its logical conclusion to where the girl was planted right front in the indoor setter's position, her macho man partner covering the entire court on serve reception. Truly a rite of manhood for the male and ideal for a small,

scrambling female setter—physically and emotionally. It was not the ideal game for a Mary Jo Peppler...unless a short male with his ego in check would agree to set every ball. Hard to find in those days.

If a studly guy with a good serve was the ideal mixed player, it is of little surprise that Butch May would reign for *18 years* as the king of the court. Without question he was one of the very top doubles players, but he found that most of the great players had committed to regular partners, sometimes for years. The mixed game was wide open, fun and no greater workout. He played with his legendary first partner when she was 12! Eileen Clancy was a shade over five feet when she was an adult; imagine the waif as a pre-teenager. But she could put the ball right on every time, where May could display his mastery of shots. They were unbeatable for over a decade.

A handful of mixed tournaments were added by the early '70s but the Marine Street Mixed was tantamount in mixed to the Manhattan Open. After a decade, it was a foregone conclusion who would win it; it remained only to be seen who would finish second. Even when May began playing with a national paddleball champion, who replaced Clancy, the streak continued. There was a good reason he switched to Barbara Grubb; he married her. And proving that combined parental genes make a difference, one of the most sought after high school girls in volleyball history, Misty May, was their talented offspring,

It was Marine Street, Rosecrans and Sorrento for the moment; the afternoon wind swept the sand clean of more memories at State Beach everyday. But nothing stays the same...even in beach volleyball.

"The night the great Ed Skorek cried..."

Moo Park didn't have to speak one of the few words of English he knew at the time. He just nodded at the "wall" of the old Pepperdine University gym and made sure he had enough balls for the drill. Go first? Get it over with? Or watch the first group in morbid curiosity? Three decisive guys in rapid succession sprinted from the wall to the net where Park would toss a ball to each diving player, barely in reach. Then get up and sprint back 50 feet to push off the wall for another one. The object was to get 30 good ones up, fatiguing but within reason. Park would count: "Fourteen!" Minus one, thirteen! Minus one, twelve!" He subtracted one every time a player didn't touch it on the dive. For a tiring wise guy who tried lagging a bit on the sprint back to the wall, the slower turn found a ball already on the floor...and the silent scorn of his two partners. "Minus one!" Ah, but the best part was that you went through the "wall drill" *twice*!

Moo Park came from Korea and instilled new life, and defense, into American volleyball. Studying English and coaching Pepperdine's team, Park was a very busy guy. Word of his notorious practices spread and he was asked to coach the Chart House team. The core of the Men's National Team had been looking for someone who could teach them something new and here he was. A new member on the squad, hard-hitting and side-splitting comic, Larry McCullough, took it upon himself to introduce the foreigner to American humor. McCullough particularly enjoyed imitating the foreigner's idiosyncracies, to the extent of planting himself in that full squat which is a resting position for Koreans. The squatting McCullough still towering over the Korean, enjoyed resting his chin on one palm and staring into the man's bewildered face...inches away...until both broke into uncontrollable laugher. "OK, now wall drill!" The restaurant chain sponsored a trip to Korea—another first in volleyball—in the spring of 1972 in a series of matches against the Korean team. Returning, they captured another USVBA Open title at Salt Lake City.

It was good practice for the summer. Scates took the well-conditioned athletes and flew off to Romania for a series of matches before the Olympic Qualification tournament in France— a last chance to qualify for Munich. The USA Men improved with competition and played with two setters, Patterson and the emerging great Dodge Parker. The two could not only set the ball but played the net unusually well for their size. The big addition that year was a healthy, stronger Jon Stanley. Having discovered acupuncture, Stanley was in better health than at any time in his long career. At 6'7" he could play all facets of the game...on the same level as the best in the world.

It all came down to the final night against Poland. Ed Skorek, Stan Gosciniak and Starie Ambroziak were the key members of the team which would be the best in the world within two scant years. They weren't yet, but unquestionably they were the favorite that night. In a torrid night in southern France, the municipal gym of Montpellier was filled and sweating when the fifth game arrived. So hot that the Americans passed around a pair of scissors and snipped off the long sleeves of their dripping jerseys moments before the deciding game started. Closer it couldn't be. At 12-10, the American team was up and *three points* away from going to Munich! A ball was dug and it flew out to the antenna to Kilgour who approached a drifting block. Kilgour still went for the line where he loosened a few boards but the lineman called it...out!

The Poles chipped away and the USA Men didn't score again...15-12, three points from the Olympics. After four hours of drenching fury, Poland's revered captain Edward Skorek sat in the corner of the gym. Sitting in a chair, his head in his hands...sobbing in relief.

For the vanquished, it had been so close...but no Olympics. The Americans even had their official Olympic sweats and IDs already—a few went on to Munich to watch. "Medal '72" would never be realized; instead, it became a bad joke. "When would things change?" the forlorn athletes wondered. Fortunately, they couldn't see the future.

"I'm goin' in!" In 1969, Tommy Haine (left) entered a match to light a fire under a somnolent Outrigger team. (courtesy of Bud Fields)

Foreign sensation. With a 40" plus jump, 5'7" Toshi Toyoda (right) was a marvel to watch.

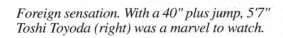

USA meets Fidel. Danny Patterson greets Castro shortly before the NORCECA finals. The Americans dropped a 3-1 match to the Cubans in an historical event. (Courtesy of Danny Patterson)

Duncan McFarland of Chart House drills a 31 set delivered by Danny Patterson, 1972. (Photo by Bob Von Wagner)

Byron Shewman of Chart House lines one off Mike Floyd, 1972. (Photo by Ron Bass)

Chart House, 1970. The team which reigns in the early '70s introduces the quicker Japanese style of offense.Back Row (from left to right): Danny Patterson, Toshi Toyoda, Byron Shewman, Marty Jensen, Bob Clem. Front Row: Budy Suwara, Mike Bright, Butch May, Larry Rundle, Jack Henn.

First NCAA championship in 1970 is won by UCLA. Front Row (left to right): Gil Doplemore (Manager), Bruce Herring, Ed Machado, Joe Shirley. Back Row: Rudy Suwara (Asst. Coach), Toshi Toyoda (Asst. Coach), Bob Metcalf, Ed Becker, Dick Irvin, Kirk Kilgour, Al Scates (Coach), Jim Welsh, John Zajec, Dane Holtzman

Too fast for the eye. Kirk Kilgour lashes another one for the Bruins, 1970.

America's first great referee, Glen Davies. Whistling more than one Olympic finals, he set the standard for the difficult job. (Courtesy of Glen Davies)

Mary Jo does it again. In 1972, Peppler leads E Pluribus Unum to a national title...and the first training program in volleyball. From left to right: Lucy Courtney, Frankie Albitz, Marilyn Mc Reavey, Mary Jo Peppler, Lou Sara McWilliams, Jerrie McGahan.

Henry Bergmann, 1972. Silent, sinewy, flawless.

Larry Rundle hammers a set from Bob Clem en route to winning the '71 Manhattan Open. (Photo by Bob Von Wagner)

Mixed machine. Butch May and Eileen Clancy were untouchable for over 15 years. (Courtesy of Dave Heiser)

Bill Imwalle passes to Matt Gage: a dominating team of the early '70s.

The King of Sorrento. Von Hagen is still strong in his second decade.

Three points away from Munich. Leading 12-10 in the fifth against Poland, the USA Men couldn't quite qualify "Medal '72" failed. Front (left to right): Doug Beal, Duncan McFarland, Dodge Parker, Danny Patterson, Randy Stevenson, Byron Shewman. Back: Coach Al Scates, Rudy Suwara, Mike Bright, Kirk Kilgour, Miles Pabst, Jon Stanley, Bill Wardrop, Burt DeGroot (Manager), Harlan Cohen (Asst. Coach).

Wilt's Big Dippers. In the early '70s, Selznick and Chamberlain barnstorm the country, four against six. (Courtesy of Bud Fields)

Chapter 13
1973-1976

"Make it entertaining..."

A spotlight! Incredible! Playing in a place like the San Diego Sports Arena was odd enough, but to be introduced with a spotlight? One by one, they stepped out into the scintillating tunnel of fame, its walls resonating with the applause of the 7,000 fans. To be sure, it was a motley crew in part. Guys who had to dust off their shoes which had been put away in the back of closets were athletes again; women who had played in college and a scatter of beach tournaments for trophies and finally been faced with that difficult choice—marriage or a career—were given a brief reprieve. Lined up and dreaming about the money they would soon make as professional athletes, the dream at once took on greater fantastical proportions and confirmation it was all true. The spotlight went to a smiling Diana Ross...then Smokey Robinson! Barry Gordy and David Wolper were at their sides as proud owners of franchises. All that was missing was Muhammad Ali!

A month earlier the league had formed and conducted an actual draft. The formula was sport...and entertainment. The first athlete selected certainly satisfied the second ingredient: El Paso took Bob Vogelsang! Vogie broke out his revolutionary jump serve but also broke too many training rules and the King of Entertainment had to take his act back to the beach even before the first game arrived. Smitty Duke, apparently at the behest of a PR manager, frizzed his hair and assumed the player-

coach position for the El Paso Sol. Mary Jo Peppler went high in Sol's choosing and a former NBA basketball player, Scott English, who had never touched a ball was recruited. That proved to be a good choice as the 6'7", 220-pound, 7-foot plus high jumper in a few years became, according to some, the country's best net player. From Brazil, Lino de Melo Gama, "the Caveman" with full beard, was an immediate crowd favorite. Local Texan, the "Amazin' Donny Maze" provided some flair. Rounding out the franchise, El Paso featured an impassioned man who was as captivating as any of the players: the mercurial "Wild Wayne" Vandenberg. Vandenberg had given up coaching the nationally ranked track team of the University of Texas, El Paso, and thrown his lot into the pro sports world as an owner. A true believer...Vandenberg became a font of stories.

On the San Diego slate, Rudy Suwara had descended from UC Santa Barbara to play and coach. The team centered around 6'7" Bill Wardrop (who detested his new stage name, "The Towering Inferno"), Jay Hanseth and Larry "Boomer" Milliken rounded out the net players. Mitch Malpee and Carlos Feitosa set the passing of Rosie Wegrich and Kathy Gregory, and to provide some amusement for the mob, Bob Hogan and his roundhouse serve was signed. Bedecked in stylish uniforms of purple and gold (there was even a poster), the Breakers had more money in the first-year budget than the rest of the other four teams combined. Barry Gordy did things first class.

Overnight, players like Bill Wardrop, who had spent most of his adult life devoted to surfing and amateur volleyball, had a reliable car and a new mortgage on a house in Encinitas. As in the song by Timbuc Three, "The future was lookin' so bright, you had to wear shades..."

"West End rowdies..."

At the '72 Munich Olympics, volleyball proved popular to the TV audience despite the fact that no American team was in it. Media moguls, David Wolper, Barry Gordy, and Barry Diller got together and decided that here was a sport which could be dressed up, sex-infused, and trotted out as a new and exciting product. Looking for some expertise in the game, they consulted with Mike O'Hara who had already been involved in the formation of the American Basketball Association and the World Hockey Association. Things were on track until the oil crisis put a bullet in the World Football League in 1974. It was no time to get into a new pro sports concept.

Yet, why not dabble in it for a year? Wolper and David Gerber who originally planned a team in Hawaii, moved it and general manager, Dick Templeman, to LA. The hoped for 12 teams which included teams in Canada and Mexico City, shrunk to five—four in Southern California. Yet on a shoe-string budget with limited travel, maybe it could grow into something...like a black hole! Gordy picked up his significant losses after the first season and walked. Wolper and Gerber, although not nearly as badly stung, joined him.

Without the heavy hitters, the second season still survived and added Tucson and Phoenix. At times it was not quite roller derby, not quite pro wrestling—owners came and went like passing streetcars. Mary Jo Peppler made sports history again as head coach and player for the aptly named Phoenix Heat. Tucson's team's raison d'etre was in reality to show league growth. The franchise was actually owned by Wayne Vandenberg who was already struggling in El Paso and started on $5,000! Les Patrick, of the famous hockey family, was called in to accept more than a challenge and set a professional sports record for trade-outs—tickets and ads were traded for merchandise—precious little cash ever changed hands.

The Tucson Turquoise had a year of tragi-comedy, a gold mine for a skilled script writer. When Craig Thompson, hired as Patrick's assistant, returned from a jog one morning, he found a huge lock on the door of his motel room. Inquiring at the office, he was informed of the unpaid bill. Patrick, ever the confident salesman in the adjoining room, convinced Thompson that he'd get the lock off that evening but right now they had to hurry to a big meeting with a potential corporate sponsor. "But my clothes are in there!" Thompson protested. Quick on his feet, Patrick generously offered Thompson the loan of his one lime-green leisure suit, 100% finest American polyester, and white patent leather shoes—the preferred sports marketing attire in that era. Though not a perfect fit, Thompson accepted and they were off to a see a local Ford dealer. Within days, Thompson's first payroll check bounced and he was happily, so very happily, driving back to his home in Corona del Mar.

The Turquoise went through almost 20 players in 1976—only two who began the season finished it. Payday was always exciting; the dispersed checks were grabbed and it was a foot race to the nearby bank. Often only the first two in line found sufficient funds in the account...the poor women usually got short shrift. What else could go wrong? The day before the opener, the 6'9" Italian import, Georgio Barbieri, blew his knee out. Patrick left town a discouraged man midway through the season; players were locked out of their apartments in addition to not getting paid. Referees went on strike at home matches for back pay; the Tucson Sports Arena even refused to sell beer to the abused players until the Turquoise office settled their debts. Rental cars were left at airport curbsides on road trips since the coach knew the team credit card was tapped out. Players even quit in airports...Nina Grouwinkel left one night when she had enough.

Leaving her sopping uniform in a plastic bag with the coach, he carried it on the plane to El Paso with the five remaining players including himself. The rules required six players to start the match, so a pretty, unsuspecting girl in the stands was convinced by Vandenberg to put it on—"please, only for a point"—so they could continue with five.

How strange that a hard-core group of 200 desert hippies, cowboys and other locals came night after night to drink beer and crazily cheer on the Turquoise's futile plays and frequent losses. Constituting half the crowd and naming themselves after the cheap seats they occupied, "The West End Rowdies," were still there a few years later when the new Tucson Sky became the darling of the league. Averaging about 3,500 fans a night, the Sky won the IVA in 1980 and was actually turning a profit! In fact, the league after 1976 would improve across the board. As for Craig Thompson, he went on to excel in international sports marketing in Switzerland...and never wore a leisure suit again.

"Triumph in Tijuana..."

Following every Olympic year, there came an announcement, a slogan, some signal from the USVBA trumpeting that things were going to change. In 1973, a benchmark occurred when the Board of Directors took an unprecedented step and hired a full-time executive director. After 78 years of operation, someone would be paid to set in train the agenda of the board. "Get us organized and make our teams competitive," was Al Monaco's brief in his own words. Monaco was a known figure in volleyball, particularly as a national referee and affiliate with the Olympic Club of San Francisco. He had also been a regional commissioner and member of the USVBA Board...he was an insider. He was a lawyer as well and that qualification would be important in his new position. Money could be saved there, and money was still a scarcity. In fact, since part of Monaco's duty was to raise corporate sponsorship money, the players hoped for a National

Team program. However, fund raising was not Monaco's background and it was a hard game to sell. Interestingly, most of the expenses of running the office the first year would be paid by an unexpected windfall. In 1973, Harry Wilson died and had left his Tachikara volleyball importing business to the USVBA...a sizeable yearly sum.

One of the first things Monaco did do was to select a new National Team coach for the men. Carl McGown was the first National Team coach ever hired, and on top of being paid to do the job, the contract was for four years. McGown was coach of the Olympic Club, had acted as the assistant coach to Bulgaria in 1970 and prior to that had been sent to Poland under a US State Department coaching grant. A professor at BYU, he assumed about half of the '72 team players who remained and complemented it with six other newcomers. The six veterans had the makings of a good squad and things finally began to jell. Patterson, the faithful standby who was selected as the MVP of the NORCECA tournament in Havana only two years prior, found himself in his perennial position—fighting for a starting position. He would prevail again.

McGown before long put the six veterans on the court: Patterson and Parker setting, Kilgour and Shewman were joined by two greatly improved center blockers, Miles Pabst and Bill Wardrop. Wardrop's improvement could partly be attributed to Italy. At the Munich Olympics, club representatives were aware of the USA Team's impressive performance in the Olympic Qualification Tournament in France; contacts were made, Wardrop and Shewman became the first Americans to go to Europe to play. Wardrop in Rome and Shewman in Barcelona. Finally, a way had been found to get paid to play volleyball, and the door now ajar would soon be kicked down by a battalion of hungry Americans.

Slipping across the Mexican border, the '73 NORCECA finals were a foregone conclusion in the old Jai Alai Palacio of Tijuana. A couple hundred gringo friends came across mostly to see the famed Cubans like Diego Lapera jump and pound warm-up balls to the ceiling. Instead, they got a cheap surprise and saw the best performance by a USA Team since Mexico City in 1968. Patterson and Parker milked the middle for all it was worth, 31s and ones, including throwing quick sets to each other since the flying Cubans were keyed on the bigger American hitters. Only six Americans played and that's all that was needed as they took their first NORCECA title, 3-0. Ruben Acosta, acting president of NORCECA at the time, would later opine that this USA Team could have become a world power as well...with proper support.

Then the US Team was off to Czechoslovakia for the World Cup with the eight best teams in the world. Picking up Duncan McFarland who had gotten married, the team got manhandled by the Soviet Union and Poland but afterwards they kept surprising themselves. They beat '72 silver-medalist Bulgaria, Brazil and Hungary, before facing the world's best team, Japan. In an impressive match, they lost 3-1 but took a game off the potent foes, 15-2! There was good reason to think that here was a team to work with—this time four years before the Olympics! However, the players had already been talking about a foreign coach—right or wrong—and were told that investigations were being made. Carl McGown surely must have taken offense to the plea...his debut hadn't been all that bad. But after years of frustration, if the National Team players couldn't get full-time training, at least they wanted some new expertise—from off-shore.

Promises, promises... Expectations, expectations... After the tournament, Wardrop, Shewman and Patterson flew off to Spain to play. Kilgour went to Italy. How wonderful to get paid for volleyball...rather than lose money. In 1974, the World Championships were to be held in Mexico City. Dodge Parker, recently married, saw no new coach and no financial help from the USVBA. The same old "show up in June, practice for a month, then go get frustrated." No thanks, said Parker. Kilgour had success and money in Italy, taking Arricia

to a second place finish. When he returned State-side, he found himself living in his van with his wife and looking at the same scenario. His wife and in-laws wondered why he kept playing this stupid game. Italy was okay...but why here? This time they made sense. He quit. Then he decided to play at the last minute, victim of a strange addiction. Parker too came back...belatedly. He didn't go with the team on a Soviet Union tour but a few begging friends convinced him to go to Mexico City. McFarland quit and stayed away. He had no interest in more frustration; married life and lifeguarding were more attractive.

Imagine: four teams in your preliminary pool—two of them the best two teams in the world! The third, Egypt...that was great. But the USA had to face the Soviets *and* Poland— the two teams which would later play in the finals in Mexico City. Inheriting the legacy of the disastrous finish in Bulgaria in 1970, the USA Men were condemned to get out of their preliminary pool as the third team. The Americans ended up a distant fourteenth in the world—playing in the same Tijuana arena where they had hammered Cuba the year before.

What had happened in one short year? Well, it was always a very fragile equilibrium. A USA Team could be brilliant at moments...but how could consistency ever be expected? They were playing against professionals! American players could jump as high, hit as hard, dig as well...at times...but they couldn't go out and do it consistently against guys who did it everyday for a living and that's all they did. In the final analysis, it wasn't the players's fault, nor were the coaches to blame. It was just a result of the system...or lack of one. Jim Coleman, in the know for three decades, said it was "a situation in '73 where the USVBA thought they didn't have to do anything. They already had a good team: 'So what needs to be done?'"

A lot needed to be done, but it wasn't; frustration led to problems. If the maddening inertia of the USVBA was the major source of complaint, what followed upon its heels was the players' criticism of American coaching. In American volleyball up until that time, it often seemed that National Team coaches would too often observe what was working currently elsewhere in the world and then try to model our players to that system: if the Polish offense was in fashion, then use it! "But we aren't made like the Poles, the Japanese...or anyone else for that matter!" For the coaches, there were always some intransigent, questioning players (usually from California) who thought they knew more than they did. With a doctorate in motor learning-physical education, was it fair for a player to question McGown's emphasis on a weightlifting program? Probably not. However, as players received no money, there wasn't much leverage for him to ply. Hence, it was often detente...peaceful co-existence.

With Carl McGown the relationship with many players grew a little worse than normal. A cerebral man—practice talks might include quotes by William James—he had ongoing problems with a couple of key players. His practice of fining a player one dollar for uttering a profanity was unpopular with more than one of those loose-lipped Philistines. Why, a flurry of bad words in the heat of the moment could lose a player his entire per diem! By the end of the World Championship, there was a distinctive lack of communication between him and a coterie of players he would need. Not a good sign for the all-important NORCECAs coming up in 1975...this time in Los Angeles.

"Strange bedfellows..."

While EPU was blazing new trails in Texas, the USA Women's National Team was mostly going around in circles...little ones. One vast improvement was the procurement of Moo Park as coach during 1972-1973. For the rest, the program was mostly two weeks training before a competition...if they went at all. "I remember working out for a trip many times, then they'd tell us there was no money to go," said Laurel Brassey. "The only trips we took were to Mexico because they had a better program

and foreign teams would come through there to play." Terri Condon, Nancy Owen, Bobbie Perry and Roxanne Demik were amongst the veteran core group; yet another disappointing blow occurred when the Canadians hired the popular Moo Park to coach their national team which was embarking on a four-year program for the Montreal Olympics.

The ambitious Peppler group was looking to expand its base; they found a willing high school football coach, Pat Zartman, to come out with his player-wife, Sharky, from Los Angeles. Peppler and McReavey arranged an agreement whereby Zartman would share coaching duties with the two. The USVBA gave its blessing to the marriage. An open tryout was held for an international trip to Japan in preparation for the World Championships to be held there later in the summer. Laurel Brassey, Beth McLachlin and some other veterans came in from California to make the team. Others from California didn't and once again the charge of favoritism was made—ironically this time against the outlaws! Under that cloud and a coaching triumvirate, the team landed in Tokyo. The awkward situation quickly turned catastrophic.

"Pat had a conflict with Marilyn and myself. He was pressured by the USVBA to keep an eye on me, I'm sure," believes Peppler. Never the twain would, or could, meet. Zartman and his player-wife, Sharky, went back to the coast. "Then the USVBA took Erbe's young team to the '74 World Championships...so we folded up the program," reported Peppler. The first resident program was a short page in volleyball history.

Indeed, right after the Tokyo trip, the USVBA pulled in its horns and quickly abandoned its support. In dire straits, they had to scramble to get a coach and team for the World Championships within a month. The Orange County Volleyball Club was already making waves with its new approach. Chuck Erbe had studied volleyball in Korea and came back to form a team of high school girls. The upstart was given the reins of the National Team.

Another tryout was held. Around the core of Erbe's teenagers were added Brassey and new talent such as Colleen Boyd and Leslie Knudsen. Brassey, in particular, was tired of being bounced around and found Erbe's style a trifle over the top. "Fast-paced, disciplined...but too much so. We missed Moo Park. I was ready to quit until Adelaide Packwood, the team manager, convinced me to give it a chance." The performance in the World Championships was less than brilliant, but a twelfth place finish wasn't bad considering the topsy-turvy summer.

And Mary Jo? Fortunately there was a good alternative. She loaded her car and drove "down to the west Texas town of El Paso..." to sign on as a pro with the new IVA franchise.

"Aztec fever...Gaucho glory..."

Still waters run deep in Duncan McFarland. Imagine Peterson gym in 1973, 4500 maximum seating capacity. Five hundred more shimmed in, outdrawing the basketball team match after match. Babes? Every long-legged blond with a tan on campus was there...if that was your taste. If not, the arena was full: Mediterranean olive, Latin brown and Scandinavian pale. Hippie chicks with wild-henna hair who didn't shave their legs or underarms were also present. This was the place to be when San Diego State played a volleyball match. What could be cooler? The bronzed Aztecs in long, flowing golden tresses, some in beards, looking more like rock musicians, or at least surfers than...athletes, and they were good!

McFarland was rolling down Montezuma Road in a hurry after practice, a good North swell had hit. A comely coed stood on the curb, holding out her hitchhiking hand-scrawled sign: Mission Beach. Well, why not? She was a geology major too. Although McFarland was reticent by nature, she somehow disarmed his shyness and they talked mountains, seas and rivers. Raised on the Strand in Manhattan Beach, he was just as home in the desert, away from the masses—an Edward Abbey type. She kept peering at him in a quizzical way; she finally asked timidly, "Are you...Duncan McFarland?" Now *he* got uncomfortable. Dropping her off at Mission Beach Boulevard, in his rear view mirror she was standing, her eyes fixed on his Volkswagen as if it was a conveyance from heaven.

Chris Marlowe, Randy Stevenson, Wayne Gracey and Milo Bekins were the Palisades guys—Steve Jensen, Mike Cote and Craig Berry were the others. They all were young and virile and enjoying the fruits of their standing. But "Darlin' McFarland" made the girls stare...and scream. That good-looking and that good too! Did he ever make a mistake? Already a cornerstone of the team that came within three points of the Munich Olympics against Skorek and Gosciniak, how did he fare against 20-year old college players? Very well.

UCLA came up way short that year. It was Long Beach State which would face San Diego in the NCAA finals. But the 49ers had a couple of men amongst the boys as well. The best setter of his generation, Dodge Parker, led a skilled group of young athletes including Tom Ashen and Mike Barton. Also the 6'4" Miles Pabst who had almost gone to Munich a few months before with Parker provided the one-two punch for Long Beach. Two teams which were cuts way above the others met in April at the San Diego Sports Arena. An insane crowd—talk about girls!—of 7,000 plus showed up at the San Diego Sports Arena for the showdown. It was close enough but the home crowd, MVP McFarland and the talented First-Team All-American setter, Stevenson, sent coach Jack Henn and the fans home to all-night parties with a 3-1 victory.

And McFarland? Did he dare attend any? Well, he'd been lassoed by his future wife, Teri, three years before and wasn't given to partying. Way up in a corner of the arena, a pretty, love-stricken geology major was quietly weeping.

The next year, the ultra-cool wave of volleyball hit UC Santa Barbara like hurricane waves wrapping around the local point, Rincon. Girls? The stands were teeming with beauties and

Gaucho players mingled freely in after-game celebrations in Isla Vista. Coach Rudy Suwara's team was loaded: Dave DeGroot, Jay Hanseth, Gerald Gregory, Skip Allen, Mark Jacobs, Gary Hooper and kamikaze Mike Moss. McFarland had some competition for the female vote with the 6'5" Jon Roberts. Broad-shouldered and big-grinned, Roberts in time would gain the aggressiveness which would make him a leading American player in his generation. He could play all parts of the game well but only Stanley and Wardrop could match him in middle blocking.

UC Santa Barbara was favored all year; it was quite an upset when the UCLA Bruins pulled out a 3-2 victory in Robertson Gym. "The Gaucho choke" stigma began to circulate. Then in the 1974 the same college team made volleyball history when they won the USVBA Open! A strange year indeed but an important one in the beautiful city.

The Gauchos aura spread to East Beach to make the golden era of beach volleyball. Bergmann was gone but most of the college players were putting in their time on the sand. The inimitable Gary Hooper was soon to harness his boundless energy and soar to the top of the beach game in a few years. Ex-basketball player Don Shaw moved up from LA to refine his beach game; legendary leftovers from earlier years made the young college kids earn their ledge on the pecking order: Rich Riffero, Rudy Perez, Jon Lee and Larry Milliken.

"Title IX...put to the test...and failed..."

In 1974, Jack Henn was feeling pretty cocky. The biggest crowds in volleyball history had attended San Diego State's matches the year before and although the athletic director, Ken Karr, had a distinct penchant for the traditional sports, he had to admit that this was something hot. Admit...but not necessarily like. Which he didn't. Apparently, it nettled the Easterner to see the masses flocking to watch so-called athletes in beards and puka-shell necklaces playing a sport which...well, was less than masculine.

In light of the national legislation passed in 1972 which stipulated that sex discrimination in education must end, women were to have equal access to the equipment, training, and competitive opportunities in sports that men had been receiving for more than half a century. Ideas were changing. The '60s for women had borne fruit thanks to Gloria Steinem, Bella Abzug, Betty Friedan and others. Or so it seemed. To pass a law is one thing; for an A.D. whose own lifelines were the well-to-do boosters of the community, to go into the office of Bear Bryant at Alabama and tell him that he was going to have to give up scholarships for *women* was quite another. It took years to coerce the legendary coach to take *black football players* into his program!

In 1970, women received only one percent of the total athletic budgets in American colleges. By 1982, women's share of the athletic budget rose to 20%. Impact on women's participation was enormous as well; during the first decade following the passage of Title IX, the percentage of high school athletes who were female increased from 7% to 35%. College women athletes increased from 15% to 30% during the same time; female athletics began to attract not only money but television interest. But when there are too many pigs at the trough, some will get pushed away. The NCAA, which had controlled college athletics since 1905, had largely ignored female athletics—as society had—but now, with the new interest, they deemed themselves the best qualified to govern the new phenomenon. A power play was made and the NCAA swept into control the ladies' collegiate sports in 1982—the AIAW was consigned to historical textbooks—much to the regret of female administrators.

So when the Aztec men took the floor for their first match with Laurel Brassey on the team, eyebrows were raised. Henn remembers a San Diego Union writer asking him, "Come on, Jack, is this a publicity stunt?" When the cat-quick Brassey went through the backrow every game for the allowed three substitutions, setting and digging ball after ball, Henn remembers searching out the journalist and getting a smiling thumbs-up approval. She could play. But Ken Karr took special umbrage at this so-called gimmick from the start. He attempted every possible blockade of the idea; Henn's only remaining avenue was to go directly to the university's president, Brage Golding. He did and won. At a price...his yearly contract was not renewed the following year. A coach who had won two National Championships in five years and seen the greatest flowering of the sport's spectator interest in history was canned. The crowds dissipated—still ignoring the mediocre basketball team—and Ken Karr eventually left for climes more clement, where there was no volleyball threat: East Carolina.

"The Medicis of beach..."

The year of the Renaissance at Sorrento was 1974. In his fifteenth year of play, the regent-in-residence, Ron Von Hagen, swept his scepter over a Southern California empire. He had withstood marriages, revolts, intrigues with Popes, even inflamed tendons, and still held onto the crown at 34. But the royal court of Sorrento was in decline, and as Henry II called in the Medicis (through marriage to Catherine) to construct the Tuileries, to beautify the Louvre and Paris and introduce the high aesthetic ideals of the Italian Renaissance, an outside influence was needed to regain prominence from those parvenus in the South Bay. Alas, it didn't come through marriage...in fact, two blond Adonises from Santa Monica and a UCLA basketball player were the agents of change. No examples of high art were laid before the king; it was simply the rebirth of the old beach lifestyle with a new face...and renewed energy. Jim Menges, Tom Chamales, and Greg Lee brought fresh blood into the game. A new breed and a new era in the game began.

At the end of the '60s, a group of high school players largely from Santa Monica High and Palisades High started congregating at Sorrento Beach to play on the second court. Randy Niles,

Chris Marlowe, and Jay Hanseth were part of the kids who observed the flawless display of Lang and Von Hagen on the main court. Wilt Chamberlain had become a fixture as well. If he wasn't playing, he would be encircled by veterans Steno Brunicardi, Gene Pfleuger, Vogie and others passing cards in either direction; the game of hearts was played for hours. Often the wind came up in the afternoon at Sorrento and the whole troop would move south to Muscle where the courts were protected.

Hanseth remembers how he and Marlowe were astonished by the skill of Lang in the wind. "When the wind came up, he would break out all these weird serves and shots. In the wind, no one was even close to Lang, and he was at least 35." Etched forever in Menges' memory is the first time he ever stepped on that court. It wasn't long. After an 8-0 lead, Lang walked off and snapped, "Next!" Menges was stupefied, didn't know about the skunk rule—nor that a guy could be that calloused. What a contrast to "Von Hagen who would come up and compliment you or act sorry he beat you. We were just kids too!" recalls Hanseth.

Menges was basically out of the same mold as Lang—an all-around player—with an intensity nonpareil. He knew and *they knew* that he had the mental edge and it would in most cases lead to their surrender. Chamales, at 6'4", was a crusher if there ever was one. He simply hit the ball so hard that it was rarely dug; what surprised most was his extraordinary quickness. He brought a lot of balls up. Greg Lee came from an established family line of players: brothers Jon and Chris were top college players and Jon was now playing on the Open beach circuit. Talent ran in the family and so did trenchant wit—a charade game with the Lees could reach an intensity of civil war. Greg was also on another heredity line as well: basketball. Keith Erikson and John Vallely were UCLA hoopsters who had scaled the heights of beach volleyball before him. When not on the sand, Greg Lee at UCLA had been dropping perfect lob passes into the waiting hands of Bill Walton who in turn dropped them into the net with an agonizing regularity against the rest of the nation's teams.

It had been almost a decade since the last dynasty of Lang and Von Hagen, fans awaited the next anointing but none were forthcoming. In 1973, Bob Jackson and Fred Zuelich delighted South Bay fans by becoming the second local team to win the monster tournament when Von Hagen and Gage let loose at the last moment in a 16-14 decider. Spectators got an extra treat that year when Kirk Kilgour, just back from the Tijuana NORCECAs, walked out on his hometown sand of Manhattan Beach and bounced balls pier-high. Had his partner, Doug Dunlap, not cramped in their last match, it might have been one more big memory for the UCLA Hall of Fame Kilgour.

But winners were changing weekly and partnership alliances were changing almost as fast. In fact, until 1974, the Sorrento faction was an incestuous one indeed. Von Hagen, incessantly looking for the right one, went through partners like Madame Pompadour did lovers...with the difference that beach players were not afterwards dropped into the Seine to remove any evidence. The habitual jockeying of partners and the ongoing innuendoes and miscues, like those in the French court of Louis XV, could hurt feelings and lose friends, and it did.

In 1974, Von Hagen settled on Chamales and it proved a good choice, although it came with a price. Earlier in the summer, Von Hagen and Menges had blown through the Ocean Beach Open in San Diego. That success bound them to playing in the Manhattan Beach Open two weeks later. With a rare, free weekend between the two events, Menges took the chance to sail away to Catalina with friends. For Von Hagen, sailing over volleyball, pleasure over playing, was too troubling. He decided to play instead with Chamales. Almost by default, an enraged Menges formed a duo with Lee. "Everytime I played either one of them, tournaments or beach, I was obsessed with beating them. It made me a better player." remembers Menges.

Still, Von Hagen and Chamales won most of that summer's tournaments including one of the king's two greatest memories—the Manhattan Open—against Menges and Lee in the finals. Would they stay together? It seemed so when they had won the first two tournaments of 1975. But money talked. Chamales, although short on indoor experience, was contacted by an IVA team and he quickly signed a contract. "When Chamales went in the IVA in '75, my career was over," pronounced Von Hagen. Not quite. But at 35, he would now see every serve over every weekend and his fragile knees would feel it.

So in 1975, the throne was vacated with no heir in sight. Who would take it? Menges and Lee grabbed and grabbed greedily. Ball control combined with fierce intensity and the pair held autocratic control of the game for 1975 and 1976 with an astounding 13 straight Open victories. Who knows how much longer it could endured had not Greg Lee gone on to play basketball in Europe in 1977. A glimpse of the next vacuum in the game happened with an upset at the Manhattan Open in 1976. Chris Marlowe and Steve O'Bradovich took the coveted championship and provided some colorful dialogue during play. That element hadn't been seen (or heard rather) in a long time. Good, early practice for the flannel-tongued Marlowe who one day would become "the voice of volleyball.'

A crucial event occurred in 1976, the first World Championships of Beach Volleyball were held at State Beach. Menges and Lee took their sweet revenge on Marlowe and O'Bradovich and pocketed the purse of $2500 put up by Cuervo. $1250 a piece! Unbelievable! Although a couple of tournaments at Lake Tahoe organized by Chris McLaughlin the year before awarded $450 per winning tea, this was big time...and the sponsors were very happy with the turnout. A promotional company called Event Concepts was put together by two volleyball enthusiasts: David Wilk and Craig Masuoka. They decided to push full-time on this infant game. Maybe there was a future...

Those two Menges-Lee summers provoked a great change in the game's play. It seems that a few of the top South Bay players set the ball "with too much spin" in that era. Always an arbitrary call, Menges and Lee felt it an unfair advantage that these dirty and disputably mishandled sets should be allowed. Lee, polemical by nature, had another rare idiosyncracy amongst players. He liked to ref! Simply by calling throws on too loose sets, he set a severe tightening up of the rules. One player, Rick Shaw, had already been using the technique of taking the ball deeper and lower in his hands, holding it and throwing it out without any spin. The "deep dish" was upon us. Unfortunately it was taken to its extreme and by the end of the decade, only a handful of players would dare set the ball with their hands. Bumpsetting was in and hand-setting was taken out of the beach game almost completely. A practice the rest of the world—and beginners—failed to grasp and could only ask with bewilderment: "It's a throw because there can't be any spin?"

"The girls show the way..."

When the Adidas girls team marched in to the Reno USVBA Nationals in 1975, there was something distinctively different about this group. First off, they were all in high school! But they didn't act like adolescent teenagers: there was no giggling and no pointing out the cutest guys (not overtly anyhow). It was all business. Debbie Green, Debbie Landreth, Sue Woodstra and Carolyn Becker counted among the Orange County athletes who lined up, then performed precision warmup drills in military obeisance under their unsmiling coach, Chuck Erbe. Erbe had studied volleyball in Korea. Taking a page out of Harlan Cohen's book—still not a best seller—he sought to find the right system, the forge to melt and form the great female talent lying all around in great pockets of ore. Discipline and dedication were the missing elements, he believed. And for a potter to shape, he needs wet clay—young girls—that didn't ask why, but just did it. "I didn't even try to explain to anyone what it was like...in high school and six days out of the week, in-

cluding weekends, all your free time was spent playing volleyball," recalls Debbie Green.

Adidas sponsored the team which had been formed under an organization, ANVA (American National Volleyball Association). Incorporated by Don Green, Debbie's father, with Erbe it was initially conceived as an autonomous organization which would eventually challenge the authority of the USVBA. If you can't fight 'em, make your own was the thinking. But the USVBA was the National Governing Body recognized by the US Olympic Committee—even though that wouldn't be formalized until 1978 by the Amateur Sports Act. The upshot was clear; any independent movement was ultimately doomed.

It's hard—especially in this country—to argue with success. Those girls shocked American volleyball by winning the USVBA Nationals while the National Team didn't even make it to the finals! Overnight Erbe's detractors were muzzled. The USVBA was once again under fire for its latest decisions.

In the spring of 1975, Arie Selinger had been hired by the USVBA to pick up the many pieces of the '74 fiasco involving Peppler's program. A loose agreement with the City of Pasadena was structured by the USVBA. The coach soon saw he had little resources to work with; he would eat crow for awhile, particularly after that initial humiliating performance in the Reno Nationals, but his long suit was persistence. An Israeli national, Selinger had come to do graduate work in Illinois in the late '60s. Born ambitious, his training as an Israeli commando taught him that ambition alone is not enough—a goal with a concrete plan must be adhered to. If the weak fall behind on the journey, the team cannot look back. Darwinian. Tough. Indeed, but the only guaranteed way to success.

When Selinger saw this new platoon of young, skilled zealots on the Adidas team, surely visions of them merging with the best players already in Pasadena filled his head. Erbe had another agenda. He had a walking National College Championship in his hip pocket; where to take them? USC was close by and had the wherewithal to do it right—especially since their cross-town rivals, UCLA, already had an early lock on women's collegiate volleyball. Tommy Trojan had a smug grin on his face the entire year as Erbe and four Orange County girls continued their climb; USC finished with the national title and a 37-1 record! Always room for improvement, a few more ANVA youngsters enrolled and they topped that the next year with a 38-0 season—the most dominating collegiate performance in the game's history—women or men.

Meanwhile, down in the suburb of Houston, the women returned from Reno in 1975 to grim conditions. Granted, the community gave them apartments, but food and all other living expenses were their own. Parents and part-time jobs supplied those other essentials. Moving around to various gyms for practice, the exhibition matches were attended by a few hundred spectators and friends. Before long, veterans who had paid prior volleyball dues were posing a legitimate question to themselves: "Is it worth it?" Many had college degrees and weren't quite enamored of the distant Olympic dream which Selinger and some of the youngsters kept warm. Most hung on until the NORCECAs and Pan-American Games; after that, Terri Condon, Bobbie Perry, Nancy Owen, Roxanne DeMik and Ruth Nelson went on to different ventures. Assistant coach, Taras Liskevych, also found disenchantment and moved on to start a successful program at the University of Pacific.

Selinger and others kept the faith...for awhile. The USVBA and City of Pasadena fighting to keep the program going, began to fight each other over misconstrued agreements made in the past. The upshot was that nothing changed for the long-suffering women, and there was no money to pay the coach. Selinger left for Israel. Things were indeed crumbling, when a Texas sugar daddy came on the scene. Bob Lindsay, a wildcat oil driller, had picked some good holes and decided to pay Selinger's salary and put in a little extra for the girls. Later elected as the USVBA president, he would con-

tribute Selinger's salary through 1984; fortunately he had the oily touch of a Jed Clampett—he would need it. When all was said and done, the benefactor contributed about $500,000 to get the women to the Los Angeles Olympics. The ladies were grateful for his generosity and the many free meals his wife donated. There were other big-hearted Texans around as well to lend a hand...and sometimes handouts; Pat "Mom" Machesky, a long-time player and supporter of Lone Star volleyball was always on call. Still, in the early days, it wasn't quite enough for some of the malnourished girls. Several of them became anemic in 1976.

Adversity makes better was somehow true this time. Hopes were high for their first European tour in 1975 when a legal bomb fell on the National Team. Don Green filed a lawsuit, claiming that the winning team—his Adidas club team—of the USVBA Nationals should be the rightful representative for the European tour. Not so, contended the USVBA and when the US Olympic Committee supported the governing body's decision, Green walked away with his first setback. For the Olympic qualifying tournament in Japan in January of 1976, they had an outside chance to make it to Montreal—until Jerrie McGahan was injured. "She was our leader and best player at the time," remembers Laurel Brassey. The next year, Debbie Landreth-Brown and Paula Ditmer joined the squad and the sentiment was a little brighter. The new blood strengthened the program and they beat Korea for the first time ever; if they didn't starve, maybe the women could become something internationally.

"Finally a foreign coach...or not?..."

The year of 1975 was meant to be a crucial year in the country where the sport of volleyball was born. The Men's NORCECA biennial tournament finally came to the US and since it was the year prior to the Olympics, the winner would go to Montreal. As '74 was a down year, something had better be done. McGown used what little leverage he could—small fines from future per diem—for players not mailing in weekly workout records. However, a successful corporate lawyer, Clint Stevenson, decided he would take it upon himself to do something substantive for the USA Team which would improve its chances of qualifying. He convinced Winston—cigarettes had a different public profile at that time—to bankroll a league of five teams in Southern California to provide competition and $300 per month for players. A far cry from salaries of the IVA—even for the women players!—but it helped pay the rent.

Other companies—one was Hamm's beer (with these sponsors, volleyball's stereotype remained safely intact)—were enlisted as team sponsors. The Winston's League director of publicity, Ray Ratelle, had his work cut out for him since the hotbed of volleyball, the colleges, wouldn't allow a competition sponsored by a tobacco company in their gyms. Neither would high schools, so matches were held in cavernous arenas as the Los Angeles, Long Beach and San Diego Sports Arenas. And, with the exception of San Diego, usually in front of double-figure crowds; it was hard to get some homecourt excitement going in that environment.

San Diego also had some other advantages. They appeared to have a generous allotment of talent, including the founder's son Randy Stevenson. Packed with former San Diego State stars, murmurings were heard around the league and those who complained felt justified when the San Diego Wave ran away with the league. Nothing's ever perfect but competition was provided; in the final word, it was a valiant effort.

At the same time, Patterson's influence with the Chart House persuaded the restaurant chain to subsidize a training squad of USA Team players beginning in the spring for several months, at $500 per month! In addition, it had been arranged to bring over a Japanese coach to train the team in McGown's absence. "Now, we'll see!" proclaimed the players. Suguru Furuichi arrived from the University of Waseda to observe the latter part of the Winston League. A man with a fine sense of humor, Furuichi's roommate was another future coach, Doug Beal. In April, afternoon and weekend workouts were held at Laguna Beach High School.

If the few attending players who had also played for Moo Park thought his workouts were tough, Furuichi's were a level beyond. Most notorious were his coach-on-one drills. From a table he could easily reduce a player to a quivering pulp on the floor, helpless to get to his feet. If it happened to be a player's birthday, he got a double dose. Never had players gone so long, four, five and later, eight hours at a practice—sometimes three hours without water. But it was new, it was challenging, it was good, and it was something believed in—right or wrong.

For the USVBA Nationals in Reno, McGown came in to coach the team which predictably brought Chart House its third national championship trophy. Returning to Laguna Beach, the squad was cut to the final 12, then moved to Wright State in Dayton for several more weeks of full-time training...the place of daily eight-hour marathons. When the Polish team came to tour, the best team in the world at the time, lineups were still under experimentation. The results were poor but in a tournament in Montreal things finally took a turn for the better when the Americans beat Czechoslovakia in an encouraging win.

Things between players and coaches, however, got worse. As assistant coach Harlan Cohen sees it today, "I think Carl tried to please everyone and he couldn't do it. A group of players—Shewman, McFarland and Patterson— liked Furuichi and wanted him to coach the team. McGown knew that but there can't be two coaches on a team." One player, Doug Beal, who eventually replaced McGown as head coach and encountered his own conflicts with players gives his perspective: "In Suguru's mind, his role was unclear. I think he was surprised and frustrated with our National Team program and the USVBA. Carl wanted bigger guys on the floor but our big guys on the team weren't ready for those roles. From Montreal, things got progressively worse and no one, including the players, faced the problem directly." In fact, a private team meeting amongst players in Montreal resulted in a majority decision to ask for Furuichi to act as head coach. Regrettably, that decision was not relayed to McGown by the team captain.

As an overview, Beal opines further, "From the '60s through the '70s, the National Teams operating under the USVBA's system were never allowed to be good. Frustration levels were high—sometimes uncontrollable. Natural targets are administrators and coaches." In that climate, the final month was spent at UC Irvine in preparation for the NORCECA competition in August at the Los Angeles Sports Arena. They were watched by Wide World of Sports and some 8,000 fans: never such optimal conditions for such an important match. And never such a horrible performance by a USA Men's Team.

"Win the vote...lose the war..."

To call that USA team which took the floor that night "fragmented" would be a gross understatement. Tension had been percolating the entire week. All through the training camp, some players were asking Furuichi and McGown, "When are we gonna scrimmage? Is there a lineup?" The players were unquestionably in shape but it befuddled some as to why no first six was out on the court working together. Yet, Furuichi must know what he was doing they thought—or did he? He was supposed to be a top Japanese coach! McGown and assistant, Harlan Cohen, were largely allowing Furuichi to run workouts which were endless drills but regarding a lineup, no one was talking much. Communication had been fraying for a long time, so the answer wouldn't be known until shortly before the first match of the competition.

The line up came. Then the unimaginable happened: the Americans lost for the first time ever to Mexico. The Mexicans were vastly improved but this caused an immediate panic in the camp. What to do? Amongst players a second private meeting was held. A distraught team threw it all out on the table. Some talked more than others; some said nothing at all. Some of those loyal to McGown's efforts overcame their apprehension and joined the tide of the more vehement critics who kept repeating: "We've got one chance left. Not much of one. But we gotta have Suguru coach us against Cuba—make the lineup and game coach." In an overwhelming vote, the rebel faction held sway. Now to tell McGown.

It was Miles Pabst, the captain, who broke the word later that day. In a hushed room, Pabst gingerly explained the vote. McGown didn't swallow it and announced he would take the team against Cuba. It probably wouldn't have mattered. The next night the excited Cubans only had to win one game to qualify for Montreal. Already having seen the miserable performance against Mexico, they also had seen that Parker and Wardrop—so instrumental in Tijuana two years before—were in the stands watching...thanking dear God that they had gone for the money the year before in the IVA. American players well over six feet with 30-inch plus jumps not only spiked, but *dinked* balls into the net! Passes were shot off forearms into the floor, the Cubans hammered away at a block which might as well not been there at all.

It was an already defeated team that started the game; it was a humiliated one which finished it. Fans hardly got their money's worth. After the first game it didn't matter, since the Cubans were going to Montreal. McGown emptied the bench. Every player on the team got some time on the floor...except one. The guy who had been at loggerheads with McGown for two years, the hard-headed firebrand who led the team three straight years in profanity fines, the one player McGown probably should have ridded himself of long ago. The author of this book: Byron Shewman.

"The decks are cleared..."

In November of 1976, a slick publication, *Volleyball Magazine*, rolled off the presses in a first for the game. The brainchild of Jim

Bartlett, an entrepreneur and former beach player from Santa Barbara, the editorial staff was largely filled with volleyball buffs. Don Weiner was appointed editor, and former UCSB graduate players including Jon Lee and Dean Nowack, filled other positions. Each edition featured an interview and the pilot profiled the dissenting player who had not entered the match against Cuba in Los Angeles. Little venom was spared...for coaches, the National Team program and the USVBA hierarchy as well. Now safely with an IVA contract, he along with many other players from the '75 USA Men's team which self-destroyed in Los Angeles—the six starters and three others quit the team immediately after the Cuban match—jumped to the pro league. The interviewee and targets of his criticisms were more than happy to be done with each other.

The ten-year National Team career of Danny Patterson ended. He says, "A number of us were close. If one left—all would go. It was probably a neccessary flushing of coaches and players. The players had played poorly; there was no synergy between coaches and players. It was bankruptcy. After ten years, my personal disappointment was that it ended on the low point." Typically, the sprightly dynamo didn't dwell on it. From a fabulous home in Aspen, he today runs an impressive company and raises a family.

And the head coach, Carl McGown? Admirably, he muddled through the debris of '75 and became an integral part of the later successes of the USA Men's Team. An Olympic advisor to Beal, Dunphy and Sturm, he now serves as head coach for the BYU men's team—one of the top teams in the nation last year with a 21-6 record.

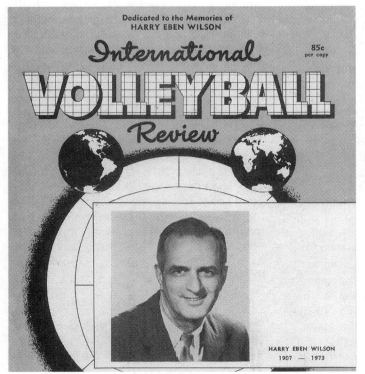

Harry Wilson passes, 1973. The publication he started.

After 78 years, the USVBA hires its first full-time employee. Al Monaco, Executive Director, 1973-1988.

The best hitter in the world, 6'8" Dimitri Zlatonov cranks one inside block of Kilgour (14) and Wardrop. USA 3, Bulgaria 2 in World Cup, 1973.

South Bay heroes. Buzzy Swartz nails one. Swartz-Gage became the first local team to win the Manhattan Open in 1972. (Photo by Robbie Hutas)

Straight down! Bobby Jackson teamed with Fred Zuelich to win the '73 Manhattan Open. (Photo by Robbie Hutas)

"Hit it!" Intensity in femine form arrived with Kathy Gregory. She controlled the beach in the '70s—here with spiking Mickie McFadden. (Photo by Robbie Hutas)

Tom Chamales in 1974 was simply overpowering. At 6'4", his speed in the sand was unparalleled.

The beach game flourished in the mid-'70s at Sorrento. Jim Menges (right) and Greg Lee set the standard for team excellence, 1975. (Courtesy of Dave Heiser)

MVP of the World Championship, 1974. Stan Goasciniak of Poland passed on a gold medal in the '76 Olympics for the IVA.(Photo by Richard Mackson)

Rosie Wegrich, one of the IVA's best female players, pops up another one for San Diego's Larry "Boomer" Milliken.

Barry Gordy gets instructions from the "Taz," Rudy Suwara. In 1975, Gordy's San Diego Breakers led the new IVA pro league...in class and cash.

"Guttin' it out in Texas!" The USA Women's Team coached by Arie Selinger wins its first national title in 1976. Hard work and little pay...but dedicated. Front row (left to right): Laurel Brassey, Paula Dittmer, Joyce Kapuaala, Leslie Stall, Cheryl Engel, Joyce Visser. Back row: Diane McCormick, Patty Dowdell, Flo Hyman, Sharon Grigsby, Janet Baier, Nicki Jessup, Coach Arie Selinger.

Jon Lee of Volleyball Magazine (the first one) interviews Kirk Kilgour after his disabling accident in early 1976. Both went on to TV broadcasting.

Chapter 14
1977-1980

"The Blond Angel...falls..."

In a dead sprint, he bolted for the spring-board. His normal 40-inch vertical jump was augmented tremendously before he catapulted off the leather-bound apparatus toward the ceiling. Soaring upwards his taut muscles relaxed while he felt the envious eyes behind him mysteriously lift his body even higher. It must have been what Icarus sensed as he climbed towards the sun, for Kilgour's exhilarating ascent spawned a dizzy notion. "Why not come out of it with a flip?" he thought. It will blow these guys away! It was the same hubris which led the tragic Greek flyer too close to the melting heat of the sun that now robbed Kirk of a precious instant he needed.

Routinely he dropped his arms which were spread parallel to the floor and simultaneously brought his scissored legs back together. But it was a split second too late when he started his roll forward. Inverted in midair he tucked his chin as hard as he could against his chest. Hitting the mat, all the weight of his 28 years mercilessly compressed down on his vulnerable neck. He saw a flash of lightning and in his ears there was a prodigious crack like an oak tree being riven to its very roots. He screamed once.

"Hey Kirk! Good thing your volleyball is better than your gymnastics! Andiamo! Get off the mat or we'll jump on 'ya!"

Kilgour lay on his back motionless some 50 feet away. It was Mario Mattioli, captain of the team, Kirk's teammate and best friend in Italy who peered at his distant comrade and guessed that he might not be playing a joke on the rest of them. He gushed, "Wait a minute! I think he's hurt!"

The raillery hushed as the Italian captain raced to the side of the supine Kilgour. Mario looked down on his friend and whispered, "O Dio!"...

In January of 1976, Kirk Kilgour was hanging by a thread for his life. He had cheated death, and after several months in a Boston hospital, he was transported to Rancho Los Alamitos Hospital in Downey, California. There he continued his long, arduous program of rehabilitation. An indomitable will was put to test as he faced obstacle after obstacle: of the body, of the mind, of a divorce, of society at large. In 1978, he assumed the head coaching position of Pepperdine University during Marv Dunphy's sabbatical to BYU. That was a challenge too. Assuming a tough job—he was coaching the defending NCAA champions—it was a disappointing year for a guy in a wheelchair who had taken on a position that no one had ever done in history...anywhere. No quadriplegic had ever been hired for a head-coaching job at the NCAA level.

In 1978, the Italian Federation invited Kilgour to Rome for the World Championships. A handful of other Americans were now in Italy, which had already emerged as the top market for international players, but Kilgour was the first giant from the USA. Winning the national championship in 1975, Kilgour's team was leading the pack when his fateful accident occurred in his second year. In testimony to his stature as the first American star abroad, the Italian Federation made him their special guest at the World Championships. In one of those rare moments in sports, the "Angelo Biondo" was introduced and wheeled out right before the finals between the Soviets and a surprising Italian team. *For 20 minutes*, 20,000 people stood and applauded for the American who was rushed and embraced by the Italian team including several of his teammates. Draping an Italian jersey on his colleague, the team captain Mario Mattioli wheeled his former teammate around the floor as the crowd thundered. Not a dry eye in the house.

"We are family...I got all my sisters with me..." (Sister Sledge)

Meanwhile on another part of the planet, a group of female athletes were working their tails off to realize an impossible dream: go to the Olympics! And if you're gonna dream...dream big! Go for a medal. They trained day in and day out; six, sometimes eight hours of practice and physical training was undertaken everyday. Neither job nor school was permitted; simply a life built upon, revolved around, and focused on one singular subject: volleyball.

"God, it would be nice to have two days in a row off," they might complain at times. Yet, what was more important? An extra day besides Sunday or a gold medal? They accepted purgatory to make it to heaven. But even Stygian and celestial realms are relative...early in 1978, the women's program was moved to the new USA Olympic Training Center in Colorado Springs. Wow! For those migrating up from Texas, this was close enough to heaven: dormitories, good food, and a monthly allowance for incidentals like laundry and gas. "Not that we ever drove anywhere. From morning till night, we practiced, ate and slept. If there was any free time, we were usually too tired to do anything. Good thing, we were all broke by the end of the month," recalls Laurel Brassey. A lot more was sacrificed than was planned upon, the setter added, "I don't think anyone

who had a long-term relationship like a boyfriend, kept it during those years." Some couldn't handle it and left.

"It was easier for us who had been with Chuck Erbe. That's all we knew since we were 14. For girls 17 and 18, it seemed a much bigger sacrifice," reflects Debbie Green. However, for the women who arrived from sunny California, the adjustment wasn't quite as easy in other ways. Admittedly, they were used to the full-on training, but the move from the comfort and warmth of Los Angeles to dormitories in Colorado brought some anxiety with it.

But what talent they had now! Some of the fabulous USC women were convinced to come down and join the Olympic quest, Chuck Erbe in tow. Erbe was to serve as the assistant coach. A country can only allow one dictator and soon Erbe was gone, Salinger's rule still intact. Debbie Green, Terri Place, Sue Woodstra, Debbie Landreth-Brown, and Carolyn Becker were now trudging through the snow to practice. "It was an adjustment for both groups," recalls Woodstra, "for the girls already there and for those coming in from California." It soon worked out. By that summer, the USA Women reached an historic goal when they finished fifth in the World Championships. Although the fabulous Lang Ping was not on the team yet—soon to become the greatest female player on the globe—a 3-0 victory over China was cause to celebrate as well. The USVBA President at the time, Bill Baird remembers, "After that win, I felt this was a team of destiny." They were on their way.

The same year a phenomenal jumper from Houston, Rita Crockett, came up to join the ranks along with big Flo Hyman, 6'5", the biggest and baddest hitter in the world when she was on. A strange phenomenon: African-Americans in the game! Sure, track and field and basketball but volleyball? A lily white sport of the Southern Californian rich and well-heeled...somewhere between tennis and polo? Still, it was Jackie Robinson who finally proved that winning was more important than prejudice in the land of the free and volleyball was one of the follow-ons. It had been slow going. Jim Coleman remembers the first great black male player in Chicago, Gayle Hunt, humorously saying in the early 60s: "I'll get you to the gym, if you get me back into the hotel!'"

If Flo Hyman was volleyball's first female superstar, the first male superstar was even a greater attraction—far greater—and an African-American as well. If any athlete besides Muhammad Ali could have as much world recognition in the early '70s, it was Wilt Chamberlain. When the wear and tear of a record-setting career in the NBA forced knee surgery, the Big Dipper took to the beach in Santa Monica where he found that the sand and water was good rehabilitation. As his knee got better, he ventured out on the court. Hundreds would stop and stare at the 7'1" man with colossal strength playing mixed doubles with Jean Brunicardi. Wilt got the bug and was soon doing some socializing with that all-time socializer, Gene Selznick. They formed the Wilt's Big Dippers and began the first professional tour in volleyball. Barn-storming through the Midwest, Wilt's four-man team would typically play against six—often an Open or college team. Using a variety of well-known players such as Keith Erickson, Larry Rundle, Butch May, Rich Riffero, and Kirk Kilgour—many people saw the sport for the first time solely because of the legendary Chamberlain.

In the second year of the IVA, Wilt was made President of the league. Because of other commitments, he would play in a half-dozen matches per year: still, his debut in El Paso in 1975 drew over 5,000 fans. Probably his greatest value materialized in the annual All-Star Games; it was Wilt's presence which attracted a TV network to cover part of the match. In 1978, a flap occurred in the All-Star Game in El Paso. A local journalist who had been critical of Chamberlain in the past was looking for a volleyball story which would raise eyebrows as well. In a clever twist of words, the headlines the day of the match shouted that the opposing team was planning to go at Wilt's weakness—ball-handling. The article was composed in a less than flattering way and suggested that the man's fame rather than his playing was the determinant of his All-Star selection.

League officials soon learned there was lot of anger in a man that size; during the introductions, a quiet smoldering had replaced the normal garrulousness of Chamberlain. In an awesome hitting performance, the towering giant hammered away at helpless blocks of former Olympians only reaching 6'7"—killing almost 80% of his spiking attempts while getting the most sets of any attacker on the floor. He was rightfully given the MVP and left the smallish players pondering what could this guy do if volleyball had been the game of the NBA...

"Lesson of a 16-year old..."

Fate is funny sometimes. Who would have ever guessed that in Sinjin Smith's first beach tournament he would meet Karch Kiraly on the same court! It happened in a AA tournament at Rosecrans in 1977. The lanky kid from Santa Barbara, still in high school, was off to an early lead with his partner, Marco Ortega—thanks to Smith's older partner, Mike Normand.

Long before the world heard of "Stormin' Norman Schwarzkopf," volleyball had it's own Stormin' Normand. A player more intense than Mike Normand probably never stepped on the court. Maybe a few more eccentric...but not many. He could have even been raised by the other "Stormin'" since his father was a rigid military man. Mike, with all that energy and enormous physical strength in addition to a demanding father, found a suitable crucible in the US Army. When they found a guy with this much speed and brawn, with brains, who would charge straight at the pointed barrel of a Russian tank, they used him...especially in Vietnam. Normand quickly found himself sneaking up the Mekong River as a member of Special Forces trained as a demolition expert; he was also highly trained in all the lethal martial arts. An ample source for an Oliver Stone movie. He survived and UCLA's Al Scates—a noted specialist in holding rein on guys "on the edge"—molded Normand into the MVP of the 1974 NCAA National Championships.

Staying on after graduation as an assistant coach with Scates, Normand hooked up with the younger star, Smith. However, in the first game at Rosecrans, Normand had a sporadic hitting spree which prompted the reticent kid to whisper to his serving partner, Ortega, "keep it on him, he's choking." Smith attests that it was louder than a whisper...obviously it was, because Normand heard it!

Oh, my! His eyes protruding from his head, he screamed at the crowd: "What! Did you hear what that punk said!" No one moved...much less answered. He marched to the net and riveted the 16- year old, "If you win, you're gonna..." (in deference to good taste, the rest can be imagined...it was foul and something the young kid would have never offered to do on his own). "If you beat me...I'm gonna kick your ass!" A classic example of being on the horns of a dilemma.

Trembling and ducking from the eyes of the most ferocious human being he'd ever seen, Karch returned to play and the lead understandably slipped, then quickly went to a victory for the other side. Even Laz Kiraly, the proud father, on the sidelines was shell-shocked by the compact strongman spewing insults between his foaming lips. One thing for sure: no one was about to say anything. The second and final game was 11-2. According to Karch, "I had never been intimidated before. Not knowing his past...later I found out about what Normand could have done to me! After that, the Cubans, the toughest guys on the beach screaming through the net...didn't matter; after that match with Normand I could handle any kind of intimidation."

In 1977, Lee left the beach scene for the hardwood of basketball in Germany. In swept a local Sorrento player, the glib and entertaining "Big Sy": Chris Marlowe. Having won a tournament with Von Hagen—his 63rd and final Open victory—Menges asked Marlowe to replace Lee. He did in a heartbeat and very little was lost with the substitution; they won every tournament except one. Menges faced abandonment again, however, when the flamboyant Marlowe left for New York and a role in a soap opera. He settled for Matt Gage, an experienced player who was the "best bumpsetter I ever played with." An important asset now since only a handful of setters dared take the ball with their hands to set it—the slightest rotation was a throw.

In the '78 World Championships, Menges was dethroned as an athletic Steve O'Bradovich and Gary Hooper outlasted them in a double finals—the last game a 16-14 see-saw affair where several throws were called on Gage's hands. "OB and Hoopie" were suitable replacements for throwing out the off-handed remarks formerly provided by the absent Marlowe. Masters of beach trash-talk, they elevated the tradition of verbal intimidation to the highest level of competition. The crowd ate it up; in turn, they turned it up. The brash O'Bradovich was particular boisterous, screaming at referees incessantly. When he was tired of that, he could turn to closer objects...like his partner. With Hooper prone to cramping, he would fight off the attacks by filling himself with liquids continually. By Sunday afternoon, the blond dynamo would be showing an inflated belly as if he was heavy with child. Jay Hanseth remembers the scene vividly: the cramping Hooper writhing on the sand while his bug-eyed partner hovered over him, howling in his face, "Get up!"

The year 1978 was the last for longest-reigning king, Von Hagen. He was an old warrior now—scarred, strong, proud—but the best players were passing him by for younger blood. He could still pull out some great performances...but where was the future with a 37-year old, no matter what shape he was in? Every dog has his day and Ron Von Hagen took his beloved hounds to Sun Valley where he would try and supplant sand with snow. Never had the old adage rung truer: Youth must serve.

"A most likeable fella..."

In the 1977 playoff finals in El Paso, the Orange County Stars took down the host Sol 3-1 for the IVA crown. It was quite a feat in one visible sense—there were only Americans playing on the Stars. Robin Irvin and Hilary Johnson passed the ball impeccably while Roberts, Pabst, Larry Vocke and Bob Stafford picked apart the block of Tom Read, Lino de Melo Gama and the great Ed Skorek. There was a certain cohesion on the Stars team: in the first place, they were paid! The owner, David Whiting, was not only an enthusiast of the game but a nice guy as well. But the key was the player-coach and setter: Dodge Parker. It was Parker's third IVA title, moving from Los Angeles to San Diego to Orange County in consecutive years...chasing the dollars...or rather franchise owners chasing him. Not that there weren't other great setters around. Money had worked its charm: in 1975, the best setter and the MVP in the '74 World Championships from Poland, Stan Gosciniak, had given up the Olympics to stupefy the fans of Santa Barbara. In 1977, Bebeto DeFreitas from Brazil appeared as well as Valdemar Valdez of Mexico. Soon there were a dozen world-class foreign players in the league—playing side-by-side by women in a zany format which began to grow on athletes and fans as well.

Yet, it was Parker who kept surfacing as the winner. "He was technically the best American setter ever, up to that time," was the opinion of Jon Stanley. "He could put up consistently a hittable ball." Growing up in Hawaii, he earned his stripes at the famed Outrigger Club before starring at Long Beach State and the USA Men's Team (1970-1974). As much as his skill, that native Hawaiian insouciance combined with his uncontrollable love of the prank made for an unusual gift of endearing himself to everyone around him. He was loved dearly but somehow could use his fierce competitiveness to make others around him play better. An intangible defying definition...that which every coach pines for. In 1978, married with a young daughter, he retired to work on the league level in an expansion role of selling franchises. His charm would not be employed for long. After an early morning jog in 1979, Parker was the victim of a heart attack. His sudden death stunned the sport—it's most loved player gone at the tender age of 29.

"Coaching by the book..."

Doug Beal has an impressive library in his home. Huge. As would be expected, many are of the sports genre: college textbooks to autobiographies, anatomy and physiology to the story of Vince Lombardi. But the hundreds of hardbacks and softcovers which line four walls go far beyond the world of the physical. It reveals an eclectic taste. If the reader preferred history, Toynbee and Spengler could be found. Psychology: Freud, Maslow, Rogers are there. The range of literature is vast; Nabokov to Pynchon and much in between.

On an end table rests more than Time Magazine; the New York Times is daily fare. A framed art poster on the wall announces a Left Bank art exhibition in the 1920s. The self-portrait of the artist in the poster turns out to be an accomplished uncle, rubbing elbows in Montparnasse with Modigliani, Gris and Hemingway. Could he have been in the Gertrude Stein salon? He has the look.

Beal had set himself on an early path to coaching volleyball—an occupation which was less than relished by his family. His grandfather was a leading dictionary publisher; besides the business successes in the family, there was a liberal sprinkling of artists and intellectuals. Banker, lawyer, doctor, even a musician...but volleyball player? Didn't fit in the elitist enclave of Cleveland's Shaker Heights. So, Beal set out on his lonely trek and ended up as an early star for Ohio State. In the late '60s, many of the men who would later fill USVBA Board positions were from the Midwest and Beal got to know them well. He also was snatched up by National Team coach, Jim Coleman, who was impressed by his play on the Open team—the Columbus Caps. Next step was the USA Men's team in 1970 on which he would play many years.

Intelligence and ambition joined to lead the way to Beal's lucky star—a trail fraught with setbacks. It was one thing to be in the midst of the USVBA hierarchy—an outsider coming out to Southern California and integrating oneself to the volleyball community was another. Especially when the person is of intellectual bent and given to thoughts of the future. When Beal was on the USA National Team during the '70s, he was simultaneously working on master's and doctoral degrees. Most of his teammates' reading was confined to daily tide charts and surf reports in the local rag. Beal was serious, analytical and goal-oriented. Sport, pleasure and the immediate were what the other Californians focused on. It was a disparity which would be a continual affliction in his ensuing career as USA Men's coach and USVBA administrator. The regional breach in American volleyball would not be closed...it would have to be lived with.

So when the USA Men's Team was eviscerated in 1975, the void was calling to be filled. One of the few who decided not to jump to the IVA, Beal stayed on as a player under McGown until the head coach resigned after his term was up in 1976. Again, the USA National Team job was open for applicants. Who in the hell wanted it? Not very many. But Beal did; in fact, he had subconsciously been waiting a long time for it. He got the job.

"Stuck in Dayton...with the West Coast blues again..."

When Doug Beal arrived in Dayton, Ohio in January of 1977, as the new head coach of the USA Men's Team, the weather itself was a harbinger of things to come. It was one of the most dreadful winters in history. Similarly the late '70s (1976-1980) would figure as the veritable Ice Age of volleyball for the USA Men's Team, on many levels. When Beal took the job, the decision to move to Dayton and establish a Men's National Training Center had already been taken; a local enthusiast, Frank Gunn, had somehow convinced the city fathers to adopt the foundling. If things were bad in Pasadena

for the women, they weren't any better for the men in Dayton. Things were worse in fact; there was no philanthropist like Bob Lindsay around with a wad of money to plug up the elusive holes in the dike.

Over the next few months, a skein of players would roll out and into Dayton. Ralph Smith and Joe Battaglia were the first to arrive from California—in a Volkswagen bug with no heater. For four years, any guy who ever dreamed of wearing a USA jersey had a reasonable shot to at least get a try-out. The eight-hour shifts of manual labor and night practices at Roosevelt High School were in more cases a deterrent than motivation for young players. Some raw talent did arrive; soon a dozen Californians and a handful of Midwesterners were vying for the team. Tom Ashen who won a starting setter spot stayed for about seven months. "We got there to find no apartments and no money. Most of us got working manual labor jobs, sometimes graveyard shifts, then worked out afterwards. But it wasn't enough—we were going into serious debt. I was down almost three thousand dollars so I told Beal that things had to improve. They didn't so I left."

He wasn't alone; still, survivors of the period such as Paul Sunderland, Marc Waldie, Aldis Berzins, Gerald Gregory, and Rick Duwelius would eventually figure as Beal's diamonds in the rough. Yet, it would take years to polish some of these before they were store-ready. In 1977, the USA Men lost to Canada and Puerto Rico in the NORCECAs to capture a lowly fifth place. The fact that Beal's good friend, Bill Neville, was the coach of the Canadian team wasn't any kind of salve for the bitter disappointment.

In 1978, the team plummeted to an all-time low of 19th place in the World Championships in Italy. Lack of support by the city, sinking player morale and a consistent hammering by critics set in. According to Beal, "Besides the other problems, the biggest one was that we just couldn't get any good new players. They were all in the IVA or still in college." Since players in the IVA were banned from playing any kind of amateur competition, the only relief in sight were the college players. There were a crop of exceptional college players in fact, but that wouldn't happen for awhile. At least they had been exposed to the international game. In 1976, a team was sent to the first NORCECA Junior Championships: Craig Buck, Dusty Dvorak and Rod Wilde were on that team which was Beal's first USA coaching assignment. The following year, Karch Kiraly, Sinjin Smith, Steve Salmons, and Tim Hovland joined Dvorak in the Junior World Championships as well as the Pacific Rim Championships in a glimpse of what was to come. Kiraly remembers the finals in Brazil: "I was the last guy on the team; I mostly took stats. I remember the warmups in the finals between the Soviets and the Brazilians...guys only 18 and bouncing balls to the ceiling. It was unbelievable!"

When Beal lamented that most of the talent was in college or the pros, he wasn't far off the mark. Not only were the USVBA Nationals gutted of many of the best players, but the amateur side of the sport itself seemed to be going nowhere. In 1979, adult membership of the USVBA was reported as 14,993. For the next five years, the number barely rose above 15,000; in 1984, the total number of adults paying registration dues were 15,530—a paltry increase of 600 players in five years! How could it not be considered a moribund game? It seems a blight had even infected Southern California. The number of teams entered in the Nationals began to tail off dramatically. The top male college players and recent graduates would eventually assemble under Chuck's Steak House or Nautilus Pacifica for a few days of play and fun at the nationals, but the national title was doing anything but gaining stature for competitors. Despite the efforts of a few standbys like Catalino "Iggy" Ignacio, a man who was a top referee and coach in Los Angeles for decades, the USVBA was stuck in the mud.

If nothing else was going too well, at least the USVBA had become more sensitive to internation rule changes and showed a willingness to adopt them. In the '76 Olympics, the FIVB instated the four-touch rule (off the block) as well as a new placement of the antennae—moved inside and aligned with the line. Both were adopted to blunt the surging advantage of the sport's offense. Points were difficult to come by, and the USVBA changed its own rules in 1977 to improve matters.

"I'm goin' to Graceland, Graceland..." (Paul Simon)

It can well be imagined what Patti McDole felt that day in 1980 when her husband, Stew, announced that he was going to put up the house as security for the loan. Loan for what? Laid off? Severe illness in the family? Future college tuition for the kids? No...for his volleyball camps. But wait a minute! The guy had four youngsters, a good job at Western Illinois University, and he was going to risk the house? She had been a good partner and rolled with the punches in the past, but a *$90,000* loan to bail out the camps? Wasn't this over the top for even the most dutiful wife? Maybe, but for a devout man whose strongest utterance was an oft-imitated "ouch," McDole's passion was overwhelming—for the sport of volleyball and young kids who wanted to play it.

In Lamoni, Iowa, sits a small religious university, Graceland College of the Reformed Church of the Latter Day Saints. One bar, Rim Fire, stands on the periphery of the small town where only local derelicts or a few "Jack" Mormons habituate. The landscape is clean and flat like most of the Great Plains. It's also the place where Bruce Jenner ran past endless cornfields on abandoned roads daydreaming of the gold medal in Montreal. A good place to train...a minimum of distractions.

Nevertheless, Stew McDole loved the place and the game. In 1971, it was suggested by Region 8 Commissioner, Bruce Wilde, that McDole attend the new volleyball camps organized by Val Keller out in California. As one of five interested coaches, he attended the separate "camp directors' camp" which was also included. The next year he arranged to use his alma mater, Graceland College, for two camps. The first high school session had 33 attendees. Expanding numbers every summer led to a concept by 1977 whereby camp proceeds would establish three training centers throughout the Midwest: St. Louis, Kansas City and Des Moines. Linda Dollar was enlisted as the coach who would drive to each of the three sites one weekend per month and train an all-star team of high school girls from the region—and further away—from Tennessee to Wyoming, some 10 states contributed players who came to get better and compete in USVBA regional tournaments. Phil Shoemaker became McDole's assistant and the Mid-America Juniors program was born. There were other zealots: John Kessel, Matt McShane, Brian Funk, Connie Truelove, Mike English, Blase Czerniakowski and Jim Callender attained Graceland sainthood.

Quality coaching was sought out. Attending coaches such as: Doug Beal, Chris McLachlin, Laurel Brassey, Miles Pabst, Mick Haley, Mike Cram, Jim Smoot, Sue Gozansky, and Scott Luster were some of the many who brought their expertise. Thousands would pass through the four-day camps, bruised, beaten and tired, but better volleyball players at the end. A few nuggets were found: Lori Endicott, Caren Kemner, Cathy Noth, Jennifer McFadden, and Jan Bolin are among the notables.

By the mid-'80s, 12 training sites were established around the Midwest and 20 camps per summer were run, some outside Iowa. Four teams were being sent to the increasingly prestigious USVBA Junior Olympic National Championships and two passenger vans were bought; the quality coaching continued. But they almost didn't make it past the summer of 1980. "Ouch!" An economic crunch came down and significantly reduced the normal 1400 campers—yet McDole felt committed to the coaches and the coaches came. The summer's $300,000 budget came up short almost by a third. The fiddlers had to be paid and Patti McDole signed her house away, probably hoping that her husband would simply confine himself to teaching and coaching. Fold it up? Stew? Sorry. The next summer rebounded and growth thereafter continued. The McDole house was never lost

to the bank, and the man never to the game. Today, he serves as the Treasurer of the USA Volleyball.

Thanks to people like McDole and other like-minded enthusiasts, volleyball did undergo growth in the '80s in the group that would be most important—the youth. In 1979, a total number of 2,846 juniors were registered with the USVBA. By 1981, junior registrants reached almost 5,000 and by 1984 that number was almost 8,000. Something was being born here and the '84 Olympics would provide the vital nurturing for kids...stars to emulate.

"Two Bruins on the beach..."

"I've never seen anything like it," mused Al Scates. He was talking about his newest recruit. The kid who was already a AAA beach player and had just led Santa Barbara High School to a state championship without a loss. He had some help, John Hanley for one, and coach Rick Olmstead had imparted the lesson of hard work and responsibility in the youngster. It happened in the very first Bruin practice when the freshman was a shagger, dutifully carrying a double armful of balls to the bucket while two teams combatted in a controlled scrimmage: a ball was dug far off the court, impossible to chase down by even the most arduous defensive specialist on the court. As the ball was flying overhead, Karch abruptly dropped the load he was carrying and in a dead sprint, caught the errant ball and lifted it up in a dive. Coach and team watched in quiet wonder...this guy was different.

The team captain took note. Sinjin Smith quickly took the wunderkind under his senior wing, immediately making him his pepper partner—a tacit seal of approval of the indoor game. It was a duo of destiny on a team of destiny. That year the team went undefeated for the first time in history and according to Kiraly, it was Smith who made the play of the season in the back-and-forth finals against the other powerful team, USC. Smith's foot inadvertently landed over the centerline on a block and Dusty Dvorak landed precisely on it to break his ankle.

Pat Powers still smarts from the incident, "We were kicking their butts!" For his part, Smith remembers Powers in particular, "I've never seen a guy go over the block like Powers that night."

In the summer of 1979, Smith and Kiraly entered the five tournaments permitted by their schedule. They won all five including the completely dark finals of the World Championship against Dane Selznick and Andy Fishburn, 18-16. When the two whiz kids weren't there on the sand, it was open slather. Menges and Gage, Fishburn and Selznick—not the ageless Gene but his quick-armed son—would both win their share and the same pattern continued into the next year. In 1980, Kiraly-Smith won six out of ten Opens. No question in anyone's mind that this was the team to be reckoned with—and at their young age—the brightest future of any pair that ever jumped out of the sand. But the sport was much more complex now. There was increasingly more money on the beach and there was promise of glory in the encroaching Olympics. A choice would soon be inevitable.

After the summer of 1979, Smith, Dvorak, Powers and Hovland were asked to come to Dayton to increase the chances of a final Olympic qualification tournament in Bulgaria in January, 1980. The couple of months there sufficed to create a rift between these new Californians and the "Dayton guys." There were some interesting living situations as well. The most piquant was the case of Tim Hovland: "It was horrible, but we were so young we didn't know any better. Here I was living with two Mormon guys...me! No car. Freezing at 7:30 in the morning, hitchhiking ten miles to get into town to practice. Someone would pick us up, drop us off on a freeway ramp, and we'd run to the gym."

After asking players to suffer in the Midwestern city, the classic dilemma American National Teams had always faced, and which continues until today, surfaced. What to do with players who are better—ones who can get you to the Olympics or even win gold medals—than the existing players who have gutted it out

for months or years? There is no easy solution, to be certain. Plus, this new group contained a couple paragons of those California players who had historically clashed with the USVBA mindset. Smith was one: "It was the worst time in my life. I don't think Beal could handle different personalities, especially West coast ones. I had too good of a time on the court and he didn't like that." With most of the other Californians, the seeds of conflict were immediately sown, particularly with Doug Beal.

"We gotta get outa this place..." (Eric Burdon)

By 1979, Beal agonized over the question; he finally convinced the USVBA that perhaps he could provide some badly needed court leadership as a player and leave the coaching duties to Jim Coleman. "According to many sources, things were getting worse than better," recalls Beal. The plan was accepted but it was an answer which fell far short of the mark. The vets were left to compete in the NORCECAs. Unquestionably, the nadir of American Men's volleyball—they finished seventh—losing to, amongst many, the Dominican Republic.

The only glint of hope came from the fresh troops arriving from California. Most were still in college: Dvorak, Hovland, Powers, Salmons and Smith gave up the better part of a Mediterranean summer for the humidity and morning gnats of Dayton—to play for the USA in the Pan-American Games. The 19-year old Kiraly, a freshman at UCLA, tried out for the team as well. He was cut from the team...the only time in his life he would ever have that experience. Alternatively, Jim Coleman would share the dubious distinction as the coach who did it. "I thought I had a great tryout; they cut me and Brian Ehlers,who was a great player." Pat Powers has another memory, "I remember Karch crying after he was cut." The rest of the boys of summer played well but not well enough for a good finish.

The bolstered USA team took off for China and Japan in late 1979 before landing in Bulgaria. Still almost all college players, they played well but couldn't pull the team out of the sinkhole it had helplessly fallen into. In January, the Olympic Qualification Tournament was held in Bulgaria. The small Soviet satellite itself would have had a better chance of invading and defeating the United States than their respective National Volleyball teams obversely achieving the same goal.

The year 1980 was relatively uneventful, thankfully for Beal and the humiliated team. However, Beal and the USVBA made a hard realization—things weren't looking good. Sometime during this darkest hour of men's volleyball, the Board of Directors had a moment of enlightenment. The powers that be realized that they better go to where the action was and the talent: California. The decision would make sense on another level. The Olympics were coming to Los Angeles.

"The final paint brush..."

It was a tie-breaker to six points. The fifth game was short but volleyball like this had never been played in the United States. In the 1979 All-Star Game in San Jose, the Eastern team had the slight edge when Hilary Johnson brought a ball up, and Gosciniak put it up to his compatriot Ed Skorek. The defense dug in, getting the block up around ten feet in hope of just deflecting the bomb everyone knew was coming. But no, the spidery limbed Skorek with bald pate and big grin, took the big swing but, like no one else in the world, purposefully hit only the bottom part of the ball with his fingertips. The ball fluttered over the block and dropped in mid-court for the final point and an Eastern All-Star victory: the "paint brush." Eddie laughed widely, somehow knowing how mere mortals must feel in the face of an invincible shot—no matter how good you are or how well prepared.

How strange that while the Men's National Team was still stuck in its Dark Ages, the IVA in its funny format was attracting world-renown foreign players. With salaries reaching $25,000 for a four-month season, the competition was a serious affair and turning Americans in the league into very good players. Besides the former USA Team players, previous college stars like Jeff Reddan, Jay Hanseth, Larry Vocke, Larry Benecke Gary Sato, Reede Reynolds, and Bernie Hite were improving yearly. Tucson's Scott English at 6'7" in four years had become a phenomenal middle hitter, and he blocked and served as well as any player in the league. This was impressive considering some of the other imports: All-World hitter Luis Eymard and Brazilian National Team stars, Fernando d'Avila, Lino de Melo Gama, and Bebeto DeFreitas (1984 Brazilian Olympic Coach), Canadians Peter Stefaniuk, Greg Russell and the magnificent jumper and player, Garth Pischke, Top Mexican players: Valdemar Valdez, Meliton Jimenez, Jose Luis Garcia, and Pischke's jumping nemesis, 6'4" Martin Castillo. Several single season appearances were made by other highly reputed Poles, Yugoslavs and Brazilians.

Foreign women made an impact as well. Most notable were the two Peruvian backcourt sensations, Olympians Meche Gonzalez and Irma Cordero who would stand in against men who hit as hard as anybody. "The six-pack rule" was initiated the first year when an enlightened announcer of one of the teams declared a free six-pack to any guy whose spike took off the face of an opponent. Not surprisingly, it was the women who got "six-packed" the most and out of self-preservation the ladies sent crowds into a frenzy when a slugger like Skorek, D'Avila, Pischke and Garcia were either dug by one of them or lost a limb. The female salaries increased with each season as well and so did the play of the American women. Linda Fernandez and Rosie Wegrich performed almost flawless passing and defense.

The league was looking stronger than ever, personnel-wise, in 1980. Laurel Brassey had signed to play in Salt Lake City. A young rookie, Mike Dodd, signed on with San Jose. The financial footing was less solid. The league had been assumed and operated by Jim Bartlett's group since 1977 and although bills were paid on time, the constant shoring up of weak franchises had the league office running in the red. Operating both Volleyball Magazine and the IVA proved too costly; the magazine was folded in 1979. The same year, the league paradoxically received national publicity as well as a damaging blow when police sporting printed "Operation Spike" T-shirts poured out of the seats of Denver Auditorium and descended on the scorer's table at half-time. As local television news cameras were rolling they deftly handcuffed the owners of the team and whisked them off to jail. Players on the Denver Comets were understandably dispirited...they had always been paid on time. As the young, long-haired owners of the team in their 20s were always afloat in cash with loads of free time, players had wondered but didn't ask too many questions. The press, some national, soon explained it. The team had been financed from the proceeds of bales of marijuana coming from Florida.

No one was shocked when Denver was soon scrambling for a white knight. As the '80 season began, Albuquerque and San Jose were already awash in red ink. Almost half way into the season, the sole hope to rescue the league rested with Don Sammis, owner of the Salt Lake City franchise. Too young a man to become a martyr, Sammis opted to instead put his money behind the USA Men's National Team in San Diego where he was a real estate developer. On a hot night in Tucson, the old West End rowdies would have their last chance to cheer. The league was already in shambles; Salt Lake City flew into town at the last minute with six players and without a setter. Laurel Brassey set and player-coach Shewman played the back row. It was a full-house and a sad night. Owner Doug Clark and the city which had so warmly embraced the poor foundling, had to watch the league and its own team go down in an inglorious farewell, 3-1. Like a fallen Saguaro cactus, pro volleyball was cut down and gone— leaving only a hot Sonoran wind to silently blow through its seared, spiny skeleton, the chants of the crowd and memories already whistling away like spirits in the desert.

"Politics and sport..."

In Colorado Springs, a myth was being built. The USA Women's Team kept climbing the celestial ladder to the 1980 Moscow Olympics. Beyond their impressive play, they were making a name for themselves and for American volleyball. Finally, a team wearing the red, white and blue commanded respect from opponents everywhere they went. They were sought out by fans as well—particularly the tall Flo Hyman was mobbed in countries around the world. "A big girl with a big personality," remembers Laurel Brassey. Yet, to go to Moscow, they had to qualify in the NORCECAs. They still hadn't beaten the physical marvels of Cuba with Mercedes Perez, the 5'6" dynamo who could hang from a basketball rim with ease—both hands. Fortune smiled on them when the Cubans earlier qualified for Moscow at the World Championships in 1978. Predictably, the favored Cuban women also won the '79 NORCECAs leaving the Olympic berth to the next highest finisher, probably Canada or the USA.

It was no hayride but the first part of the dream came true in a harrowlingly close encounter with the Mexicans. Down 2-1 to Mexico, they were perilously close to elimination when the Mexican ladies sped off to a 11-7 lead in the fourth game. "That's when Patti Dowdell decided to take over. She was unbelievable!" recalls Sue Woodstra. The tall co-captain showed the way that game and the next as the USA snatched back a victory. Their confidence regained, next came a 3-0 blanking of the Canadians—they were in. For the first time in 12 years, an American volleyball team would compete in the Olympics...and more, be expected to win a medal!

A few scant months before the Moscow Games, the USA Women were touring with East Germany, the team that would eventually win the silver medal in Moscow. The Americans were consistently beating their guests and had just arrived from the airport at their San Antonio hotel when they heard the news on the radio: President Carter had decided to boycott the Olympics in protest of the Soviet invasion of Afghanistan. Decidedly an improvement over such foreign policy maneuvers as the appointment of his brother, Billy Carter, to negotiate peace agreements with Colonel Moammar Khadaffi of Libya; still, the strategy caused immediate worldwide controversy as well as here. For the athletes, it broke hearts.

Shock, disillusionment, then bitterness befell the women. Some of them had worked five hard years...and then this. With the single-minded vision they had bought into the program, they had sweated and cried and made enough money to survive until they were counted amongst the top four teams in the world. It had finally been done...it wasn't pretty...but *that* was the beauty of it. And they had done it largely by themselves, under the determination of a couple of stern-minded men and a generous wildcatter. Instantly, it was gone with a political gambit. And a lot of tears.

USC celebrates. The Trojan women were 37-1 in 1976, 38-0 in 1977—the only undefeated women's collegiate volleyball history. (Courtesy of USC)

Luiz Eymard, world-class Brazilian of Santa Barbara Spikers, blows by the Tucson Sky block, 1977.

*Kiraly-Kiraly. First lesson at six, first tourna-
ment at 11, first trophy at 15. Third place,
Muscle Beach B, 1976.*

Green to Hyman...a lethal combination. (Courtesy of USA Volleyball)

Ladies lead the way. Debbie Green sets the pace on the road to 1980 Moscow Olympics.

Dayton, 1979. "Stop by for a tryout..." Top (left to right): Klostermann (Asst. Coach), McFarland, Berzins, Corbelli, Richards, Wilson, Richards, Gregory, Olbright, Coleman (Coach). Bottom: Waldie, Sunderland, Beal, Duwelius, Carpenter, Bryant, Battalia, Shaw, McLean, Sorenson.

Doug Beal exchanging gifts with Greg Russell of Canada. USA Men's coach-player- administrator, Beal was in charge through the dark days of Dayton.

Help is coming! Dusty Dvorak sharpens his setting skills at USC in 1978 before joining the USA Men's Team. (Courtesy of Volleyball Magazine)

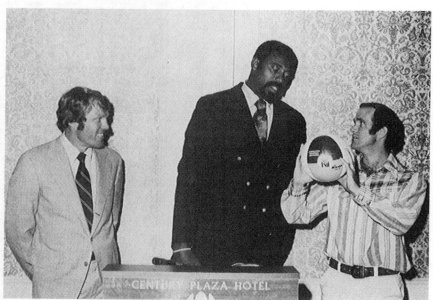

Orange County Stars. A new franchise in 1977, owner David Whiting, league president Wilt Chamberlain and player-coach Dodge Parker. (Courtesy of Volleyball Magazine)

Orange County it is! After '77 finals, a happy team: (left to right) Dodge Parker, Bob Stafford, Jon Roberts, Miles Pabst, Hilary Johnson, Robin Irvin.

Ed Skorek, captain of the '76 Polish gold medalist Olympic team. The El Paso star slices the line against Dave Schakel.

Paul Sunderland decoys for setter Mike Cram—two early USA Team members in '76 Nationals action. (Courtesy of Bud Fields)

Chris Marlowe. Beach or indoors, Marlowe excelled...with flair. (Courtesy of Dave Heiser)

Hooper and OB. Colorful, dominant team of the late '70s. Steve O'Bradovich, the referee's ulti-mate nightmare, questions another one. (Courtesy of Doug Avery)

Gary Hooper tries it inside against a young Sinjin Smith. (Courtesy of Doug Avery)

Jim Menges. The top player bridging the amateur '70s and the money game of the '80s.

The first one for Marv Dunphy. Pepperdine wins the NCAAs in 1978. (Courtesy of Volleyball Magazine)

Running down another one. Nina Matthies took her muscled game to pioneer the WPVA. (Photo by Robbie Hutas)

Reede Reynolds connects with Brazilian set-ter Bebeto DeFreitas. Santa Barbara beats Tucson for the '78 IVA championship. (Cour-tesy of Volleyball Magazine)

A human marvel: 6'7", a 7'4" college high jumper, former NBA forward. In four short years, Scott English became arguably the best male American player, leading Tucson in re-venge to the '79 IVA title.

Chapter 15
1981-1984

"Days of Balboa..."

The Seven Cities of Cibola... Eldorado... Where was it? The river of gold, wide like a fat serpent winding back into granite mountains, blinded the avaricious eyes of those who peered too long. Musket followed cross and crown, sailing out of Sevilla down the Guadquilivir River in search of man's holiest grail—wealth. If it wasn't found, there was a noble consolation: Christian converts who translated into human labor. The conquistadors came to the New World and plundered their earthly treasures quickly. The search for souls, and bodies, in the new land required much more time.

Junipero Serra founded one of his many missions on one of the most heavenly spots on earth: San Diego. Presidio Hill overlooked the wondrous bays, the gentle hills which folded back into mesquite-covered mountains. In 1915, the city fathers hosted the Panama International Exhibition and looked not surprisingly back to their Old World conquerors for a motif. Further back to the Alhambra, the Alcazar. Dusky Moors who had invaded the sun-scorched Iberia and established cool gardens in irrigated courtyards of elegant design, preserving the admired tradition of Islamic mathematics and science. The result was one of the most beautiful parks in the world: Balboa Park.

One of the many remaining buildings of Balboa Park was referred to as the Federal Building; its dark, cavernous expanse with molasses-brown spring loaded floors had served the community as a basketball, volleyball and badminton center for decades. There in the spring of 1981, Doug Beal like Hernando Cortez looked over at his first lieutenant, Bill Neville, who nodded smugly at the exotic prizes of the New World. "I was almost giddy with the talent out there," recalls Beal when thinking about that first tryout.

Dusty Dvorak was setting warmup lines. Pat Powers at 6'5" jumped some three feet off the ground, coiled his notorious hand and bounced balls as high as anyone in the world. The blond Craig Buck, three inches taller, cut 31 sets inside not the ten, not the five, but the three foot line! Randy Stoklos looked like he could do anything, Sinjin Smith the same in a smaller version, Mike Dodd a fluid element who appeared a coach's delight...big and smart; and the most irrepressible was the remarkably fast, volcanic 6'5" Tim Hovland—a magnetic field, stand next to him and your hair curled. Finally like an ace in the hole, there was that kid from UCLA who would join them after school was out: Karch Kiraly. In fact, he too was in the warmup lines, but only for the weekend—the icing to come on this delectable cake.

There was even more talent! "But who cared?" thought the stoical coaches. Come what may, everyone knew that the Games were only three years away...the USA would be playing...families, friends and hods of beautiful girls would be in the stands. The team would be living in San Diego. Could things be better?

A quick reflection upon the days in Dayton declaimed an emphatic "no!"

For 90 years, the sport had limped along. Astoundingly, the USA Women had finally achieved worldwide respectability through a Herculean effort, but the USA Men had degraded to a doormat abroad...a source of derisive joy for cynics at home. Maybe we deserved this unimaginable stroke of luck! A new crew of male athletes sent from the gods and a guaranteed berth in the Olympics...in the US...in LA! In the understated words of executive director Al Monaco: "The Los Angeles Olympics changed everything..."

"Smaller might be better..."

The team was tested by fire within a month when they toured with the Brazilians; they won the series 5-4. Not bad. Their test by water was the NORCECAs in Mexico City; the new group dropped the fifth game to arch-rival Cuba, 15-13. Pained but hopeful, the team prepared for the Canada Cup in November where they beat Brazil to face the dreaded Cubans in the finals. In recent years, the notion reigned among American National Team coaches that since the best teams in the world were putting huge Slavs and Cossacks out on the court, what was obviously called for was size. Could they pass, could they play defense, could they play ball control and could they compete? "Well...maybe not now, but they can learn," was the response. On the USA Men's Team, too many tall guys rarely learned...or perhaps they just couldn't.

The same problems were recurring against the high-octane Cubans when Beal strained his neck to look down the bench where two of the shorter players, Aldis Berzins and Sinjin Smith were swearing under their breath as a ball almost landed on the foot of one of the taller starters. That was followed by the all-too-frequent delayed dinosaur response, a grimace and shaking of the head: "Dang, I shoulda had that!" In went the two short-stuffs, and soon balls were popping up and the badly needed passes off the serve were arriving precisely in Dvorak's waiting hands. The USA turned it around and beat the highly regarded Cubans, 3-1. Ball control was the key, and that remained in Beal's head.

Back in San Diego, a three-year routine leading up to Los Angeles began. At eight o'clock in the morning, practice began in the cold, dark Federal Building. It didn't take long to heat up. "There were 16 guys who could probably start at that time. Practice was intense," understates Craig Buck. Kiraly added, "What we needed was a lot of hard work and discipline...and we got it." Not that they got paid for it. "Half a dozen guys were sleeping on the floor of friends' apartments. A few guys took part-time jobs in banks. The rest of us just lived poor and played. I think we got a little money every few months...not much," remembers Buck. Kiraly adds, "They promised us a couple hundred bucks a month...I don't think I ever saw a dime of it. But my goal was to go to the Olympics at all costs."

For the coaching staff, it was all new and strange: all that ability to work with, and more importantly, guys boiling over to compete. An important training concept was soon born; Beal and Neville decided that if these animals were going to go for each other's jugulars regardless, "then let 'em go but raise the stakes!" "We decided to do a lot of team-oriented, highly competitive drills—to create a very competitive situation over a long period of time," according to Beal.

Many iterations of the idea evolved and as was the wont of Neville, a notorious nicknamer, a catchy name was attached to each. So it was no surprise when the "wash drill" in time surfaced as a new buzz word in American volleyball circles. It was based on a simple concept: two teams in a type of controlled scrimmage; a sideout must be followed by a point scored in a free ball opportunity. Thus, one defensive and one offensive success in a row counted for a single point, if not, the play was a "wash"— start over. Perhaps a game to three points was the goal. The fierceness between the two teams for the precious points might take an hour before one achieved the goal—center blockers who had to jump in the middle everytime suffered particularly. Pat Powers gets a gleam in his eye when he remembers, "It just got mean. A guy would make a mistake and five guys would scream at him. The great thing was that when practice ended, it was forgotten." The drill would eventually lead to a competitive advantage over everyone else in the world. Craig Buck believes that it did: "There was a difference when we got a free ball or dug a ball in a game. Everyone elevated. It could take 40 minutes of killing yourself to get one point to get out of a practice drill and some rest...now this was absolute pleasure. We usually scored."

Done around noon, a few players showered and went to part-time bank jobs found for them by Sammis and his contacts. Four others routinely headed for South Mission Beach: Kiraly, Smith, Hovland and Dodd. Kiraly humorously recalled an incident which illustrated the two separate cultures on the team. At one point, he and Dodd had decided to drag along their 15-pound weight belts down to the beach to try and even the games out with the locals. They wore the belts in the sand. One afternoon, Waldie and Berzins decided to come down and see what the beach game was all about. "We beat them 15-0," Kiraly laughs. "I never let them forget it either." For the easy-going Berzins, it rolled off his back like so many grains of sand. Kiraly remembers his passing partner from Ohio State amusing the beachies with his comments: "I hate the beach. Everything gets sand in it! It gets in your sandwiches—through plastic baggies—through anything. In your socks..." In a group of ego-driven, high-spirited young men, the quiet kid with a dry wit was a needed buffer. "We called him the 'sponge', recalls Neville. "He could take it, and give it out too."

Sinjin Smith remembers driving down to the Mission Beach Open with Karch Kiraly on Saturday after a four-hour workout in Balboa Park. Arriving about noon, they persuaded the tournament director, George Stepanof, to let them in—with an automatic loss. No big deal; they blew through the losers bracket and finals without breaking a sweat. The oldest existing Open beach tournament trophy which dates from 1949 was awarded to them by the late Ed Teagle, a superb athlete and congenial man who won the tournament its inaugural year.

The uneasy social rift that had started between the players in Dayton continued out on the coast as well. "Beal hated that we had a closeknit group of guys that didn't include the whole team...but it couldn't include the whole team. A few were married, some of the guys from back East were just different from us. We were single, young and having a great time playing volleyball and seeing the world." says Kiraly. Rod Wilde who grew up in Iowa, later joined the team, and remembers, "Yeah, they had this Eastie thing. Like if someone screwed up, that was an Eastie play. We just lived with it." After the Dayton experience, Beal had learned his own limitations in intra-player relationships: "It never worked for me to get close to players. I always surrounded myself with a coach who did that role." In this case, it was Bill Neville.

The first year of practice ended well. Although Stoklos had quit during the first tour in 1981— he was "maybe our most promising player," according to Beal—they had picked up another player with promise: Karch Kiraly. The year 1982 started well but soon turned sour. It began with Smith. Embarking on a modeling career with his brother, Andrew, the Smiths were being called by GQ and Esquire to shoot big-time photos. One shooting could make him more money than six months at the so-called "jobs program" a few of the players took. Smith had the perpetual complaint as most of the others, "I was out of money." Beal let him go with many admonitions. Admittedly the relationship had started deteriorating the moment Smith arrived at Dayton in 1979—neither liked the other from the get-go, but it had become progressively worse. Smith arranged to keep in contact with the Beal through his mother. Apparently wires were crossed in communication. When the team took off for a tour in Canada, Beal received a late-night phone call from the photogenic star asking what the hell the team was doing in Canada. "We're playing in an international tournament, Sinjin!" One claimed ignorance, the other claimed irresponsibility. The coach had final say and Smith was gone from the team; however, he soon found solace in a tremendous beach partner in Randy Stoklos.

The next controversy centered on the MVP of the Canadian Cup, the first American who ever banged away at will from the backcourt, the abundantly gifted Tim Hovland. Southern California High School Athlete of the Year in 1977, he could do anything: quarterback, play forward or guard, pitch...instead he opted for a volleyball scholarship at USC. After his sterling display in the '81 Canadian Cup, "The Hov" asked for money to live on: "I had about $100 in my checking account. I was told to get a loan from my parents. No...sorry." Beal tells the story differently; he contends that Hovland had been found a part-time job in a bank. Regardless, for Hovland, taking loan applications or working as a teller wasn't the solution. A better idea was to permit him to finish his degree at USC, staying in shape and joining the team when time permitted.

The situation was not ideal but feasible. Beal could live with the other two lost players, Stoklos and Smith, but this guy was crucial. During the spring, physical tests were performed. Hovland, the fiercest of competitors, would normally win any contest, but during these competitions he'd win a mile for time and immediately be throwing up on the side of the track. He lived hard and he played hard was a cliche for Hovland. A college teammate, Pat Powers, reflected about the flamboyant badboy, "Back then, I don't think volleyball was big enough for Hovland. Today it would be."

Hovland's behavior became intolerable; Beal cut him, but not without regret. "All the way up to '84 I had second thoughts about Hovland. I do know that if he would have stayed, he would have been on the court in '84—I don't know in what position but he would have been there." Also revealing are Beal's comments about the ferocity of intrasquad scrimmages which came

to mark the team. "Everyone seemed to give Kiraly the credit for the verbal stuff which erupted in the competition. But with Kiraly, it came later. I give Hovland the credit for starting it." The coach distinctly remembers a Japanese film crew coming in to film a USA workout when they were visiting there. "They immediately turned the cameras on Hovland. He'd been a football player and he liked confronting in competition. And he liked to be confronted too. I didn't have a problem with his practice or match play; he just refused to conform to the rules off the court." Kiraly also holds Hovland in a special place: "Nobody has ever competed as hard as Tim Hovland. In any game...in any venue." Despite his great abilities and his MVP performance, the '81 Canada Cup was the last time Hovland ever wore a USA jersey.

One other player was released after that tournament: Pat Powers. Chided for immaturity and lack of discipline, he was suspended for a year. The big hitter didn't take lightly to the decision. Since he hadn't been paid for the months of training in San Diego, he took the team to small claims court to get his back pay—and won! However, it was a Pyrrhic victory. After a year's suspension, he was given another chance to don a USA jersey... to get back on the team, he had to forfeit the payment. He accepted. Good thing for American volleyball.

In the summer, Hovland teamed with Dodd to form one half of the first great rivalry of pro beach volleyball. The other half was comprised of the other two USA Team delinquents: Sinjin Smith and Randy Stoklos. The summer ended and the restless Hovland boarded the plane for Torino, Italy, an immediate star who wowed fans and players alike in the top professional indoor league in the world. The Hov lit up the court...and the discos as well.

The air was cleared at last, or at least cleaned up for awhile, thought Beal; now get back to work. He and his staff were back on the job with renewed intensity when all of a sudden Beal got wind of a plot to rid him of his job. Who was behind the seditious scheme? Some parents of players—notably UCLA players. Two principal individuals were Laz Kiraly and Ron Salmons; letters of complaint were being written to USVBA president, Bob Lindsay, asking for serious action. As it turned out, it was more than a crank's fantasy. Even a head coach was approached by the dissenters to fill in for the soon-to-be-beheaded Beal. No surprise that it was UCLA's own Al Scates. For the Midwesterners at the team's helm, Dayton in a mid-winter freeze didn't seem as bad as this environment. Bill Neville remembers, "We'd go home at night, wondering if we would have our jobs the next morning." Beal and Neville prevailed. Understandably, the affair did little to palliate the already uneasy trust between the Eastern coaches and Western players of the team.

The summer of '82 provided little time to the players for beach tournaments since the team took an extended trip to Korea, China and Japan. Not that it mattered. Beal laid down the law; there would be no more beach. "I think it probably made me a better indoor player...but I sure could have used money from a few of the tournaments," Kiraly commented. The USA Team's play appeared to be catching up with its raw talent. New tryouts were held while at the same time amateur status was given back to former IVA players. The decision was too late for Mike Dodd, who after spending the preceding year in limbo waiting for his renewed amateur status, decided to join Hovland on the beach and hardcourts of Italy where the money was becoming very alluring. But ex-pros Rod Wilde, Jon Roberts, Jay Hanseth, Reede Reynolds and Larry Benecke jumped on the Olympic wagon headed for Los Angeles. The team was now ranked within the top six of the world in Beal's opinion, and it's focus was on the World Championships in Argentina.

In a domestic tour with Italy, the good cop/bad cop routine of the coaching staff was vividly impressed on the team. Kiraly distinctly remembers the Italians getting out of control in warm-ups. Finally one stray ball wrapped around the face of Reede Reynolds; as soon as

his vision returned, Reynolds retaliated with a direct hit on one of the Italians. Beal angrily summoned Reynolds and the entire team over to the bench. "Don't you *ever* hit at another team! I don't care what they do to you." Beal's warning came only seconds after Neville's rousing praise of Reynolds blast into the Italian camp. "We'd get conflicting signals like this. We got along with Neville well...I think he was kind of a foil for Beal," remembers Kiraly. They handled the essential, however; they beat Italy and flew down to Argentina.

The World Championships were "the single most frustrating event I've ever been associated with," recalls the head coach. Still unable to shake the specter of poor seeding, the enduring legacy of 1970, the Americans found themselves in a tough pool. With the Soviets—the best team in the world and some claimed the best of all-time—and Bulgaria, always a tough opponent of ample height and muscle. So, the USA had to beat Bulgaria.

It was looking good. They were leading 12-5 in the fifth game until they got caught in a cross-fire and couldn't get out. It began at that point when a free ball was given to the Americans; a right X play was called for and it worked—no blocker was up. Setting one of the biggest American spikers, the sight of no hands must have been too much for him as he blasted the ball not only out, but into the stands. The Bulgarians crawled back and when a dink dropped over the block to the same big blocker at 14-13, the Americans had a chance to get out of the nightmare. This time, he inexplicably spread his joined arms and let the ball drop untouched to the floor. The team was dismantled and soon lost, 16-14.

So close, but the team was still too green. Kiraly, for all his talent at 21 still needed some maturing...and the offense, it was now painfully apparent, required more flexibility. Dvorak threw set after set outside to be rejected by the two huge Bulgarians or else touched, dug and converted to points. To see Kiraly in trouble sent the rest of the team all atwitter. Passes began to be sprayed. As the precious points ticked away, Beal went to the bench...a partial bench. Marc Waldie, a sometime starter, certainly could have contributed his excellent passing skills to relieve that problem but he had gone down on a slippery practice floor the day before and severely sprained his ankle—he was not even in uniform.

Substitutions, timeouts, prayers...nothing could prevent the boat's slow sinking. As the hull slipped beneath the placid, chilly water, a wave of disgust and disappointment quickly rose and swept over the coaching staff. Not unexpectedly, they lost to the Soviet Union as well, 3-0 (15-11, 15-12, 16-14). Tolerable. More than tolerable, the champions did not lose *a game* that tournament, and the Yanks, in fact, scored more total points than any team against them.

Over the next three days in a hotel room, Beal, Neville, Crabb, and McGown analyzed and agonized. They knew big changes were imperative. An immediate enlightenment was to take Kiraly out of setting two positions. Why not have one of the best passers in the world performing only that duty? Then there was another quiet kid, an astronomy major, who passed and played defense on the same level as Kiraly. When was the last time either one of them had missed a pass? No one could remember. So let Kiraly and Aldis Berzins try and take as many serves as they could between them. This could utilize the great speed and lateral jumping of Kiraly as well—when he got locked into the left side against Bulgaria, it was the offensive system which was at fault, not the 6'2" spiker— there simply were no outlets. Find some, they determined. Finally, full control of the offense was given to the smart and capable Dusty Dvorak who had been chafing at the fact of not having it. He had wanted to set a 5-1 and be in command; now he got it. Many other changes would soon follow—systems and personnel— but the other important decision made in Argentina was to somehow get this fractious team into one cohesive whole. A novel solution would appear but not until months away.

Bitter as the preliminary losses were—particularly to Bulgaria—a good augury ascended from the ashes of disaster. A show of character. The USA rolled through every remaining match, 3-0, except for one. They finished in spot 13, as high as their secondary round would permit. And one of the Americans would be selected to the All-Tournament Team amongst the countries of the final pool battling for places between 13-24. Not the first time that Karch Kiraly would demonstrate an uncanny ability to rebound after an altogether rare, sub-par performance.

"Workers unite!..."

In the 1982 World Championship at the end of the summer, a new scenario was taking shape which like an old film classic, would in time get played over and over, summer after summer. There might be some color enhancement by a few newcomers, a captivating interlude if Karch Kiraly could sneak away from the gym, but the movie was pretty much the same: Smith-Stoklos versus Hovland-Dodd. The only change in the story was the ending. Even Jimmy the Greek would have found a challenge in picking the odds and winners on any given weekend.

Randy Stoklos had been in the eye of every aficionado, top player, and most of the girls since 1981 when he won his first tournament with Jim Menges, the Manhattan Open and the $5,000 first-place prize. When the 6'4" beefcake paired up with Andy Fishburn, pundits proclaimed this the greatest thing since Lang and Von Hagen, and even better. What's good on paper is not necessarily good on sand, and early in 1982, the duo's acclaim was already vanished, as quickly as the green flash of a Sorrento sunset. At the same time, Sinjin Smith was not in sync with his partner Mark Eller. In June of 1992, Smith and Stoklas combined to win their first Open in Santa Barbara. They were off and running on a destined path to meet up with another team that was only a year old. The Manhattan Open of '82 is compared to the great finish of 1968. In the finals, Tim Hovland remembers being down 8-0 in the first game before scratching back to win 11-9. Second game down 7-0, 12-10 steal. Now the sudden death game to 15. But it was getting dark. Totally dark when Smith served match point at 14-13—underhand. Just get it in and it was a point. "No way Dodd and I could see it—we had no choice but to let it drop. Out!" The Hov stood back and looped two straight rainbows over the net. The sound of the plopping balls were followed by the groans of the benighted Smith and Stoklos. Today Hovland grins with the memory, "They called their last timeout. So I kinda sang out: 'Oh Sinjin, you're gonna lose...'" Hovland dropped in the third lob which landed untouched.

Bitter, bitter is defeat. Yet, how sweet was the nectar of revenge a month later at the World Championships when in a similar shoot-out just as close, Smith and Stoklos walked away chortling after the last point. "Oh Hov!..."

Another summer of change. The court of the Medicis at Sorrento had aged and lost vital contact with the new changes in the game, namely money. The last of the Sorrento kings, Jim Menges, won a few tournaments but his shoulder had simply been ground away from too many years on the sand—"300 days a year, nine in the morning until sunset." His dukes and nobles had either been overthrown or given up in fear their Parisian apartments and taken to their country estates to live out their lives in unkempt castles with memories of the beach fading with passing summers. "My old Sorrento crowd was gone now, all my friends. We used to play in the mornings; the new guys like Sinjin, Karch, Stoklos and Selznick played in the afternoons. They were playing at State Beach now," said Menges. Ah, the winds of change. The Sorrento Grill was boarded up; its yellowed photos stripped from the walls. The Sorrento wall was now a palimpsest: the ancient words like Von Muscle and Gazelle were lost under new graffiti spray-painted over hieroglyphs gone forever. Leaving only invisible sprites, souls of the old masters sitting sadly around the courts, nodding in silent approval at the movement of youth over the sand...what was once theirs but never again.

By 1980, the promotional efforts of Event Concepts had taken seed. The number of pro tournaments had grown to seven while the major national sponsor was Jose Cuervo Tequila. In 1981, Miller Brewing Company saw that the sexy image of the beach volleyball lifestyle could also sell beer, and bumped the prize money of some tournaments to $20,000. By 1983, the tour had gone national: 13 sites including Florida, New York and Colorado and the total prize money reached almost $200,000.

And to add a little spice to the affair, a beauty contest was held at each site. Miss Cuervo was selected to the howling delight of young men in the audience; the tournament shut down and *somehow* the promoters cajoled four players to sometimes help judge. Imagine Smith, Stoklas, Dodd and the Hov volunteering! Somebody had to do it...

Minor irritations arose: the scoring system and then the new ball became points of contention. Event Concepts was trying to raise more money, please sponsors and expand the already interested ESPN television coverage of beach volleyball—changes were asked, some say demanded, of the players to go along. For example, television programmers didn't have time for this sideout business which could make a game endure fifteen minutes...or 75. To get the time element somehow manageable, Event Concepts announced the unpopular "rally-point" scoring system: a point was scored after every play, and matches in the winners were to 35 points, 25 points in the losers. Next, players were serving and passing the heavy, "Mikasa Suede Spike" volleyball. Mikasa obviously put up money for the rights but what wasn't foreseen was the weight it would take on when it got wet with sweat and sand clung to its hide. Players screamed in protest, most audibly Menges, who believed it was this bowling ball which ended his career prematurely. The players wanted the old, trusty Spalding Top-Flite 18 and, while they were in the feisty mood, a peek at the books of Event Concepts as well!

The first labor dispute was set in train and predictably the leading players were involved: Smith, Hovland, Dodd, Kiraly, Selznick, Stoklos, Hanseth, Fishburn and Jon Stevenson marshalled the group. In July, 1983, the AVP (Association of Volleyball Professionals) was formed after several meetings to protect the interests of the players. The organization was mostly academic, until the following year at the World Championships in Redondo Beach. The relationship had been deteriorating for a year; Leonard Armato, a pro sports attorney who had played beach volleyball and was a friend of the first AVP president Kevin Cleary, agreed to represent the organization. Specifically they wanted more prize money, access to financial records,and a greater say in such areas as licensing and merchandising. "Most of the guys were in their early 20s. I was 31 and Fishburn, 28. They had no business experience. The meetings were like a bunch of junior high kids throwing out one-liners," recalls Jay Hanseth.

Finally, a type of manifesto was fashioned. More prize money, more representation—if not, strike! "What we found out the week before was that a demand was also made that the AVP have complete autonomy to deal directly with the sponsors—get control, then contract Group Dynamics to run the tournaments. I knew Wilk and Masuoka; I thought they had done a good job. Sure, I was all for more money but I wasn't confident these players were more capable," adds Hanseth. Yet, the AVP was set to strike at the World Championships in Redondo Beach. Neither side budged.

Some of the players even arrived with picket signs Saturday morning, expecting the worst. They promptly received a chance to use them. Two top players, Fishburn and Hanseth, had decided to break ranks and play. "I called Armato to tell him the night before," recalls Hanseth. In the parking lot, the two received the treatment of traitors. While Fishburn was trying to explain their position, Sinjin Smith approached and held up an opened newspaper in his face as a barrier. The two shrugged and

walked off to play. The word had gotten out to the AAA players in the beach community of the impending strike and there were plenty who now entered the tournament with an unusual chance to make some good money and a reputation. Even Vogie showed up! The weather, like the mood, turned bad and threatening clouds began to sprinkle. A silver bolt flashed, a clap of thunder; Vogie turned to the crowd: "They said it would be a dark day in hell when I won a tournament again. This is my kinda weather!"

For the others, it was less cheery. Paying a heavy social price, the participating players were called "scabs by association" by the AVP players. Meanwhile, the animated discussions between AVP players and their attorney, Events Concepts and Jose Cuervo officials began to ratchet up as the morning bell approached. Finally, screaming insults were exchanged and reportedly a few obscenities were even uttered, but nothing was settled. Fishburn and Hanseth easily went home with the purse...and put a double lock on their doors.

"Beauty and the beach..."

Nina Matthies, formerly Grouwinkel, was a volleyball junkie as a teenager. Growing up in Manhattan Beach, she played down at the Manhattan Pier where Charley Shakley lowered the net and gave coaching hints from time to time. A cute girl in a cute group. But Nina was even crazier for the game than her friends. In the late '60s, instead of rock posters she pinned up beach volleyball tournament schedules and recorded the results faithfully—not just the Opens—but every tournament: B, A and AA, men's and women's as well. When she saw the '68 USA Women's Team play the Japanese women in an exhibition in Los Angeles, she became more hooked.

At the Manhattan Open for women in 1967, Nina was milling around dazed by her idols when Kathy Gregory came up to the plucky 15-year old and asked her to replace her partner who hadn't shown up. Kathy Gregory! The best on the beach? Yup! They took a fifth, and for the next four years, the two assumed the throne vacated by Brunicardi and Latreille as the dominant female duo. Matthies was a new element in the game; tremendously strong, she combined an ability to read hitters with unmatched leg power to run down balls, and hit with surprising force. Out of her teens and playing at UCLA, Matthies' style of play—at least verbal—was a lot more subdued than her partner's; for that matter, *everyone's* style was more subdued when juxtaposed to Gregory's. Style difference aside, what nettled her more was being in the shadow of Gregory's reputation as the top player on the beach. "I figured I'd rather beat her than be her partner," reflects Matthies. Beat her she did...sometimes...and lose to her she did sometimes. With only about a half dozen Opens in those days and usually before small crowds except for the Manhattan Open, there was a lot of partner switching. What was the reason to try and dominate with one partner?

After three years in the IVA, Matthies returned to UCLA as an assistant coach. There a long, lissome and pretty player, Linda Robertson, impressed her coach with her athletic ability as well. In 1980, the pair gave an added attraction to the game, not to mention the male spectators, as they began winning tournament after tournament. Matthies and Robertson put their stamp on the first half of the '80s as the predominant pair—only Gregory and Kathy Hanley would offer any real resistance—the greatest obstacles to the team's reign were Matthies' pregnancy and finally the marriage of Robertson to pro beach player, John Hanley.

Although the women's game still paled beside the bronzed males in terms of money and media interest, sponsors still took notice. Matthies and Hanley were invited to play exhibition matches at some scattered AVP tournaments—attractive interludes to the men's competition. It was better than nothing, at least they got paid something for it. And it got the active mind of Nina Matthies working...her ego as well. She set out on a path to set things right for women.

"Greed is good...in volleyball as well!..."

Solidarity was called for—there was strength in numbers. The old collective bargaining idea was resurrected and dusted off, ironically right there in that bastion of free enterprise where Ronald Reagan was out front leading the charges like US Marines up Sam Hill. But the '80s was mostly about money and getting it quick—maybe not at any cost—but get it. Ivan Boesky, Michael Millken, The Donald: these guys were the real American heroes now. The Puritan ethic had come full circle; God smiled on those who made it, and if you made it big, then flaunt it. Others might take the cue...the cream would rise. Just don't look at the debit side of the ledger.

Leonard Armato in the off-season contacted a host of promotional companies. One of these was Group Dynamics, run by Jack Butefish. An arrangement was made with Group Dynamics whereby it would operate the tournaments in 1985 and represent the AVP with corporate sponsors; although, they were not to negotiate directly the sponsorship deals...or so it seemed. Suspecting that wasn't the case and demanding to see the books once again, the players found that Groups Dynamics, just as had Event Concepts, refused to divulge their financial secrets. Armato pursued and obtained an out-of-court settlement in the AVP's favor against the promoters. It had become a three-ring circus and often the sponsors and promoters were on the same side, preferring to deal with one another and by-passing the AVP. They were brash, they were arrogant, they were protective and they were at times provincial...but it was the players' game and they were going to keep it that way. Ironically, it would eventually be seen that the actions of Fishburn and Hanseth were not a total anomaly. Money and egos were a volatile combination. This same compound which governed the affairs of men from time immemorial would in time split the nascent organization. Easy to talk equality when the stakes are low...things change with bigger cash.

"What's better than undefeated...?"

At UCLA, Kiraly was rarely tested. During his four-year tenure, the Bruins lost only five matches—one was a loss in the 1980 NCAA finals against one of the greatest collegiate teams in history: USC with Dvorak, Hovland, Timmons and Powers. Coach Scates still claims that the back injuries suffered by Steve Salmons and Rick Amon in the '79 Pan-Ams were responsible for the loss...plus, the team had a bout of mild dysentery from a contaminated water supply at Ball State, host of the tournament. Yet, Scates rarely received sympathy from anyone. In Karch's senior year, UCLA bid farewell to the pre-med student with a perfect 37-0 season—only its second ever—the first came in Kiraly's freshman season of 1979. "He was a bad sport," laughs Scates. "Karch didn't like to lose."

"That '82 team could have been the best ever," added the coach. Considering four future Olympians—Kiraly, Saunders, Partie and Luyties—were on the court at the same time, it seems a scant surprise. The other team which vies for the all-time in Scates' thinking came two years later in UCLA's third—and last—undefeated season in NCAA history. This time they were 38-0. "Since the NCAA rules now prevent more than 28 games, that record will never be equaled," reports Scates with that half-wicked smile which has rankled other coaches for three decades. If Scates decided to lean a shade toward the '84 team, it would be due to the fact that a foreign factor was added to the Luyties/Partie backbone of the team. Ossie Volstad, a sensational hitter from Norway, riddled blocks all season long. Finally, before 9,809 fans at—where else?—Pauley Pavilion, the Bruins took down Pepperdine making Ricci Luyties and Doug Partie the only players to ever play on four NCAA championships teams...even Kiraly hadn't done that.

But it was on the women's side where college volleyball was booming. Title IX, after a decade, was having a delayed effect and a big one. Men and women were clamoring for the well-paid coaching jobs and every middle-class parent in a major city who had a tall, ungainly teenager daughter, entertained the notion of getting her on a Junior Olympic volleyball team if there was one around. Clubs like the Orange County Volleyball Club, Sports Performance of Chicago and ASICS Tiger were growing monthly.

If UCLA had a big season in 1982, there was another female dynasty which was making history thousands of miles away. Talk about domination! The University of Hawaii chalked up a 67-3 record over the two years between 1982-83—barely off the incredible legacy of the USC teams of '76-'77.

Counting the '81 season, the Wahines totaled 104-5, although they were knocked out of the NCAA playoffs by USC. Coach Dave Shoji fashioned a methodical team which would systematically take opponents apart. The hometown Hawaiian crowds were enormous and rowdy; imports Dietre Collins, Kori Pulaski and Lisa Strand joined local girl, Joyce Kaapuni, to form the hottest show in Honolulu since Don Ho. It would be the last extended run by any college...probably forever. Title IX, besides fostering a national phenomenon of interest in collegiate volleyball, also ensured parity. From there on out, it would be an even playing court on which women would compete—coast to coast—and to the furthest islands beyond as well.

"Magnum in Memphis..."

What price fame? There he was sore and wet but comfortably ensconced in the back of a Lear jet...alone. His broad shoulders almost touched the sides of the dark, needle aircraft; nothing to hear but the subtle brushing of a Tennessee rain. To see...only the tiny mesmerizing lights of the instrument panel. Waiting for takeoff to New York City where he would jump on the Concorde back to London and resume the shooting of a film he was starring in. An enviable position for most mortals but one which left him ambivalent; in truth, right now he preferred to be celebrating with his Outrigger teammates on Beale Street. Or wherever they could all gather and shield him from the ogling public and adoring females. No, it couldn't be. Television's biggest star, an athlete at heart, had just helped Outrigger Canoe Club win the USVBA National Championship in the Master's Division. Selected as Honorable Mention, All-American, his primal lust for competition was throbbing. Wow, they had won it all!

"I didn't like taking second the year before," Tom Selleck recalls. So the cast of former All-Americans, the great Jon Stanley, Chris Crabb, Charlie Jenkins and company grabbed the gold that year in 1983. It was crazy that he was even there. The megastar of "Magnum P.I." had convinced the director of the film he was shooting in London, "Lassiter," that it was imperative for him to go to Washington D.C.—fast. "Why?" the director demanded. Well, Bob Hope was calling. The icon of entertainment had personally asked Selleck to play a big part in his own honoring by the Kennedy Center—to be graced by Presidents, billionaires and every Hollywood luminary who had the good fortune to get an invitation. "You just didn't turn down Bob Hope." Reluctantly, very reluctantly, the director let the movie's lead interrupt shooting and jump on the fastest jet to Washington for four days. Via Memphis...a detail the actor left out.

Not that he was shirking his obligation to Hope's extravaganza; a chartered jet flew him back and forth between the capital and Memphis daily. During some matches, the Outrigger team would be warming up when their 6'4" outside hitter, more like Superman than Magnum, burst through the door to join the hitting lines. Mayhem. That was his life: cameras in his face, interviews begged for, intrepid women dashing in for just a word, an autograph. Pile on all that the friendly jibes of his teammates: "the guys on the team would really give it to me then. Rookies carry the balls...and I was willing to do that. But it just didn't work out like that."

Selleck's volleyball career followed a similar path to that of his acting. A long climb fraught with pitfalls. His introduction to the game was happenstance but a likely one in the late 50's; a trip to the beach and of course the lively Sorrento Grill. Beach volleyball's Hall of Fame already hanging from the walls, most of those same demigods could be seen in real life out back or further up at State Beach. With his older brother, Bob, Doug Plowden and Dennis Berg, he watched in awe and finally mustered the courage to step out on the B court. After a couple of high school summers, he pursued the more established sports of baseball and basketball at Valley College near his home in Van Nuys. He also took a Theater Arts class at the junior college "because it was supposed to be easy and I needed good grades to transfer somewhere. I got an A, but sports was what I lived for then." While his brother went on to play baseball for USC and the Dodgers, Tom transferred to USC where he played basketball for two years. "I wasn't a great shooter, but I could jump...and rebound." At 6'4", he could take a basketball and stuff it easily with either hand.

In the spring of 1966, he and a handful of other players put together a volleyball team to compete locally and make the trip to the USVBA Nationals in Grand Rapids where they entered the Collegiate Division. Ex-Trojan great Dick Hammer was asked to coach them, and the Olympian had some brute—albeit unpolished—talent on the floor. Selleck's best buddy, Plowden, was setting along with Jack Hines who had grown up playing on the beaches of Santa Monica. When he unfurled his long right arm, Dennis Duggan could knock down almost any block; the leaper Selleck summoned his spring and a fast arm to make up the rest of the Trojan offensive arsenal.

It was a tournaments of upsets in 1966. The shoe-in, UCLA, with a hired coach and an actual scholarship given to Ernie Suwara, also had Larry Rundle in their stable of stars. In the finals they would go down against SMCC led by Danny Patterson; yet another surprise were the two teams which battled for third place: BYU and USC. If Keith Erickson had shown that basketball players were suited to this game, the twin towers of BYU's Stanley and Alstrom combined with Selleck to confirm the theory. The next year in the Detroit nationals, his team came within a breath of knocking off arch-rival and eventual champion, UCLA. The USC team was bolstered with Bill Wardrop and Bob Clemo, "we had them for the win and someone served out," today Selleck winces with the memory. Returning from Detroit, he was in his last semester as well as in a United Airlines management training program when the phone rang. It was 20th Century Fox. "You wanna be a star? Sign right here!" He agonized over the decision. Play it safe and go into business..or take a shot at acting? His father convinced him to use his natural gifts and go for broke in Hollywood.

Broke it was for many years. Concentrating on his dramatic skills, he signed and got on that famed treadmill: appearing, disappearing and reappearing in the Hollywood shuffle. Seven television pilot shows went south almost as fast as the disappearing credits of the final scenes. However, his one venture into the world of commercials was undeniably a smash. Although the blue eyes weren't his, the rest of the virile "Salem man" was indeed him and plastered around the world's billboards. Several millions of dollars for the billboards, but "something like five hundred for me."

Finally at 35, the roller coaster ride ended when he was signed for a new TV series to be filmed in Hawaii. So he thought. And everyone else did too until the Screen Actors Guild went on strike right before shooting the first episode. Like a ripe tropical fruit within inches of his grasp, it was all so tantalizingly close but as far away as any Hollywood fantasy. "I had this big house to live in but no money. I was working for the landlady for seven bucks an hour and going down to the Outrigger to play." Ten agonizing weeks to wait. Maybe bad for Selleck but a coup of good fortune for volleyball. He picked up the game after leaving it for more than a decade. "Dennis Berg and Tommy Haine really helped me. It wasn't easy to go down and fail a lot more than succeed, at the begin-

ning, and be embarrassed." He paid his dues in full and soon the top Masters' team in the country asked him to play.

"I never had learned good fundamentals. I didn't even know the new type of rotation," he laughs. "And a lot of the guys were coaches too! But most of the time they were too busy playing to stop and coach me. It was a competitive situation but I loved it." The Outrigger guys loved it too—especially the bachelors. Could it be any better than to venture out on a balmy Honolulu night with the hottest sensation in the islands. "Trolling" is what some of the bon vivants like Tom Madison and Randy Shaw would come to call it. Selleck could walk into a bar and step out in five minutes, a trail of sun-tanned lovelies in train as if someone had pulled the fire alarm. There was a price to pay. "I was working 80-hour weeks on Magnum but I still loved playing."

Between 1981-1985, Selleck played in four Nationals with the Outrigger Masters' team. Two championships and two close seconds. Two honorable mentions and one second-team All-American. "That meant a lot to me. To play against and with All-Americans and prove that I could play with them." So much that he surprisingly says, "winning those championships and the All-American awards meant as much as the Emmy I would get." His playing meant a lot to teams on the other side of the net too. At 35, guys were now playing before the biggest crowds of their career; training was called for and the level of play rose dramatically.

"Magnum P.I." would go on to etch itself in the mythology of America in the '80s. Mustachioed, in Hawaiian print shirt and Detroit Tiger hat, Selleck drove his red Ferrari into the nation's imagination. As a testament to the increasing power of television, Selleck's adulation and fame reached heights rarely known before. Somehow he kept playing through it all—including fund-raising matches, even once in an intra-squad match of the '84 Olympic Team in Honolulu. An injury found the benefit one player short and Selleck was asked to play; "there I was with Karch,

Timmons, Dvorak, and Berzins!" Gary Sato attended that match, "I was amazed. They started out kinda playing around him. Then he got a one-on-one stuff and things got more serious. He started banging away and balls were going down...consistently. He could deal!" And not just playing but promoting as well. The only posters Selleck ever appeared on would figure as the sport's most famous as well as lucrative. Posing in a USA uniform, and then in shorts playing at the Outrigger, the two posters raised more than $100,000 for the USA Men's program—a big and needed slice of the annual budget. Such an impact he made—both as a player and supporter—that the '84 Olympic team players asked him to serve as honorary captain, a position he held through 1988 and two Olympic gold medals.

The captain was usually seen during the Los Angeles Olympics, up in the VIP section, cheering on his compatriots. Although the constant flash of photographers and leering ladies transfixed his presence, Selleck's own vision was glued to the court. In the high-security area, he sat next to his brother Bob while nothing could dim the electricity of the historic night when the USA battled Brazil. For some of the dignitaries in the exclusive section, the spectacle was to be enjoyed...but in moderation. Not so for the Sellecks—especially Bob. After every floor-rattling spike, Bob was springing out of his seat, fists flailing and voice screaming in wild cheer. Tom says of his brother, "I'm competitive. But my brother is as competitive as they come."

Apparently too much so when a stately Brazilian gentleman didn't ask, but told the wild-eyed brother to "shut up!" "What are you kidding?" replied the incredulous older brother who sat back down. When Pat Powers nailed the next ball for a point, Bob launched himself once again out of his seat in pure joy. Protocol out the window now, the distinguished official stood up and kicked Bob Selleck. Oh, no! International incident...and what timing! "For the first time in my life, I saw my brother control himself!" his younger sibling smiles. Constraint being the better part of valor, indeed Bob

chomped on his tongue, restrained his clenched fists, and sunk down to his seat in deference to his famous brother. Just as Tom stepped over, grabbed the guy by the collar and gently lifted him off the ground! Every VIP jaw dropped to the floor. A frozen moment, this was bigger than the movies as the diminutive man, hunched and helpless, looked up into the famous, now furious eyes. Today the actor known for his gentility, sheepishly recalls, "maybe I shouldn't have done it. But..." Surely over 15,000 hooting Americans would have loved it. His brother Bob in fact did...immensely.

Today, Tom Selleck has a trail of feature film successes behind him. "Three Men and a Baby" put him in that rare category of actors who have mastered both television and film. Through it all—accolades, fame, money—there's an uncanny sense of the real about him. What is striking about the most famous personality to ever play volleyball—and as an individual, arguably had more impact than anyone putting it on the American map—is that a compassionate element has remained alive. In the schizophrenic mind-set of Hollywood, Selleck's perspective still allows him today to head up a new organization called "Character Counts Coalition." Comprised of such disparate national leaders as William Bennett and Barbara Jordan—that alone an accomplishment in a more and more politicized nation—the idea is to include ethical values in the American educational system. Ethical values? *Whose* ethical values? Talk about a can of worms! Yet that's just it; a consensus approach, over 50 organizations representing 36,000,000 children—fundamentalists to neo-humanists and every stripe in between—somehow have hashed out a simple agreement on basic ethics to teach American kids. A testament to Selleck's ability to moderate extremes, find the middle ground...and do something about it. After tireless lobbying, Congress has approved a national "Character Counts" week for October, 1995.

Friends still matter too. When the untimely death of the legendary Tommy Haine shocked the volleyball world in September of 1994,

Selleck flew to Hawaii to attend his friend's memorial service and help comfort family members.

The jet eased out onto the runway. The sole passenger replayed those last few points, projected in his mind's eye his Outrigger teammates toasting another National Championship— basking in that rarefied, warm aura of victory. Lifting off from Memphis, the lights of an upside-down sky glittered. Invisible in the darkness, but on the fringes of starlight stood a colossal, Southern ante-bellum mansion. Home of another American star, Graceland became a garish tomb of America's greatest rock-and-roll force; a self-destroyed victim of too much fame too fast. A prisoner of his own dream: Elvis Presley. Tricky up there when you make it—fame can turn on itself. A man or a woman better have an anchor, a line back to the past, a finger on the pulse of mortality, a sense of meaning in the human scheme of things.

Tom Selleck was pressed back with the acceleration of the climb. Early memories rose, thrilling prospects of the future seeped down. A heady mixture. Ah, that last cross-court kill felt good! He reached down for one of the ice-cold beers in the six-pack his teammates had given him for the trip. He took a long draught of the cold nectar, smiling in the night.

"Soccer's loss...volleyball's gain..."

In 1980, Paula Weishoff graduated from high school with a problem. What to play? Soccer or volleyball? Actually she had played everything else growing up in the shadow of two athletic brothers and she was good at everything. Better than good, but"There were more scholarships in volleyball at the time so I went that way." Predictably, she was highly courted in the Southland, already a star with friends Dietra Collins and Dale Keough under Dale Flickenger's program at ANVA. Volleyball it was. Imagine the jubilation of USC coach Chuck Erbe when this 6'1" frame of quickness, strength and agility walked on the court...and the chagrin when she left after one semester!

She was just too good. Coach Selinger convinced the phenom to drop out and migrate south to Coto de Caza, an up-market planned community, where the USA Women had moved their program from Colorado Springs soon after the 1980 Olympic boycott. Selinger had seen, as Beal did, the attraction...and danger...in keeping Californians away from their beloved sun and sea. Another Israeli and friend of Selinger, Gideon Ariel, had already established an advanced computer analysis lab at the recreation center of Coto de Cazo to study biomechanics. The high-tech stuff was being used in Vic Braden's tennis camp at the same facility. The one-court gymnasium was a sweetener — a donation by Coto de Caza developers rolling out "little pink houses" communities in that booming era, and a welcome home for the girls. The dream was once again real and the $250 per month that was raised to $500 was enough enticement for the tall spiker and a dozen others. That measly stipend was over and above an apartment with a roommate—it was largely still "pay to play" in American volleyball— but it seemed a safe bet that at least Americans weren't going to boycott their own Olympics in Los Angeles.

The National Team was an adjustment for the 19-year old youngster: "I was used to Erbe's Asian style of endless reputation. With Arie, we did more weights; we worked very hard." Dietra Collins, who had come on the team with Weishoff, couldn't tolerate the authoritarian control of Selinger and she soon quit. Those who stayed got better. "Erbe taught me fundamentals; Arie taught me style," recalls the small setter, Debbie Green, who ran the offense during another quadrennial. By adding physical training, the coach sought out a combination of Soviet power and Japanese quickness. "We and the Chinese mostly dominated...Cuba and Japan could at times," was Weishoff's evaluation.

Today, Jeanie Reeves is an assistant coach with the USA Women's Team. In 1983, she was Jeanie Beauprey out of UCLA and had a good showing in the World University Games.

Good enough that she and Kim Ruddins were asked to join the USA Women's Team. At 22, she was a bit apprehensive joining the revered program and the rumored multi-hour training under the ironfisted Selinger. "Would she be ostracized?" she wondered. On the contrary, "They welcomed both of us with open arms. It was almost like they had lost touch with what was going on outside the world of volleyball. I was just out of UCLA and Kim out of USC, so we were kind of representatives of the world outside. You have to realize that people in this country weren't used to women competing on that intense of a level—with a program like that. It was still bizarre to most people."

Was she prepared for what she would encounter? "It was more intense than anything I'd ever imagined. We were traveling a lot but at Coto de Caza, it was at least six hours a day during the week and four to five hours on Saturdays. We were playing a five-game scrimmage everyday, besides other practices and a lot of physical work. Today when I think of the physical stress that was put on our bodies, it scares me. No medical and training expertise or facilities to speak of—that's a huge difference in today's game," Reeves remarks. "I remember times driving home to El Toro after a day's workouts and just sitting in the car...too tired to get out."

And the coach? Genius, Svengali? "Arie was incredibly knowledgeable about technique. He could watch you play, analyze it and correct it," Reeves says. What no player denies is that the Israeli demanded to be in control. It had to be his way or no way at all. "I think Arie sincerely believed that was the only way to reach our goal. I don't think it would work today," thinks Reeves.

Almost three months before the Los Angeles Games, the Soviet boycott was announced, and the road to the gold looked as smooth as if a new coat of pavement had been evenly spread over it. Although the ride would be more comfortable, it was pretty clear where the highway was leading: to an ultimate clash against the other top-ranked team in the world. The USA/

China was what most experts predicted anyway, so there would be less naysayers than on the Men's side tisk-tisking: "Well...remember the Cubans and the Soviets weren't there..." It would unfold thus...but in one of the strangest episodes in Olympic and volleyball history. Not surprisingly, it all centered on the controversial coach, Arie Selinger.

"The Canyonlands...in the dead of winter..."

"...learn to draw on the best in themselves in times of challenge and decision." reads the brochure. Just what the doctor ordered thought the coaches. Outward Bound, a program which claims to bind businessmen and students into a cohesive group, came out of an English program during World War II which was designed to bolster confidence and cooperation in young merchant seamen facing the ever-present danger of finding themselves on a sinking ship in the freezing waters of the North Atlantic. Nothing can match that for cold terror but the Canyonlands in Eastern Utah can get very cold in midwinter. In January, 1983 the USA Men's team sans Karch Kiraly (still at UCLA), began a 21-day trek on mostly snowshoes through the breathtaking beauty of the National Park. Not that most of them were admiring the raw, awesome scenery over the 100 miles and ascents to 11,000 feet peaks lugging 70-pound packs. Much of the familiar whining and moaning continued but the coaches hoped that a prickling problem would be mitigated at least: up until that point during intense, high-stress situations of international play, the team succumbed too easily to adversity, blaming each other or the officials for failure. The goal was to make them a mature unit—a true team dependent upon one another.

Following the trip Beal commented, "Some of the guides let us know the team members realized they weren't particularly close and admitted privately they wished the situation would change. It did change, not spectacularly, but at least enough for us to function as a cohesive unit." Even today some players disagree with the coach, questioning the wisdom of forcing highly-competitive individuals to expend energy in psycho-babble exercises...especially in zero degree weather. Today Beal still holds firm, "It was absolutely good for the team. I can tell you one thing—they remembered it!"

For some of those who made the trek, it would be an excruciating memory followed by a worse one. All of the former IVA players were let go except for setter Rod Wilde. In their early 30s, their better days were behind them in the estimation of the coaches and a better idea would be to go with some of the younger talent coming out of college. A coach's worst job...but as the dawn of the Olympics neared, cutting the last players doubled the pain.

Besides Kiraly, one other player turned down the invitation to survey the sweeping sandstone vistas, the red and ocher arroyos—Tim Hovland. Kiraly had two legitimate excuses: he was finishing his last semester at UCLA and the trip conflicted with his acceptance speech for the five "Scholar-Athletes" selected by the NCAA (including John Elway). Hovland's was a bit more sketchy. During a break in the Italian season, he met with Beal and convinced him of his desire to play before returning to his team in Torino. Beal's estimation of the ebullient talent was continually supported by other players, even parents of players. Yet, in the back of his uneasy mind, Beal knew he was dealing with a half-cocked cannon on deck. And how could it be fair to let one guy go and make money on the beach and in Italy, then come back to play when it was convenient? A true dilemma.

Late in the spring of 1983, Beal came up with a solution...so he thought. To get the untoward child in line, make him put up a bond: a healthy sum to be held by the USVBA and repaid monthly against good behavior...or bad...which meant fines. Like many best-laid plans, this one backfired. Novel and unprecedented, it was also perfectly ripe for multifarious interpretations. "It was play by extortion. I had just come back from Italy, finally had a little money saved up and they wanted all my savings—something like $25,000! Didn't

take long to see this wasn't such a good deal. I wanted to keep the money I made; just leave me alone and let me play." What about his propensity to stay out too late and show up tardy to practice from time to time? "Hey, I was willing to live by the rules...and the punishments. I was a little older. And if I was late, I was ready to go the ten minutes with coach-on-one." No one could deny that the Hov could pay the band at the end of the night's dancing.

Beal and the staff saw it as a reasonable insurance plan. Hovland and soon the press read it as something entirely different. "Trying to make a player to buy his way on an Olympic team!" The story and Hovland's plight became the cause celebre of one particular Los Angeles Times reporter, Jerry Crowe, and the greatest thorn in the side of Beal's coaching experience. It garnered much media attention and Crowe wrote a series of critical articles on more than just Hovland. Finally, Hovland filed a grievance with the US Olympic Committee. The athlete eventually lost and Beal's relationship with the media would be blemished until the Games. As for the brilliant irritant, he went back to Italy where he won the MVP of the Italian League in 1984 which already featured many of the top players anywhere. "Sure I wanted to play. But I had the best time of my life in that period. In my 20s in Italy, and I got to play against the best players in the world every week."

Meanwhile, things of greater importance like playing were at least improving. The two-receiver system gave rise to a new "swing" offense where attackers were approaching the net almost parallel, moving inside to outside, as opposed to the old perpendicular, straight-on route. In particular, this system utilized the unusual ability of Kiraly to get to the left front on the run, jump and float outside while cranking the ball back inside. Thus, in new and sometimes complex starting positions, Kiraly would pass five or six positions from the left side of the court and Berzins the same number from the right. Berzins would be utilized more as a secondary hitter on right-side combinations. At the same time, both Powers and Timmons began perfecting the attack out of the backcourt. Soon, the three-against-three 10-foot games in practice became a dreaded exercise if you were on the other side of the net of either one. To stand in and try to dig Powers on the fly, with no block, was a rite of passage...and sometime's a direct menace to one's manhood.

The backcourt attack quickly changed the game of international volleyball. Effectively, a new hitter was added to already complex offensive patterns—now it could be three blockers against four hitters! And by the time those big monsters floated forward and unloaded their crane-like arms on the small ball, they were practically hitting a regular set. It was a blast which was particularly hard to block. Craig Buck remembers, "the offense changed. You couldn't commit to one hitter anymore." Coaches, like Star Wars scientists, were scrambling to come up with efficient ways of stopping the new weapon. The Russians, traditionally using a "commit" system of blocking, used the "stack" variation more and more—essentially, they put a blocker behind another where the front one commits to the first quick set, and the blocker behind steps to stop the second attacker either crossing or flying from the backcourt. The Poles had perfected the "read and react" system whereby blockers bunched close together and attempted to read the setter's hands—often arriving an instant late but deflecting many balls to be dug in the backcourt.

At 6'9", Craig Buck became the best in the world at all types of blocking but no player could touch his "soft" blocking ability. "My job was to touch the ball. Especially with the backrow guys coming in now, we couldn't commit as much. And I knew if I just touched the ball, I had Karch and Aldis behind me. If we dug a ball, we scored." The coaches soon decided to employ both systems and at times a blend of the two. It was a complex system and required discipline but the many hours of practice would pay off. The astute Buck was given the unusual privilege of not only deciding the system, but moving players to whatever posi-

tion he wanted. "Buck's the best blocker I've ever seen," complimented one of those grateful for the many thousands of balls he touched—Karch Kiraly.

The coaching staff of Beal, Neville and Tony Crabb, who was added in 1982, saw that some of the guys were responding positively to responsibility on the court. Dvorak had taken complete control of the offense and it worked swimmingly. It was no great revelation either to discover that two guys were getting the bulk of the digs on defense. Kiraly had close to a 4.0 GPA and as Berzins had figured out red shifts and Hubbel's expanding universe concepts, they were well equipped to understand opponent's hitting tendencies. They let the two run open-range; they went wherever they wanted to on defense...and none of those big guys could say a word.

Every month they seemed to get better. In the NORCECAs of 1983 they beat Cuba in the finals at Indianapolis although the Cubans left some of their team home. A better indication of their improvement came at the prestigious Savin Tournament in Russia when they lost a tough 3-1 match to the top-of-the-heap Soviets. Getting closer.

"Spiker"...

Olympic fever was rising. Volleyball was receiving attention never before imagined...some of not necessarily positive but who cared! The men were getting better everyday. Those morning drills at 8:00 when you could see your breath in the dark Federal Building were starting to pay dividends: things like the "flinch" drill where Powers, Timmons and Blanchard were given 50-50 sets right on the net to pulverize. The object of the drill was for the two defenders beginning inside the ten foot line to come in and try to dig the impossible shot, risking life and limb. "Quien es mas macho?" If you could just *touch* one of those bullets, then it was demonstrably possible to dig one in a game—in the Olympics!

The intensity was contagious and the father-in-law of Dusty Dvorak decided to make a dramatic volleyball movie based on the USA Men's quest for the Olympic gold. Sounded good; the most publicity the sport's players had received to date had been mug shots in two-page programs. In the end, it wasn't a major Hollywood production but there were real cameras and a bonafide actor. Sort of. The lead didn't have a big name, but he had a history of acting, although his city looks, his short stature—well under six feet—and his lack of physical prowess didn't qualify him as the quintessential volleyball player. Well, this is the movies...let's improvise!

They did; a mini-trampoline was sought out and after three hours of trial and error, the little guy was hitting the ball down over the net—closed fist and all. Someone suggested that they lower the net but that had been done before...this was a chance to forge new cinematic trails. Before long, the allure wore off. Even the 15 bucks players earned for hanging out three hours in the afternoon to act excited when, and if, the guy connected on one wasn't doing it for them. Mission Beach was 15 minutes away, the sun always shining, and local girls who could vie with most starlets in looks. The film did come out. It was not a candidate in the Cannes Film Festival, but "Spiker" got a limited showing in a limited amount of theaters...very limited. Today it's available on video, like almost every other film ever made, and figures for posterity as a accurate reflection of where volleyball was in 1983. Intentionally or not.

"Volleyball...monthly?..."

If not on the silver screen then maybe on the printed page. In 1982, two guys just out of Cal Poly San Luis Obisbo and working as journalists took a look at the future and it scared them. "Are we gonna be writing stories on dog attacks for some local rag in 20 years?" they asked each other. Jon Hastings, a AA beach player who had grown up in Hermosa Beach, said no. His partner, Dennis Steers, agreed. So they mustered enough cash to print the first newsprint edition on a subject they loved—volley-

ball—and somehow sold enough to cover their costs. "We probably made a mistake calling it "Monthly," remembers Hastings. "Now we had to print one every month!"

Not such a bad idea after all. While the Olympic interest heightened, the AVP formed and women's collegiate volleyball began its explosion; there was finally a substantive base to support a magazine. And enough controversy to feed the new reading animal. Determined to walk that old fine and contentious indoor-beach line, the two facets would maintain an effective balance—despite the beach junkies and hardwood zealots screaming that there was only one brand of true volleyball worth reading about...their own.

"Simply Red...and deadly..."

The final piece of the Olympic Team puzzle was put in place almost by accident in February, 1984. During a tour in Cuba, Craig Buck went down with an injury. The other starting middle blocker, Steve Salmons, was holding his own but who could replace "Biggie"? Well Steve Timmons was interested. Beal recalls, "We had almost cut Timmons many times up to that point. He definitely didn't have a spot on the team." What happened?

Whatever the cause, the result was dramatic. The red-haired Billy Idol of the sport, the guy who would take the flat-top to new heights and fame, world-wide and even attach it to a sports apparel logo, was let loose to stuff the Cubans off the court. And as Dvorak started pitching a short lob behind his head—Timmon's favorite set because of his extraordinary quickness, the 6'5" spiker proceeded to tomahawk with a frenzied violence never seen before in the young man...nor any young man! Even Beal admitted, "I don't why! But it gave us a dimension not there before with a backrow hitter." Buck thinks he knows what happened with Red, "he changed his mental image of himself." Outward Bound? Was their a vision up there, an appearance of a silver crow to prophecy the great change? Best it remains a secret. Simply there was a transformation. According to Karch

Kiraly, "he became the most versatile hitter in the world."

"Eighty percent of our preparation was geared to beat the Russians. We felt that we were finally ready." says Beal. In a tour of Russia in the spring of 1984, he would see. After four hours of the fiercest battle of their volleyball lives, the Yanks bested the Soviets in the fourth game 16-14 after losing the third, 15-13. The fifth game would surely be like no other. But then, wait a minute! What was going on! the dumbstruck Americans wondered. They rolled over a suddenly impassive Soviet squad 15-6! Nevertheless, the joy of the celebration in the locker room was overflowing. For Beal an the other coaches, it was somehow blunted even though it was the first win over the great team since 1968—and the second time ever. Within minutes came the announcement in Russian of the 1984 Olympic boycott by the Soviets. Beal was told privately.

About a year later over a few sips of vodka, a Soviet player confided the truth to Kiraly: "They told us about the boycott before the fifth game." Beal had guessed it the same night; the marked change was too dramatic. It was a sad evening for the coaching staff even though they allowed the team to revel in their victory; the disappointing news was related to the players the following morning. The USA Team was deeply disheartened; the great test in the greatest arena only three months away would never come. For the Soviets it was worse. Overpowered by the news, they dropped the remaining three matches 3-0 in less than lackluster interest. In the last match, backup setter Wilde got a chance to show his stuff. During a long rally, the Huck Finn kid from Iowa landed on a Soviet hitter who passed far under the net while chasing a close, inside set. Both bones were broken in Wilde's ankle; a harrowing experience in a Soviet hospital and a long ride home made things worse. His Olympic dream was shattered. Yet one man's pain is another man's pleasure, and Chris Marlowe, who had been cut a few months earlier, was suddenly on a rare trip to his local church of preference to give thanks.

Both teams bade a saddened farewell. Of course the other Soviet Bloc countries followed in lockstep. "We had been about 50-50 with Cuba up until then; they might have even been more worrisome than the Soviets at LA," reflects Beal. It wouldn't matter. Politics...once again the enemy of sport.

Two passers. Karch Kiraly and Aldis Berzins (right) revolutionize international volleyball by taking every serve reception on the way to the '84 Olympics. (Courtesy of Bud Fields)

Pat Powers. Greatest high ball hitter on the planet, 1983. (Courtesy of Bud Fields)

At 6'9", Craig Buck and setter Dusty Dvorak were a world-class threat. (Courtesy of Bud Fields)

Born to be wild. Tim Hovland holds the MVP award of the 1983 Nationals...but he'd never make it to LA '84. (Courtesy of Bud Fields)

Big Flo and Sue Woodstra leave little room for a Canadian spiker.

No challenge. Out of the gym, down to the beach and their fourth straight Cuervo San Diego Open, 1982. Karch Kiraly and Sinjin Smith were virtually unbeatable together.

Pro beach goes to Florida. In 1982, Dane Selznick and Andy Fishburn win the Cuervo Open on the other coast.

Miss Cuervo of Los Angeles...every site had their own.

Sinjin Smith pounds a Kiraly set. (Photo by Doug Avery)

Hovland-Dodd, 1982. One-half of beach volleyball's greatest rivalry. (Photo by Doug Avery)

Biggest block on the beach. Wilt Chamberlain makes Mike Dodd go around him, 1983. (Photo by Doug Avery)

Randy Stoklos. Ferocious blocking half of Smith-Stoklos. Demonstrating why Kiraly names Stoklos as the best he has played against. (Photo by Doug Avery)

Magnum, P.I. warming up at '83 USVBA Nationals. (Courtesy of Bud Fields)

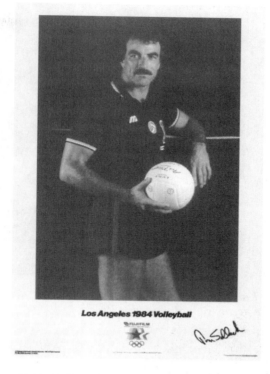

Poster perfect. Tom Selleck loans his image to the '84 Men's Olympic team—a needed windfall. (Courtesy of USA Volleyball)

Tireless...another benefit match: Outrigger versus USA Staff. Back (left to right): Tony Crabb, Mark Warner, Tom Selleck, Doug Beal, Rudy Suwara, Ed Machado, Marv Dunphy. Front: Kerry Klostermann, Bill Neville, Dick Templeman, Dave Weston.

Strike! Karch Kiraly and Tim Walmer picket for AVP at World Championships ,1984. (Reprinted with the permission of the Daily Breeze © 1984)

Strike or no strike! Jay Hanseth crossed the picket line and won the '84 World Championships.(Courtesy of Jay Hanseth)

Chapter 16
1984 Los Angeles Olympics

"In the tunnel..."

"What is going on!" was repeated in many languages. All ten thousand athletes were sitting in the sports arena next to the Los Angeles Coliseum, aligned by country and waiting to march in. The USA as host would enter last. Four hours of an impossible fanfare—a brainchild of David Wolper—kept the 100,000 spectators entertained while waiting for the athletes. It was indeed the first high-tech Olympics; three huge video screens in the arena displayed for the competitors the incredible show going on outside. Until all three went blank five minutes into the ceremony! Groans of disappointment, but four hours of seeing nothing unquestionably built up the suspense for the Americans. Finally Australia departed, the procession moved along alphabetically and slowly on down to Zaire. The American women were in the front of the USA athletes, ranked short to tall; then came the Yankee men in similar order. Obviously, the tall USA Men's volleyball team was at the back of the 150 foot tunnel leading into the Coliseum when the first American lady stepped out onto the track.

The sound of 100,000 thundering voices blew back through the tunnel, literally blowing back the athletes' hair and pressing their clothes against them. Karch Kiraly will never forget it. "It was the most incredible rush of my life. Everytime I think about it I get goosebumps."

If the moment was magic, it took on another aura of unreality. In a rare display of mass spontaneity, the American team somehow unconsciously declared their greatest tradition. In the most formalized and disciplined of ceremonies in the world of sports, the Yanks broke ranks! They sprinted out on the track, seeking family and friends, waving wildly and yelling, even obstructing the runners carrying the fabled Olympic torch. As the rest of the world's teams duck-walked in unison and watched in slack-jawed wonder, the noise of the crowd reached San Francisco. The behavior quickly drew reproof from the protocol-minded Olympic officials. "It was awesome," recalls Kiraly.

"Conspiracy...at the Olympics?..."

"Rolf, you better get down here. Quick! There's twelve guys in USA sweats with the Women's team—and they all got guns!" Engen flew to the entrance tunnel before the first match of the Olympics. My god! It was true. A dozen guys with USA warm-ups flanked the women...a private guard for each one. To Engen's relief, they were officers of the Fountain Valley Police Department and had volunteered to escort the women to the matches at the Long Beach Arena and back to their residence. They also would stay close to the team while they were on the floor; any attack, whatever type it might be, would be hard to pull off.

Engen had to think quick. The Commissioner of Volleyball calmly invited them into a side conference room. "I appreciate your interest but we have very good security here. After all, this is the Olympics. And I would be happy to get all of you good seats to watch the game...but fellas, you *can't* take those guns out there." The voice of reason had spoken; the dozen armed men silently concurred. Although any possible heroics were quickly quashed, the troops would still escort the team to and from matches—guns and flak jackets replete—leading interference for the team bus on the freeway up to Long Beach. Any highjacking attempt would be foiled. Somehow, the idea of Olympic fraternity suffered in this atmosphere; on the other hand, it indisputably strengthened the coach's outlook that it was "us against them."

The final night at the Long Beach Arena was almost beyond imagination for American volleyball fans. Both the Men's and Women's Teams in the finals! The ladies were, as expected, more on track than the men. They had beaten China in pool play, 3-0. In a sense the match was moot, since it was certain they would meet again; in fact, the perennial argument remains as to which team has the advantage in the second encounter as this: the first winner...or loser? But the USA Women had waited so long. Some, like Flo Hyman and those Adidas women like Debbie Green and Sue Woodstra, had waited almost a decade. Selinger had as tight control as possible on his team and it seemed to be working. He even had them stay outside the Olympic Village in a complex near their practice gym in Fountain Valley—an experience a few players did not warm to. Still, they marched in and the air was electric. My, how those women bounced balls in warmups!

Both teams were introduced and the 16,000 people clapped and cheered. Fears of plots and violence had disappeared from all suspicious minds...where could danger lurk? Magnum P.I. was in the stands! Back and forth in the first game; Selinger was up off the bench at the end of the tight affair, gesticulating like a traffic cop in disapproval of calls. At 14-14 there came the moment of truth: the Chinese prevailed in a 16-14 victory. China's momentum swelled in the second game as the marvelous 6'2" Lang Ping spiked and blocked in a resounding display of volleyball skill; the bee in the bonnet of Selinger was still astir and now he was up and down like a squeaky piston. Clearly the American squad was unraveling. "Some of our stars

didn't play well," remembers Weishoff. "We were more tense than when we played them four nights before," added Green. The normally effective hitting of the two hammers, Hyman and Crockett, wasn't there.

In the huddle before the third game, an irate coach was fulminating amidst the distraught girls. The head referee blew his whistle for the teams to take the court. The American girls didn't budge; their eyes glazed over with confusion at the sight of the remonstrating Selinger. He was demanding that they not go out on the court! The man had pulled off a few similar ruptures of rules in the past, in protest of biased refereeing or something not right in his eyes. More than once he had yanked the team off the court as a demonstration of his conviction that his team was getting the shaft. But this was the Olympics! And more...the gold-medal finals! Well, if you're going to make a point, is there a bigger forum?

From the seats behind the bench, Al Monaco and USVBA President Bob Bender saw that something was going down—something serious. Bolting down the stairs, Monaco was instantly in the coach's face. An ABC camera closed in on the confrontation as orders, threats and counter-threats were flying...on national television. Abruptly, Selinger desisted and nodded to the girls to take their positions. They did and went down in a miserably played third game. "I remember after the final point that Flo gathered the six of us to walk off the court. She told us to keep our heads up; we had nothing to be ashamed of...kinda like a big mother," recalls Debbie Green. But on the stand, the Americans were flushed with tears receiving their medals. "Second just didn't seem good enough. It took me years to get over it."

The next day was one of the strangest in many of their lives. All the years, filled with the daily routine, was suddenly stopped. There was the pain of losing like a wicked hangover that wouldn't go away but there was also an eerie sense of emptiness, a vacuum, no sense of orientation. "Nobody from the USVBA even talked to me. I felt they didn't care," remembers Paula Weishoff. Not much reason to talk in the opinion of Al Monaco, as earlier in the spring the USVBA had learned that Selinger had already arranged a deal for Hyman and Crockett to play for big money in Japan shortly after the Olympics; Selinger would eventually go to Holland to coach as well. Debbie Green was scheduled to perform a series of clinics in the Orient. Still, there had been talk of a post-Olympic tour to Hong Kong sponsored by the FIVB. "We were looking forward to that," said Green.

"How could we plan a tour when three of the top players and coach weren't even available?" seemed a justified response to Monaco. In fact, a team was finally sent to Hong Kong but with only two of the Olympians on it. Finally, there was disillusionment and disappointment everywhere, and quietly the saddened ladies slipped away to new lives, many to play in Italy.

And what was that spat all about right before the third game? Selinger thought that the referees were doing a number on them; apparently some higher powers preferred that the American women lost. At least he believed that...

Almost universal praise exists for the knowledge and determination of the man who spent nine years climbing the mountain. Every fiber of his being seemed dedicated to winning a gold medal, but he was from a vastly different culture and volleyball was a team sport. The captain of the team, Sue Woodstra, sums it up best perhaps: "I think Arie made the mistake of thinking we didn't want it quite as badly as he did. We did."

"Is the lineup right?..."

The morning after the Olympics the USA Men were nursing hangovers as well but a different kind than the women—for some of the men champagne and beer played a role. But the headaches this time were unusually welcomed. "I've never felt that high," remembers Kiraly. "It lasted about two months!" Strangely their odyssey to the Olympic finals was almost a mirror image of the American ladies.

Nerves were still unsettled when the first match of the USA Men finally took place in the Long Beach Arena. A good team from Argentina would give them the first test. It didn't start too well when Beal put in the wrong lineup to begin the match—"the only time I ever did that in four years." Tight. "At the first timeout, I looked over at Timmons and he was completely flushed, almost hyper-ventilating," Beal adds. They settled down and put away that awful case of nervousness, 3-1. On the third night, they faced a tenacious Korean team but, barring a complete letdown, expectations were high. In fact, Beal decided to rest the recently operated foot of Craig Buck as well as highball slugger and warmup king, Pat Powers. He started Sunderland and Salmons in their places—a 3-0 whitewash for the favored Yanks.

The next day was the Americans' day off, and they were shocked when Korea ambushed Brazil, 3-1, in a surprise upset. The other favorite of the tournament, Brazil, in two days would face the Americans in the pool's final match. The Brazilians had to win this one or they would be eliminated, and the final-four competition would look more and more like an American cakewalk. Beal felt confiden and allowed the team to stay at the Olympic Village at USC before matches, the team was lodged in a hotel near the arena after night matches.

Against Brazil, the USA team started the match with the knowledge that once they scored the first few points, they were qualified for the semi-finals. Probably the coaching staff playing in suits and ties could have pulled that one off; yet that same comfort seemed to melt some of their intensity. "It would have made sense to try and get rid of the Brazilians that night...but we didn't." Kiraly recollects.

When the six starters hit the floor, a lot of American pundits wondered if Beal had screwed up the lineup a second time. He started the same team which had started against Korea. "I didn't think Buck and Powers played particularly well against Brazil," admits Beal. "Yeah, but Doug..." came the collective thought as the restless crowd murmured. The Brazilians came out like they would never see Rio again if they lost this one. Brazilian leader Bernard Rajman, only six feet but with footspeed and an armswing so quick it could barely be seen, was as a man possessed. Brazil's Montanaro led a barrage of jump serves never before displayed with such speed and accuracy in volleyball's history. Fireballs were hitting both lines. The bench was emptied. Kiraly confessed that "I had one of the worst matches of my life." The first two games were long skirmishes, the third game was 15-2. Fans trooped out of the arena, shaking their heads after the 3-0 blowout and wondering if all the pre-Olympic criticism of the coach wasn't justified. And how in the hell were these Brazilians ever going to be stopped!

Was Beal worried? Surprisingly, no. "Right after the match I saw a good sign. Normally these were guys who liked to second-guess a lot, but they weren't upset. Instead they talked about what they had to do next time we played them." And the coaching staff made the inevitable lineup change. Buck and Powers were back in there...and did they go to work!

The semi-finals saw a different team and a different story. The guys readily handled Canada, 3-0, and predictably, Brazil put away Italy, 3-1. After the terrible disappointment of the Women's finals, the final hope for gold rested on the men. A few adjustments were made including the decision to block the bullet serves of the Brazilians. It hardly mattered. Brazil had peaked and more, two nights before...no way a team could ascend to that level again. Even their fierce jump serves were often hitting the net and going long. And this was a different USA team! Buck and Timmons shut down the Brazilian attack, and Powers was going *over the block* with deep court rockets from the left side. A flawless match. It was 15-6, 15-6, and 14-7 in the third when Rajman got a shoot set on the left side. With a final torque he fired away, right into the hands of the captain, Dusty Dvorak.

A couple players fell to the floor. Timmons rushed, leaped and catapulted off the referee's stand—it was pandemonium, American style. Chris Marlowe, photo op maestro, unfolded an American flag and began his famous traipse around the floor. Beal coaxed the two alternates, Rod Wilde and Mike Blanchard out on the court. It had taken 89 years to reach the pinnacle. Were William Morgan and Pop Idell somewhere up there in the cheap seats smiling?

"Little pieces of the gold..."

At the Marriott, a couple hundred people were slapping backs and shaking hands. Comely women discreetly peered at Tom Selleck, larger than life, sharing a beer with the gold medalists. Even the normally somber Al Monaco was wearing a grin ear-to-ear. Parents, girlfriends and wives of the players and coaching staff, former All-Americans and National Team players who had suffered and complained, toasted in triumph. Earlier coaches who had tired of the constant and unfair criticism for doing a job with no pay raised their glasses. As did USVBA officials—good ole boys from the Y—who sincerely believed they had always done the right thing...and got ripped for it. Lifelong fanatics of the game and neophytes newly on the bandwagon all gushed with victory. Rolf Engen whose own Olympic dream had been foiled 20 years prior by a bad Achilles and shadowy politics was beaming too. As Commissioner of Volleyball, he was an integral part of the most successful Olympics in history...and volleyball as well.

Thirty minutes into the party, Kirk Kilgour rolled up in his wheelchair commandeered by his chin. Bedecked in his ABC blue blazer and sweat on his forehead, he had just come from the announcer's booth where he had performed the broadcast with Bob Beatty. Peter Diamond of ABC had liked what he saw earlier in the week, and an inordinate amount of volleyball was shown—the ratings had soared. Offered a beer, a grateful Kilgour slaked his thirst from a straw. Eight years ago his fateful accident abruptly ended his life-long dream of being in the Olympics. Who could have known that he would be a part of it too? Not on the court with those twelve, but a part of it nonetheless...like a lot of others that night.

They did it! 1984 Olympic gold medalists.Back row (left to right): Bill Neville (Asst. Coach), Chris Marlowe, Dave Saunders, Craig Buck, Steve Salmons, Steve Timmons, Paul Sunderland, Rich Duwelius, Coach Doug Beal. Front row: Karch Kiraly, Pat Powers, Marc Waldie, Dusty Dvorak, Aldis Berzins.(Courtesy of Doug Beal)

Chris Marlowe with his famous traipse around Long Beach Arena.(Courtesy of Doug Beal)

Two by two. 1984 USA Women's Olympic team. Left to right (by pairs): Linda Chisholm /Jeanie Beauprey, Kim Ruddins/Debbie Green, Julie Vollertsen/Rose Magers, Flo Hyman/Carolyn Becker, Laurie Flachmeier/Rita Crockett, Sue Woodstra/Paula Weishoff.

A single tear betrays Rose Magers. Left to right: Flo Hyman, Magers, Julie Vollertsen, Debbie Green.

Chapter 17
1985-1988

"The Wisdom of Solomon..."

Beach versus indoor. USVBA versus AVP. Southern California versus the rest of the world. All were manifestations of the same conflict, the same dichotomy which marked volleyball in the United States, and had marked it for a half century. A nation divided...a family split...a sport riven. In 1985, the game was following two separate vectors, two brilliant laser beams shot into space but on separate paths and in separate directions. Sad.

In 1984 at the Los Angeles Olympics, Ruben Acosta assumed the presidency of the FIVB. Born in Mexico, he was a lawyer by profession but had an abiding interest in volleyball: player, coach, administrator, and the driving force of the NORCECA zone. A man of enormous ambition, intelligence, and a master of the political game of international sport, Acosta was eager to make volleyball a truly world-class sport—one which had been hidebound by tradition. Paul Libaud, the previous FIVB president, had overseen the sport from his sunny home in Cannes, France for 37 years—since its inception in Europe in 1947. It was a game which had been dominated by the Soviet Bloc from the onset of the first World Championship in 1949 and was only challenged on a level of influence by the powerful Japanese Volleyball Association. Yet unless the sport took hold in Western Europe and the US, particularly amongst corporate sponsors and television, it would continue on as an outmoded, colorless and minor sport. Acosta knew he had to get it into the '80s.

American volleyball limped along as an amateur sport like all the rest...struggling under antiquated rules which were simply circumvented by nations of the Communist Bloc and Japan. The upshot was an exciting game in those parts of the world, but one which still suffered under a staid and unimaginative image in the country where it was invented. A lot of people played it, but for most it was still "bat ball." Knocking a piece of hard rubber back and forth across a sagging net.

The '84 Olympics awakened a sleeping nation to a new sport. Recently so had beach volleyball. The American public was confused by the differences: "Yeah, I've seen it on TV...but mostly on the beach. They play with only two people, right?" In time, the distinction was made clearer: Karch Kiraly and Sinjin Smith became names someone might pull out at a cocktail party if knowledge of the subject were called for. For the converted, the adherents of the game, there was a deepening line of demarcation. Play one or the other...argue about which was better. Union or Confederate? Which side you on? Pick your heroes and heroines accordingly. Occasionally a figure cut across borders—the inimitable Karch Kiraly became widely revered as the best in both arenas.

The discerning eye of Acosta quickly saw the situation in LA '84. From a loftier perch and one untainted by American history, he recognized two versions of the same sport: one indoor which had six players and one outdoor which normally had only two. So what's the problem? Let's play both...and promote both!

235

Every other National Volleyball Federation around the world agreed since other than Brazil there was no beach volleyball to speak of—and even there the beach game was already under the federation's hegemony. But what did he mean, "promote?" The concept of taking the sport, dressing it up—as well as appreciating the lack of dress on the beach—and presenting it to the public as new and dynamic was a unique one. A sport of today! Something that corporate sponsors could hang their hat on and maybe even have their marketing people design hats around...like colorful beach visors with corporate logos artistically printed on them.

The man didn't tarry. The first World Volleyball Championship was held in Rio de Janeiro in 1987. The event was not only wildly successful, it was wild.

And here on home shores? Marv Dunphy, a native Californian and the new coach of the Men's National Team, relaxed Beal's hard stance and allowed players to play on the beach if no direct conflict existed with his own agenda. But he was an oddity in the scheme of things. The USVBA and AVP came to loggerheads time and time again and the beach game, even on an amateur level, was not embraced by the USVBA. Most of the offical caretakers didn't put on shorts and run around in the sand during the summer. "Don't do it...don't like it...don't care."

The battle for the public favor was on. It wasn't even close. The AVP, with Miller Brewing Company staunchly behind them, pushed the new sexy lifestyle portrayed by beach volleyball to unforeseen heights. Beach doubles was seen weekly throughout the summer. Chris Marlowe and Paul Sunderland became known broadcasters. A pro women's tour was formed in 1986. Although IMG snapped up the USA gold-medalists within twelve hours after Los Angeles with the promise of money—contracts were signed—by the end of 1985, the USA Men's National Team came within hours of boycotting the World Cup. IMG's one-year deal with the Olympians had run out. The USVBA asked the players to take big salary cuts; the

players countered with lesser ones. The USVBA said no, and the players were united in a hard stance. They practiced a week without coaches and threatened to strike. At the airport in San Diego, the team begrudgingly decided to go and play, still disgruntled on the plane.

Ruben Acosta and most of the volleyball world couldn't understand the beach-indoor rift, or why the USVBA was not capitalizing on the blond, tan and articulate gold medalists who had captured the imagination of America in the Olympics. The USA Women of '84 had disbanded; over half had fled to Italy and Japan to play. Italian impresarios had waved huge bundles of lira in front of the American Men as well, but they had stayed on except for Dusty Dvorak who decided to take the cash. However, things would get better in 1986...the USVBA was shaken by the close call in the airport.

The window was open; the sport was hot. Yet it seemed that after 90 years, the shadow of the same YMCA mentality hung over the USVBA. The same old "go slow; don't change the sport's image—let the world instead conform to it." It hadn't worked for 90 years...it didn't work in 1985. In contrast, pro beach was cool. Off and running, it continued stretching its lead on the indoor game every year...never even looking back.

"Can't buy a thrill...or a partner..."

If there were rumors—and there were—that Fishburn and Hanseth "broke the strike in the last tournament of 1984 because that's the only way they could win," that theory suffered a setback when the duo won the first AVP tournament of the 1985 season in Santa Cruz. They also won another in Redondo Beach and took several seconds including the World Championships against Hovland and Dodd. But at a heavy social cost. Particularly for Hanseth since Fishburn retired after that season to embark upon a career as a lawyer. Hanseth, who won the Laguna Beach Open in 1973 as a 20-year old, had excelled both indoor and out, and wanted to keep it going...especially with the bucks now in the game. But it's hard to find a partner when they won't even speak to you; was he wearing the mark of the beast? The mirror told him no but in 1987 he was asked to pay a fine to the AVP for his three-year old transgression; afterwards he was absolved. "Guys who wouldn't talk to me now asked me to play." But it was the end of a long career; the last flame flickered when he took a second with Leif Hanson. They were defeated by Jon Stevenson and a kid who was good but a little too cocky for his age most thought—the first win for Kent Steffes.

Another player was looking for the right partner in those days. Already considered the best player in the world on hardwood, Karch Kiraly was considered by many to be even better on the beach. Here was an athlete: in the 1985 Super-Stars he tied with NFL All-Pro, Marc Gastineau, only to lose the contest on a technicality. But he could only play *half* the summer's tournaments at best. It was tricky: play with a full-time great partner, which could be counted on one hand, or go with the best for half a season? Then what about the other half? Mike Dodd went for it and played five tournaments with Kiraly in 1985, winning two. At the season's end his old partner, Hovland, asked for a full commitment in '86 or forget it. The great duo reformed, the great rivalry with Smith and Stoklos revived, and Kiraly was feeling a little alone for the first time in his life. In 1986 he won only one tournament. In '86 and '87, he went through a whole stable of partners looking for the right one, including such notables as Luyties, Hanson, Hanley and even Timmons. Where was the one player who could rise to the challenge? The frustration was only broken by the approach of the 1988 Seoul Olympics...even Marv Dunphy wouldn't let his boys touch the sand that year.

"Volleyball Gods..."

In July of 1985, the sport of volleyball received a national boost. Well, if not exactly a boost, a flap. Płayboy's edition that month featured a lengthy article on the sordid lifestyle of beach volleyball heroes. "Volleyball Gods" depicted a lifestyle which seemed instead to be a day in the life of a decadent rock star. On the other hand, since it was based on the quotidian habits of Tim Hovland, the old adage "There must be *some* truth in it" applied. Hovland now admits, "That took me right to the top of the charts! I was set up by the writer." While it might have made Hovland an even greater anti-hero, the AVP's corporate marketeers blanched at the article. "Sex sells...but subtly, my men. Sex *appeal* is what we're talking about—you've taken it too literally," complained the masters of free market propaganda. Still, it was a safe bet that some of the PR men were silently rhapsodic over the article: "any publicity is good publicity." Likely the same ones who most appreciated Miss July a few pages away.

Beach volleyball was racy, Playboy or no Playboy, and about the same time it began to impact fashion. Suddenly, it was cool to wear the colorful shorts and silk-screened images of spiking beach players on T-shirts. The trend started in California but before long, "volleywear" was being sported in airports, bars and colleges in Milwaukee, Phoenix and Atlanta. Sports apparel merchandisers kept a close look on the styles; in a few years, the sport ushered in the "neon revolution"—those day-glow nylon shorts which helped make jogging on the streets safer. Southern California companies formed overnight: Burmys, Spot Sport, Club, I Dig and Mossimo were joined by older surfwear outfits like Quiksilver, Gotcha and Maui and Sons to cash in on the beach volleyball look. Industry giants as Fila, Nike, Adidas and Speedo would try their hand as well. In 1985, Sideout signed Sinjin Smith to a full-time annual contract to promote its volleywear. Soon the other companies were throwing around big money to get the stars to wear their gear...and name.

Since 1979, Sinjin Smith had been chipping away at what was once thought an impossible record to break—Von Hagen's 62 Open victories. Admittedly, Smith's seasonal tournaments numbered more than twice the amount of summer Opens when Von Hagen started in the early '60s, but that did not detract from the fact that he had proven a consistent winner. Sideout was a good company for him; siding out was his game. Sporting the same mental toughness of the greatest sideouters, Lang and Menges, Smith, like them, put a mite less heat on the ball and jumped a little bit lower...but he got the ball down...time after time after time. Hovland compliments his arch-rival, "He was the hardest worker. On defense...he came up with some unbelievable balls." In 1986, Smith won his sixty-third Open to surpass the great Von Hagen. The new king remembers, "I never imagined when I started playing that the record was even touchable."

When he hooked up with Randy Stoklos in 1982, the brute power of Stoklos would soon force most of the serves to Smith. Strangely, the 6'4" Stoklos was blessed with one of the most beautiful pair of hands that ever played, and fed the sideout machine that was Smith, impeccably. On offense, Stoklos exploited his great jumping to fire dangerous jump serves as well as put up the most feared block in the game. Using one hand on close sets to get over farther, the "Kong block" became a daily term of beach jargon. In what is probably the highest compliment in the game, Kiraly has singled out Stoklas as the best beach player he has played against.

As a team, their play was superb. Smith would deftly stand in the open zone to pop up dig after dig, or run around the monstrous Stoklos scavenging for dinks. Soon television viewers were listening to the weekly broadcast of Prime Ticket's Chris Marlowe and Paul Sunderland as they explained the various hand signals used by blockers to direct the digger behind. The game was taking on more strategy. And beach volleyball was reaching a growing national audience on a consistent basis...America was learning about a new sport.

"Different coach...different style..."

"I'm just not real sure you *really* want this job," one of the panelists kept repeating over and over. The guy in the interview seat, Marv Dunphy, stayed true to his own character: consistent, direct and honest. He admitted to the 12 people conducting the interview that in fact, he did enjoy his current situation. Living in the Santa Monica mountains and coaching the men's volleyball team at Pepperdine University where he had built a national reputation as a respected coach was enjoyable...but he would also certainly enjoy the position of head coach of the USA Men's Team vacated by Doug Beal. Like a mosquito, the question of zeal by the evangelical panelist kept coming back. Dunphy didn't waver; at the end of the meeting he was approved.

The man fond of such axioms as: "Coaching is not knowledge," and "People like to do the things they're good at," is one of the most admired volleyball coaches who ever put in a lineup. He is also one of the most liked. His hallmark of positive reinforcement became apparent to him at age 22 when he was a graduate student teaching swimming for two summers at the Northridge Swim Club: "Whoever got more kids to come back the following week, got a quarter an hour raise." Dunphy won it every week. Later, completing his doctoral thesis on the coach he most admired, John Wooden, he had to learn an unsuspected and difficult lesson. "I tried to be Marv Wooden the first few months...it didn't work. You have to be yourself."

Dunphy's own style was a good alternative. In his first year as head coach in 1977, he took the small Pepperdine University to a third-place finish in the nation. The following year, Pepperdine won its first NCAA championship. Part of his conditions for taking the National Team job was that he be allowed to finish coaching Pepperdine that season. It was conceded, and led by the play of Bob Ctvrtlik, the Waves won their second NCAA title in 1985.

In May, 1985, Dunphy joined his Pepperdine assistant, Gary Sato, in San Diego to face the Olympic gold medalists. The team had been in good hands with Sato even though his choice as assistant was a hard sell for Dunphy. "They thought he was too young for one thing," remembers Dunphy. Sato, the former great player who starred at UC Santa Barbara, was from a family who could have beaten most volleyball teams in the country. Sister Liane and Eric would become Olympians, brother Scott was a leading player at San Diego State and another sibling, Glen, played at Loyola and now serves as assistant coach of the USC Men's team...for a sixth member, their father, Richard, was also an accomplished player. And if he or one of the kids went down, the mother, Elissa, was less practiced but not fearful of taking the court. Of a mixed Japanese, Chinese and Filipino descent, they all shared the same distinguishing traits: small, incredibly quick and dynamic. Bring on the best, but better bring your lunch and flashlight—it could take a long time—because the Satos may not block a lot of balls, but you could be sure that a lot of balls would be coming up...more than a lot! Fans loved to watch the Satos play, together or alone.

Gary Sato had to walk across the coals as well as Dunphy to get the job. When hard-nailed National Team Director, Doug Beal, posed the standard corporate questions: "Tell me what you consider your strength and weaknesses." Sato had an interesting reply. "Weaknesses? Two. This young face I was born with, and I don't have any suits or ties. Strengths? I know a lot of the young guys coming up, and I've seen the way these guys play defense...I can help!"

Dunphy didn't embark on his new job starstruck by any means. Most of the players he had coached at one time or another, many on Junior National Teams. Within a week they were on tour with the powerful Cubans in a four-match series. Dunphy remembers Doug Beal, holding up two fingers on each hand as Dunphy left the office for the airport. "He predicted two and two. I held up four fingers and a fist. I was right; we won all four matches."

A few months later, the USA Men went to the Dominican Republic for the NORCECAs. "Vacation in hell" would be a euphemism for the trip wrought with mishap. After all, these guys were prima donnas from Southern California, and rain water showers took some adjusting. When Doug Partie was awakened by an excruciating tarantula bite one night, he stumbled through the dark to find the light switch—a direct shot of 220 volts from the bare wire knocked him back several feet and made him forget for a few seconds the pulsating pain in his leg. The housing facilities weren't quite finished; Pat Powers found his most comfortable spot for sleeping in the bathroom.

The sudden death of Dvorak's mother prevented the starting setter from making the trip so the backup setter, Jeff Stork, was thrown to the lions. Stork, a left-hander, had starred at Pepperdine under Dunphy; still, he had been on the team less than a year and even the limited time he'd spent in practice with the world's best hitters had its trying moments. Things however were going fine in the finals against the Cubans—up to 2-0. But the heat was stifling in the hothouse gym and players were losing water at an alarming rate. If sweating is good for you, then Stork is probably the healthiest player ever to play in a USA uniform. As early as a second game timeout, Dunphy noticed that his setter was starting to stoop. His abdominal muscles were cramping. Quickly Dunphy forbade him to do any more jump serves.

In the third game, the setter was playing bent over. In the fourth with a 6-0 lead, Stork went to his knees in a contracted ball. They had to slide him off the floor to the bench where all his muscles were now going to stone—the hell of full body cramps. Getting him to the locker room, the doctor for the Canadian team attended the man and saw that he needed help fast.

Out on the court, the Americans understandably were struggling. The Cubans were elated...especially when they saw there was no backup setter. They quickly ran off six straight points; it was 6-6. At Stork's exit the master of control and calm, Dunphy, had been confronted with an unusual situation. He subbed in Dave Saunders for Stork, but Saunders was a hitter! Powers' reaction was a vein-popping bellow, "What are you doing!" as if he had suggested rolling Stork back out. Six hitters on the court and no setter within a thousand miles except for Gary Sato, who by now had grown accustomed to the tie he was wearing. In trouble? Then go to the miracle maker; Dunphy instructed Kiraly to step in and set every ball. Keep it simple; high sets forward or behind. Fine, but Saunders was playing in the setter's position so the lineup was haywire. Talk about play by feel! "We just improvised on the court," recalls Kiraly.

Somehow Karch got to the net from wherever he was; Saunders passed flawlessly and the wave of panic began to subside when Powers sided out with a backcourt kill. Time to breathe. Kiraly who had set four years at UCLA began hanging up perfect lobs which Powers and Timmons bludgeoned time after time. The Cubans halfway into the game became edgy—points weren't coming fast enough. Frustration led to errors and to a 15-12 victory for the red, white and blue. "The most incredible match of my National Team career...including the Olympics," states Powers. This team was pretty good.

They rushed the rolled up Stork to a local hospital; by the time they arrived his eyeballs were rolling in their sockets. The doctors managed to get an IV in one arm, although the muscles, hard as wood, kept repelling the needle. They then worked on penetrating another into his other arm. Only the needles were too small! Not enough fluid was getting into the man; it was getting perilous. The Canadian physician frantically called around to other island hospitals in search of bigger hypodermics—finally some arrived. The necessary solution was immediately injected...Stork came back from the brink of no return.

It was a trip to remember and one Dunphy was glad to put behind him—yet not without a unforgettable instances of humor. After the last point of the match, Dunphy remembers rushing into the locker room to see Stork in agony and the Canadian team physician bent over him. Shortly after, the jubilant players filed in, unsuspecting of the gravity of Stork's situation. In particular, "I remember Powers coming over

to Stork lying on the table and kind of innocently asking, 'What happened to you?'" The same question could have been asked of Powers much later that night. Awakened by a constant thud followed by a bizarre cackling, the two coaches got up to look out their window. There was the great outside hitter, a beer in one hand, a big rock in the other. He was repeatedly hurling the rock up at a terrified rooster clinging to the top of a palm tree—at three o'clock in the morning, howling with laughter.

Gary Sato proved the critics wrong very quickly when he took the USA Men's Team to Japan for the World Cup in December of that year. Since Dunphy's daughter was being born, the head coach stayed home. It was there at the highly esteemed competition in Tokyo, after being down 11-5 in the fifth game, where the Americans pulled out a 15-12 victory over the Soviets—the first victory over them in a major official competition since the 1968 Olympics. The youthful face of Sato beamed as he held up the trophy for Coach of the World Cup. The '84 Olympic gold medal took on a new luster as well for the veterans. Yet, imagine the reaction of Ruben Acosta and other FIVB luminaries had the gold medalist team not even shown up for the gala event! They almost didn't. The highly reputed marketing firm, IMG, which had a history of burnishing some of the world's brightest stars as John McEnroe, wasn't having much luck in establishing Olympic volleyball stars as household names. There were some good crowds on a post-Olympic tour with the Soviets: over 10,000 in Seattle, Portland and Los Angeles. The top players averaged about $50,000 for that first year. But now the term was expired and although IMG would stay on to promote matches of their preference through the '88 Olympics, they weren't putting up any money for salaries the second year. The honeymoon was over.

There was however, a healthy windfall from the Los Angeles Olympics—all National Governing Bodies of Olympic sports received $1,300,000. The USVBA which had always operated on a hand-to-mouth basis, now with some cash decided to play it safe; a decision was made to not touch the loot, put it in an interest bearing account for a rainy day—for an emergency. In addition, the USVBA under Monaco was making headway in garnering corporate sponsorship; in particular, the merchandising of Tom Selleck posters, T-shirts and other apparel was a source of revenue "which reached six figures faster than anything else," states Monaco. Yet when time came to re-negotiate another year-contract for the players, they were asked to take pay cuts—big ones. They had been planning to ask for *raises*! "Something is awry here," collectively cried the players. "The USVBA has $1,300,000 from the success of the LA Olympics and now they don't want to pony up the cash to pay us for year two?" The USVBA pointed to IMG as the stingy culprit. The marketing pros had made their bundle..or lost a little as they might claim—and the pot was now empty.

"No way!" screamed the gold medalists. The entire team huddled together and hashed out a pay scale from top to bottom. Kiraly is still impressed by their next step, "We decided between ourselves what the new salaries should be for every player. That was pretty amazing. We all agreed." Rookies like Doug Partie were exceptionally pleased. Playing for $450 a month up to that point, the veterans stood behind their teammates' sorry plight and demanded substantial raises. According to Partie, "I wasn't expecting those guys to stand up for us. Karch especially took a strong stand for us new guys."

Numbers decided, it was time to take pragmatic steps to force the issue. In effect, they boycotted practice for a week even though they showed up at Balboa Park and put themselves through their own workouts—hard to argue that they weren't motivated. It turned into an eleventh hour showdown. After several hours of haggling on the final day, Kiraly recalls, "We decided at the San Diego airport to go—with big pay cuts. It caused some divisiveness on the team; I remember Powers and I got into a pretty good argument. We mostly went because we wanted to prove ourselves as the best team

in the world amongst all the best playing. But we weren't happy with the USVBA."

Returning from Japan with yet another accolade, some of the USA Men were still smarting from the bad blood created before the trip. Dunphy was also alarmed. He asked the USVBA to sign players through 1988...cement a two-way commitment which wouldn't be broken before the Olympics. Hard for them to argue the soundness of that idea after the recent scare. Kiraly quickly went to ProServ and soon some of the other players signed agents to represent them. Doug Beal, who served as National Team Director (1985-1986), was suddenly confronted with fast-talking agents, many with MBAs and law degrees. A couple had little time or patience to hear out what the USVBA's problems were. "Do you want my boy or not? If you do, this is the price?"

New contracts were signed which bound most of the top players through the '88 Olympics. Two notable starters who weren't signed were Dusty Dvorak and Pat Powers—simply a case of the USVBA not coming up with the same money they could earn in Europe. The exhibition matches attracted good crowds around the country in certain places, but many players felt that the USVBA and IMG weren't doing a great job exploiting their gold medal. "It was a frustration we just learned to live with. Between 1984 and 1988, we had the best team in the world, the best players, the most marketable ones. They didn't reach one-fifth of the marketing potential," is Karch Kiraly's assessment. However, if the attendance wasn't overwhelming in some places, the USA Men certainly played a lot of matches. Travel became a brutal part of playing. "Between 1981 and 1989 I averaged over 200 nights a year in some other bed than my own," recalls Kiraly. Quite a switch from even a decade earlier when the strongest complaint by National Team players and coaches was the lack of international matches. With contracts safely signed, the team could now concentrate on the World Championships in Paris.

"Where's my Coke?..."

Thirty-two years earlier in Paris, Gene Selznick taught the Soviets how to make bubbles out of chewing gum and in return took home a new offense and criticism of American rules. Now the USA Team was the team to watch. "By then, we were probably 20% better than any other team in the world," reflects Dunphy. Dvorak had returned after one year in Italy and regained his starting position. With Stork playing behind him, Dunphy believes "our second six would have finished in the top 10 of the world." The finals were once again between the Soviets and the Americans. The Soviets still had the phenomenal middle-blocking Alexander Savin, who at 6'7" could still turn it on, and the ultra-smooth, swarthily handsome Alexander Sorokelet could finish a match without seemingly committing an error. Yet, with the great Soviet coach Platonov now retired, there was visible dissension on the Soviet bench—something rarely seen. When the starting setter, Zaitsev, was pulled, his stormy reaction spilled onto the court.

Not that things started all that smooth for the Yanks. With Berzins retired, Bob Ctvrtlik had been selected to take the demanding position of passing every ball with Kiraly and he was having real trouble in the first game. Craig Buck today laughs "we were giving Marv looks like...get him out!" Even the unflappable Dunphy was concerned and yanked the newcomer for a few points. "I just needed to settle him down for a few points."

He put him back in and Ctvrtlik turned golden, grabbing the confidence which would keep his spot unthreatened for many years to come. A stellar job by every player and that intense style which marked this world's greatest team was a stark contrast to the other greatest Soviet, Japanese and Polish ones in the sport's history—Kiraly barking out orders, Timmons running back to serve with the ball in one hand, pumping his other fist and screaming out a direct challenge to the fans as if *they* were the adversary. However, the one to watch in Paris turned out to be Powers; he had an all-time best performance. Earning Kiraly's praise "as the best high ball hitter he ever saw," he was virtually unstoppable on the left side, turning high sets time and time again into valuable points. Gary Sato says that there was always a can of Coke in the ice chest on reserve for Powers. If he had one of those spectacular nights of bludgeoning the better part of 80 sets, late in the game his face might blank and he would erupt, "Where's my Coke!" In Paris, they had a six-pack ready. It was fitting perhaps. Soon after, Powers left for an Italian contract as did Dvorak for a second time. Their brilliant careers as USA players were over.

"A clean slate..."

After the USA Women's finals in Los Angeles, the American girls emptied their lockers and looked around...for someone...for something...for a sign. None was there. The captain of the team, Sue Woodstra, still remembers: "We felt very proud of how we represented our country for many years...without much support. It would have been nice to have our efforts acknowledged after our very last match. No one...nothing." In lieu of a USVBA celebration, some parents of the women arranged a party at their Los Caballeros practice gym in Fountain Valley—cops and all. Someone requested a Linda Rondstadt tune: "...everybody loves a winner, but when you lose, you lose alone..."

Hyman, Crockett, Magers and Woodstra quickly flew off to Japan. Weishoff, Julie Vollertsen and Linda Chisholm got off the plane in Italy. The USVBA was suddenly without a team and without a coach...ostensibly not a bitter disappointment to many of the organization, at least the veterans thought. The trip to Hong Kong was made by a team coached by Selinger's assistant, John Corbelli. Only two Olympians went, Corbelli's future wife Laurie Flachmeier and Sue Woodstra—both in the roles of assistant coaches. A couple of the remaining '84 Olympians were interested in continuing on the USA Team, but in Corbelli's words, "They weren't welcome."

Perhaps it was better to start over. Interviews were held for the coaching position and Taras Liskevych, son of Ukrainian parents, who had dropped soccer to play volleyball in his hometown of Chicago, was selected. Having coached nine years at the University of Pacific, not only had he been a successful coach but he was a proven promoter. When he arrived in California in 1975, UOP had not even heard of the great Stockton Y teams of the '50s—it was football and the rodeo. Within a few years, Liskevych had garnered big donations and big crowds as well—both imperative to draw talent to a city which was no Los Angeles nor San Diego.

Without one returnee from the '84 USA team, Liskevych scoured the landscape for new flesh. There was plenty out there although all were young with no international experience. In terms of athleticism, the new coach had little to complain about in Caren Kemner and Angela Rock. They could bench press and jump with many of the USA Men—the trick was to get their technique perfected. Height arrived with Kim Oden and the young marvel, the 6'2" Keba Phipps. Versatility came in the form of Karolyn Kirby, gifted at everything but also a 5'11" setter who could jump close to 30 inches. Liskevych and assistant Jim Iams decided to go for it ; besides, they had four years to work it all out.

"The Filipino Bomb...returns..."

The Rawlings glove which flicked off the curve sign was less than top-of-the-line. Try a change-up? Waving that off too, the catcher realized what it was gonna have to be. A fastball on a 3-2 count—just what their best hitter would be looking for! With only a one-run lead and men on second and third. He disagreed but what could he do? Nothing. He gave the fast ball sign.

That's what Liz Masakayan wanted. The 10-year old kicked her shoe against the rubber on the pitcher's mound and stared down at the burly slugger, a big wad of pink chewing gum pushing out one of his cheeks. No ruses, no gimmicks she decided. Her best against his...blow it by him or not. Besides, this was the same kid who when they were younger wouldn't let her in the tetherball line; "Go play jacks!" he would scoff at her. Curling her index and middle finger over the red stitches, she rocked back and pushed off the rubber strip with her powerful right leg, came straight down with her arm past her left knee and twisted her hip towards first base in a full follow-through. The kid lunged at the white pill with all his eleven years of strength. And whiffed. The infield rushed the pony-tailed pitcher; the batter slinked off in double ignomiy. He could live with striking out to lose the game...barely. But against a girl! Where would he find the strength to live out the rest of his life?

"My upbringing is what made me competitive," believes Liz Masakayan. Funny, the burning drive to compete belies her sunny exterior—smiling, courteous, gracious, she has all the markings of a privileged childhood. Not even close. Her Slovak mother left the Phillipines with four young children to settle in Santa Monica and raise them by herself. Liz, who was five at the time, afterwards only saw her Filipino father a few times. Her mother was trained for adversity. A veritable coal miner's daughter from Pennsylvania, she had fled to the Big Apple the first chance she had at eighteen. Having sewn clothes by hand in her humble home, she plied the same trade in New York initially, before long she was designing apparel. And off to the Phillipines. Later, in Santa Monica, eighteen-hour days were not uncommon in her efforts to fill the cupboard of the two-bedroom apartment they lived in.

The Los Angeles beach communities have always had a wide range of wealth. Kids from Pacific Palisades might drive a Mercedes-Benz to high school; those toward Venice have less extravagant means of getting around. For Masakayan and her siblings, sports was a means to achieve some social standing which the lack of clothes and cars denied. She played soccer, little league, beach volleyball and then indoor volleyball in the Lincoln Junior High gym at night. By the time she was a senior, she and a little setter who would gain her own share of fame, Liane Sato, led Santa Monica High School to the State Championship. When college coaches began to call in recruiting efforts, the surprised mother tried to politely explain, "I don't think you understand. We don't have *any money* to send Liz to college."

One interested coach was Fred Sturm. Head coach at Stanford, Sturm had come close to shaving off the side of Masakayan's face in a mixed doubles beach tournament the preceding summer. He explained to her mother that the university would pay for the schooling—everything! Maybe he shouldn't have hit that overset so hard that summer day. She chose UCLA and after an All-American career was asked to try out for the USA Women's team in 1986.

In early '86, Masakayan accepted the $600 a month salary and a part-time job in a bank as well. Liskevych began experimenting with lineups and with her spot as well. Finally her right-side hitting position was decided upon. For the team, things jelled slowly. Only in the summer of the 1987 NORCECAs did they qualify for Seoul by beating Canada. They were still behind the Chinese, Soviets and Cubans who had world sensation, Mareya Luis. At 5'8" Luis could soar 40 inches and bounce balls with the same force as most men.

"Staying on top..."

The Pan-American Games came to Indiana in 1987. It seems the same rabid basketball fans were willing to take a look at any game with a ball, so 14,500 people filled the famous Hinkle Field House, the same gym where the movie, "Hoosiers," was filmed. What a surprise! The Men's volleyball finals pitted rivals USA and Cuba. In probably the most intense match ever played by many of the competitors—Dunphy included—it was a slugfest with lots of fireworks. And it was hot and humid. Spectators were sweating through their clothes, Stork was sweating through his shoes—squishing in them

until the water squirted on the floor and a new pair was provided. At least he didn't cramp, this time precautions had been taken. Kiraly and the phenomenal Cuban spiker, Despaigne, began a shouting match. Although Dunphy had made a point when he took the team to curtail this kind of display—corporate sponsors and television didn't cotton to it—that night it was too hot and too loud to matter. Let 'em go. They went at it big-time.

It was a turning point for the USA team with three new players: Ctvrtlik, Stork and a 6'6" center blocker from UCLA, Doug Partie, cemented their positions through the '88 Olympics. Timmons was moved to opposite the setter where he could wreak havoc in six hitting positions. Other than these few changes, Dunphy didn't overly tamper with the offensive system. Stork claims, "Everyone in the world knew what we were going to do, they just couldn't stop it." That night the Cubans were sure trying. At one moment during the match, the rowdy crowd hushed almost to a complete silence. It was eerie. They waited in suspense to see if the disappeared Timmons was coming back up. Playing on an elevated floor, the big blocker went in chase after a ball past the sideline—right over where the floor ended in a three foot drop to bare concrete. Timmons went straight over and down...head-first! Landing on his head he got up, that famous red flat-top a little flatter but no redder with the sign of blood.

There was a lot more room behind the court. In a play which many swear as the most spectacular ever seen, Karch Kiraly, in a dead sprint off a dug ball some 40 feet back *behind the endline,* reached a dropping ball with a flying leap. Planing out parallel to the floor, Kiraly backhanded it with a mighty swipe. Now traveling backwards 50 feet, it descended on a confused Doug Partie in mid-court. Not hearing the screaming players to bump it over the net, instead he *bumpset* the ball on his side—a reasonable set but the fourth touch! If looks could kill... Luckily Kiraly had continued his slide almost out of the county and besides, he was too out of breath to berate anyone.

"Most of the best teams in the world would stay with us, then hit a point where they would just crumble," remembers Dunphy. This time it was an exception. "The best finals I ever played in," recalls Jeff Stork. "There were times when Buck could take over a game by himself. At the end of the fifth game, he made three or four stuffs in a row...straight down!" It was a fight to the death, a great match. The USA prevailed in the end.

Dunphy knew that there was only one thing harder than getting to the top...staying there. His biggest challenge was to keep these guys fresh and hungry for four years. Four *more* years, since they had been going hard since 1981. From the onset, he and Sato designed a four-year plan, alternating intensive periods of important competitions with periods of more relaxed training and rest. He also began to slow the intensive practices down, devoting more time to teaching and refining of technique. "They had a hard time with that at first. They were so used to the daily go-for-the-throat scrimmages." Craig Buck believes that "the team matured with Dunphy. We only needed three hours a day in the gym now; the players were so self-motivated." Pat Powers compared the two coaching giants of the game: "You'd play with Marv out of respect. With Beal, you played out of fear." The new plan worked splendidly; every year Dunphy's winning percentage was well over .800. He would finish the quadrennial with a 196-31 record.

However, no road is without bumps and Dunphy remembers a rocky spot in the middle of China. They had been on a tour in 1988 with the Chinese and landed in the small town of Chendu; in warmups they could see snowflakes falling through the broken windows of the small gym. It was cold and they were as far away from home as they could get. Already in a sour mood, when the official started blatantly favoring the home team, tempers frayed and then snapped. Weren't they the best in the world? And now here in some God-forbidden, jerkwater

town, they were getting homered by some crooked bozo on the stand? They kicked balls, bounced nets, and swore at the ref in an unknown tongue. Dunphy's admonitions were feckless; it was a bad night all around.

In the locker room, Dunphy was deeply troubled. He'd seen this attitude building during the past month. Better to confront it right then and there. The frigid air went tense with the coach's words. Hey, Marv was serious about this! He cut to the quick: no more net grabbing, cut the swearing at the ref, never kick a ball, and ignore the officiating. Play volleyball the way they could, every night, despite the conditions. "If anyone has a problem with any of this, speak up now. After we walk out of here, I'm considering it settled. Alright, anyone not like it?" The twelve guys knew two things about Dunphy: first, he would stick by his word. And two, if you didn't agree, now was the time to say it. They knew a third thing too—he was right. Heads were down but no one spoke.

The relieved coach thought it had blown over, proud once again of the unparalleled character of this team. Until the official scorer ducked in the small room to get the captain's signature of the score sheet—a requisite of international volleyball. "I'm not signin' it!" declared Kiraly. Dunphy now saw *he* was serious. "You have to, Karch." Still, the captain couldn't stomach condoning the outright cheating of the referee; he resisted. "You mean after the meeting we just had, and nobody objected...you're going to refuse this?" Dunphy looked in the eye of the world's greatest player. A standoff. Kiraly grabbed the pen, clenched his jaw and scribbled. At that moment, losing a finger would have been preferable for the captain.

What a night! The thought kept returning to Dunphy as he assiduously pored over the score sheet in the darkness, tabulating points per rotation in the ugly match. As the bus jostled in the icy rain on a country road, every player was asleep dreaming of San Diego sunsets shared by spouses or girlfriends. Maybe it was a jolt of the bus, but for some reason the coach's vision fixed on the required signature of his captain. Technically a full signature was required—protocol in international volleyball was something universally respected and something the circumspect Dunphy would defend to the hilt. What Dunphy saw instead was a hen-scratched mark that looked something like an "X." He glared...then smiled, then chuckled lightly. Careful not to wake up his champions.

"Beach goes world..."

In 1987, teams from eight countries were invited down to Rio de Janeiro to compete in the first World Championships of Beach Volleyball. A portable stadium was put up on the beach of Ipanema, thousands of Brazilians sang and chanted and screamed like only Brazilians can. Television covered the event extensively and live. It was major league stuff; great athleticism and beautiful girls in those string bikinis only found in Brazil. In stifling heat, Smith and Stoklos took down Kiraly and Powers in a close match—two American teams—which showed the world early on who commanded this sport. The next year was even bigger. In 100 degree weather, it was Kiraly and Powers who proved American superiority again on the sand, but this time a Brazilian team finished second with the national hero, Bernard Rajman and his partner.

Meanwhile, back home beach volleyball kept getting hotter. Television viewers normally saw Smith-Stoklos against Hovland-Dodd, but sponsors and TV weren't complaining. The AVP, under Armato's tight stewardship, dumped Group Dynamics and was now in complete control of the show—from setting up nets to promoting the mammoth weekly extravaganzas. The beauty contests were now transformed into "Miss Miller Lite" but the entertainment was still the same. In 1988, the AVP agreed to a three-year deal with Miller Brewing Company: $4,500,000 for 23 events in conjunction with the three Jose Cuervo Tequila $100,000 "Gold Crown" series. Prize money and apparel deals were making guys, who in former times

were waiters at the Chart House, now drive BMWs and take speech lessons in order to appear articulate for TV interviews.

And a glimmer of new, young ability began to appear for those bored with the same old two teams always in a face-off. Brent Frohoff, 23, and Scott Ayakatubby, 21, were two Manhattan Beach kids when they came out to claim an Open victory in 1986. Besides giving the South Bay locals a new team to cheer on, they broke out the first new weapon which would widely impact beach volleyball: the jump serve. It was a common feature of the indoor game and the easiest way to score a point, but when these two guys started firing for points on the sand, it made heads spin. The 25-year old invention of Vogie had reached respectability even though the inventor went woefully unappreciated...at least, Vogie saw it that way.

The summer of 1988 supplied an unusual addition to the game, albeit an entertaining one. Pat Powers, now liberated from indoor except for winters in Italy and France, came into his own as a leading beach player. In the early '80s, he had occasional appearances, mostly to leave heads shaking at the cannon arm. No American ever hit a ball like Powers—*ever*—indoor or beach. But Olympic gold medals had been more rewarding for him; so no surprise that the sand game could be mastered by a soaring 6'6" who could vaporize a ball from practically anywhere on the court. And since the game went to blocking over in 1986, Powers was an instant threat at the net. In fact, all he had to do was block. Opponents weren't going to serve him! When the much shorter Jon Stevenson hooked up with "PP" in 1988, he would scamper around the towering barrier and pick up the garbage for valuable points—a la Smith-Stoklos. The proven formula worked under the new regime; Powers-Stevenson captured six Opens and played in six other finals. Had not Powers torn a rotator cuff in Italy months later, the celebrated detonater might have won a lot more...and been a lot richer. He would hang on with respectable finishes, but the heat of those nuclear blasts was gone, to the chagrin of spectators everywhere.

If toward the end of the '80s, beach volleyball had entered the American consciousness—and it did—it was largely through the weekly contests of the same two teams. Smith-Stoklos versus Hovland-Dodd emerged as living icons on the TV shrine in millions of American households. Since 1982, the two pairs traded off points, games and tournaments like squabbling merchants at a weekend swap meet. And after some 10 years of fighting in the sport's greatest and longest-lasting rivalry, the argument over which team was better still continues. On numbers alone, Smith-Stoklos were clearly the winners—they won about twice as many tournaments. Yet, if the bigger tournaments are given more weight, the nod would go to Hovland-Dodd. Counting up the richer and more prestigious events: Manhattan Opens (5-2); U.S. Championships, (2-1); World Championships, (5-1). Only in the Cuervo Gold Events did Smith-Stoklos reverse the trend with a 4-3 record. Is more necessarily better? Or is there more greatness found in winning bigger titles? It's a classical argument of sport itself. If ever there were this same polemic played out on sand, the Hovland-Dodd, Smith-Stoklos confrontations must be studied as the model. One thing cannot be argued: their intense battles week-in and week-out put a new game on the American map.

"Women need greed too..."

"Basta!" said the fair maidens finally. By 1986, American fathers were getting used to almost every high school girl in the country coming home to announce that they were on a team...if some of the more macho males hadn't subscribed to it in earlier times, legislation had made them open their eyes. Richard Nixon's Title IX had made a tremendous impact even though it would take over a decade to effectuate the changes. It slowed down dramatically in 1984 when a Supreme Court decision, Grove City versus Bell, severely limited the scope of the law; Title IX wasn't gutted but it was un-questionably maimed. Legislation often reflects the zeitgeist of the era and it is safe to say that the '80s were not a time of great social change. Money rolled...so did the national debt but it was the salad days for conservatives. When the First Lady, Nancy Reagan, deemed the *Beach Boys* too radical for a White House concert...those were astringent guidelines.

Toward the end of Reagan's terms, the bloom was starting to come off the rose a bit and Congress put forth the Civil Rights Restoration Act of 1987—an attempt to revitalize the weakened '72 legislation. Politics are not immune to irony and one occurred when Ronald Reagan vetoed the legacy of another Republican, Richard Nixon. However, in 1988 the veto was overridden by Congress. There were new teeth in the old legislation and Title IX as well. Girls were going to compete, so move over, boys!

By 1988, the number of full volleyball scholarships for women had soared. The NCAA reported that year over 260 Division I colleges with a women's volleyball program. Combining Division II and Division III levels, over 450 smaller colleges funded women's programs. Many of the Division I schools were handing out 10 full-rides and the wealth was spread far beyond the west coast. Predicting the Final Four in the NCAA championship was no longer an easy task: Nebraska, Texas, LSU, Penn State—there were now great collegiate teams from every corner of the nation. In contrast, in 1988 only 51 total men's collegiate programs existed in the country.

On the sand things might have gone on their uneventful way lost in the shadow of the AVP, had not Nina Matthies realized that sex sells...and the ladies' beach game could be sold to sponsors. She was right and like Susan B. Anthony of the feminist emancipation movement of the early 1900's, she led the charge which would eventually form the WPVA (Women's Pro Volleyball Association) and make pro beach volleyball for women a separate reality in 1987. Matthies marshalled the troops around her and even enlisted her husband and his friend, Scott Hubbell. Hubbell, already involved in sports promotion, was able to allure Budweiser into a tour sponsorship and Danny Matthies took charge of setting up the tournaments. For the next four years, Matthies would serve double duty—overseeing the tour and playing. Both jobs were demanding but she surprisingly hovered near the top—in the top four on the money list until she finally hung it up after 1990.

In the first season of WPVA, an astoundingly agile and quick player came out of nowhere—nowhere in America, that is—to dominate the tour. Jackie Silva, an Olympic setter from Brazil, found the sand of Ipanema and Bahia not too distinct from that in California. Teaming up with an Olympian from the '84 USA team, Linda Chisholm, they won most of the ten tournaments that year and pocketed about $8,500 a piece. The following year the same pair ruled again and came away with about $12,000 for their bank accounts. If the comely ladies could play on the sand, why not on the hardwood?

Major League Volleyball. Major league name, no question...anything else, questionable. Despite the hurt feelings of the men who played in the old IVA, in February of 1987, a new pro league was announced which featured only women. Strikingly similar to the IVA in its original grandiose designs, the league planned to have six franchises in six major media markets: New York, Chicago, Los Angeles, Dallas, San Francisco and Minneapolis. Major media markets...well, kinda. Player-coach Mary Jo Peppler found herself in the outer boroughs of Long Island the first year, then the team was transferred to White Plains. Minneapolis began in a downtown arena but ended up in a suburban high school gym. San Francisco was really San Jose and Los Angeles was anywhere a cheap gym could be found...including out of state. It was called playing fast and loose with the news media...which was rarely around anyway.

There were no Barry Gordys or David Wolpers to bankroll the league but there was a devoted and well-heeled financier who kept it

afloat and made sure the women got paid. Robert Batinovich funded the league and owned one of the few reasonably successful franchises in San Jose. Minneapolis was the other and with a league-leading average attendance of under 1500 the first year, the prospects of muscling out the NBA weren't encouraging. The more customary two hundred fans and family members at the other sites weren't grabbing headlines either. They had the stars: Peppler and Kirby in New York; Brassey and Dowdell in Dallas: Green and Crockett in Los Angeles (somewhere). And ESPN broadcasted occasional matches. An example of overreaching perhaps; you can fool some of the people...but not for long...and rarely the media, especially when they can't find you.

"The biggest star..."

Out of breath again, she was wobbling on her feet. The head coach of the Daiei team in the Japanese women's league in 1986 quickly substituted her out. Flo Hyman sat on the bench, head bent forward resting on her forearms. Next moment, she was prostrate on the ground; physicians knelt over her in attendance but it was too late. A victim of a rare disease, Marfan's Syndrome, which normally afflicts tall people, Flo Hyman died where she made such a tremendous world-wide impact—on the court. Sue Woodstra and Rose Magers, playing for NEC, would see the awful event on television later the same evening. In those images, Rita Crockett was seen as well, a shocked teammate at the side of her big friend. Woodstra remembers, "We talked to Rita all night on the phone."

The most recognizable American woman volleyballer in the world up to that time, Flo Hyman was gone too soon. Still, she had been a big pebble...and the ripples of her magnetic personality would spread...and keep spreading...

Sassy, classy, Brassey..."

She'd gone through enough she figured. She had been on the first USA team in 1972, broke the sex barrier at San Diego State in 1974, suffered in Pasadena in the mid-70s, got shot down like a U2 pilot over Moscow in '80, went into the IVA a few months before it folded, played in but didn't see the Major League Volleyball dream come to truth, and ventured to Italy in the early '80s when the money wasn't so good but at least the pasta was marvelous. Finally Laurel Brassey was comfortably ensconced in Albuquerque, a cushy job as head coach at the University of New Mexico, a decent car, a mortgage...and no more grueling, knee-wrenching, shoulder-ripping workouts! Finito!

Then the phone rings and it's Terry Liskevych. We need you, your country needs you! he cried. "Ah, come on. I'm 34!" she countered. That's okay, he'd seen her in Major League Volleyball: the great hands, the remarkable defense, the court savvy. "Oh, man! pack up my car again to go play volleyball?" To leave that wonderful state the sport had never let her know...stability. But like a bad dream...the best dream...the Olympics kept recurring. She arranged a leave of absence and in the spring of '87 was out in her hometown of San Diego setting thousands of balls once again.

Paula Weishoff had come back as well the year before to play in the World Championships in 1986. "But my heart was in Italy," she declared; plus the eleventh place finish probably did nothing to keep her stateside. The original setter, Kirby, left in a huff as well after the World Championships—soon in the middle of Italy's boot. Her replacement wasn't working as planned and Liskevych was getting nervy about the most important position. My god! they still hadn't qualified for the '88 Olympics. That was soon coming in the NORCECAs. If no rising stars, then what's recently descended which can be salvaged, shined up and shooed in? Brassey. She was feisty—one of those who couldn't handle Selinger a second stint but she was a proven winner...and still good. Real good.

Vision with ambition. Ruben Acosta becomes president of the FIVB at the LA Olympics. (Courtesy of FIVB)

Nowhere to go! Perfect block by Timmons and Kiraly. (Courtesy of USA Volleyball)

Right-side terror. Steve Timmons punishes a Cuban block...and most others.(Courtesy of USA Volleyball)

Bob Ctvrtlik rose to the occasion in the '86 World Championships in Paris. (Courtesy of USA Volleyball)

Turistas. Kiraly and Timmons in downtown Havana. (Photo by Bill Frakes, ALLSPORT USA)

Best in the world. Craig Buck (7) roofs another. (Courtesy of USA Volleyball)

Gettin' down! Sinjin Smith in relentless pursuit, surpasses Von Hagen's 62-Open win record in 1986. (Courtesy of Doug Avery)

If it's close to the net, Stoklos will win it. (Courtesy of Doug Avery)

Pat Powers. The most awesome hitting machine ever...indoor or beach. (Courtesy of Doug Avery)

Jackie Silva, the first off-shore threat. (Photo by Peter Brouillet)

Company man. Jon Stevenson goes from player to AVP president. (Photo by Robert Beck)

Linda Chisholm teamed with Silva to dominate the first year of the WPVA, 1987. (Photo by Peter Brouillet)

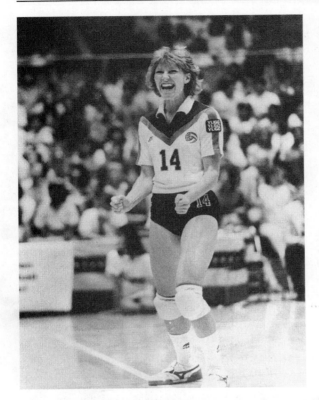

Laurel Brassey. Called out of retirement to set for Seoul. USA Women's Olympic Team, 1988.

It's a famiily affair. In Seoul '88, Liane Sato, Assistant Coach Gary, Eric Sato (Courtesy of Bud Fields)

Chapter 18
1988 Seoul Olympics

"Seoul on ice..."

"I wanna watch myself when I was a good hitter." Marv Dunphy couldn't believe his ears. Worse, the timing of it. The night before the gold medal match and Steve Timmons was standing there, the world's most consistent hitting machine during the past quadrennial, and asking for a year-old tape of the USA Cup. The coach had noticed some mounting frustration—it happened in all thoroughbreds—particularly as the race neared. But this tingled his spinal column. To go in the tank for the '88 Olympic finals? Perish the thought!...but the thought was there.

Dunphy reached for the tape lost in a whole wall full of video matches. Handing it over, he abruptly stopped his arm. The familiar serenity and calm in his baritone voice was worth more than a thousand videos. He sat the big red-head down. He explained that for the last two years the world was against the spiker—literally. Timmons' attacking had proven so devastating that other teams had been putting their best two blockers on him. Of course it had an impact on his effectiveness...but it provided almost open range for the other hitters around him. Timmons spirit lifted a bit but still not satisfied, he reached for the video.

"Steve, I don't care if they put one guy...or no guys on Karch...and three on you tomorrow. I know what you can do. Just go play." Dunphy still holding the video, tossed it against the wall.

"Stork's back!..."

It had been smooth sailing for the Americans until the third game of the pool. Not that there wasn't a great worry in the back of everyone's mind. Jeff Stork had thrown his back out—unable to play during the first ten days of September. On the bench during the preliminary pool play, Ricci Luyties—the big, great UCLA setter—came in and performed admirably. Then they ran up against Argentina: three hammers, two-meter guys with big jumps and heavy arms. Raul Quiroga was one of the threesome; another was Hugo Conti with the Van Dyke beard who was giving them fits, unstoppable out of the backrow. They'd never quite seen this before; the two 6'7" attackers were varying their right side approach out of the backrow—the deft Cantor would set the ball one time on the line, the next five feet inside. And Conti from the back middle was flying so far forward he was hitting a low two-set almost on the net, a normal front row attack. The USA blockers couldn't get a beam on either of them and they were slicing up the American block at will. The best team in the world was down 2-0 and losing the third game.

"Stork! Get ready to go in and serve!" Dunphy shouted down the bench at the injured setter. He was up in a flash, without wincing he happily noticed. Ten days left in the Olympics...he had to go for it now. Play or not play. Stork took aim and fired—five straight points! He stayed in and set, the Americans revived and took a 3-2 victory which was their only close call of the Games. Stork wouldn't come out another play the rest of the Olympics. "There was never a doubt about the outcome," remembers Buck. "It was almost anticlimactic."

Still, the finals were no foregone conclusion; although there was not the same emotion that the Yanks usually played with against other teams. "We and the Soviets respected each other so much that there was never any yelling through the net. Our two teams were head and shoulders above the rest of the world during that time; in fact, they had beaten us a couple times before Seoul in big competitions. But we were closer to them than any other team. We'd gotten to know them pretty well," says Kiraly. "Some great battles...and a lot of vodka afterwards," Powers recalls. Not that the gold didn't mean much. Kiraly adds, "Seoul was much more meaningful to me even though it was much less euphoric than Los Angeles. It's always harder to repeat, harder not at home, and harder when it's a full tournament."

The close call with Argentina had some of the television heavies concerned. Volleyball ratings as in 1984 were outstanding. But some other things weren't going well; it appears that the handing over of gold bracelets by Korean agents to boxing judges, for some reason, seemed to have an effect on the outcome of matches. In uproarious results, some American favorites were losing. A few other upsets in track and field and it was getting a little thin towards the last days of Seoul. The volleyball semis were terribly crucial now for NBC—the USA Men needed to win to guarantee an American team finalist on the final broadcasting day of volleyball. Dunphy vividly recalls walking down the television control center when he crossed paths with program director, Peter Diamond. The man who had done so much for the game in Los Angeles by giving volleyball tremendous coverage was now hoping for a payback. Dunphy espied the main man approaching down the hall and held out his hand. Diamond instead slumped to both knees. "Oh, my God!" thought Dunphy. Diamond lifted his head slowly and softly spoke, "Marv, you gotta win tonight." Dunphy promised they would...thankfully he was right.

For the gold medal match, there was only one insidious element of fear to upset Dunphy's game plan. On the international level there is a facet of coaching, like in all team sports, which is much like chess. Endless scouting and tabulation of statistics, analysis in search of tendencies, both for teams as well as individuals. The Soviets had a lefty with a whip arm, Yuri Antonov. He was the one unknown variable—a little unorthodox—but if he got hot, he could drill it or hit off hands and find ways to kill you all night. He'd done it a few times before. The best defense for Dunphy was to get the right guy lined up against him...in this case, have Timmons follow him across the front row. To do that, he had to guess where the Soviet coach would start him. Dunphy guessed that the southpaw would start right front—he started Timmons in the same spot. When Antonov took lined up right front, Dunphy and Sato gave a discreet high-five.

Good omen and a good strategy. Timmons got to the wiry Soviet in a couple early stuffs; Antonov wouldn't bring on the nightmare match they'd fretted about. The team was up 2-1 and one point away when Eric Sato was substituted in to serve. He launched a jumper which was passed over the net; substitute Scott Fortune hadn't played much but he got the sweetest kill of his life when he drilled it for the match. Gary Sato remembers, "I was more relieved than happy." As for the lost form of the worried Timmons, he had over 40 kills. Stork added several more on second balls and kept up his wicked serving.

It was a dynasty...the greatest in the sport's history. It seemed that the phenomenal USA Men's Team could have gone on...and it could have. Yet the undercurrents of change were already coursing, a tide carrying along the flotsam of beach dollars and Italian lira...and easily sweeping away the underpinnings of the USVBA's National Team program.

"3-0, under 32 points...and we're in!"

The women had some ill fortune from the outset. Liz Masakyan had hurt her back in a pre-Olympic tournament in Japan the week before Seoul and would not practice during the ten days before the competition. Not to be denied, the spunky Masakayan came out fearless and turned in a good tournament. Some of the other pillars of the squad did not. In a pool with top-ranked China, they also had Brazil and what would be the tournament dark horse, Peru. All went well against Brazil when the Yankee ladies pulled out a 3-2 victory. As expected the Americans got white-washed by the Chinese and worse. Keba Phipps, who at times displayed as much talent as any woman in the international game, started with a bad case of the jitters against China. Although Liskevych yanked her early in the first game, the unnerved 19-year old was unable to get out of her playing funk. Kemner was at times brilliant but erratic. Angela Rock played well off the bench troubleshooting but one player's performance could only do so much. As for the 34-year old setter, Brassey, she held a cool and steady hand but the offense was not risk-taking enough in her mind, "too predictable. We had a real young team but I thought we needed to take more chances and use more variation." Masakayan agrees, "I thought Terry didn't give Laurel enough freedom to run the offense." Liskevych counters, "We were young and didn't have the passing skill or setting to run a varied attack."

Well, no one expected them to beat the Chinese anyway. Neither were the little, digging Peruvians with the one huge 6'5" Gabriella Perez, when they pulled the rug out from under the gold medal favorites. Somehow, China had 14 match point attempts and lost. So now it all came down to the last pool match, USA versus Peru, which required the American Women to not only win...but win 3-0 and give up less than 32 points!

They had a better chance to win a decision against a South Korean boxer, or outstrip Ben Johnson on steroids than to pull this one off, most experts thought. However, it was a very gutsy display by the USA Women; coming out with both guns blazing, they took the first two games while giving up a total of 23 points. Now, if they could stave off the frightened Peruvians with a 15-8 win or better in the third game, they would qualify for the medal round. Perhaps the young ladies might have thought it too much themselves as they dropped the third, and understandably, the next two. After that, it was a dispirited team which played through the secondary pool. The USA Women finished seventh out of eight.

More gold. USA Men celebrate their second Olympic gold medal in 1988. (Photo by Bruce Hazelton, ALLSPORT USA)

USA Men's Olympic Team, 1988. Front row (from left to right): Craig Buck, Scott Fortune, Doug Partie, Jon Root, Troy Tanner. Middle row: Asst. Coach Gary Sato, Bob Ctvrtlik, Steve Timmons, Jeff Stork, Dave Saunders. Bottom row: Ricci Luyties, Karch Kiraly, Gary Moy (Manager), Coach Marv Dunphy, Jim Coleman (Statistician).(Photo by George Long)

Young and inexperienced.USA Women's Olympic Team, 1988.Back row (from left to right):Melissa McLinden, Caren Kemner, Keba Phipps, Kim Oden, Jane McHugh. Middle row: Kent Miller (Manager), Tammy Liley, Laurel Brassey, Deitre Collins, Jim Iams (Asst. Coach). Bottom row: Terry Liskevych (Coach), Debbie Landreth-Brown (Asst. Coach), Liz Masakayan, Kim Ruddins, Angela Rock, Liane Sato. (Photo by George Long)

Chapter 19
1989-1992

"Can Sinjin come out to play?..."

In Hermosa Beach at the US Championships in 1989, a bizarre event occurred which illustrated the influence—some said over-influence—of the players...or one of the players at least. The finals of the winners were set for Smith-Stoklos against Hovland-Dodd. The crowd gathered, Hovland and Dodd were warm but where were the opponents? Sinjin stayed in the tent. Unmoving until a linesman, Jon Lee, was removed. Not a head referee but a linesman! Few were critical of Lee's expertise or eye; he'd been a major figure in the game long before any of these players on the court had played their first tournament. Articulate and witty, he had also been asked to contribute articles to Volleyball Monthly and a couple had smacked of criticism—namely of one ranking player, Sinjin Smith. Ah ha! One in particular covered the Santa Barbara Open where Lee was acting as head official. The article further explained the antics of Sinjin Smith at East Beach, refusing to play with any of the new dozen balls. After 20 minutes of plying technicalities in the rulebook, Smith finally relented. Apparently, he didn't forget.

They began to count points; Smith still refused to come out. At 11-0, he emerged and his team went down 15-0. Never known for lying down, the guy whose success Pat Powers attributes to being "too egotistical to lose," came roaring back. Even vengeance came up short and they lost in a double finals. Still, a similar incident occurred earlier in the season in Rhode Island—and to Karch Kiraly of all people! Tied at 6-6, the next point scored by either team meant victory. Kiraly served and rushed to the net to block; the ball Stoklos buried past Kiraly was brought up with a stupendous dig by Brent Frohoff. Kiraly set it and Frohoff swung for the seventh point—what an ending, what a match! What a call! The referee was signaling something; a touch on Kiraly's block which would make Frohoff's winning-spike the fourth touch. You only get three in the AVP. "No!" howled Karch.

To no avail. The serve went to Smith who served up a floater to Frohoff. Waiting like a famished animal at the net, Stoklos put the roof over Frohoff's cross-court spike. 7-6 to Smith-Stoklos...and this time it was final. Kiraly went off again. Somehow most of the beach, the television audience and all of the AVP players derived some perverse satisfaction out of the ensuing spectacle. The captain of two Olympic gold medalist teams, the guy who rarely remonstrated, the paragon of volleyball rectitude...clutched the net and ripped it to the ground in one awesome act! Did he feel remorse? "It felt great," Kiraly reminisces today with chuckles.

Yet, the outcome of Smith's actions was more vociferous and critical. How could a player have such pull...and gall for that matter...to oust a referee, a linesman, he didn't like. Even Magic Johnson didn't have that clout! It added fuel to the smoldering rumor of Smith's power. Matt Gage recalls, "The perception at the time was that Sinjin was having too much inside influence with the AVP. Both he and Stoklos were being represented by the same attorney who represented the AVP." And more, not only was the attorney acting as legal counsel but his office was performing the accounting and other functions as well. The AVP again wanted to see the numbers; Armato came out clean in an audit but there were paid tasks being performed for the AVP by other companies which Armato was a stockholder in. Somehow this had slipped by the playing members of the board. It was finally looking way too incestuous and players were grousing more than usual—especially "those from the South Bay" in the opinion of Smith.

On the heels of the audit came the renegotiation of Armato's contract and he took a hard line. Gaining a high profile in the pro sports world with representation of megastars like Kareem Abdul-Jabbar and later Shaquille O'Neal, the man had plenty of work. To continue with the AVP, he wanted a seven-year deal with a seven-year option...and a big chunk of ownership. "Wait a minute!" came the players' chorus. "The AVP is owned by the players!" The whole affair called for a new board election and after an unsavory canvassing campaign, Smith was replaced on the board. "It was the only time I ever served on the board," recalls Karch Kiraly. "Seven months of energy wasted on the whole issue." Another power play, another change. Sinjin was out of the inner circle, Armato was out the door. What was most sacred in the AVP—the players' ownership—would stay intact.

Miller was understandably a little jittery with the news. With minimum prize money for an event in 1989 set at $50,000—the U.S. Championships paid a record $150,000 purse—they sat back with a fat sigh when the richest event at Hermosa Beach attracted more than 30,000 fans. Money talks. And it was talking all they way down to the 17th place in tournaments; good college players upon graduation often made the same choice. Forego an up-and-down USA Mens' program—or a year in Italy to pay off student loans—to spend time playing in the sun, on the sand, before mobs of beautiful girls and weekly television. A hard choice?

Adam Johnson, Mike Whitmarsh, Kent Steffes and Brian Lewis were names more and more mentioned by Marlowe and Sunderland on Prime Ticket and ESPN, as well as printed in the two monthly magazines, perennially below the same two teams which owned the sport for most of the '80s. An ongoing argument accompanied the longest rivalry of the sport; was Smith-Stoklos versus Hovland-Dodd a good thing to see every week or not? In 1989, there came a needed relief on the air when Kiraly found Frohoff able to live up to the living legend's impeccable play. They won a handful of tournaments. Tailing at the end, the superstar next recruited a stripling, Kent Steffes, for the '90 season. Not yet the perfect pairing, they won only two out of ten events and a frustrated Kiraly backpedaled a bit and went back to Frohoff to finish the season. A man can't have two brides—at least in this country—and Kiraly flip-flopped again in 1991 after his return from establishing himself as the reigning indoor monarch in Italy. A jilted but more seasoned Steffes found the magnanimity to accept Kiraly's renewed offer of a partnership. After all, he wasn't crazy. They won six out of ten tournaments and those who sensed that there was a new team of destiny in the making—that the greatest player in many minds who ever touched a volleyball—would now get a chance to stamp his lasting imprimatur on the sand...were right.

In 1989, beach volleyball proved to be "very, very good" to some foreign women: Silva found another South American, Patti Ortiz (later Dodd), and they swept most of the tournaments and almost $30,000 per lady. Matthies and Elaine Roque took seven seconds—Matthies at least able to show some $18,000 for her efforts. By then however, the sport was on solid footing—swimwear companies were signing up tanned beauties to sport their latest and all the players were wearing Ray-Bans or Bolles—smiling all the way to the bank.

"You are a little early...but one day you will be an Olympian..."

"Treat me with respect and you get a lot out of me." Who said it? Diane Feinstein, Kathleen Brown, Hilary Clinton, Ann Richards? A campaign slogan from 1992, "The Year of the Woman?" No, Karolyn Kirby in a reflective moment. Still, she says it with an edge: sensitivity, bluff, bitterness, challenge, hurt, all of these and more? Until now, the best female beach volleyball player to have ever stepped out on the sand...or leaped out of it...or spanked one, angle, line, hard. She's pretty as a picture, hard as nails—but it is best to throw out the cliches and trust fate to tell this story.

It was an unlikely route which lead the 5'11" athlete to the top of the heap. One mixed up with destiny...of the strange vicissitudes of life which befall mortals and make for greatness or not. The ancient Greeks were obsessed by it; the events of a whole year could swing on the messages in the entrails of a goat, read by the oracle of Delphi. Kirby was raised in the athletic shadow of two stud brothers yet her father kept saying, "She's the athlete in the family." Did he have extraordinary foresight? Or did he himself will it in part?

What was empirically true was that the local star from Brookline, Massachusetts, had no money nor a lot of options when she graduated from the Boston suburb high school in 1979. A gifted swimmer in childhood, she was a burnt-out case by high school and under the long arms of the Boston Celtics, was leaning toward a college career in hoops. It was weird that she even went out for the volleyball team— weirder, when they won the state championship. Fate...and talent: a powerful combination and it kept happening. Scott Mose, an early volleyball enthusiast out of New York who was coaching at Rutgers, conducted a couple of summer camps in the Boston area and did a double take on this kid. How could he not? The camps made her better and there were offers of partial scholarships to Penn State and of course, Rutgers in Newark, New Jersey. It didn't matter anyway—she didn't have enough money to go to either.

Destiny. Made...or do we make it? Her high school coach fired off a letter to the obscure school which had just won the National Collegiate Championship in 1978—Utah State. The school was irrelevant; the coach was everything—the notorious Mary Jo Peppler. An unlikely place to be for the outsider but Orleans was a strange place for Joan of Arc to hail from. Besides, Brigham Young demonstrated to many that here was the place where one could carry out a dream—a full-on dream of the Church of the Latter Day Saints by the time Peppler arrived in 1977. Still she found a place. Peppler and assistant McReavey were interested in the Bostonian. "Could you come out for a tryout?" Are you kidding? That's five hundred bucks! "How about a tape?" They agreed to give it a look. Obviously, Kirby was good but she was raw; yet, Peppler was sharper than any women's coach in the country. Still, to offer a full ride on a tape? That same combination—fate and talent—stepped in. Kirby was soon in Logan, Utah. A starry-eyed kid with a Boston accent and deep in grief. Her father had unexpectedly died at the age of 49.

"Mary Jo was a great role model." Kirby joined many others to sing the praises of the head coach. Peppler, the eternal peripatetic, having conquered one more frontier was off to another in 1983. This time to the deep South, the University of Kentucky. She took Kirby with her and they finished a respectable fifth in the nation. The result was enough attention on the brilliant captain, who could set or hit, to get a tryout with the USA Women's Team in California—six months before the Olympics. After a few months, Selinger took her aside: "You are a little too late...but one day you will be an Olympian."

It sure looked that way when she made the '85 team under Terry Liskevych. Setter and captain, she was an integral part of the rebuilding of the new Women's Team. But progress was coming too slow and in 1987 Liskevych invited the great Paula Weishoff back on the team as well as setter Michelle Boyette. Three weeks before the Goodwill Games and the World Championships, he changed the whole lineup: Boyette setting and the versatile Kirby now playing as a starting hitter. An eleventh place finish and a disillusioned Kirby—she wanted to set and to lead—quit the team.

So what about Selinger's prediction? Well, soothsayers had been put to the stake since time immemorial for predicting the wrong outcome—even the vestal virgins of Delphi. Where to go now? Amidst a lot of tears but "a feeling of power I'd never felt" the moment she quit, she cast it all to the wind. Destiny. She was off to Italy to get some cash and have some fun like every other American who wasn't into the Olympic dream. Two years in Reggio Emilio, a new language and a good time. She had also discovered the beach. In 1988, she darted out on the sand, white skin and all; that year she paid her dues with Jo Ellen and with Dale Hall the following.

In 1990 she arrived: "I developed that year." Starting the season with Patti Dodd, she finished with Jackie Silva who after nursing a career threatening injury suggested Kirby play with someone else. That suggestion coincided with the realization that she was as good as anyone on the court—Californian or not—and in 1991, she chose Angela Rock and they set a modern standard for women's beach volleyball. But big jumpers get big knee problems and Rock got hers the next year. In '92 they suffered a ninth place finish in *Cape Cod* before every distant Kirby relative and childhood friend. Something told Kirby that maybe another change was in place. Rock agreed and Kirby finished the year with Nancy Reno, dominating the WPVA and more—the two heavyweight FIVB tournaments in Brazil and Spain, an Olympic demonstration event. It wasn't quite Barcelona—and the true Olympics—but it was an international tournament with the world's best. She and Reno won it. Was that Selinger's prediction?

"Sideout...the movie (gag!)"...

Volleyball Monthly featured it. All the tanned heavies in tuxedos, arms draped over buxom blonds who appeared to have one eye on the lens and one roving for the agent skulking behind the potted palms. Dude, this was it! The game had come home...to Hollywood. Bernie Holtzman, eat your heart out. His father was a purveyor of costumes to the Hollywood studios but the game he pioneered at State Beach had now hit the movies. The sport was hot, hot, hot! Players were all of a sudden getting screen tests and voice lesson teachers in Manhattan Beach couldn't handle the surge of incoming phone calls.

The budget was ten million bucks for "Sideout." Director Peter Israel assembled an acknowledged cast; television's "Thirty-something" star, Peter Horton, looked the part. Blond, tan and...well, he could run, actually jump off two feet, and land without falling. The other star, C. Thomas Howell, was about as miscast in appearance as looking up on a tournament board and seeing that same *name* entered as a competitor. At considerably less than six feet, dark hair and moon-skinned, Howell was somehow passed over in the year's Oscar nominations. John Travolta would have been a better choice for the role...even in bells and elevator shoes. If the script, crew and actors deserved panning, only one person deserved more: the casting director. Admittedly the cast members were not self-avowed thespians—Shakespeare, Shaw or Beckett would never be a temptation—but this was a movie about *beach volleyball*.

Trite? Moreso. A cocky white-skinned kid from Nebraska or thereabouts arrives for a summer in Manhattan Beach. That happens. What doesn't happen is that the guy who has as much visible prowess as Pee Wee Herman takes to beach volleyball and cajoles an aging AAA to re-get a life. Predictably...oh *so predictably*...they climb through tough teams to the top in a few scant weeks. Kathy Ireland, the heroine, was admittedly something to gawk at but she was far more suited to pre-talkies. Throw in the other chicks and the South Bay bars and then throw up. Jon Stevenson, hired as technical consultant, had the greatest challenge in making Howell look like he even belonged on the beach, much less function on it. Sagging nets below women's height ("Spiker's" mini-trampoline was not employed) were unconvincing even to the kids slumbering in the audience. The best acting job was done by Randy Stoklos who emoted a realistic emotional state of being pissed off in a bar.

The poor script writer, David Thoreau, got a first-hand experience in what Hollywood does to screenplays; seven writers were called in after him to doctor his script—before calling him back again to try and salvage his original idea. "A good concept never realized," Thoreau laughs today. If it was the gold rush for every volleyball player and camp follower on set, one player refused to participate...and he was offered a lead! Karch Kiraly was originally to play himself; he and Timmons would act as top dogs and finally succumb to Howell's latent athleticism and Horton's resurrected rage. "I read the script and couldn't justify some guy coming out from Nebraska and beating me after taking four weeks to learn the game. If I was playing another character...maybe...but Karch, no way!" Kiraly passed on some good money but his integrity stayed whole...as well as an unblemished acting career.

The movie lasted at best a month in nationwide theaters. "Now available in video" was subsequently true and in the final analysis, a stunning example of how not to make a film. Even for the American public.

"Bulldog tenacity..."

He tells a great story. That's a valuable asset in tough times; the ability to articulate, to embellish hurtful events somehow can make them more palatable. And Bill Neville had some tough times during his tenure as USA Men's head coach between 1988-1990. He picks one like a favorite arrow out of a crowded quiver. "This kinda typifies what it was like. Adam Johnson was new to the team and was having a good year in '89. He was showing signs of be-

coming a very good swing hitter—all the necessary tools. So he came to me about Christmas of '89 and said he had a problem," Neville snickers. "Oh, really?" he adds in impressive mock seriousness. "Tell me something new."

"Adam tells me that he has gotten an offer from Italy for six figures...for five months. As a first-year player, we are paying him $12,000 for 12 months! And he sincerely wants to stay. He asks if we can at least increase it some. Of course I tried but the USVBA said no. He probably would have stayed for $25,000 but the USVBA couldn't pay it. How do you compete with that?" Rhetorical question. Answer: You don't. "Up to '84, there weren't the same options for players. The beach was not paying that much and the Italian salaries hadn't taken off yet."

Money was probably the greatest problem for Neville but by no means the only one. When Al Monaco resigned after 1988, the USVBA decided to hire another insider. Cliff McPeak had served as the Associate Executive Director for the USVBA for several years. Prior to that he worked as the Chairman of the Department of Health, Physical Education and Recreation at Wright State. It was there during the dark Dayton days that his interest was piqued in volleyball; soon he was out in San Diego with the associate position. McPeak took over the USVBA with a challenge. By the end of '80s, the AVP and beach volleyball had firmly fixed itself in the American public's awareness of the sport. Meanwhile, the fabulous USA Men's Team of the era and the world-ranked Women seemed to have the habit of almost going underground...only to appear during Olympic Games. "A fourteen-day appearance every four years," as Karch Kiraly would say. And to add insult to injury, foreign club teams were waving huge contracts in the faces of the best players.

With some luck and some insight by Al Monaco, the USA Men held together between 1984 and 1988. As Al Monaco would say, "I feel lucky that Karch Kiraly and Flo Hyman were born when they were and played during my administration." This next quadrennial didn't look so promising. Given the setting, it was with some skepticism and tongue-clacking that many received the news of McPeak's appointment in January, 1989. Those who wanted the old USVBA network to be finally broken—to go outside the sport and get a professional from the sports marketing world— were disappointed again. "Oh well," thought many indoor enthusiasts, "turn on ESPN or Prime Ticket, crack open a beer, and watch 'the Hov' and Dodd go against Sinjin and Stoklos in another weekend battle."

To oversee National Team affairs and international relations, Doug Beal was rehired soon after McPeak—Beal's title was now Senior Director. It was another new beginning and fortunately, Neville was left with some of the residual talent of 1988. Stork, Ctvrtlik, Troy Tanner and Scott Fortune would stay full-time while Kiraly and Timmons would come and go with a whim. Both center blockers, Buck and Partie took the money and ran to Italy. Not that Buck wanted to go. "They wanted to pay John Root more money than me! So I told them what they could do with that idea. Besides, here they had over a million dollars in the bank from the LA Olympics. Did they invest it in two gold-medalist teams? No, it sat there collecting interest. Is that a sound business investment? During the '80s!"

If the post-'88 era didn't begin propitiously, it got worse. For a second time, IMG came in for a multi-year contract to market and promote the National Teams. After a lackluster tour featuring patch-work teams, they were looking for a way to give volleyball back to its nominal guardians. "I finally told the USVBA, how long do you think we can keep bringing back these all-stars to bail us out in important competitions? How long do you think Karch and Timmons are going *to live?*" Undoubtedly, they hoped forever. Neville found the domestic exhibition schedule woefully inadequate as well. "There was no purpose for most of the matches." IMG seemed to agree. "There were a couple of times I arrived at the gym and there

was nothing set up—no net, no lines, nothing! IMG was always trying to save money. Once it happened in LA—against the *Japanese*, of all teams. Over there we get treated like royalty. I spent hours apologizing to them."

Finally Neville went to the powers that be and made three strong suggestions for improvement: make home international matches mean something, develop a viable program to train young players which feed into the National Team, and develop a book of protocol—standards to follow in setting up and promoting an international match (and give a copy to IMG).

"I was told I'd never get any of these." Money, always money—or the lack of it— raised its ugly head on a continual basis. Too much going out, not enough coming in. Al Monaco feels one grave error was committed by his successor McPeak as soon as he came in "and raised office salaries significantly...across the board." The USVBA executives were happy, the players less so. Another dizzying blow fell when it was discovered that indeed the second deal with IMG was negotiated but *not signed* for some reason—a technical loophole which the marketing company slipped out of after a year. Those decisions and others would raise the question of priorities, not immediately, but within two years; accountability would eventually be called for by a group of disenchanted regional commissioners of the USVBA—a novel undertaking in itself.

In 1989, Kiraly and Timmons played in their "farewell tour," and within a year were in Milan rolling in the dough. In the 1990 World Championships, the USA Team went on with Stork, Ctvrtlik, Fortune and Tanner. They got some help from young players Bryan Ivie and Mark Arnold but the best they could do was 13th. Later that year most of the team, including the starters, flew off to Italy. Neville is a compact man, stout, bulldog constitution. A doughty breed, he likes the outdoors and has spent a lot of time there. But every man has a breaking point and Neville reached his in late 1990. Tired of fighting for the same conditions enjoyed by his opponents, he looked around at the bunch of new, young faces. Next, he thought of the American greats—guys he had helped groom since 1981—over in Italy, fat and happy, playing against the other best players in the world. He found it too hard to look these new fledglings in the eyes and give one of his rousing orations...to go for it, get the gold at any cost. They were now empty words. Let some other miracle worker come in and try his hand— someone who didn't know how the odds had so heavily shifted against what was the best team in the world only a year ago.

He handed in his resignation. "It was the only way of making a statement," he thought. After all, he had been to three Olympics: team manager for the USA Men in 1968; head coach for the Canadian Men in '76 and USA Men's assistant in 1984. Today Neville is head coach for the women's team at the University of Washington; he is also Secretary of the FIVB Coaches' Commission. And he still tells a great story.

"A year to forget..."

The year of 1989 was a "nightmare" for Liz Mazakayan. Three surgeries on her knees— ten major surgeries for the entire team! "The medical care was terrible. When you work out four to seven hours a day, you need to get rubbed out. You're so full of lactic acid. We had one trainer. He was good, but he had to do everything. Training, rehab, insurance...for maybe 18 girls! It was the same old story. Not enough money." After sitting out four months in 1990 after having a torn cartilage in her knee misdiagnosed, the frustration became too great. She left.

Following the barrage of injuries, Liskevych was finding a fate similar to the Men's coach, Bill Neville. Of course, players were more than ever looking for the best deal and more than not, they weren't found here. Caren Kemner went to Italy; Rock decided to work on her tan and prolong her knees by playing on the beach. In December, 1989 tragedy struck the sport again when a new addition to the team, 24-

year old Judy Bellomo, was struck with thyroid cancer and unexpectedly died of complications during surgery. A perky and fiercely competitive player, Judy's college coach Cathy Gregory fondly remembers her as "the player who mirrored the player I was."

In February of 1990, the 21-year old Keba Phipps failed a drug test and was subsequently removed from the team with a "lifetime ban." The starter and one of the most highly touted physical talents to ever play women's volleyball was not banned in Italy. There she seemed to flourish and has been selected MVP several times in the professional league. Her ban has since been rescinded but the gifted athlete has returned to American competition only once on the Budweiser four-women beach circuit. To top it off, Liskevych encountered conflicts with his assistant coaches. A nightmare was now part of Liskevych's daytime reality. It lasted almost two years.

In 1990, the winds of change brought some good fortune. Greg Giovanazzi, former All-American player from UCLA, brought some needed levity and new perspective to the team as assistant coach. It was an immediate good mix, Liskevych could concentrate more on strategy and "Gio" could take charge of practice and serve as counselor, confessor and friend. Blessed with an infectious sense of humor, the current coach at University of Michigan also had a rare sensitivity which the women warmed to...and had found wanting before his arrival. Kim Oden says, "he expected a lot of you. Gio instilled confidence."

Plus, a bumper crop of thousands of big, strong college women provided an exceptionally good harvest. Lori Endicott, Elaina Oden, Tara Cross-Battle and Teee Williams were plucked from the abundance of the bin. Caren Kemner decided to come home, and in 1990 the Women finished an impressive third place in Bejing, beating Cuba for the bronze. More importantly was next year's NORCECAs, but the automatic berth to Barcelona was scotched when the women lost to Cuba in the finals. One last shot remained—the World Cup in 1991 in

Japan. Liskevych could take no chances. Paula Weishoff got a call in Italy: "We need you!"

Weishoff enlisted for the Barcelona Olympics, provided they qualified, but part of the deal was that she could finish out the '92 season in Italy. Flying back and forth every three weeks was hard but she had made the commitment. "It was nice being older; playing for Terry was a radical difference from Arie too." Still, the travel was hard on her and hard on Liskevych who commented, "The system of players coming back from foreign leagues at the last minute just doesn't work. Paula was different but most of them come back in terrible shape. And to play internationally, you have to play hard four nights in a row. That's not the system over there and it's a serious problem besides just the different playing styles." True. But the dilemma remained: leave your best players off because they can earn a far better living elsewhere? Cut off your nose to spite your face? Liskevych and the Men's coaches, Neville then Sturm, had some common frustrations and little answers.

When the American women took off for Japan, nerves were high. Upon arrival, the veteran recruit Weishoff, who had enough frequent-flyer miles to last many lifetimes, before long was experiencing a veritable rarity in her world. Playing for fourth place against Peru, and a do-or-die trip to the Olympics, she was having a bad match—"even Paula has one occasionally," remarks Liskevych. Yet, to have your best all-around player, the rock of steadiness have a shaky match is, if nothing else, troubling, especially in the most important match outside the Olympics. What to do? He brought in the winsome Tammy Wiley. Off the bench, the sub went in and hit, blocked, served, dug and everything else to get the team to the fifth game. "She was the spark," understates her coach. In rally scoring, the ladies pulled through in a 15-12 tussle. They were going to Barcelona and Liskevych looked out his window on the long flight home—eastward over the broadest expanse of the dark Pacific, he saw the faintest rays of morning. Was the long night finally over?

"Beware the zealots!..."

John Kessel could have been Johnny Appleseed. Well, he is Johnny Appleseed for the sport of volleyball in the United States. The consummate clinician, he has spread the gospel of the game from the northern border of Alaska to Tasmania, about as far south as you can go on the globe. Lecturing, demonstrating, proselytizing, indefatigably teaching and preaching: "Isn't this the greatest game in the world!" A man so impassioned he forgets to eat and sleep; he has been found catatonic under bleachers in National Junior Olympic Volleyball Championships after not sleeping for 72 hours. Running, answering the phone, sending out his computerized witticisms, making personal loans...*anything* to make another convert, to help someone to see that *this* is the game, brother and sister! Sell your possessions, give up your daytime job, sacrifice your firstborn! But play! Play, my children! Play volleyball!

John Kessel was about a good a deal as the USVBA, or any organization, could get. Cheap...more than cheap...here was a guy who didn't really care about money. As long as he could keep spreading the word. In 1990, the Australians liked his act enough to offer him a real contract for a real job as technical director Down Under. After watching him run clinics from Brisbane to Perth, they would give whatever he wanted. "We'll match your USVBA salary and more!" You mean, four hundred dollars a month? For a minimum of 70 hours a week? "Hang on, mate! You talkin' four hundred...or thousand?" The former—for five years with the USVBA.

From 1985-1990, John Kessel served as "Consultant for the Youth and Junior Division" of the USVBA, at about the monthly salary of a part-time Junior Olympic Club coach—working around the clock. Fortunately, the man didn't eat much...he didn't have time. When the regional commissioners of the USVBA learned of his Australian contract, there was an immediate uproar. So indignant were the members in the meeting that one declared, "He's a national treasure!" Others chimed in: "We can't lose him." Honoring his word, he worked six months for the Aussies and then convinced them to let him come back. Heartbroken, they did. Their loss...our gain. And John Kessel suddenly had an *office* and a *salary* in the land where he was born.

He was a tireless crusader—passion in a man is seen too rarely in an ordinary world. His quest began early; as a student at Colorado College in Colorado Springs in the early '70s, he organized both a men's and a women's team. A lefty with an exceptional jump, he had a serious future as a player and attended his first USVBA Nationals in 1973 with the Pike's Peak Y. Then a serious knee injury beset his playing career. He could play but not totally; the thwarted dream would continue but not surprisingly he found himself always coaching, always teaching. Abruptly one day a friend on the Pike's Peak team, Mark Eastman, almost lost his leg...and life...in a freak accident at the gym where they were practicing. In a dead run, Eastman splintered a heavy glass window chasing down a ball. In the hospital, Kessel made a prophetic statement about the sport to the other fanatical player: "I'll go as far as I can for both us...since you can't now." Quite a ways, and Eastman is still playing with the same zeal they both shared before that fateful day.

After a couple of years in Italy playing, Kessel filled his empty days at the computer compiling "Kessel's Coaching Encyclopedia"—a guide for young players filled with humor, aphorisms and off-the-wall comments meant to loosen up kids and coaches and get them devoted to this game. Today the man has spread his influence to greater spheres; he is the active Secretary of the Technical Commission for the FIVB. A sought after FIVB Clinician, he has exported his zeal to every continent in over 20 nations; with 210 countries in the FIVB, he has miles to go before he sleeps. Here in this country, he is now in charge of "putting the grass in the grass roots" of out-

door volleyball—a new program, albeit belated, by the USVBA to embrace the beach and grass game. It is an effort to bridge the historical chasm between the two versions of the American sport. Having grown up in California, he understands both worlds. If commitment and caring can span gaps, if passion can infect, his is a good choice to lead this new movement. A close friend of the great Lang Ping who now helps coach at the University of New Mexico, Kessel likes to quote her favorite Chinese proverb: in this instance assuredly one not fallen out of a stale fortune cookie, and one which befits her passionate friend. "Winning and losing are temporary; friendship lasts forever."

"We're in the finals!..."

The mob was clamoring for seats on the fifth day. Every parent, relative, boyfriend, or friend of the thousands of teenage girls weren't disappointed—their player was "still playing and had a good chance to go all the way!" How could it be? After four days of playing, there should be maybe a couple hundred at best left in the competition. The rest all gone home...days ago. Ah, that's the way it used to be! Until Dave and Bernice Epperson joined forces with Gary Colberg to develop the Nike Festival—the biggest junior volleyball tournament in the world—into an annual extravaganza held every year at UC Davis.

Festival is a good name. The event celebrates all the right things in the sport. De-emphasizing the modern precepts of winning, ego and money, this event is designed to have girls compete, to win, to lose, to make new friends, to get motivated, and ultimately to walk away from the affair nodding their heads and saying, "This is a great game!"

By 1988, over 3,000 girls were attending the festival which had its humble origin in 1980. The brainchild of Gary Colberg who ran the intramurals at UC Davis, the event was a one-man show the first two years. The man needed help and found a plethora of it in Bernice Epperson, a trained accountant, and a mother of two teenage volleyball players. Her volunteered expertise helped get the event into the black by 1983 and also ensnared Dave Epperson to use his business acumen to start on a hunt for corporate support. Making a small profit was great but developing the concept of "multiple levels of success" was even greater. Every team plays the same amount of games: simply, a team is ingeniously placed in a division of similar ability which is decided by the actual playing. If a team loses every game, every day, on the last day it finds itself with teams of the same record—and they battle it out. The finals are equally exciting for everyone. One great reason is that the divisions' names, "Championship Division" or "Character Division", does not denote a team's level: the traditional "top, middle or low."

Today a staff of 350 are required to pull off the event; the Eppersons work year round on it and there is an annual "Woman of Achievement Award." Such outstanding women as super model-pro beach player Gabrielle Reece is a recent honoree. In 1994, over 7,000 players came to UC Davis.

The US Junior Volleyball Championships are held annually as well. Catering to the more traditional idea of determining the top teams in the nation, it soon became serious stuff and college coaches combed the premises for talent, dangling full-rides to their colleges. It was all a part of the phenomenal explosion of women's volleyball in the past decade. Title IX started it; an emerging attitude in the national psyche welcoming the idea of girls competing was another ingredient. In the mid-'70s, no full scholarships for women volleyball players existed. In 1988, there were hundreds available and the numbers increase yearly. It's a hot sport for women. Recruiting and winning take on more importance every year; ego, money, and prestige are waxing and it makes the competition fiercer with each season. Yes, that's all well and good. But the Nike Festival has remained a refreshing break—an event unique not only in volleyball but sport itself. Oh, that it continues...

"Volare, cantare...pagare..."

On the last day of 1990, Fred Sturm was on the plane to Italy. New Year's Eve in Rome? Champagne in Capri? Spumante on the canals of Venice? Hardly. He was on a mission; his first job as the new head coach of the USA Men was to find out what were the playing plans of the nine veterans off the '88 Olympic team—six of the starters—were all in Italy. Even Doug Beal was over there! In 1990, he left his position as Senior Director to play a small role in Sylvio Berlusconi's business empire. The media magnate who would become prime minister, Berlusconi bought national championship teams like toys—from soccer to basketball, including volleyball. No expense was spared to get the best players and coaches in the world.

When Beal left for the mega-bucks to coach in Milan, it looked as if the USVBA office was about to ship out as well...or would like to. But other than players and coaches, nothing else interested them; the Italian Volleyball Federation knew how to make big money and to push the sport to a national success. Here at home, the USVBA was in the throes of financial anemia. The IMG deal had gone sour; lawsuits were filed in quest of holding IMG to its implied commitments but that was just more money going out the door. Loose financial reins continued to slacken in the front office.

By 1991 the organization was seriously sick; even the Olympic slush fund had been tapped into deeply. Al Monaco contends that "three-quarters of a million dollars was lost in the in the year of '91 after McPeak's resignation;" other board members thought the sinkhole had opened months earlier and just continued to drain in 1991. Ostensibly, financial controls were more than relaxed. One board member states, "The word bankruptcy was mentioned in board meetings. Regions were talking about disassociating. The bank was talking about withdrawing the USVBA's credit line. Cash flow problems were so severe that it was hard to pay the staff. The annual deficit was finally projected at $700,000 if we continued the way things were going." It was no secret. The house was bust and players fled American volleyball like the plague had been announced. Articles and letters from laypersons to the editors around the sport became more scathing and finally a bunch of USVBA regional commissioners assembled to take some action. McPeak agreed to resign, a buyout of his remaining contract was negotiated, and an executive search was on for someone with a professional sports background to get the foundering ship in workable shape.

If USVBA finances were in shambles in 1991, where was the game in terms of people playing? In the sport's golden decade the average growth of registered adults increased every year about 10%; it had required a decade to double USVBA adult registration from some 15,000 in 1980 to 30,000 in 1990, with men still holding about a 55% lead. That rate of growth might allow the parent organization to keep up with the consumer price index in paying their bills but it wasn't going to do much more than maintain a status quo. But the kids, wow! In 1980, registered juniors were recorded at 2,754; a decade later the number of volleyballers under 18 had soared to 26,084 with 85% of them female. Like young Neros, the youngsters kept playing while Rome was burning.

In the meantime, Kerry Klostermann was trying to hold things together in the wake of disaster. A Canadian Olympic volleyball player before serving as assistant USA Men's coach in 1978, if Klosterman had been one thing since his USVBA involvement, it was consistent. Executive officials, marketers, secretaries, board members, coaches, appeared and disappeared with ever fortuity like the Olympics or Italian windfall, but Klostermann stayed on. His doctoral in psychology would serve to assuage the recurring maelstroms of trouble. Joining the USVBA front office in 1980, he serves as Senior Director of USA Volleyball and gives daily thanks that the '96 Olympics are back in the good ole USA. Still, 1991 and 1992 were dark years which rocked even Klostermann's steady keel.

To understate Coach Sturm's plight, he didn't have a lot of tricks in his bag—certainly not much money. So what do you tell a two-time gold medalist like Karch Kiraly, who is making in Italy a yearly salary tantamount to a healthy percentage of the entire USVBA budget? If he were to throw in his beach winnings and endorsements and he could have bought the entire organization—certainly in 1991— had he wanted it. Well, "appeal to their pride," thought Sturm. Go for a record third gold medal. But some of the vets were now raising families and as far as the competitive angle, the prevailing attitude was much like BB King's first popular blues anthem, "The Thrill is Gone." A hard sell to put it lightly and Sturm was not well practiced at the art of bamboozling. One thing was sure. They weren't coming back in '91...maybe in '92...maybe...

So it was make do. Sturm was no stranger to new beginnings. After being an All-American at UCLA and contracting hepatitis as a player on his first USA National Team in 1976, he decided to get into college coaching instead of playing. A glance at the map told him that Northern California had promise so he volunteered his services as an assistant at Stanford in 1977. By 1978, he was the head coach of men's and women's teams and built a successful program until 1986. That year his assistant, Don Shaw, took over the women while Sturm stayed with the men. The whole time at Stanford he was active helping out with the USA Men's Team in San Diego; he coached the World University Team in 1987. He was well versed in the job he took over from the resigned Neville.

In January, 1991, Sturm had 16 young guys who wanted to play volleyball. Sixteen guys with very little international playing experience. In the spring, a needed boost, and experience, was added when Eric Sato came back on the team. Meanwhile, in 1990 a "flex policy" had been devised whereby veterans could come back—a formula equating the number of years already played to the date a player could rejoin the team: the more experience, the later the date.

For the world-class stars who already had two gold medals—Kiraly, Timmons, Buck, Saunders—this formula would give them deferments until six months before the Olympics. Bryan Ivie and Dan Greenbaum would soon come on board as promising college graduates and collegiate players such as Tom Sorrensen and Brent Hilliard were being used even while they were still in college. However, as the '91 NORCECAs approached, Sturm was getting nervous. Experience was called for. After a month's practice, Buck, Stork, Ctvrtlik, Partie, and Saunders were reactivated for the tournament in Canada. They took second but got murdered by the Cubans, 3-0, who didn't even send their strongest team.

Most of the older guys were soon back on the plane to Italy, and Sturm was left with assistant coach, John Cook, to mold anew with wet clay. At the World Cup in Japan, they surprised everyone with a third place finish, beating Cuba, 3-1, enroute. With Partie and Fortune serving as the pillars, Bryan Ivie was causing waves with his play and a gutsy little Uvaldo Acosta had a sensational tournament. That was the peak, there were more valleys. With a 26-31 record in 1992, Sturm was praying for a change of heart by those American studs in Italy.

April 27. That was the date in 1992 when the vets must decide. Before that eventful day, Buck had decided to return and then Timmons announced his rejoining the team after his second year in Italy. But more volleyball eyes were turned towards the captain, Karch Kiraly. Bets were made...arguments went late into the night. Would he play or not? Was he burnt out on indoor? Did he just want to play beach? How could he turn down a third gold medal when he was the most critical element? What about his wife and two young kids...would she frown on him being away once again? Kiraly's answer came at the eleventh hour. He wasn't going to Barcelona.

Kiraly cites more than one reason for his decision: "First I thought Timmons and I had played our best indoor volleyball ever in our first season in Italy (1990-1991)." No argument there. Playing for Il Messaggero in Ravenna, they set an Italian league record by winning 25 straight matches; had they won their last match, it would have been an undefeated season—they lost it 15-13 in the fifth! "Italy was nothing like I'd ever experienced. The passion of Italians for sports, and to play every single day against the best players in the world. Our second year, I thought our game had dropped a little and that was a factor. But mainly, I'd had it with traveling and gym time. I knew I wouldn't be one of the most 12 motivated players and that wouldn't be fair to the team. And I'd already missed seven years of beach volleyball in my career—things like overall wins were on my mind. Steffes and I had a great second half of the '91 season. I liked the beach schedule and the time to stay at home with my family." And of course, there would be no way that the USVBA could match the money he would lose if he went to Barcelona. He had paid his dues...regrettably. As close as the USA Men came without him, it is hard to imagine them not coming home with a historical third gold medal had he been there.

Another blow. Buck, a temperamental sort, was not seeing eye to eye with the coaching staff. Disenchanted with his initial role on the second team and wondering whether he would have the chance to regain his spot as a starter, he quit within a month. It would prove to be particularly costly when Bryan Ivie injured his knee in Barcelona. One encouraging addition was the inclusion of Gary Sato on the coaching staff. Positive and well-liked, he would make his second Olympic appearance in Barcelona along with his two siblings, Eric and Liane.

Still, the team came together in less than three months. In a crucial meeting, Sturm recalls the attitude: "They only wanted to talk about the gold medal. They were confident they could win it." They came quite close.

"And now...live from Hermosa Beach..."

Three live telecasts on NBC! Unbelievable. But true in 1991 when beach volleyball came of age in the nation where it was engendered.

In 1992, there would be five. New sponsors were knocking on the door to get in. Under the newborn entrepreneurial eye of Karch Kiraly, Old Spice was brought in to sponsor the "King of the Beach" event in 1991 where the top players were continually changed and paired over a weekend; in theory, it provided the most objective test as to who was the best. You couldn't hide behind a partner in this one. Not too many were surprised when Kiraly walked away with a lifetime supply of deodorant—stick and can—that first year and the next two as well.

Live TV was at once the crowning glory of the game's golden boy and the fade-out of the two greatest rivalries in its history. Hovland and Dodd broke up in 1990 while Smith and Stoklos were on the downside of their fabulous career's curve. In 1992, Kiraly and Steffes planted their flag on the first court and rarely did anyone touch it, much less remove it. Thirteen victories in a row! "That might not be broken for a long time," admits Kiraly who is not known for self-aggrandizement, "especially since the talent pool is so much deeper now." Sixteen out of 19 for the two. If viewers tired of seeing the same two complimenting each other in post-final interviews, at least they got the chance of watching a variety of second-place finishers. Even though the comments were the same studied, stock replies: "Well, we're playing better every week. If we keep it up, maybe we can knock Karch and Steffes off. They're pretty tough." The remarks may not have been terribly elucidating...but true.

If the bronzed boys of summer were laughing all the way to the bank, the ladies were turning a whiter shade of pale. The hapless ladies finished the '92 season awash in bickering and disillusionment. If sponsors wanted an example of the dangers of allowing players to run their own organization, here was a textbook case. As the left hand did not know what the right was doing—or even where it was—the competitors finished the season drenched in debt and unable to even pay a substantial amount of prize money. Some veteran players tired of it all and abandoned the board; a clamor for in-

fluence ensued which hadn't been seen since the time of the Borgian Popes. As many of the better veterans shook their heads in dismay, some of the young lionesses leaped for the throne, but one which had lost much of its glitter—Coors Brewing was feeling as if they had just poured a million six-packs down the drain. Cut and run? they wondered. At the same time the male-dominated AVP saw an opportunity. Why not include the belles of the beach in their revue? Perhaps a kind of pretty sideshow to begin with but a real tour eventually. At least that's what was proposed—to six of the top WPVA finishers of the '92 season. Sounded good, especially when WPVA checks were bouncing like overinflated balls—and soon the telephone lines were heating up.

Before long, six of the leading women were invited into the plush offices of the AVP. Kirby, Mazakayan, Chisholm, Silva, Reno and Rock were listening to the AVP pitch of Dankworth, Stevenson and Billy Berger, "Get on board with us now and we'll take you ladies to the same dizzying heights as the men." Just sign here for five years. The half-dozen looked at each other with a wary cast in their eyes. Kirby posed a penetrating question: "What about representation?" It appears that some of the women wanted a say in their own future besides cash.

Kirby adds, "Here we were, six of us in a room, some without agents. All they were offering was money...no positions on the board. They only wanted four teams and already had already gotten one committed. I felt a responsibility to the women's game and had to take·a stand. I would have been selling out if I went with them." Liz Masakyan was experiencing the same uneasiness in the pit of her stomach. She recalls, "We were given a deadline. I decided I wasn't going to sign; there was the Olympic conflict as well which the AVP hadn't worked out. The night before I thought only two others were jumping to the AVP. All four went over—except for myself and Karolyn."

That wasn't all that bad. Since Nancy Reno had signed with the AVP, Kirby needed a new partner. Having won the most money in the

1992 season, she could take her pick. No one was surprised when Kirby selected Masakyan, the MVP of the '92 tour, to team up for the '93 season—a formidable alliance in theory which would prove even more devastating in real life.

"New York state of mind..."

It was perfect. So perfectly the "Hov." Madison Square Garden, February, 1993: the coldest day of the year. Pristinely clear, sunlight as pure as Manhattan ever gets, polished ice crystals in the gutter in a whipping wind down around 34th and Broadway. It was a beautiful day for a Sunday stroll, from the ice skaters in Central Park, down to more fashionably attired ones in Rockefeller Center to the Garden. The place Willis Reed and Walt Frazier made famous and where Pat Riley is getting so close. But today there was a weird gig going down...even for the City. *Beach volleyball* in the cold heart of a New York winter.

Inside muscled guys (with tans no less!) were playing volleyball—right in the middle of the Garden. Running and jumping on imported sand dumped on the hallowed floor and some 7,000 warmly clad New Yorkers were into it. A little mid-winter revelry or fantasy perhaps, but in the summer, beach volleyball on Long Island and the Jersey shores was booming. Local stars and zealots like Eric Pavels and Tom Gould were every bit as fanatical as any crazy out in

the other Manhattan, on the West coast. Even more so...these guys were known to play beach doubles on Long Island's Atlantic Beach...in the snow!

In the finals of the losers against Smith and Stoklos, Tim Hovland made a great dig and Mike Dodd ran the ball down. A high arching set fell from the lights and the mighty Hov took a mighty jump and swing. It caromed off Smith's forearm, who receiving a perfect set, cranked his own best shot. Hovland dug it again and every alabaster-skinned coffee-talker in Manhattan watching the first game in their life somehow knew the 6'5" Hovland would put this one way. Not so...into the net! The crowd gasped. Hovland lifted his clawed hands in rage; his contorted face emanated an anger which could be felt up in the highest seat, blood looked to be spurting from his ruptured eyeballs. Even the other three players looked on in silent awe, waiting for some catharsis—some blood-letting sparagmos—to vent the nuclear fury. The volcano had to erupt. The clenched fingers hooked on to his sponsor's tank-top and hunching over in a blasphemous uttering, he ripped the cotton apparel cleanly in two—a piece in each hand. The crowd went crazy. The noise somehow neutralized Hovland's mania; he suddenly broke into a big grin and tossed both pieces of the shriven raiment to the adoring crowd. They screamed for more.

*Queen of the beach, Karolyn Kirby.
(Photo by Peter Brouillet)*

*Versatility unbound: Ricci Luyties. All
the skills, in the gym or on the sand.
(Photo by Doug Avery)*

The Hov takes it hard. (Photo by Doug Avery)

But not for long...after tournament action.

Rock steady. Angela Rock, phenomenal on both surfaces...leaves the hardwood in 1988. (Photo by Peter Brouillet)

Pros' favorite. Spalding balls have been around for 100 years. (Courtesy of Spalding)

Ex-Trojan goes to world-class hitter. Only injuries stopped Bryan Ivie's ascent. (Photo by Robert Beck)

Lori Endicott, All-American setter, leads USA Women's charge to Barcelona. (Photo by Robert Beck)

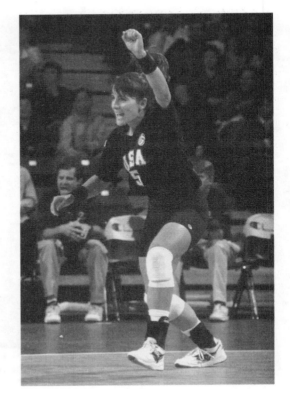

Chapter 20
1992 Barcelona Olympics

"Bald is beautiful..."

First match Japan. Shouldn't be too hard. "I decided to let the players who wanted to, attend the opening ceremonies; they were long and tiring and I think it hurt us the next day," Sturm believes. Japan wasn't tired and in the fourth game at 13-13, one of their spikes hit the line...or out. "I thought it was in," says a fair-minded Sturm. Samuelson who was in the game, didn't agree and went nuts. The linesman who was berated so roundly by the shiny-headed American, awarded a yellow card—Samuelson's second card of the fourth game. However, a second card according to the rules calls for a red card and a point. Technically, the game was over. Fourteen on the ball out, 15 on the red card. But the head referee didn't award the red card and point; later he confessed that he didn't want to end any important match on a technicality—especially one so hard-fought as that one. Lofty thoughts but it didn't escape the scrutinizing eyes of the Japanese officials who swept down on the scorer's table like a kamikaze raid a second after the match. Meanwhile, the Americans were leaping wildly in the narrow escape from infamy—they had recovered from the 14-13 deficit and in a see-saw tussle finally triumphed. A 17-16 thrilling victory. That set up the final fifth game which turned out every bit as exciting with the Americans squeezing out a 16-14 win.

So thought Fred Sturm and everyone else...until a call that night to inform him that he and captain Scott Fortune would have to attend a meeting the following morning: the reason was that a protest had been filed by the Japanese. At the meeting, the protest was elaborated upon. In short, the Japanese held that rules were rules and accordingly a 15-13 score should have ended the fourth game and match. The bewildered Americans mustered the argument that the technical was not recorded on the score sheet. How could you count a point which isn't accounted for? "Well, just because the officials didn't call it by the rules, didn't mean it didn't happen!" was one of the many strident replies. That's the way it would go four hours later in a separate FIVB meeting which decided the outcome—a victory was given to Japan. And the best the frustrated American team could do was to return to their dorms and mope.

Sitting around in an informal circle, the talk was of some kind of protest. "We can't take this lying down;" they decided a statement had to be made. Doug Partie offered a joke to lighten things up: "We could shave our heads." The younger guys looked around at each other: "Yeah!" Partie quietly added, "Ooops!" Timmons volunteered his ever-present clippers for the rookies; Partie and Cvrtlik trudged off to the village barber to get a flat-top...albeit a short one. Upon returning, they found a band of young skinheads and the two vets succumbed immediately to a revised coiffure. Not long after, a full-haired Timmons returning from a live NBC interview had announced that the sports world was going to see a visible protest by the team, which he would keep secret. Recapitulating the interview to the shaven team, he handed his clippers to the naturally bald Bob Samuelson and mandated, "Do me!" Samuelson responded with a wide strip right through the center of the most famous hairdo in the Olympics. Didn't change the score but overnight they were seen around the world—bald guys in blue uniforms.

The oldest team in the tournament, it wasn't wise to play five-game matches but they kept doing it—and winning them. After Japan, it was Canada and Spain, and then the first big upset of the tournament: the USA knocked off the gold-medalist favorite Italy in four sets. Next, they would face their long-time nemesis, the Soviets. The greatest team tradition in the sport—never finishing less than third—the Soviets lost to the Americans. Wow! Could it be three Olympic golds in a row?

It looked that way. Sturm remembers, "We knew every other team well except Brazil. We hadn't played them much the past few years so I didn't have a good feel for them." When the Brazilians came out, they displayed their familiar Latin fire but it was augmented with youth and height. Great hitters and booming jump serves, the Americans gave them their best fight in the tournament. "We won the first and were up with a good lead in the second," Partie recalls. "Then the momentum changed; you could feel it just slipping away through your fingers." Not totally. It was 12-12 in the fourth game; had the USA pulled that one out... They couldn't and the heart-broken team would have to meet another rival the next morning for the bronze. In an admirable display of character, they took down the Cubans for the bronze medal—a team they hadn't defeated in the last 12 times they faced them. "For me," states Doug Partie, "that match was as satisfying as winning the gold in Seoul. Going into the tournament, we had no idea how we'd do. It could have been first...or eighth. A bronze was at least a medal." All in all, it was a surprise finish, but also a disappointment. Jeff Stork believes "we could have won it if Timmons and Ivie were healthy." They weren't. And had they played with Karch? In the end, they were tantalizingly close to Olympic history with a third straight gold medal.

"Bad rotation..."

The USA Women were rolling as well in Barcelona. Taking a bad cue from the men, they dropped a 3-2 heart-breaking opener to Japan. It wasn't anger and poor sportsmanship that did the ladies in—something more insidious—a virus had attacked setter Lori Endicott who had to come out in the first game, too sick to play. She and the team rebounded to a historical victory the second day—they beat the Soviet women. The two Oden sisters, Kim and Elaina, were holding down the middle blocking positions; Cross-Battle and Williams were popping away from the outside, Weishoff did everything well from opposite the setter but it was Kemner who was providing the heavy punch. Getting more sets than anyone, she was hurting teams with relentless pounding.

Other than the Japanese, the Americans were now the only team to ever beat the Soviets in Olympic competition—a 3-2 drug-out affair. Spain and Holland went down like renewed victims of the Hapsburg Dynasty, and suddenly our women were looking at Olympic immortality. Against the ball-crunching Cubans in the semi-finals, the momentum kept on for the Americans. Up 2-1, they dropped the fourth game. Touch and go, they lead 8-7 and then the rope to the prize for some reason got slippery.

Getting caught in a dangerous position—two hitters at the net—Endicott continued to fling out sets to Kemner on the left side. Why not? The big hitter had been punishing teams with a 35% hitting percentage. But not that night. The big Cuban block knew where the ball was going and they kept pushing it back, for valuable points. A play which had worked all year, had gotten them to the semi-finals...broke down. Weishoff compliments the Cubans, "They had a good strategy. Serve Caren long, make her run a long ways to get to the ball. It worked." The ladies sadly dropped the fifth game, 15-12. Yet they roared back the next day. A 3-0 smear of Brazil gave them all bronze medals—and it gave a remarkable second MVP of an Olympics to Paula Weishoff.

Intensity personified. Paula Weishoff, the MVP of the Barcelona Olympics, lines up behind Kim Oden. (Photo by Mike Powell—ALLSPORT USA)

*Barcelona Bob. Could antics equal play?
(Photo by Mike Powell—ALLSPORT USA)*

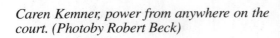

*Caren Kemner, power from anywhere on the
court. (Photoby Robert Beck)*

Bald power. Stork throws a quick set to Doug Partie in Barcelona. (Photo by ALLSPORT USA)

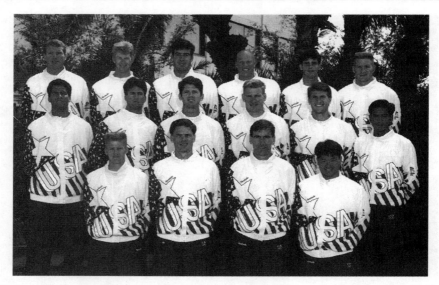

Before the haircut. 1992 USA Men's Olympic team Back Row (left to right): Doug Partie, Scott Fortune, Bryan Ivie, Bob Samuelson, Brent Hilliard, Steve Timmons. Middle Row: Carlos Briceno, Dan Greenbaum, Jeff Stork, Bob Ctvrtlik, Bick Becker, Eric Sato. Front Row: Kevin Ringermanger, John Cook (Asst. Coach) Fred Sturm (Coach), Gary Sato (Asst. Coach) (Photo by Robert Beck)

The bronze for the ladies. 1992 USA Women's Olympic team . Back Row (from left to right): Terry Liskevych (Coach), Caren Kemner, Elaina Oden, Kim Oden, Paula Weishoff, Janet Cobbs, Teee Sanders, Dan McDonough (Sports Medicine), Dave Sims (Manager). Front Row: Kent Miller (Asst. Coach), Tammy Liley, Yoko Zetterland, Ruth Lawanson, Lori Endicott, Tara Cross-Battle, Liane Sato, Greg Giovanazzi (Asst. Coach).(Photo by Robert Beck)

Chapter 21
1993-1994

"Man for all seasons..."

One thinks of a DaVinci drawing. Compass, ruler, proportion, Euclidean exactitude. He even speaks in measured control. Yet as in the works of the greatest mind which the Renaissance produced, there's more than meets the eye. Humor tempers a sharp intelligence; an absence of self-aggrandizement—a distinct graciousness all too rare. Harking further back to the Greek ideal: robust of mind, body, and spirit. If you prefer a musical analogy—a Puccini opera? Sublimity of language...how about Marcel Proust? What is hard to find are detractors...anywhere...of Karch Kiraly.

Coaches from the USA National Men's Team have thus spoken. Marv Dunphy: "The best ball shagger, the best floor wiper, the best net setter-upper on the team." Doug Beal: "The drill didn't matter. Every time Kiraly touched the ball, he tried to do it perfectly. You could turn your back and know that he would work just as hard." Gary Sato: "If Buck or Timmons didn't feel like shagging balls, when they saw Kiraly do it, they'd follow." Bill Neville: "He never had a bad practice; nobody focuses like Karch."

And players: "He has a computer mind, a great body and he destroys you," reports another great one, Tim Hovland. Adam Johnson who holds the distinction of being the only player besides Kiraly who has won the King of the Beach event, after his victory in the 1994 event told Volleyball Magazine: "Karch is the greatest beach volleyball player." It's found in print everywhere, magazine covers with the following letters: "Karch Kiraly: A Dying Breed?" "The Sand King." "King Karch" "The World's Best Player Says No to the '92 Olympics" "Karch Kiraly: Man of the Year?" Which year? Name almost any one for the past 15 years. The best American to have ever played volleyball—indoor and beach. Take it a step farther: on the world level, the best ever on the sand. Indoor...well, that one is too close to call. But he would certainly receive a lot of votes.

If only one vote was sought out—one most valid—that of Paul Sunderland would be hard to surpass. The sports broadcaster who has been around more great athletes than anyone in volleyball, places Kiraly in the company of a few select men. "Michael Jordan, Sergei Bubka, Alberto Juantarena: they're special human beings. These guys have more ability than the rest...but they also work harder and are more competitive. Karch is in that group."

"I've seen guys who are underachievers—physically limited—who compensate by hard work. But Karch had more physical ability than anyone in volleyball, and mentally as well. He has an incredible ability to focus and compete everyday. I've talked to Magic Johnson, to Barkley—the great ones are all the same. They've got the total package. So does Karch."

"Rise and hit!..."

"Rise and hit!" is a familiar one. "Yes, my friend!" is another one of his sonorous exhortations if you make a good play and happen to be the beach doubles partner of Laszlo Kiraly. Chances are, you won't be. The renown physician who serves as medical director of the Rehabilitation Institute of Santa Barbara is fastidious in choosing his partners. In fact, he organizes a daily game with only four players at East Beach. At a designated time and a certain court; serve it up, play hard and no nonsense. Most likely you'll be playing on another court; one more laid back and none of that screaming. "Relax, dude!" was meant for Dr. Kiraly but it goes unheeded. When members of the foursome take breaks between games—maybe a dip in the ocean to cool off—Laz marches to his beach chair and reads a medical research article. Never a wasted moment...intense as intense can be.

It's in his voice. Two dollar words carefully enunciated, immaculately clipped in perfect syntax but there's a foreign shine on it—and that burning intensity. No wonder. At 21, a member of the Hungarian Junior National Volleyball Team, Laz Kiraly left his Budapest home during the Soviet invasion of 1956, and sprinted to freedom over barbed wire under the sparkling light of rocket fire. With all his possessions in one bag, he arrived in the land of the free and set about to demonstrate the immigrant dream. He did. Scraping and scrabbling, he finally walked away with a Master's Degree in engineering from the University of Michigan. His wife, Toni, who helped support his schooling was ecstatic...until Laz decided to enter medical school! In the era when the adage reigned, "behind every great man...," here was a woman qualified for sainthood. But how could anyone withstand that man's volition?

Finishing medical school, the Kiralys headed west. When the lad was six years old, Kiraly began teaching him the Hungarian volleyball fundamentals he had brought with him from the old country. Having played USVBA competition with Ann Arbor Y during med school, the father was interested in this new beach game and between games at East Beach he would bump the ball with the little towhead. Karch remembers his first game when he was nine: "I played with a guy called "Jack the Rat" against Bill Conway, who was called 'the mayor,' and my dad." Karch's first beach tournament came at age 11 in a "novice"—with his father. "Initially I pushed him. But whether it was genetic or learned, he would eventually gain his own intensity. Something between his mother's which is quiet and personal, and my own—I'm much more of a hothead," admits the father of the most accomplished American who ever played.

Laz pushed him but soon the kid pushed himself...like very few had ever pushed. They competed together: in 1976, the father-teenager took a third in a B tournament at Muscle Beach. Back on East Beach, the word was getting out. Rich Payne, a AA player, asked Laz permission to play with the kid. One year later, the father distinctly remembers a phone call from his 16-year old son who was now playing in Open tournaments. "He called us Saturday night; he was kind of down since he had gotten beat in the second round. He told us not to come down to watch him, so we didn't. Sunday night he came home and said he had finished second—against Menges and Lee. I knew then...he was something special."

Laz watched the never-ending ascent of his scion with pleasure. Under coach Rick Olmstead, "I learned how to work out," remembers Karch when he and John Hanley led Santa Barbara High School to a California championship in an undefeated season in 1978. Then it was UCLA and on and on...and the prodigious conclusion of 100 years of an American sport was here. Today the proud father still plays everyday at East Beach, screaming and fierce. Yet upon reflection he softly claims, "Toni and I are equally, or more, proud of Karch as a husband and father." And what if... And what if Laz Kiraly, so deftly and determinedly, failed to dodge those Soviet rockets that night in 1956?

Looking out into the second century of volleyball, it is indeed hard to imagine another Karch Kiraly, a player who could do it both on the floor and on the beach. Money in the game alone, as well as its accompanying commitments, have allowed players less and less the chance to play the two. The actual play of the sport's double versions have diverged more and more. "Indoor is a game of specialization. You cannot be a specialist on the beach," declares Kiraly. And how does the sport's brightest luminary see himself amongst the panoply of stars in the game's history? Typically of Kiraly...in perspective...and modestly. "I've heard how great Selznick was on the beach for example. But I never got to see him in play. So how can you make a judgment?" You can't. Rather you don't. Or better yet, you let other experts dare to judge. When asked about the indoor game, the two-time gold medalist moderates his reply, yet with no discernible dodging. "Timmons, Negrau, Powers on any given night can dominate a match—people will always focus on the big hitter-blocker—that's the way it is. I could never play that role nor did I try. I did most of the other things," he adds. That he did but what most distinguished Kiraly was an intangible, a rare quality which defies quantifying—what is heard over and over by the greatest coaches and greatest players alike: "Karch made *everybody else* around him better."

If aspiring kids modeled their indoor game after Kiraly in the '80s, what does a youngster in 1994 who aspires to be "King of the Beach" one day have to look forward to? A lot. The AVP season which just ended gave away almost $4,000,000 to needy players. Kent Steffes walked off with some $460,000 while his partner, Kiraly, who missed a couple tournaments due to injuries, had to settle for $430,000—together they won 17 of the 20 events. Kiraly is one of a handful of players who can bolster winnings with another $500,000 per year in endorsements. An easy million bucks a year and it's climbing. "We're playing for $4,000,000; I gotta be happy with that." says Kiraly. Especially when only a year ago the purse was at $2,500,000. In 1993, Kiraly and Steffes won 18 of the 23 tournaments and took home most of the bacon again: some $400,000 for Steffes and $470,000 for Kiraly who won The King of the Beach event again. The next

players earned about $100,000. There seems to be good reason the rich dynasty will continue; "I have as much confidence in Steffes as I do Timmons indoors." What more requires saying?

"World beaters..."

In the spring of 1993, Karolyn Kirby was flying back to Colorado to meet with Coors and work out the many kinks in the WPVA tangle. By summer there was a new regime at the top of the WPVA and the brewery felt more comfortable about the management; they would give it another go but at a reduced level—the season's purse was reduced to about $300,000. Negotiation behind her, Kirby and her new partner took to the sand with Mary Jo Peppler as their coach. Reeling off 13 straight Open victories while only losing one tournament, the two earned over $60,000. That amount well exceeded the next two teams which found themselves alternating as grist for the rapacious mill of Kirby and Masakayan: Fontana/Kotas-Forsyth and the other team of Castro-Roque hovered around the $25,000 mark.

Meanwhile on other beaches, with bigger crowds and more hoopla, a spectator might have to look hard to find the eight women playing on the AVP tour—and if you were patiently waiting for them on NBC's live broadcast of the weekend competitions, a mistimed trip to the refrigerator for a snack could have ruined your plans. It was not uncommon to see the final three points of the final game and then..."get the men back on!" Prime Network was much kinder to the ladies with several hours of coverage. Not that the money was something to blink at: Holly McPeak topped the list with contract plus winnings of $65,000, Cammy Ciarelli walked off with $55,000, Reno earned $50,000 which was $10,000 more than the fourth-placed Rock.

Both tours were enticing players in the '94 season with increased prize money; the WPVA's purse totaled some $500,000 and the AVP was giving away over $600,000, but it was still paltry compared to the men's game. The AVP held tryouts to increase the road show to a 16-team tournament but the women were already grumbling when the season began. "Where was the live TV? How about those big-time sponsors who were supposed to make us all rich?" Unable to procure that elusive sponsor by the 1994 season, the prize money was cut almost in half during the summer. The vibes became bad enough that the AVP President, Jon Stevenson, offered to allow the ladies to walk away from their contracts. "Sure, they offered to let us walk," comments Angela Rock. "But unlike the men, we were on 10-month contracts; they could just stop payments and we'd lose even more money." The season was to linger on to the unhappy end.

At least, the field was much closer than in the runaway Kirby-Masakayan derby, Ciarelli and McPeak finished the summer with some $41,000 a piece; Reno and Rock were close at just over $38,000 in winnings. Both teams Chisholm-Hanley and Silva-Pires almost reached $30,000 in pay before a steep dropoff for the remaining competitors.

The Karolyn-Liz show continued in '94 with them swiping 11 out of 13 Open victories. Although the prize money was not providing anyone with early retirement, the women of the WPVA seemed happier than their counterparts of the AVP. "If I had to do it again, I wouldn't have gone over to the AVP," one player reveals. "The AVP front office made what we thought were promises...later we were told they were goals. We thought we would get a stand-alone tour under the AVP—not just be a sideshow for the men. They didn't get us a major sponsor—maybe they were too busy selling the men." Both parties have since mentioned that a fusion might be needed to attract sponsors and television interest alike. Unless the AVP comes up with that big sponsor, the sentiment seems to be swinging towards the WPVA as the '95 season approaches. Some of the leading AVP women are currently investigating ways to get out of their existing contracts, ideally gaining free agent status.

One great advantage the WPVA has enjoyed is the allure of the Atlanta Games as well as the increasing prize money of the FIVB beach circuit. If Kirby and Masakayan have found the domestic competition a trifle lacking, they have found some surprising competition abroad, particularly from two Brazilians. Maria Salgado and Roseli Timm have been the most consistent challengers to Kirby and whomever she has teamed with since the FIVB Beach Volleyball World Series was initiated in 1992 at Almeria, Spain. Kirby took the first crown with Nancy Reno against fellow compatriots, Linda Chisholm and Angela Rock. For Kirby, it was a position she would not relinquish easily; since Almeria, there have been nine events held by the FIVB. Kirby has played in eight and won five. She had number six in the bag in the most recent event in Brazil when Liz Masakayan's knee locked up on her—a mere three points away from victory, winning the first game handily and cruising with an 12-8 lead in the second. Hobbling around the court, it was a sad and futile effort as they dropped that game, and the third—a tie-breaker.

The FIVB is upping the ante of beach volleyball dramatically in its quest to establish a world-class sport. For the women there were three events in the 1993-1994 season which offered a $300,000 purse. The number of World Series events doubled in the '94-'95 season and the prize money grew to $550,000. But the big boom will begin next year; for the '95-'96 season leading up to Atlanta, the gold-paved road today offers a confirmed eight tournaments and a planned ten events—$50,000 for each contest with a few $100,000 purses. Top that off with a "Bonus Pool" of $500,000 to be finally divvied up according to individual standings, and the ladies are genuinely smiling. At least a million bucks in cash prizes—traveling to tournaments in Portugal, Brazil, Japan and Bali isn't all that bad as far as scenery either.

As a precursor to the '96 Atlanta Games and the growing interest in beach volleyball, the summer Goodwill Games were shown around the world from St. Petersburg. On the shores of the Gulf of Finland with the Peter and Paul fortress rising behind, who would have ever guessed that men and women, all with the prototypical Southern California look, would be bouncing around in the sand in Russia? But there it was. And Kirby and Masakayan made quick work of all comers. At this point, a likely showdown for the first Olympic gold medal in beach volleyball could be the USA and Brazil. However, if the AVP women are liberated to play, it could well be an all Yankee finals. If Masakyan's knee holds out and the world's dominating beach player, Karolyn Kirby, stays on her same steady path, the team which has put their indelible stamp on international beach volleyball will be the heavy odds-on choice for Atlanta.

"Unlikely, unholy alliance..."

Vice-president of the FIVB World Beach Council, 1994. Member, USVBA Board of Directors, 1994. Former AVP President. Time out! A Baptist Pope, a Jewish leader of the PLO? Considering the old sentiments and rising stakes of the Atlanta Olympics, as unlikely as the feat of having positions on both sides of the rivalry, is the likelihood of the only person pulling it off—Sinjin Smith. Smith has always applied his energies to more than just playing. A driving force of the AVP, he was a hands-on guy. Before his ouster as president of the AVP, Smith admits "I was known as a complainer." If the signs were too close to the court, if the PA system was too loud, Smith's antennae were perpetually out looking for imperfections and he tried to get them corrected. "I cared about the sport and that it was presented professionally."

Ego, money, power: dangerous elements in the new admixture of pro beach volleyball. Some players admired Smith's actions as caretaker; others construed it as the whining of a self-serving, ambitious star. What cannot be denied is that no other player during the '80s, the first decade of pro beach volleyball, would have the same national impact as Smith. Upturned bill on his visor with a printed Sideout—

part owner of the leading volleywear company in the world—on posters, television interviews, magazines...Smith was the guy most seen. The gadfly of officials and consummate self-promoter in the eyes of his detractors, what finally got Smith in the eyes of the public was more than his big-time modeling good looks. He won more than anyone else: 135 tournaments to be exact. Maybe not all of them, or even many of the big ones, but week-in and week-out, he was the winner. With partner Randy Stoklos—who ranks second in all-time wins with 117—in the first decade of the pro circuit, they pocketed the most money.

Yet Sinjin pushed hardest off the court where he won the most as well. Sinjin Smith was the first to get a big clothing deal, the first to publish an autobiography and the first to play in an FIVB international event. It rubbed many people the wrong way—Sinjin saw it as a result of two things: petty jealousy and regional rivalry. After being the protagonist during the opening chapter of the pro game, Smith, in the same voice of any deposed ruler, admits, "they pushed me out." And like a cat on a rain gutter, he has been on a precarious path ever since his ouster from the AVP board in 1989. Still, his nose always to the wind, something told him that the FIVB was going to make a move toward beach volleyball in a big way. In fact, the head body under Acosta already had: by 1990, FIVB sanctioned tournaments had been held in Italy and France...and were attracting TV, crowds and sponsors. By 1992, he had won several of the FIVB World Series events—Smith-Stoklos were the first Kings of the International Beach—and had become friendly with various figures of the FIVB and other National Federations. In turn, he was a taproot of information for the inexperienced promoters of beach volleyball in other parts of the world...including Ruben Acosta.

Yet the push offshore would cost him...figuratively and literally as well. In 1992 he was still a leading AVP player when he and Stoklos asked permission to play in the appendage to the Barcelona Olympics—the tournament in Almeira, Spain. Denied the right, he and Stoklos went anyway and won. It was a costly victory: a $70,000 fine and suspension from a subsequent Cuervo event were slapped on the two renegades. However, the $70,000 fine was later waived.

Although the conflict did nothing to increase his popularity with the AVP, Smith was not the retiring type...nor would he ever be. In 1994, he took a bolder step by recruiting Bruk Vandeweghe to play in the prelude to the Atlanta Olympics, the Goodwill Games. From serving as the original Patrick Henry of beach volleyball amongst the AVP front office and many players, he now went to being Benedict Arnold. Having undergone two recent knee surgeries—"I tried to play on it too soon"—he and Vandeweeghe took home the bronze medal while the other American duo, Jeff Williams and Carlos Briceno won the silver. But oh my, the Americans didn't win the gold? If their names are not pronounceable—Bjoern Maaseide and Jan Kvalhelm—be it known that the gold medalists were from Norway. Beaches up there but not a lot of sun; still, the sport is obviously producing good players around the globe.

This time for his transgression, Smith and his partner were given a one-year suspension. Presently recovering from his third knee surgery, it probably didn't matter. What does matter is that the AVP-USA Volleyball (or FIVB) feud which appears to reach detente for brief periods, continues to retreat to heightened tensions...which keep getting higher. At the eye of the hurricane, Smith thinks he's made the right move. He could be right. The FIVB is raising the bets furiously. For the men's '95-'96 World Series Championship, a scheduled 15 events are on the calendar with a lot of money in the purse—doubled from the year before to about $2,000,000. $100,000 minimum for most and $200,000 for a few tournaments; the bonus pool will offer $500,000.

The bucks are big but so is the prestige. The first Beach Volleyball Olympics in Atlanta will be something special and the sport has arrived

at the pinnacle of competition in breath-taking speed. Sinjin Smith was certainly amongst the few who helped push it there. His own role was marked with ambition, controversy...and winning the most beach tournaments in history. As he will be 39 years old in Atlanta and is presently nursing a dicey knee, some people have counted him out. No one can count him out as a tour de force in the future of beach volleyball, playing...or otherwise.

"From playing to talking..."

Perhaps the greatest measure of the growth of volleyball, and an immediate yardstick as well, is its increased exposure on television. The great American assimilator—the filter of society's needs, mores, and fantasies—all quantifiable too. Success is quite simply determined...what's the ratings? To get on the tube means there is some intrinsic value there, something that some part of the country views as worthy of their attention—from Oprah Winfrey to the MacNeil-Lehrer Report and every stripe in between. Sports are no different and if an activity can keep the fickle American public long enough, personalities can emerge to capture the audience's fancy too. So powerful is the medium that those who deliver the message can loom as large as the performers on the field or court.

On the cusp of its second century, American volleyball can boast its own two talking heads. Chris Marlowe and Paul Sunderland began climbing up the television rope—cable to network—in the early mid-'80s. Today they talk to each other without missing a beat...joined at the hip...or rather at those ubiquitous microphones they share. Glib, witty, incisive but something more, they're into it. Sure, there is a certain dash of that mock sincerity which nowadays passes over sports viewers like so much residual radiation from the screen, but in the final take, these guys are pros—TV-wise and they know the game inside and out. They've been there and back, competed against many of the same athletes they are interviewing. It's a young sport in terms of television, and its acceptance argues a new stature in our TV-driven world.

Sunderland, with the slicked-back hair, handsome and brimming with confidence, has recently signed as anchor for Prime Network's national sports show. Well-versed in all sports and at ease in any situation—he will soon be seen expounding on topics ranging from ice hockey to NCAA football. The corporate image, ephemeral, saying the politically correct thing while still dredging for the deep secret at the same time. "Volleyball opened the door for me. Then I was successfully able to cross over into football and basketball, as well as hosting and the studio."

Marlowe? Different breed. He's as ambitious as his talk-mate, but there is more of the ham in him. Son of recognized Hollywood actors, "Big Sy" learned the value of flamboyance and grabbing the headline as an infant journeyman. Still, there's an originality in the man. He was not a leading player on the '84 team—not close to being the starting setter—but he was the captain. As Kiraly said, "Everyone could relate to Marlowe, Eastie or beach guy." On one side of a bus touring East Germany there might sit the dour Beal, hovered over statistics in quiet study. On the other side a passel of mostly Southern Californians raised on fun. All of them in agreement: "Play it hard but geez!...enjoy it! Life is short!" Marlowe was the bridge. He was as stingy with a point as any guy who ever played the game on wood or sand, but he had the gift of walking away and having a beer—or two—and entertaining the whole mob. Humor. The glue of life and Marlowe had more than a normal dose.

At the 1996 Atlanta Olympics, volleyball fans will be able to sit back in their easy chairs and enjoy the action. Chances are that the same two guys who brought us coverage of the last two Olympics will do the same...and more. This time it's beach volleyball as well and there's more than one educated guess that the new off-beat sport will be Atlanta's darling. Americans will already be an educated audience; millions have seen and listened to the two Olympians on NBC's live coverage of the AVP summer events. Should be great fun...especially if America's best are in it. If for some reason Karch Kiraly is home watching with the rest of the world's top players, that will be a sad day for everyone...despite Marlowe's inevitable one-liners.

"Barcelona Bob goes south...then east..."

There always seems to always be a blue period following the grandest of competitions, but 1993 was abnormally severe. Sturm, as previous Olympic coaches, found the ship all but abandoned. Although off-shore salaries—especially in Italy—were going flat as pizzas, the money was in most cases better there than here. Stork, Partie, Fortune and Ctvrtlik went back to Italy; Ivie went as well but stayed only for a week since his recently operated knee developed an infection. The retired Timmons was spending his time between surfing in Mexico and rolling out thousands of T-shirts with variations on the same Redsand theme. A couple key players remained but it was an emasculated team for the most part; Ivie would not return until early 1993 and Brent Hilliard was only partially available between periods of rehabilitation. Ivie's knee and Hilliard's shoulder were well worn. In January of 1993, two new coaches as well came on board. Former playing legends and top college coaches, Rod Wilde and Rudy Suwara were now trying to teach new dogs their old tricks.

With John Carroll fully at the helm now, a new marketing strategy was set in train. In wake of the sensational media coverage of the shaven head protest in Barcelona, why not take "Barcelona Bob" and make the distinctive looking spiker the new quintessential star? That meant obviously a raise in pay and showering much more attention on the lad. Some of the volleyball community was immediately astir. Pick for stardom the guy who cost his team an important victory in Barcelona? More importantly, what about his ability as a player? Should that be part of the criterion? Many thought yes. The USVBA and IMG thought no.

What made it worse was that the new star was approached at the eleventh hour. The irony was that the hitter would have been happy to play for much less money. "I went to the USVBA two and a half months before to get Sammy a contract. He wanted to stay: I wanted him to stay and take advantage of his marketing ability here. We asked for far less than what he eventually got," reports his agent, Tom McCarthy. But we were contacted the actual day before he was leaving for Italy." The deal was signed and Sammy was driving a new car.

He soon appeared nude in a magazine ad, the traditional fig leaf supplanted by a modest...volleyball. "Big Bad Bob" exploded the cover in yellow letters of Volleyball Magazine's edition of April, 1993. Subtitle: "Just how good is the good life for Bob Samuelson?" With a $97,000 base annual salary, life seemed indeed not too bad. Up until then, a seventh player who would come off the bench to spark a team in trouble, Samuelson was known for hard hitting, hot blocking and fiery antics—all in indeterminate streaks. He could raise a team...but he could also make no difference or worse. Consistency was not his strong suit. The gambit proved a problem with the other players as well. Some were asking themselves which would produce a salary raise? Ten stuff blocks, a 70% kill rate or a complete body tattoo? "It was unfortunate. He was somehow put in a role he wasn't prepared to fill. Samuelson could be great but he couldn't carry the load on an everyday basis," reflects Sturm.

In the World League of 1993, there was some proof of the miscast pudding. Finishing ninth out of twelve and with a record of 7-13, the same scenario of those former horrible off-years reappeared. Besides the repeated challenge of building another team for the next quadrennial, Sturm more than previous coaches, had to live by IMG's stepped-up scheduling agenda. Matches, including several World League events, had to be played when the marketing company set them up; a lot of balls for a coach to juggle. It would get worse before it got better.

"Six long weeks." That's what Sturm uses as a euphemism for the hell of the World League '94. Another headline on Volleyball Magazine: "0-12. Are the USA Men *Really* That Bad?" Many thought so. Dwindling crowds, low morale, for Sturm it was the nadir of his career. With a 19-38 record, "coaching change?" innuendoes were heard. "Since 1989, Italy, Cuba, Japan, Brazil and Russia have all kept their teams together. Ours was basically new...once again." Same ole song. Could the USVBA ever keep a team together for four years? With the Atlanta Olympics around the corner, "they had better" was decided in July, 1994. Besides the flak from the volleyball community, the central office had IMG and corporate sponsors to answer to for the poor performance. Once again, it looked like the governing body was in the precarious position to deal with National Team problems on a reactive basis.

In July, Fortune was finally signed and Ctvrtlik had already committed in the spring. Thank god! Ctvrtlik made an incredible difference the minute he walked in the Federal Building. That was it...the connection which reached back into the glory days of '84 to '88, a missing filament which galvanized that world-beating tradition once again. Assistant coach Rod Wilde views the dismal performance of '94 not as a lack of physical aptitude, just a bunch of young guys not really knowing how to compete on the world's top level. You can show videos, old photos, read books and talk...and talk...but "Ctvrtilik *showed* them on the court how to do it."

Wilde remembers the first week and the team's reaction to playing pepper. The warm-up exercise as old as the game itself can be played just for that—an exercise for preparing to play while at the same time taking some leisurely minutes to chat. Or...two players can take every ball as a matter of winning and losing, total concentration on spiking, digging and setting. "We had ten minutes of nonstop pepper every practice and I moved Ctvrtlik to a different partner every day. Guys were sweating, getting yelled at, and taking this as a serious drill. Now when we play pepper, there's a whole new level of concentration." Wilde continues, "There are guys out there with much more talent than Bob but no one has near his intensity. We really needed that."

Other things got better. Ivie was becoming healthier; "injuries kept breaking his cycles," says Wilde. "Right now he's our one world-class level hitter." The versatility and experience of two-time Olympian, Fortune, was another blessing. And once again, the gods smiled broadly when Lloy Ball and other collegians like Jeff Nygaard came to San Diego. In a four-match tour of the country with Poland, the new team with the big setter took every match. Well, better but the real test would come in Athens at the World Championships. Pass the test they did and more. Doormats for the world's best teams six months before, the revitalized team steamrolled through world-powers as Cuba and Brazil which they hadn't beaten in 18 months to capture the bronze medal. In the recently released FIVB world rankings, the USA Men had risen to sixth place; the powerful Brazilians are still at the top of the heap with Italy close behind.

"Tokyo Roses..."

In the fall of 1992—long before Bob Samuelson happily penned his name on his USVBA contract, USA Women's coach, Terry Liskevych, approached the USVBA front office for a similar treatment of his own chosen star. There was a difference. Samuelson's appearance and incendiary antics would figure heavily in his salary; however, the number of the world's great female outside hitters could be counted on one hand, and Kemner's value was attached to her membership in that select group. She was ready to commit for four years through the Atlanta Olympics. She wanted $90,000 per year for the quadrennial. Turned down, she went to Brazil to play. Liskevych went away shaking his head—once again, a

victim of a short budget, along with shortsighted judgment and gender inequity, he felt.

On the judgment side, at least, he was right. In October, 1994 at the World Championships in Sao Paulo, Brazil, Kemner's hard-hitting would have been worth tons. Staying within the top four in the world since their bronze medal finish in Barcelona, Liskevych was hoping to pull off a win this time. One affliction which kept rearing its ugly head was inconsistent outside hitting: Teee Williams, Tara Cross-Battle and Elaine Youngs had stretches which sparkled but dark lapses as well. Things started well enough; the Americans won the preliminary pool mowing down Japan, 3-1, in the process. But in the quarterfinals, the wheels started to come off and the ladies fell victims to the always robust Russians. The disappointed Americans recovered to put away Japan a second time and place themselves in their final match for fifth place—disappointing but liveable. Instead, they dropped a 3-1 match to Germany. Germany? Yes—an improved Germany—but the red, white and blue bus had slid off the road and lay in a forlorn ditch.

Outside hitting...and team leadership. Well, Kemner was in Japan to hypothetically answer the first riddle. Where was the second? In Japan too! On the same team! Today Paula Weishoff and Kemner are part of the latest stampede to the newly opened pro leagues in Japan. From lira to reais to yen, the MVP of the '84 and '92 Olympics and the most decorated American woman to ever play volleyball, Weishoff has followed the money trail to the Daiei team. Coached by Arie Selinger no less. Would Liskevych like to have the marvelous athlete although she will be 34 by Atlanta? He has wisely left the door open to two athletes: Kemner and Weishoff. "It depends on how I am physically," says Weishoff about Atlanta '96. The USA Women's coaching staff is less concerned about her marvelous physical talents; they need her her experience and proven ability to win.

Still, the women will need more than these two additions to upset the formidable Cubans with the ferocious pounding of Mireya Luis and incomparable blocking of Regla Torres. The Chinese, Brazilians and Russians as well seem a cut higher than the Americans at this juncture. But there are pipe dreams in the offing. If Natalie Williams can recover from a recent knee surgery, a bundle of raw ability awaits to be molded for the Atlanta Olympics. The lethal attacking of the woman who led Long Beach State to last year's NCAA title, Danielle Scott, has many bettors throwing money down on her odds to rise to Olympic stardom in '96. How about the youngest of the phenoms, Kristin Folkl, of Stanford? And that marvel over there in Italy, Keba Phipps—now older, now maturer. Who knows? There are two years to work it all out. That's more than double the time Liskevych had to assemble his last two Olympic teams. There's more talent than ever, albeit spread around the globe; the Olympics are home again. Will the proper financial support arrive from USA Volleyball to optimize the ladies' chances? Again, who knows? It can only be hoped.

"Four is better than two!...or is it?..."

If Kiraly believes that you can't be a specialist on the beach, he was clearly referring to the doubles game. Not the hybrid of four-person beach volleyball. In 1991, there were plenty of good indoor players, corporate sponsorship funds and a promoter, Craig Elledge to put it all together. It was a nice break and extra money for USA Men's team players like Stork, Buck, Partie, Salmons and Fortune. To ensure parity, a captain was selected by each team sponsor who in turn formed his team by selecting from a pool of players in a draft. Club Sportswear won the title that first year and the MVP was the left-handed setter, Jeff Stork. Each year increased prize money and cable television coverage; in '92 a newer and younger name, Tom Duke, grabbed the MVP for his Ocean Pacific team which won the tour. A women's competition was introduced with a partial season in 1992.

The Bud Light Pro Beach Volleyball League was in full swing by 1993 with a full nationwide tournament schedule for men and women. Five teams battled in some major American city almost every summer weekend before ESPN cameras and bleachers full of local enthusiasts. The top man and woman who received the MVP that year were ones already familiar to indoor fans. Bob Ctvrtlik and just what she needed—another award—Paula Weishoff.

How much would players stand to win? Nothing like the AVP purse, but it was not a bad way to spend your summer. The winning Team Paul Mitchell for the men in 1994 split almost $110,000 between themselves over 14 weekends, with the captain getting a little more of the gravy. After the 10-tournament season for the women ended, the winning Sony Autosound team split up about $75,000. Jeff Stork was selected the men's best player for a second time and Kim Oden proved that tall middle-blockers could also play on the sand.

And for 1995? Bigger and better. An even 12-tournament schedule is slated for both genders according to CE Sports, fighting for over $1,000,000 in prize money and visibility on the renewed ESPN coverage. The garrulous Kathy Gregory strafing comments on the women while Jon Lee will add his incisive comments on the boys. Adherents of the four-person game claim that it sits in a better position than even beach doubles for international allure. Foreigners will have a much easier time with this game since adapting from indoor is simpler, and rumors of an international tour are heard. A line in the sand, is there enough beach to battle for? In 1994, the answer appears to be a function of that TV/corporate dollar continuum—the shifting tide seems to be going out today and there's more room, and more interest, to play on the sand than ever.

"Tyger, Tyger, burning bright..." (William Blake)

Faces have launched thousands of ships. Homer told us of an exquisite one but it's now a little threadbare. Besides, this modern beauty strays from classical Troy; calls for the French Symbolist poetry of Mallarme or a dream-engendered painting of Puvis de Chavannes. The more mannered feminine beauty of Klimt? Nah, even that doesn't get it. It's the Pre-Raphaelites! A lurid, haunting beauty of a woman's face by Rossetti...or moreso...the poet-painter who turned the nineteenth century idea of art upside-down. William Blake. "The Marriage of Heaven and Hell"—that stirring idea that the life force lies in the primal energy of the noble human spirit *and body*, not the stale fusty confines of stone cathedrals. Lurid poems of feral beasts in the jungle, trenchant eyes of tigers impaling readers with frightful questions.

Gabrielle. Picked by so-called experts like Elle magazine as having "one of the world's most beautiful faces." As absurd as that exercise is, there is a beauty there which captures; large, luminescent eyes, resounding like steel drums of her half-Trinadadian father. Raised in the Virgin Islands, she was gifted as both a basketball and volleyball player. At 6'3" and with a good jump, she had her choice and finally plumped for a volleyball scholarship at Florida State. Besides attracting sizeable crowds to their matches, largely male, it was there that her tall prettiness was marked for world recognition. Soon she was taking junkets to New York, Paris, Milan and exotic islands for fashion shoots. Such a splash the long-legged island girl made, she had to forfeit the last two years of her scholarship and pay for her own education.

In 1990, Gabrielle Reece finished college and said good-bye to indoor volleyball. Where was she to play...even if she had the time? Well, eventually on the beach between stints of glamour. Picking up doubles games in Florida when she could, she bravely decided to enter a WPVA event. She knew she was being thrown to the lionesses; that was okay. But she had just picked up a bout of dysentery on a shoot in Morocco and dropped a quick 20 pounds. Skinny and shaking, she took the court, and to her surprise, she and partner didn't embarrass themselves.

More, she got the bug to play beach volleyball...at all costs.

That could be a heavy cost. Leaving the fashion mecca of New York could only jeopardize some of her modeling career opportunities. She might be walking away from some megabucks when she moved to Los Angeles for her apprenticeship, but so be it. And had anyone told her that a woman her size, whose only volleyball experience was four years indoor, would have as much chance in beach doubles as becoming a ballerina? "I've always done what I wanted to. Besides, I hated living in New York." She jumped into it, and playing with Holly McPeak and other top pros, she slowly got her sand legs and ball-handling skills.

Enigmas seem to surround Gabrielle. Certainly beach doubles allows for more of the star quality, the fine focusing of individual faces. But no, she enjoys the teamwork part of the game. "Sure, I'm better suited to four-women than doubles. But doubles isn't a team sport. It's very individualistic and I didn't like the vibe of it all. And I think for women, fours is a better game for TV."

At 24, she has become a savvy promoter of the Bud Light Pro Beach Volleyball League and its four-women circuit. Gabrielle has TV visibility and that translates to *power* in today's world. She knows it. "I try to use my position to advance the sport. We've got a game for taller women like myself—players who specialized in college can now play on the beach. I impose my ideas when I can. For example, I think they should be concentrating more on the Olympians on our tour like Liane Sato, Tammy Liley, Keba Phipps and Natalie Williams." Yet invariably the cameras keep coming back to the same center blocker. Despite her own view, "There's a lot more pretty girls in volleyball than there are athletic models." Yet to have both gifts in such abundance has gained her a distinct position in the world of glamour...as well as a decision to only appear in the image of an athlete. The Nike woman, the MTV paragon of beauty, talent, and *sports*. "It was a direction I worked toward."

If the TV cameras are homed in on her beauty, they are also seeing a phenomenal talent...getting better every summer. Chosen MVP in the inaugural '92 season, admittedly thinly talented, Reece captained the Lady Foot Locker team the next year. After a frustrating beginning, she was instrumental in getting Gary Sato to take over coaching the team near the end of that season. They won the last tournament at Seal Beach and finished third in the league. Perennially pushing herself to get better, Sato observes: "She works hard. She's the most improved player on the tour." In 1993, she led the tour in total kills and blocks. In the past '94 season under Sato, her Nike team finished in third place and Reece was selected as the Offensive Player of the Year as well as the Most Improved Player—an award which is decided by the players themselves. Her '94 statistics again bear out her dominance at the net: in the kill category, her 454 kills ran away with it—the next player totaled 322 put-aways. Her 55 blocks put her in third ranking and she finished fifth in service aces. "This year's award meant a lot more to me. We had many of the best players in America on the tour."

Gabrielle's prowess has even caught the eye of Olympic coach, Terry Liskevych. Will she try out for Atlanta? Once again an odd, almost anachronistic, sense of fairness influences her thinking. "I thought about it a lot. But I wouldn't want to go out at the last minute and take someone's place who had spent years working to go to the Olympics." Yeah, but she's 6'3", can hit and block...and has a proven work ethic.

Ethics. Not a word heard much today in the moneyed world of sports. Well, the word is often found...only the *practice* is scarce. Probably why she's like a cool zephyr, skipping off a warm Caribbean Sea. Down in the tropics, in the Virgin Islands. Where tall beauties sometimes grow.

"New name...new game?..."

In 1994, after 66 years of service, the old title which was commonly used, "USVBA," was retired. A new moniker, USA Volleyball, was conferred upon the organization...not only a trifle more hip but hopefully someone who had never heard of the organization—which probably included most Americans—now had an immediate clue as to the purpose of its existence. "Volleyball" was now actually spelled out for the uninitiated.

Does the new name suggest new changes? Well, yes and no. In 1992, when John Carroll brought his extensive background with ProServ to his new job as Executive Director, he was faced with an enormous challenge in setting the dishevelled house in order. With the reserve fund from the '84 Olympics running out fast, it was hard to kick-start the money side of things. So he contacted the USVBA's old standby, IMG, and after months of negotiation the governing body like an inveterate drunken sailor re-upped for a third hitch with the firm. It appeared the easiest way and perhaps the only way—at least for the National Team program—to have some kind of promised floor underneath it until the Atlanta Olympics. The deal guaranteed the USVBA a minimum of $1,900,000; well, almost. If IMG spent too much money in their duties—players' salaries, match expenses and the like—the company could actually dock the USVBA's guaranteed sum for additional expenses, but nothing too extraordinary. For IMG, if they hit a homerun with the sport, they would stand to skim the cream...way down into the bucket, before the USVBA would get additional dividends from any resounding success.

It was clear who had the position of negotiating strength; Armand Hammer or Ross Perot would have been pressed to get any more out of the marketing company. However, what did raise eyebrows more was the term of the contract: IMG could walk at any time—something they had done in the past as was well known. Or they had the option to stay if they chose...*for 12 years!* With an optional four more! That's a long time.

In November of 1994, Volleyball Magazine reported that IMG was asking to renegotiate the deal, stating it suffered losses over $1,700,000 over the last two years. Expecting to lose another $800,000 this year—largely from poor domestic National Team tours and a disappointing FIVB Beach World Series event in Miami in January, 1994. At that rate, there appears to be scant chance that the company will stay around the dozen years it signed up for—but then again, the rocky marriage has already gone through three trips to the altar.

Grassroots? That's a plus for the governing body. About 60,000 registered members held cards in 1990; today that figure is over 97,000. With some 55,000 junior memberships! In the '94 Junior Olympic National Championships held in Austin, a record number of 423 teams entered from 37 states, Puerto Rico, Guam and Canada. In the Nike Festival this year, total participants reached almost 7,000.

Although not on the same dynamic growth rate, adults are playing more as well. And everywhere. In 1993, the first ever Outdoor National Championships were held in San Jose. A co-ed affair open to both juniors and adult, the number of teams and divisions doubled in '94: 223 teams and 21 divisions. In fact, in certain parts of the country, grass and sand are overtaking the indoor interest. Players are finding that it's a lot easier to put up a portable net than to find a gym—if one can be found—to wait in line to play. Ann Davenport, who has run the Southern California region for many years, says "The number of adults playing in tournaments are down. They're playing outdoors more." While the hotbed of the game has some 6,000 registered juniors playing, the adult membership has slipped to about 1500. Alas, it seems those days are gone, or at least going, when teams traveled to some high school for a regional USVBA tournament which would last all day...and often late into the night.

As far as the old "Nationals," in 1989 the diminishing interest in that competition reached a point of crisis. Total number of teams entered in Toledo was only 117. Granted the sightseeing attractions of that chosen city were limited but there were 135 the year before in Salt Lake City—and 188 entered in the Berkeley Nationals in 1987. Not a good trend. What was

wrong? For one thing, the NCAA refused to allow college players to compete anymore. "That killed the Women's Division. Over half of the teams were gone," reports Glen Davies. And besides that, the tournament had become...well, boring! Same ole thing, same ole teams, different year. While juniors, college, and beach were getting hotter every year. The famous ref and holder of every other USVBA position over the decades, Davies, came up with the idea of creating more divisions. "We had to do something," he admits. So if you went to play in Raleigh in 1990, you could play in the Open Division or: Seniors (30-35), three divisions of Masters (35-49, 40-44, 45-49), and four divisions of Golden Masters (50-54, 55-59, 60-64, 65 and over). The "festival format" was borrowed and a consolation bracket was used to provide more play as well as more even competition. The format continues to undergo slight alterations but the concept has proven successful. In 1994, a record total of 232 teams entered the U.S. Open during the week-long tournament. Fourteen divisions ranging from ages 18-75 played "under one roof" in Tulsa.

Under one roof has undeniably been a factor in improving the tournament. No longer required to drive cross town in search of obscure high school gyms, the portable Sport Court flooring has allowed up to 25 courts to be put down on huge convention center floors. Manufactured in an array of colors, the synthetic material has taken volleyball to places never conceived of before—Grand Central Station in New York was one—both for tournaments and exhibitions.

"Women rule..."

Has Title IX had an effect since its passage? A simple statistic: in 1971, a reported 294,015 girls participated in high school sports. In 1994? 2,124,755! Compared to boys? In 1971, the number was 3,666,917; the '94 figure came in less at 3,478,530. For volleyball, the sport ranks third amongst high school girls with over 327,000 players counted this year. For high school boys, about 25,000 play the sport which ranks somewhere well below the top ten. In testimony to the efficacy of the legislation on the college level, this year there were almost 300 Division I volleyball programs reported by the NCAA; 240 in Division II and 343 programs in the Division III category, as well as numerous NAIA Colleges. Still, the designed impact of Title IX has not been fully implemented, and in fact, it looms as the biggest shadow over NCAA sports today. How is gender equity to be defined in college sports, particularly financial? A static state now reigns and although women's programs continue to grow, minor NCAA sports for men are stagnant or in some cases being eliminated altogether. Only 64 NCAA men's volleyball programs are around today—there were 63 in 1981.

Women's volleyball is where the great growth is in the sport today. Since the NCAA took over women's volleyball in 1981, the college interest and growth has soared. It's big-time. Recruiting is a year-round activity; college coaches are seen regularly at junior club competitions on the lookout for the next Paula Weishoff—the search for talent is so intense that coaches are also looking offshore. And when NCAA playoff times begin in November every year, the intensity gets heavy. In 1992, the NCAA playoff field numbered 32. Not bad. This year for the Fourteenth Annual Championship held at the University of Texas, it was 48! And it has truly become a competition national in scope. The talent pool has expanded so much that teams from the Big Eight, Southeastern, and Big Ten Conference are fully capable, and oftentimes do, knock off the once perennial powers of Southern California.

With no end in sight. Especially when the base level is surveyed, almost 1200 Junior Olympic clubs have been formed in the country to date. Considering that a full scholarship in this day and age can amount to a couple hundred thousand dollars of value, parents are more and more willing to invest in club dues to advance their daughters' chances. Clubs in turn clamor more and more for the best local talent.

Some of the established clubs like the Orange County Volleyball Club, ASICs Tiger and Sports Performance of Chicago have been around for more than a decade and have become local institutions. High school girls dream of starting on one of their club's top teams. The first and largest club in its city, the San Diego Volleyball Club, is perhaps the leader in placing their young players in colleges. Janet Kramer, a former All-American at UC San Diego, has been a director of the club for five years: "When I graduated from high school 12 years ago, there wasn't a club in San Diego; now there are nine. In nine seasons we've placed 150 girls into college programs with about 110 receiving scholarships. It just gets bigger—this year we have 21 teams."

"Ebony among the oranges..."

There she was; 13 years old, 5'11", her body weight not quite in triple figures, and trying out for the Orange County Volleyball Club in 1978. Charlie Brand was continuing a legendary program in the wake of Chuck Erbe's departure, so at the behest of her Marine father, who was impassioned by volleyball, Kim Oden stepped out on the court—long limbs flailing, askew...and the only black girl in the tryout. This was Orange County, one of the most conservative places in the country at the zenith of the Great Communicator's reign, and John Wayne keeping law and order from his burnished dais at the airport. "I had five great years in the club. Race mostly seemed not an issue. I had lots of fun playing." The bright perspective on life Kim Oden brings to any situation must have been a factor. Articulate and sensitive, she thinks similar to how she plays—balanced, smart, consistent. Plus, she's 6'2".

An All-American at Stanford where she was one of four presidents of her senior class, Oden was on the USA Women's Team by 1987. By then, her experience as the "guinea pig" in her family had been exploited by a talented sister, Elaina, who was also playing for the National Team via UOP. The Seoul Olympics were admittedly a disappointment for everyone but by

Barcelona in 1992, "We knew a lot more about the other teams by then. And we were a more mature team." She also credits the addition of Greg Giovanazzi on the coaching staff: "He expected you to do well; that instilled confidence in us." After a bronze medal, she was off to Italy to play pro and then to play in China in 1993. Her versatility took her to the four-women's beach tour where she was selected MVP in 1994.

A third sister, Bev, followed in the oldest pair of footsteps: Stanford and the USA National Team. "We're all so different physically—just like our playing styles. But if we weren't sisters, we'd still be friends." Kim says it convincingly. There is a palpable strength of character, of dignity, in the 30-year old star. And the future? She's excited about it; "There's a big positive difference in the women's game now because there are many more women coaches who were ex-players." As far as her own role in the sport she has so strikingly imprinted, she is very conscious of the black athlete in America and would like to further African-American participation in volleyball. "It has to happen. The question is not if but when the kids in the inner-city will play, but they need good coaches from the people who live there. Exposure to and proper teaching in the inner-city will be crucial to our international success." Could it be the same ungainly colt who walked out on that court for the first time at 13, center of attention, will be the one who leads the charge? Likely. It's a quiet fire in her; one senses a person cut from the same mold as another woman she admires: Wilma Rudolph. Tall, she carries her height with pride, as she does her gender, her race and her chosen game.

"Hall of Fame, 1994..."

The ring. "Not until you get the ring, baby!..." It's the symbol par excellence of American sports—Super Bowl, NBA and on down. In 1989, Barbara Boskovich was chatting with Kathy Gregory who had just been inducted into the Volleyball Hall of Fame in Holyoke. "What did you get?" Barbara asked.

"A plaque," replied Kathy. The ASICs Tiger representative to volleyball since 1987, a fervid supporter who has her own distinction of being the person probably asked the most times for sponsorship funds, Barbara nodded. "Hmmm, that's nice but you can't really wear that and show people." She was right there. Boskovich's thoughts strayed to TV images of the epic heroes of America, brandishing on their fingers one-pound chunks of glitter and stone— the circular proof of immortality. "These people are the ambassadors of the sport; they should have something to show people. So I worked with ASICs to get approval of the idea to give rings to inductees." Kathy Gregory as well— the award has been made retroactively to honored members of the institution.

This year at the honorary banquet in Holyoke there were four who received rings: Patty Dowdell, Marv Dunphy, John Koch and Larry Rundle. An organization founded in 1985 where the sport was born, largely through the efforts of the community of Holyoke, the Hall of Fame is located in a small building that now houses historical information and memorabilia of the game. In addition, 24 individuals have been recognized for their contribution to the sport: players, coaches and administrators. The Hall of Fame also awards the "Court of Honor" award to outstanding teams or organizations.

In 1994, the American Volleyball Coaches Association (AVCA) was distinguished with the "Court of Honor" Award. It is indeed a worthy recipient. In 1981, college coaches Terry Liskevych and Andy Banachowski huddled together and decided that some type of overseeing body was needed in the growing collegiate game: to share ideas, promote the sport and disseminate information. They contacted Sharon McAlexander for her assistance and the original Collegiate Volleyball Coaches Association was formed. Interest and growth was immediate and a full-time director, Sandy Vivas, was hired in 1983. As the sport boomed in the '80s, high school and junior club programs were crying for information as well. The board and staff increased; a seminal event occurred in

1986 when a new name was adopted to reflect its expanding universe: the AVCA. Today its member organizations number about 3,000 and the AVCA has emerged as an efficient educational organ of the sport in this country.

The William G. Morgan Award is a brand new one. Its first and only recipient was recognized this year—designed to honor manufacturing companies, or professional organizations, which have supported volleyball for an extended number of years. To no one's great surprise, it was received by Barbara Boskovich for her own ASICs Tiger Corporation. Since the early '70s, the company has sold volleyball shoes and apparel in this country and has used its resources to support countless teams, sponsor tournaments and underwrite special projects as the ASICs Tiger Men's and Women's Collegiate All-American Posters. Boskovich's own interest has led her to chair the SGMA (Sporting Goods Manufacturers' Association) volleyball division which is an assembly of companies that manufacture volleyball-related products. In turn, the group supports selected activities. In perhaps a twist of irony, some wondered what Barbara Boskovich would receive on behalf of ASICs at her acceptance speech for the first company ever inducted into the Volleyball Hall of Fame. Would the lady be granted her own invented ring? Nah...she got a plaque.

"South of the border...down Mexico way..."

People from as far away as Maine fly out to San Diego, rent a car, and invariably get lost on the road to Ensenada. Part of the Hadji, or the Dark Age holy pilgrimage to Compostela— every sojourner must pass through the obstacles. "Toll road? What's that?" Finally, after several payouts, a lot of confusion and possibly some margaritas to defuse the frustration, they arrive at Ensenada. Hawkers sell everything to sombreros to day-glo portraits of Elvis and Jesus—all signed by the original sitter. Finally, they get to Estero Beach. The holy trek of beach volleyballers is ended; now to give homage to the sport they adore and its unholy tradition.

Tan bodies barely covered, sweating in the sand, drinking cervezas and tequila, dancing to rock and roll under a million Mexican stars. "Viva la...who cares? Let's party!" It happens year after year...increasingly so.

But if you want to play too, it's suggested that you get in your fifteen dollar entry fee before arriving. *Weeks* before to be safe. And if you haven't made a hotel room reservation in Ensenada several months before, you could be back on the toll road looking for a hacienda. Or join the revelers who rock around the clock...or simply crash a few hours on the wide beach. If you show up early Saturday morning hoping to sign up in the overflowing tournament, your only chance is to ask for George Stepanof, tournament director. Say you're an old friend of...uh, Jim Callender or Ed Teagle or Nate Parish. Stepanof, a member of the California Beach Volleyball Hall of Fame, has been running the tournament for about 20 years and has run Opens north of the border for 30. Every year the organizing committee haggles over closing the entries and every year they seem to let everyone in. "Just put up another court!"

Last year they put up *135 volleyball courts!* To accommodate 792 teams: 552 pairs of men and 240 women's teams. The largest beach tournament in the world was the brainchild of one brainy guy over 20 years ago, Jack Elliott, amongst some other San Diego buddies who decided to go down and spend a weekend in Ensenada. Drinking beer, eating lobster...naturally! But also playing a little beach ball. It got bigger every summer and another local from La Jolla, Mike Brown, stepped up and took over the organization of the growing creature. By the mid-'80s it was a huge, Frankensteinian affair; a rock band had to be moved outside to accommodate the party. By the late '80s if you were looking for that old friend in the tournament, forget it! Try checking out 100 courts of six-team pools to find someone. Amongst only players it could be done...not with everyone else who comes down to the Woodstock of beach volleyball.

And they come from all walks. MTV crews, pros like Brian Lewis or Steve Timmons whose Redsand is now the official sponsor. Pros and legends. It had to be; a 40-something 6'7" guy started showing up, at the bar hustling the young lovelies and offending their escorts. Upsetting and entertaining the whole way, one year he won the whole thing. Who else...but Vogie!

"The other Hall of Fame...beach..."

In 1965, the California Beach Volleyball Association (CBVA) was formed. That year, tournament organizers from the main volleyball beaches in Southern California convened to coordinate scheduling, establish ratings and standardize rules for the growing game. They quickly approached the Santa Monica Recreation Department for institutional support, and through its efforts the CBVA was born. The CBVA underwent another dramatic change when it became a non-profit organization in 1987. A few years later, a former president of the CBVA, Rick Jennings, got together with a colleague, Ed Montan, and formed FOVA (Federation of Outdoor Volleyball). Attempting to implement a nation-wide, grass-roots outdoor program, the ambitious effort flourished before finally failing in 1993.

The CBVA, staying only in the Golden State, now had the beach game to administer by itself. Today under president Dale Hoffman, it is an association of tournament directors who have taken the responsibility to run hundreds of beach and grass tournaments in California. Besides establishing a calendar of events, the CBVA provides instructional clinics and monitors a player rating and ranking system. Recently it has extended its borders to scholarships as well as an outreach program, "Beach to Street," to reach under-served populations.

Another upshot of the CBVA's efforts has been the creation of a Hall of Fame—just for the beach. Although one beach legend, Ron Von Hagen, was already in the USVBA's hallowed halls: "I couldn't believe it," says Von Hagen, it was a safe guess that the institution on the other side of the continent situated in eastern Massachusetts didn't have their blanched fingers on the pulse of beach volleyball. As of 1994 now, 19 men and women have been honored in the CBVA version.

And get ready for this...a deal has been struck with USA Volleyball! No! Never! But the twain have met. John Kessel, a native Californian whose father played beach volleyball in the '50s, used his native ability to relate to the traditional renegades out West. So he wisely asked the CBVA to work hand in hand with the governing body on the sand—a move that for many would have made sense long ago. And now with the Atlanta Olympics featuring beach doubles, even the old guard from the USVBA men who never touched a Spalding Top-Flite 18 are now recognizing the beach game. Jerry Sherman, current USVBA president says, "we're excited about beach volleyball." As proof, the first CBVA Youth Beach Volleyball Championships, the UNOCAL Cup, was held in July of '94 at Capistrano Beach. Together with USA Volleyball, the two organizations ran a week-end tournament which drew almost 70 teams—high school seniors on down.

And the AVP which still views USA Volleyball like an alley cat views an excited Doberman, has made a foray into its own grass roots program. Affiliating with the AVA (Association of Volleyball Amateurs), this new organization heads a program in principle structured to capture the minds and membership dues of sand players. One of the ploys is the Spike-It-Up program—patterned on the outdoor 3-on-3 basketball tournaments of Hoop-It-Up—and invites novices out on the sand to try and hit the ball hard for money. The sand race to Atlanta is on. Sponsors and TV have already shown that the greatest allure of volleyball is on the beach—even USA Volleyball has come around to that.

"Power of the press..."

In November, 1994, it was learned that Volleyball Magazine acquired its older competitor, Volleyball Monthly. Having run a close head-to-head race for the past few years, it seemed to make sense, financial and otherwise, to join forces and make one bigger, better publication rather than two smaller ones. And it was an amicable deal as well; Volleyball Magazine would continue with Rick Hazeltine heading the editorial side and Jon Hastings, former co-owner of Volleyball Monthly, was now publisher.

For Volleyball Magazine and Hazeltine, it has been a quick ascent. Beginning in 1990, Western Empire Publication, which is part of a media-based conglomerate owned by Australian Clyde Packer, decided to jump into a hot new sport. Editorial Director, Dave Gilovich had made successes out of Surfing and Bodyboarding, so why not a volleyball magazine? Looking around for someone with expertise to run it, they were led to Hazeltine who was working for the LA Times, San Diego edition. Hazeltine certainly knew the sport; for several years he had been in charge of the NCAA men's national statistics, and served as information director of the CIVA (California Intercollegiate Volleyball Association) begin-

ning in 1983 when he was still at San Diego State University. "Our starting point was where volleyball was going—towards more corporate interest and a sophisticated game. We also made it instructional-based. Anybody who plays wants to get better and that has been the unifying thread."

Philosophy intact, Hazeltine recruited a crack writer, Don Patterson, who was a colleague at the LA Times, to come on as executive editor; he also would enlist accomplished photographer, Peter Brouillet, as photo editor. The first year the magazine gave away 14,000 one-year subscriptions to coaches around the nation. It would pay eventual dividends. But the big payoff is around the corner. Hazeltine says, "I'd like to have a circulation of 125,000 by 1996." The Atlanta Olympics should bring lots of news, and the ever-present controversy of beach volleyball, promises to provide much material for avid readers. Entering its second centennial, a grown-up sport will have a grown-up look...provided by a big-time publication.

Lady killer. Gabrielle Reece leads the '94 four-women circuit in kills for the Bud Light Pro Beach Volleyball League The athlete-model. (Photo by Peter Brouillet)

Keba Phipps returned from the Italian pro league to also star on the four-women tour. (Photo by Peter Brouillet)

Craig Buck, untouchable on the four-men circuit when he's on. (Photo by Peter Brouillet)

Kim, Bev, Elaina: the fabulous Odens. (Photo by Robert Beck)

Future trends—6'8" setters. Lloy Ball. (Photo by Robert Beck)

Danielle Scott. Hard-hitting All-American looks to be a key in Atlanta in '96. (Courtesy of Volleyball Magazine)

One half of the top pro beach doubles team in the world. Liz Masakayan. (Photo by Peter Brouillet)

Holly McPeak. Top AVP money winner. (Photo by Peter Brouillet)

Indoor-outdoor threat. USA Women's Team Captain and pro beach, Tammy Liley. (Courtesy of ASICS Tiger)

Only other King of the Beach winner besides Kiraly. Adam Johnson. (Photo by Doug Avery)

Kent Steffes has grown into the role as partner of the world's best beach player, Kiraly. And getting better every year...(Photo by Doug Avery)

Proving there's still room for the little man, Brian Lewis. (Photo by Peter Brouillet)

Always room for a good big man. Mike Whitmarsh teamed with Mike Dodd in 1994 for an impressive season. (Photo by Peter Brouillet)

Flannel-tongued Olympians, Paul Sunderland and Chris Marlowe.

Chapter 22
1995 and on

"On the cusp..."

As 1995 begins, volleyball starts the celebration of its big birthday bash—number 100. Looking out on the Centennial year, the sport seems to be undergoing rapid change...especially with the '96 Olympics so close. Within the past decade, the amount of progress witnessed could possibly equal that of the first 90 years. Yet will the future be a gradual return to the old inertia of the game...the only growth coming in fits and starts externally imposed upon it? A sport which has slowly flourished, almost in spite of itself? At least the mind-boggling growth and TV profile of beach volleyball says a resonating, "no!" The older indoor game appears to have a few things up its sleeve, but in the gym it looks like the resounding impact of women's indoor volleyball—especially junior and collegiate—will lead the game.

What are the visible trends?

"Bigger, faster, better..."

The indoor game is undergoing a facelift. For fans who saw their last international men's volleyball match a decade ago, today's game would provide a couple of noticeable surprises: the increased size of the guys and the serving. With a running forward leap, young men of 6'9" are blasting the serve...and *controlling* it! In the '80s, the jump serve strategy was "mostly blast away for a point," remarks Fred Sturm. Today the trick is to pick out the weakest point in the reception pattern and deliver it to that precise area: either line, deep or short. "And now we're starting to see the jump float serve," adds Sturm. Terry Liskevych sees another huge innovation in the serve resulting from a rule change recently adopted by the FIVB. Serving is now allowed anywhere along the endline. "Many more serving angles will be created," he remarks. And points will come faster.

Plus the game itself is speeding up. "We're seeing quick sets everywhere and the four-hitter attack system is now standard. A team is as good as its sideout ability," Sturm believes. "That's why the serve is so important." What the USA Team strives to do is serve well enough to cause a bad pass—ideally keep an opposing team under 65% efficiency. If they achieve that, the number of quick sets are reduced to a beatable level. "We have to be effective in stopping the quick sets," says Sturm. Obversely, today's USA Men's Team has marked improvement in one very important area—passing. Before Ctvrtlik and Fortune joined the team, it hovered around 60%. It is now about 70%, good enough to beat most teams.

On the defensive side of the ledger, everybody has to dig now. "You can't have a big guy anymore who hurts you in the backcourt." To help close the perennial gap between offense and defense, the FIVB has also just changed the rule to allow multiple hits on the first contact. Liskevych believes "This will create many more rallies."

After the surprising bronze medal in the '94 World Championships, the steady march to Atlanta for the USA Men is much more upbeat today. A medal looks promising but the fatal flaw could be one which afflicts many teams. They need a Pat Powers: a guy who can bang high sets from the left side—score those difficult points when the ball is dug. Nggaard, Fortune and a rehabilitating Hilliard are the best prospects to fill the important role before Atlanta arrives. And of course, in the setting area for the men, American fans have been talking a lot about the 6'8" Lloyd Ball. "He is going to be the next great American player," Sturm mentions offhandedly.

For the women, many of the same current trends are apparent—the ladies are bigger, stronger and faster. "We'll see new blocking schemes for women," predicts the head coach of the Women's National Team, "Stopping the slide is very critical." We are also entering the high tech age of volleyball. "Computer analysis will be in real time right on the bench," Liskevych observes. As far as the missing link, it is the same outside point-getter who is sorely missed, as with the men. There's a world-class one in Japan, Caren Kemner. Yet, it is still undecided whether she and current teammate, the great Paula Weishoff, will be seen playing in Atlanta.

As the game continues to spread its influence geographically, it has seeped into new sociological areas as well. The sport is beginning to reach, albeit on a very limited basis, the inner-city and there are hundreds of top black athletes playing the women's collegiate game. In fact, nine out of the 18 women on the USA Women's team are African-Americans. On the other hand, there has been a valid argument that the junior club program is fostering an elitist sport. Considering that it costs between $1500 and $2000 annually for a girl to compete, that is a pretty convincing point. Still, with the huge player base, tons of new talent is guaranteed unlike in the men's game.

One nettlesome area according to USA head coach, Terry Liskevych, is the lack of top setters in the country. Perhaps a fairer assessment, is the lack of *setting emphasis* amongst the junior players. Stands to reason, one thing that hasn't changed since the days of William Mor-

gan is the pleasure of jumping and smacking a volleyball. Talented girls enjoy that too but "we need to get the top athletes—especially the leaders—into setting as well." Another thorny issue for the women is the diminishing playing season as defined by the NCAA. College women are getting excellent coaching but only for a period of 22 to 26 weeks. The rest of the year they are not allowed to compete or have any organized training. For a National Team coach, that's a restriction which the rest of the world does not have to abide by. Yet, the competitive tussling for national titles is so fierce that tough restrictions are required to make it fair, feels the NCAA. It is a problem with no immediate solution. Again it is Lisvevych who sees the problem most severely, "We must develop Junior National and Youth National Teams to participate in these age group world events. We can no longer just get kids at 21 or 22 from college and expect them to compete against players starting at 14 or 15!"

"Pro leagues...again?..."

In December, 1994, USA Volleyball announced plans to launch a men's pro league in the fall of 1996, following the Atlanta Olympics. The plan calls for 12 teams in two divisions; to be played in major cities in major league facilities: the National Volleyball League. A franchise start-up fee was cited at $250,000 with a 10-man team to cost an owner $400,000 for player salaries. Ain't the first time words like "pro" and "league" and "franchise" have been announced—but there are some differences here.

Besides the fact that the game is bigger and that the Atlanta Olympics should optimize any opportunities, this time the league is to be under the auspices of the sport's governing body, USA Volleyball. Admittedly that in itself could blow out any prospective investor who studied the organization's past successes, but on the other hand, there are some advantages the office brings to a pro league. One great one is the long and powerful arm of the FIVB. If the league is created in a synergistic relationship with the world governing body, the chances of success are greatly increased. Foreign players, foreign competitions, even foreign teams (talk of Mexico and Canada already exist), could all help things.

The venture is to be led by Doug Beal who has been working as Special Assistant to John Carroll. As executive director, Beal will use all his experience and contacts to make the league fly. Yet, penetrating questions have arisen by certain pundits. "Is there enough wealth of talent? Why start a men's league when the women's indoor game is so much stronger on club and college participation levels?"

Paul Sunderland has some incisive answers: "In terms of numbers, the women have it hands-down. But there still aren't any broad-based women personalities like Karch or Timmons. And right or wrong, corporate sponsors for sports are still male-market driven. The indoor game needs something like the NVL to grow." Beal adds, "If we don't get a league, I'm afraid that all we'll have in this country is outdoor volleyball."

For the disconcerted women, there already exists a pro league...once again, the name surpasses the reality. The National Volleyball Association experienced a humble birth in 1992 and since then has grown modestly. The five-team league—all in California except for Salt Lake City—invokes images of the early IVA and Major League Volleyball, with a couple of notable exceptions. First off, there is a great talent pool; in fact, 16 National Team players participate in the league. And secondly, to date there is less investor interest than even early IVA fortune hunters—certainly no Barry Gordys around.

Finally, it must be said that the indoor game needs some dressing up, a more contemporary look, to get America's attention. It has gone a long way from Harry Wilson's staid game but times have changed too. Once again, perhaps Paul Sunderland with his crow's nest view has the best perspective: "It has begun to look a little like Wimbledon. Too fast, no rallies, too boring. It needs rule changes: shorter matches (speed-scoring), and it should do away with rotation like the IVA did. Allowing specializa-

tion would give exciting players like Eric Sato a chance to play." The independent IVA was willing to make radical departures from the rules; if that is indeed needed, can USA Volleyball be expected to be the organization to try new ideas?

One wonders.

"Beach just gets brighter..."

In December, 1994, the squabbling between AVP-FIVB-USA Volleyball seemed to have come to an end...or at least arrived at a truce. An announcement came stating that the AVP would recognize USA Volleyball and the FIVB as official governing bodies of the sport; in return, AVP players would indeed be eligible to compete in the Atlanta Games. With a proviso: that they conform to the qualification guidelines established by the FIVB. Well, what were those exactly? Exactly is still not an operative word here. In principle, AVP men and women are eligible to compete but realistically they must jump through a lot of hoops on the way—FIVB qualifying tournaments. There's the rub. Competing sponsors (Miller of AVP and Budweiser of the FIVB events in the US), possible conflicting event dates and television broadcast conflicts, at this point, present quite a minefield. Notwithstanding all the problems, from the present vantage point, one top American Men's and Women's team will qualify through the FIVB World Series events. In addition, one or possibly two more teams, will qualify at a single tournament to be held in June, 1996—ostensibly the top AVP and WPVA teams will compete for these enviable spots.

The conflict is born from success, however, so ultimately it remains an encouraging sign. Beach volleyball is on a big roll. "I see a full-blown FIVB, 40-week per year circuit," predicts Paul Sunderland. He is not alone. With competing corporate dollars and live network television coverage waxing every year, the Atlanta Olympics should give the former cult-sport a legitimization. And it's not just beach...it's *outdoor*—sand and grass, at times blacktop, as long as it is under the sun and in open air. In the beach game, John Kessel even sees the possible solution to the NCAA stale-mate in men's volleyball. Amongst other advantages, the national junior director rationalizes: the beach game is cheap—two players and minimal equipment—they don't even need shoes! Health and fun...and a growing sport.

Yet for the clearest view of beach volleyball's future, the AVP must be looked to. In a scant ten years, the player-based organization has garnered more public visibility and financial clout than the sum total of a century's efforts by the national governing body. Continual turf wars will be waged, plus the organization might have stubbed a toe with its women competitors recently, but the AVP's record shows mostly wins—big ones. It remains a safe bet that the AVP will continue to lead the sport it knows so well.

"Everything must change...including politics..."

If the first president of the USVBA, George Fisher leaped from 1928 to the eve of the Centennial, the one place he might feel comfortable would be at a USA Volleyball board meeting. 28 members!

Yes, the Boy Scouts to the NCAA to the same old (albeit new) YMCA...all with a voice and a vote to exercise. Representation by such an array of influential organizations is undeniably a good thing; to run an organization—with a proposed budget of some $8,000,000—in a business-like and efficient manner in 1995, through an annual meeting of 28 scattered people, is not a good thing. Other non-profit organizations similar in makeup have found ways to adapt to modern times. It's an executive board! A selected half-dozen individuals with demonstrated expertise, business knowledge and vision to make decisions...and carry them out. They are answerable to the 28 of the inner circle, but still the smaller group could get things done better and more quickly.

In 1993, the American Sports Data, Inc., published statistics on volleyball participation in America. The amount of people playing over 25 days or more per year was an estimated 6,200,000. Women outnumbered men by a slight 51% to 49%, and hard surface volleyball is dominated by young people, with 78% of all players under the age of 35. Finally, about 24% of all volleyball players play beach volleyball. It's all there: young, both sexes, and growing. Yet it is still an unwieldy, amorphous blob waiting to be kneaded, shaped and have life blown into it. Surely that is the overriding challenge of the first decade of the second centennial, and unquestionably the '96 Olympics in Atlanta will do wonders to jumpstart the process.

As the first 100 years of volleyball ends, we are left with an impressive body of history, replete with triumphs and defeats, peppered with a host of fascinating characters. Many of the early giants of the sport are gone. Some of the supernovas who helped bridge the game from its primitive era to the modern are still with us: Paul Johnson, Dick Caplan, Bud Fields, Manny Saenz, Bernie Holtzman, Bill Friermood, Burt DeGroot, Glen Davies, Iggy Ignacio, Dave Heiser, Jean Brunicardi, Jane Ward, Alice Chambers, Bertha Lucas and many others. Some are still playing. Many of these have been recognized for their unparalleled careers. Sadly, some still aren't—particularly early stars. *Jimmy Wortham* is still not in the Hall of Fame! Neither is Manny Saenz, nor Bernie Holtzman. And vis-a-vis the other Hall of Fame—beach—who has contributed more to that game's colorful lore than the irrepressible mad hatter...Vogie! Volleyball, as many sports, has an incredibly rich heritage, and individuals as these have contributed mightily.

And lest history (and some historians) come down too hard on the stewards of the game who guided the USVBA for its first century—and been criticized so roundly for their conservative, incestuous and sometimes heavy-handed policies—progressive signs do appear. In particular, those playing rebels of the game championed by Gene Selznick should know that not all of their struggles have gone unrecognized...in 1988, Gene Selznick was the first male player inducted into the Hall of Fame.

Rod Wilde will get a chance to reach his thwarted '84 Olympic dream...as assistant USA Men's Coach in Atlanta. (Courtesy of Bud Fields)

"Spread the word!" John Kessel, Director Program Development and Services, USA Volleyball.

Mr. Consistency—through the good and bad. Kerry Klostermann, Senior Director, USA Volleyball.

"What court are we on?" Estero Beach, Mexico. World's biggest beach tournament.

The ring. Hall of Fame members wear the ASICS Tiger award. (Courtesy of ASICS Tiger)

Hall of Fame inductees, 1992. From left to right: Jim Coleman, Merton Kennedy, Ron Von Hagen, Jon Stanley.

Some CBVA Hall of Fame members...at the beach once again. Back Row (from left to right): Sharky Zartman, Chris Marlowe, Nina Matthies, Gene Popko. Front Row: Bob Barber, Kirk Kilgour, Jean Brunicardi, Jim Menges.

Epilogue

I had a vision of the future...100 years hence. I stood in a wondrous expanse of green. Sun worshippers lazing, their fatuous smiles craning at the brilliant warmth. A human mosaic: musicians, painters, buskers, people sculpting in the open air. Strange, the sun was clearer now, heaven's dome such an immaculate cerulean blue. Ah, but I had been here before! Central Park. And now here once again, gazing over Sheep's Meadow. So quiet now, only the voices of jubilant human beings. Of course! That infernal engine, the combustible one of the automobile, was long gone. And thus the pristine air. People were swimming again in the limpid waters of the Hudson and East Rivers.

I watched the spectacle all through the afternoon—people a little bigger, certainly better fit, some funny activities I didn't understand but...nothing so different than before. One game I knew well. So many courts now: sixes, fours, doubles—on sand, grass and something that looked like wood but wasn't—all up and down where the few blacktop courts used to be. And beyond, some open-air courts, stacked up vertically 10-high! What remained was the menagerie of languages—only many more now—shouts of Spanish, French, German, were joined by Arabic, Swahili and Slavic tongues. Arguments erupted—hey, this was still New York! Every color of skin I'd seen before, but here were bodies in brilliant orange, emerald and blue, of every hue. Were they dyed? Permanently? Men, women, androgynous types, others sexless to the eye. No one seemed to care. They were focused on the game at hand. And what remarkable displays of human prowess! I would tell you but you would not believe.

Hundreds upon hundreds played on through the day. The sun dipped and left a Vlaminck-smeared sunset over Central Park West—some of the Art Deco buildings of the 1930s still standing. When it was finally dark, tens of thousands sat and supped and waited...for something. Suddenly, from the children's park of Strawberry Fields, a barreled beam of light shot into the cobalt sky. It filled the entire vaulted night, theater in the round, "Sunday Night Concert in the Park"—like days of old. John Lennon night. Three hours of divine music, Beatles to The Plastic Ono Band, with interstices of the famous wit. But that was over 100 years ago! I marveled. No matter, he was as real again as life.

Imagine. I looked askance and I saw, I felt it: divine human imagination. Sure, it would take generations more before the wealth was shared fairly. And religion...well, that would even require more time. But population was now controlled; there was a sense of planet awareness I could never have envisioned. Human nature hadn't really changed—just become more refined on the collective level. Then that one phrase of Lennon's which always had struck me, "nothing to kill or die for," seemed here. I inquired about that one. Apparently after enough human wreckage early on in the century, guns had been removed from civil society. Well, not totally. Those who prized the instruments so highly had opted to move down near Antartica, where they too were free to play out their war-like fanatiasies. Their choice.

It was a better world. Something I wouldn't have wagered on, back in 1995. But here it was...right before my eyes. And a lot more people were playing volleyball.

Appendix

Men

OLYMPICS

1964	9th
1968	7th
1972	D N Q
1976	D N Q
1980	D N Q
1984	1st
1988	1st
1992	3rd

WORLD CHAMPIONSHIPS

1956	6th
1960	7th
1962	D N P
1966	11th
1970	18th
1974	14th
1978	19th
1982	13th
1986	1st
1990	13th
1994	3rd

Women

OLYMPICS

1964	5th
1968	8th
1972	D N Q
1976	D N Q
1980	Qualified, boycott
1984	2nd
1988	7th
1992	3rd

WORLD CHAMPIONSHIPS

1956	9th
1960	6th
1962	D N P
1966	2nd
1970	11th
1974	12th
1978	5th
1982	3rd
1986	10th
1990	3rd
1994	6th

Men		Women	
WORLD CUP		**WORLD CUP**	
1973	7th	1973	6th
1977	10th	1977	7th
1981	DNQ	1981	4th
1985	1st	1985	DNQ
1989	4th	1989	DNQ
1991	3rd	1991	4th
NORCECA CHAMPIONSHIPS		**NORCECA CHAMPIONSHIPS**	
1969	3rd	1969	6th
1971	2nd	1971	3rd
1973	1st	1973	3rd
1975	3rd	1975	2nd
1977	5th	1977	3rd
1979	7th	1979	2nd
1981	2nd	1981	1st
1983	1st	1983	1st
1985	1st	1985	2nd
1987	2nd	1987	2nd
1989	3rd	1989	3rd
1991	2nd	1991	2nd
1993	2nd	1993	2nd
PAN-AMERICAN GAMES		**PAN-AMERICAN GAMES**	
1955	1st	1955	2nd
1959	1st	1959	2nd
1963	2nd	1963	2nd
1967	1st	1967	1st
1971	2nd	1971	6th
1975	4th	1975	6th
1979	4th	1979	4th
1983	4th	1983	2nd
1987	1st	1987	3rd
1991	4th	1991	5th

NCAA COLLEGIATE NATIONAL CHAMPIONS

Men

1970	UCLA
1971	UCLA
1972	UCLA
1973	SAN DIEGO STATE
1974	UCLA
1975	UCLA
1976	UCLA
1977	U S C
1978	PEPPERDINE
1979	UCLA
1980	U S C
1981	UCLA
1982	UCLA
1983	UCLA
1984	UCLA
1985	PEPPERDINE
1986	PEPPERDINE
1987	UCLA
1988	U S C
1989	UCLA
1990	U S C
1991	LONG BEACH ST.
1992	PEPPERDINE
1993	UCLA
1994	PENN ST.

Women

1981	U S C
1982	HAWAII
1982	HAWAII
1984	UCLA
1985	U O P
1986	U O P
1987	HAWAII
1988	TEXAS
1989	LONG BEACH ST.
1990	UCLA
1991	UCLA
1992	STANFORD
1993	LONG BEACH ST.
1994	STANFORD

ASSOCIATION OF VOLLEYBALL PROFESSIONALS (MEN)

INTERNATIONAL CHAMPIONSHIP

1976 .... Lee-Menges
1977 .... Marlowe-Menges
1978 .... Hooper-O'Bradovich
1979 .... Smith-Kiraly
1980 .... Fishburn-Selznick
1981 .... Smith-Kiraly
1982 .... Smith-Stoklos
1983 .... Hovland-Dodd
1984 .... Fishburn-Hanseth
1985 .... Hovland-Dodd
1986 .... Hovland-Dodd
1987 .... Hovland-Dodd
1988 .... Smith-Stoklos
1989 .... Hovland-Dodd
1990 .... Smith-Stoklos
1991 .... Johnson-Luyties
1992 .... Kiraly-Steffes
1993 .... Kiraly-Steffes
1994 .... Kiraly-Steffes

MANHATTAN OPEN

1976 .... O'Bradovich-Marlowe
1977 .... Marlowe-Menges
1978 .... Lee-Menges
1979 .... Menges-Smith
1980 .... Kiraly-Smith
1981 .... Stoklos-Menges
1982 .... Hovland-Dodd
1983 .... Hovland-Dodd
1984 .... Hovland-Dodd
1985 .... Hovland-Dodd
1986 .... Smith-Stoklos
1987 .... Hovland-Dodd
1988 .... Kiraly-Luyties
1989 .... Smith-Stoklos
1990 .... Kiraly-Frohoff
1991 .... Kiraly-Steffes
1992 .... Kiraly-Steffes
1993 .... Kiraly-Steffes
1994 .... Johnson-Stoklos

WOMEN'S PROFESSIONAL VOLLEYBALL ASSOCIATION

U.S. OPEN

1988 .... Chisholm-Silva
1989 .... Chisholm-Harrer
1990 .... Kirby-Silva
1991 .... Castro-Cotas
1992 .... Rock-Silva
1993 .... Kirby-Masakayan
1994 .... Kirby-Masakayan

NATIONALS

1987 .... Chisholm-Silva
1988 .... Chisholm-Silva
1989 .... Crockett-Silva
1990 .... Matthies-Roque
1991 .... Chisholm-Masakayan
1992 .... Kirby-Reno
1993 .... Kirby-Masakayan
1994 .... Kirby-Masakayan

VOLLEYBALL HALL OF FAME INDUCTEES

VOLLEYBALL HALL OF FAME INDUCTEES

1985

William Morgan

1986

Harold Friermood

1988

Leonard Gibson
Flora Hyman
Gene Selznick
Jane Ward
Harry Wilson

1989

Doug Beal
Glen Davies
Kathy Gregory
Mike O'Hara

1990

Al Fish
E.B. DeGroot
Mary Jo Peppler

1991

Catalino Ignacio
Rolf Engen
George Fisher
Tom Haine

1992

Jim Coleman
Merton Kennedy
Jon Stanley
Ron Von Hagen

1993

Mike Bright
Al Scates

1994

Patty Dowdell
Marv Dunphy
John Koch
Larry Rundle

CALIFORNIA BEACH VOLLEYBALL ASSOCIATION HALL OF FAME

1992

Mike Cook
Kathy Gregory
Bernie Holtzman
Mike O'Hara
Gene Popko
Ron Von Hagen
Ed Montan
Gene Selznick
George Stepanof

1993

Jean Brunicardi
Kirk Kilgour
Keith Erickson
Mickie McFadden
Chris Marlowe
Sharky Zartman

1994

Bobby Barber
Matt Gage
Nina Matthies
Jim Menges

About the Author

Byron Shewman currently lives in San Diego where he is a writer.

Shewman played on the USA Men's Team between 1971-1975. Concurrently, he played in Spain: C.D. Hispano-Frances (Barcelona) and Club de Futbol de Barcelona. Between 1976-1979, he served as player-coach for the Tucson Sky of the International Volleyball Association. Shewman was selected twice as IVA Coach of the Year, 1978 and 1979. During that period (1978-1981), he also coached for the Racing Club de France in Paris, France. Between 1988-1990, he worked as Director of Marketing and Promotions for the Australian Volleyball Federation where he helped establish the professional beach volleyball circuit there.

Having lived abroad for several years, Shewman has recently worked on documentary films and continues to write poetry and fiction.